I0802047

Seasons of Nobility

Sermons on the Festivals

Michael Scharf
Publication Trust
Yeshiva University Press
RIETS

מגיד
MAGGID

Rabbi Aaron Levine

SEASONS OF NOBILITY

SERMONS ON THE FESTIVALS

The RIETS Hashkafah Series
Rabbi Daniel Z. Feldman, Series Editor

The Michael Scharf Publication Trust of
Yeshiva University Press

Maggid Books

Seasons of Nobility
Sermons on the Festivals

First Edition, 2019

Maggid Books
An imprint of Koren Publishers Jerusalem Ltd.

POB 8531, New Milford, CT 06776-8531, USA
& POB 4044, Jerusalem 9104001, Israel
www.maggidbooks.com

© The Estate of Rabbi Dr. Aaron Levine *zt"l*, 2019

Papercut Cover Photo © David Fisher Art

The publication of this book was made possible through the generous support of *Torah Education in Israel.*

All rights reserved. No part of this publication may be reproduced, stored in a retrieval system or transmitted in any form or by any means, electronic, mechanical, photocopying, or otherwise, without the prior permission of the publisher, except in the case of brief quotations embedded in critical articles or reviews.

ISBN 978-1-59264-500-8, *hardcover*

A CIP catalogue record for this title is available from the British Library

Printed and bound in the United States

In loving memory of
Sarah Levine

Contents

ḤANUKKAH

TU BI-SHEVAT

SHABBAT SHEKALIM

SHABBAT ZAKHOR

SHABBAT PARAH

SHABBAT HA-ḤODESH

SHABBAT HA-GADOL

PASSOVER – FIRST DAYS

PASSOVER – SHABBAT ḤOL HA-MO'ED

PASSOVER – SEVENTH DAY

PASSOVER – LAST DAY

SHAVUOT

SHABBAT ḤAZON

ROSH ḤODESH

Foreword

Rabbi Dr. Aaron Levine was a quintessential gentleman and scholar, embodying the values of Torah virtue and ethical behavior that he taught in his classes and writings. He was a world-renowned economist who served as the Samson and Halina Bitensky Professor of Economics at Yeshiva University, and as the editor of *The Oxford Handbook of Judaism and Economics.* His published works, including *Free Enterprise and Jewish Law,* and *Case Studies in Jewish Business Ethics,* are considered classics in the domain of Jewish business ethics and law.

In addition, Rabbi Levine served as the Rabbi of a synagogue in Brooklyn for many years, during which time he inspired his congregation with homilies on the Torah portion of the week and on the Festivals, providing timely commentary on the topics of our times. As the grandson and namesake of the Reisher Rav, a preeminent Polish scholar who was the author of *Ha-Derash ve-ha-Iyyun,* a masterful collection of insights into the Torah, Rabbi Levine adroitly continued his family tradition of extracting penetrating ideas and lessons from the weekly Torah portions.

This book, edited with love by his family, is a compilation of Rabbi Levine's sermons on the Festivals that he delivered in his synagogue. Each essay is a self-standing gem, offering timeless wisdom in both scholarly and succinct fashion. Rabbi Levine's penchant for academic precision, combined with his reverence for the word of God, enabled him to convey an authentic Torah *Weltanschauung* for the complex political and socioeconomic challenges of the modern age. We are now all able to be beneficiaries of these pithy pearls of perspicacity.

The Talmud (*Ḥagigah* 15b) teaches us: אם דומה הרב למלאך ה' צבקות יבקשו תורה מפיהו ואם לאו אל יבקשו תורה מפיהו, "if the Rabbi resembles an angel of God, then learn Torah from his lips, but otherwise do not learn Torah from his lips." One only had to gaze at Rabbi Levine's countenance to recognize the face and demeanor of an angel. Those of us who were privileged to be his students can attest that he was a man who occupied a special plane of holiness. This book, endowed with the beauty of the words that once emerged from Rabbi Levine's lips, is similarly blessed with the sanctity of his spirit.

It is thus with great pleasure that we present this important volume in homiletics as the latest installment in the RIETS Press series. We are of course indebted to our indefatigable executive editor, Rabbi Daniel Feldman, as well as to the past and present visionaries and architects of the RIETS Press, former Presidents Rabbi Dr. Norman Lamm and Richard M. Joel, President Rabbi Dr. Ari Berman, Rabbi Zevulun Charlop, and RIETS Dean Rabbi Menachem Penner. It is through their herculean efforts on behalf of the Yeshiva that we continue to imbibe the fruits of YU and RIETS scholarship.

Rabbi Yona Reiss
Director, RIETS Press

Preface

With deep gratitude to Hashem, we present this volume of sermons of our dear father, Rabbi Dr. Aaron Levine, *zt"l.*

A renowned authority on Jewish business ethics, Rabbi Dr. Levine was the Samson and Halina Professor of Economics at Yeshiva University. A paragon of *Torah u-madda,* he published widely on the interface between economics and Jewish law, particularly as it relates to public policy and modern business practices.

Rabbi Dr. Levine was also a distinguished pulpit rabbi, toiling tirelessly in the rabbinate for nearly thirty years. In his sermons, he would urge his congregants to seize nobility, to leap toward greater achievement in religious observance and refinement of character. In his personal conduct, he was the very embodiment of those ideals.

This volume is a selection of Rabbi Dr. Levine's sermons on the Festivals, transcribed from his manuscripts dating from 1982 to 2011.

We extend our heartfelt gratitude to Rabbi Yona Reiss for including this volume in the works published under the auspices of the Rabbi Isaac Elchanan Theological Seminary of Yeshiva University, and for his eloquent and meaningful Foreword. To Rabbi Daniel Z. Feldman, we express our sincere appreciation for his enthusiasm toward this work and his steadfast devotion in shepherding it though the publication process.

To Matthew Miller, Rabbi Reuven Ziegler, Tomi Mager, Ita Olesker, and Shira Finson of Maggid Books, we extend a special note of thanks for their thoughtfulness, dedication, and professionalism in bringing this book to publication.

Rabbi Dr. Levine was born on the second day of Passover and passed away on the first day of Passover. On Passover, we observe the mitzvah of *haggadah,* the telling of the story of the Exodus, so that we can feel as if we ourselves had gone out of Egypt. As Rabbi Dr. Levine noted, "We are bidden to somehow leap the generations and touch the lives of our ancestors, to make the biblical figures come alive and vicariously feel their pain and triumph, to feel the birth pangs of a nation of Hashem."

May the recounting of these sermons strengthen our Jewish identity and commitment to the Torah, connecting us not only with our father, the author of this work, but with the previous generations, back to Abraham, Isaac, and Jacob.

Family of Rabbi Dr. Aaron Levine, *zt"l*

Rosh Ha-Shanah

To Dumbfound the Satan

September 28, 1984

During the course of the year, the Satan assumes the role of prosecuting attorney in the Heavenly court. No transgression, however small, goes unnoticed by him. No less than stern justice is demanded for each offense.

On Rosh Ha-Shanah, we do something special to disarm the Satan, to silence his accusations. What do we do? We blow the shofar twice – once before *Shemoneh Esreh,* and once again after. How does this dumbfound the Satan? The hasidic master R. Pinhas ha-Levi Horowitz explains it by picking up on *Rashi*'s statement that the performance of a mitzvah twice displays that we love mitzvot.[1]

Now, we are told, for one who repents out of fear, his intentional sins are converted into accidental sins, but for one who repents out of love of Hashem, his intentional sins are converted into merits.[2] By

1. R. Solomon b. Isaac (*Rashi,* France, 1040–1105), *Rashi* to *Rosh Ha-Shanah* 16b, s.v. "*kedei le-arbev.*"
2. *Yoma* 86b.

performing the mitzvah of shofar twice, we demonstrate an attitude that we cherish mitzvot. The Satan then fears that if he dares mention some sin, Hashem will transform it into a merit. He therefore chooses silence.[3]

May I be permitted to add to this charming idea. Fully knowing that we show maximum reverence for a mitzvah at its outset, the Sages cleverly structured the mitzvah of shofar in a manner that the *reshut,* the "optional part," is first, and the *ḥovah,* the "obligatory part," is later, in accordance with the opinion of the *Ran.*[4] We maneuver the Jew to treat the *reshut* as a *ḥovah.*

Moreover, there is another view in the *Rishonim* that the first set of *tekiot,* the *tekiot de-meyushav,* is the primary part of the mitzvah.[5] If this is so, the learned person is thoroughly confused about which part is voluntary and which is obligatory. He is forced to treat everything in the same manner. Treating a *reshut* with the same urgency, enthusiasm, and awe as a *ḥovah* signifies that we love mitzvot!

The obligations that fall our way can be divided into *ḥovot,* inescapable obligations that cannot be delegated; mitzvot, obligations that can be delegated; and finally *reshut,* the whole realm of *lifnim mi-shurat ha-din,* "beyond the letter of the law." Now, it is the work of the Satan to chill the Jewish soul with the weapon of *maḥar,* "tomorrow," to drag

3. R. Pinhas ha-Levi Horowitz (*Ba'al ha-Hafla'ah,* Germany, 1730–1805), *Panim Yafot,* Leviticus 5:26, s.v. "*mi-kol asher ya'aseh le-ashmah vah.*"

4. R. Nissim b. Reuben Gerondi (*Ran,* Spain, 1320–1376), *Ḥiddushei ha-Ran, Rosh Ha-Shanah* 16b. Two sets of shofar blasts are sounded on Rosh Ha-Shanah. The first set, the *tekiot de-meyushav* (lit., "the blasts that are sounded while sitting"), are sounded before or during the personal *Shemoneh Esreh* Prayer. The second set, the *tekiot de-me'umad* (lit., "the blasts that are sounded while standing"), are sounded during the communal *Amidah* service. The universal custom, however, is for the congregation to stand during the first set of blasts as well.

5. See R. Isaac b. Jacob Alfasi (*Rif,* Algeria, 1013–1103), *Rif* to *Rosh Ha-Shanah* 34a and Maimonides, *Mishneh Torah, Shofar* 3:12 (noting that the number of blasts sounded during the second set is limited to avoid inconveniencing the members of the community as they had already fulfilled their obligation to hear the shofar during the first set of blasts). See also R. Solomon b. Abraham Adret (*Rashba,* Spain, 1235–1310), *Ḥiddushei ha-Rashba, Rosh Ha-Shanah* 16a; R. Yom Tov Ishbili (*Ritva,* Spain, ca. 1250–1330), *Ḥiddushei ha-Ritva, Rosh Ha-Shanah* 16b and 34a.

down the mitzvah and *ḥovah* to *reshut,* shifting in time, place, and person all the mitzvot.

We can counteract this only by rearranging the letters of the word *maḥar* (מחר) to *romaḥ* (רמח), a spear, and channel the *reshut* and mitzvah to the realm of *ḥovah.* This is the mindset of one who loves mitzvot.

I would submit that there is no area in our lives where the battle between *romaḥ* and *maḥar* is more intense than in the area of attending to the needs of the community. It is here that we can easily delude ourselves into thinking that anything beyond minimum participation belongs to the realm of *reshut.* The man who regards the work of the community as a labor of love, something that he can never have enough of, something that he cherishes, is the true hero of the spirit. For him, our Sages say, "His righteousness endures forever" (Psalms 111:3). Why? Because such a man silences the Satan.

On this awesome day, when we recall the most difficult trial of our Forefather Abraham, the *Akedah,* let us take note that Hashem called to Abraham by enunciating his name twice, an expression of *ḥibbah,* "love."[6] Abraham responded with a great act that conferred merit for all time. Let us today merit *ḥibbah* with *ḥibbah* from everlasting merit.

6. Genesis 22:11; *Rashi* ad loc.

The Relevancy of the *Akedah* on Rosh Ha-Shanah

October 4, 1986

Perhaps there is no episode in the Torah that is given such prominence as the *Akedah*. It is both daily fare and the highlight of Rosh Ha-Shanah.[1]

As great a trial as the *Akedah* represented for our Forefather Abraham, we know that the test will never be given to another mortal. Human sacrifice is an abomination, and there can be nothing further from the divine will than this.[2] So how can we relate to the *Akedah* today?

The *Akedah* is a story of how a great man dealt with contradiction. Hashem promised Abraham, "through Isaac offspring will be considered

1. The biblical account of the *Akedah* is recited daily during the Morning Prayer and is the Torah reading for the second day of Rosh Ha-Shanah.
2. Deuteronomy 12:30–31; Jeremiah 19:5.

yours" (Genesis 21:12). From Isaac would emerge a nation as numerous as the stars of the firmament and the grains of sand on the seashore.[3]

Now Hashem says, "Bring him up there as an offering" (Genesis 22:2). This is a contradiction! What is to be of the future? What became of the promise?

Indeed, the element of divine contradiction explains why the trial of the *Akedah* was the most difficult trial, qualitatively different from the others, as the other trials did not have an element of divine contradiction.

Did the contradiction crush Abraham and paralyze him? No. He handled it brilliantly.

On one of the holiest of days, Rosh Ha-Shanah, a day on which we do not make explicit confessions of sin, we read the *Akedah* as a gentle but powerful reproof. We ask ourselves, how do we measure up in handling contradiction, inconsistency, and conflict of interest?

Every day, we pray, "Remove the Satan from in front of us and from behind us."[4] What does this mean? When we want to perform a mitzvah, the Satan gets the better of us and convinces us that on the scale of priorities, the mitzvah is either very low or zero. But if we somehow manage to overcome him and perform the mitzvah, the same Satan drums in us a sense of great accomplishment, as if we need not perform any more good deeds the rest of our lives. So great is our accomplishment that we were fully *yotzei*. We seem to be very comfortable with the contradiction. We have no problem living with this.

Then we are transported to one of the most compassionate moments in Jewish history. It is the eloquent plea of the Prince of the Tribe of Judah that the Viceroy of Egypt release his brother Benjamin. Although the evidence is overwhelming that Benjamin pilfered the Viceroy's goblet, and there is really nothing to say in his defense, Judah pleads, "How can I go up to my father if the youth is not with me?" (Genesis 44:34). The old father will simply pine away from the anguish of being separated from his precious child.

It is then that Joseph reveals himself to his brothers. "I am Joseph. Is my father still alive?" (Genesis 45:3). "But his brothers could not answer him"

---

3. See Genesis 22:17.
4. Evening Prayer (paragraph beginning with "*Hashkivenu,*" "lay us down to sleep").

(Genesis 45:3). Our Sages see in Joseph's revelation a poignant reproof. *Oy lanu mi-yom ha-din*, "woe unto us from the Day of Judgment."[5] What is the reproof? The *Beit ha-Levi* explains that Joseph was saying to his brothers, if you are so noble and you care so much for the welfare of the delicate old man, you should know that I am Joseph, and is it possible that Father is still alive? How could Father have survived the twenty-two-year separation? Why did you not think of the torture that you would cause our father when you sold me into slavery?[6] Inconsistency is the greatest reproof for every individual, for there is no answer. "But his brothers could not answer him."

Perhaps the greatest application of the *Akedah* is in the realm of interpersonal relations. The *haftarah* of today is no coincidence. Rachel accomplished in the realm of *bein adam le-ḥavero* what Abraham accomplished *bein adam la-Makom*.

When Manasseh placed an idol in the Sanctuary, Hashem, according to Tradition, decided to destroy the Temple and exile His people. Thereupon, all the great personalities in Jewish history pleaded to Hashem to rescind the decree, but to no avail. Our Matriarch Rachel then pleaded to Hashem, "Your mercy extends beyond any mortal. Jacob worked seven years only for the right to marry me. But when my father Laban substituted Leah for me, I assisted the deception and gave her the passwords so that she should not be put to disgrace."[7]

On this very holy day, we can feel a sense of exuberant national pride that despite all the pogroms, persecution, and holocausts that our people have endured throughout the generations, we have survived and flourished in our religious beliefs, hence withstanding the test of the *Akedah* as a nation. But we must transfer the pride to a reaching out to our fellow Jew, capturing the spirit of Rachel, who did not allow conflict of interest to push aside her sister.

---

5. Genesis Rabbah 93:11.
6. R. Yosef Dov Soloveitchik (*Beit ha-Levi*, Belarus, 1820–1892), *Beit ha-Levi al Derush u-Milei de-Aggadata* (Jerusalem, 1985), *Va-Yiggash*, p. 62.
7. *Rashi* to Jeremiah 31:14; R. David Kimhi (*Radak*, Provence, ca. 1160–ca. 1235), *Radak* to Jeremiah 31:14, s.v. "*ki einennu*"; Lamentations Rabbah, *petiḥta* 24.

Yom Teruah

September 24, 1987

The Festival of Rosh Ha-Shanah is referred to by the Torah as "*yom teruah*," a day of the *teruah*,[1] and "*zikhron teruah*," remembrance of the *teruah*.[2] The *teruah* is identified by our Sages as a broken sound, either the sighing sound of the *shevarim* or the whimpering sound of the *teruah*.[3]

The focus on the broken sound of the shofar as opposed to the *tekiah* sound seems quite appropriate, for it is the broken sound that captures the essence of repentance – profound remorse or regret. But this focus on the *teruah* runs the danger of having us regard the *tekiah* as a mere embellishment, a technical requirement of the mitzvah, rather than an integral part of the mitzvah.

1. Numbers 29:1.
2. Leviticus 23:24.
3. *Rosh Ha-Shanah* 33b; Maimonides (*Rambam*, Egypt, 1135–1204), *Mishneh Torah, Shofar* 3:2.

But our Sages tell us that a *teruah* is defective if it is not preceded and followed by a *tekiah*.[4] What this means, as we see it, is that any feeling of failure that we have must proceed from a feeling that we have failed to live up to the standard set for us by the *tekiah*.

The *tekiah* was the sound at Sinai.[5] It was there that the standard of perfection was set for us. Shortcomings and frustration can be assessed only in relation to the *tekiah* at Sinai.

The connection of the *teruah* to the *tekiah* that succeeds it is also important. Our sighs and whimpering must lead to a straightening out. We must reproduce the *tekiah* at Sinai for our own daily lives. There is no *zikhron tekiah*, a remembrance for the *tekiah* of Horeb, because we must recreate it in our own time for each generation. *Kol gadol ve-lo yasaph*, "a great voice, never to be repeated" (Deuteronomy 5:19).[6]

From both a communal and personal standpoint, we face the challenge of preserving the integrity of the mitzvah of shofar. From a communal standpoint, we face the danger that organizations will push to the top of their agenda, and hence to the forefront of the consciousness of the public, concerns that are at most *zikhron teruah* issues, and, in the process, do violence to both the *tekiah* before and the *tekiah* after the *teruah* – the *tekiah* of idealism and the *tekiah* of practical living. Jewish-Catholic relations is such a case. In the process of arranging a meeting with the Pope, we did violence to Jewish pride and identity.[7]

---

4. *Rosh Ha-Shanah* 34a.
5. See Exodus 19:16 ("the sound of the shofar [*kol shofar*] was very powerful"); Exodus 19:19 ("the sound of the shofar [*kol shofar*] grew continually much stronger"); R. Zevi Elimelech Dynow (*Benei Yissaskhar*, Poland, 1785–1841), *Benei Yissaskhar, Ma'amerei Ḥodesh Tishrei, ma'amar* 3, *derush* 1 (noting that the phrase "*kol shofar*" in the Torah indicates the sound of a *tekiah*).
6. *Rashi* to Deuteronomy 5:19 (second explanation). An alternative interpretation of the phrase "*kol gadol ve-lo yasaph*" is that the sound did not stop. *Targum Onkelos* to Deuteronomy 5:19; *Rashi* ad loc. (first explanation).
7. Larry Cohler, "Jewish Delegation in Historic Meeting with Pope: Impetus Was Waldheim; No Change in Recognition of Israel," *Jewish Advocate*, September 3, 1987, 1; Phyllis Singer, "Views Exchanged by Pope and Jews during Meeting in Miami," *American Israelite*, September 17, 1987, 1.

And then there are Jewish organizations that bring to the fore a genuine Jewish concern, Jewish unity, and are swept away with a need to produce a *tekiah gedolah,* but with no connection to the *tekiah* of Sinai.

From an individual standpoint, there are two challenges. We must be sure that the *tekiah* that follows the *teruah* is a reproduction of the *tekiah* that precedes the *teruah* rather than something that is produced by the *teruah.* In retrospect, a *teruah* can be reconstructed. It is straightened out and is no longer a *teruah.* We have witnessed in the Iran-Contra hearings how people with the aid of counsel are able to reconstruct actions and are made to be exemplars of patriotism.[8]

And there is the challenge of avoiding connecting the *teruah* to only the first *tekiah,* relating only to abstract ideals and not to practical living. Such is the man who concentrates on coronating Hashem over the four corners of the world, but not over himself. Such is the man who will not eat nuts on Rosh Ha-Shanah because the Hebrew word for nut, *egoz,* is equivalent to *ḥet,* "sin," in *gematria,*[9] but forgets that *ḥet* is also *ḥet* in *gematria.*

"Praises to the people who know the *teruah*" (Psalms 89:16).

8. See R. W. Apple, Jr., "North Portrays Band of Patriots Striving to Surmount Obstacles," *Minneapolis Star and Tribune,* July 9, 1987, 09A; Adam Pertman, "Panel Members Say North's Image Will Make Task Harder," *Boston Globe,* July 10, 1987, 10; Wilbur G. Landrey, "In the World of Oliver North, It's Patriotic to Lie under Orders," *St. Petersburg Times,* July 12, 1987, 5D.
9. R. Moses Isserles (*Rema,* Poland, 1525 or 1530–1572), *Rema* to R. Joseph Caro (Safed, 1488–1575), *Shulḥan Arukh, Oraḥ Ḥayyim* 583:2.

How to Ask and Get More than You Bargained For

1980s

The pious man, overwhelmed by both a sense of awe in the presence of Hashem and his own unworthiness, dares not beseech Hashem with his material and mundane needs without promising to give something in return. We are given a poignant reminder of this by Hannah's petition for a child. No less than three times does she refer to herself in her entreaty to Hashem as "Your maidservant" (I Samuel 1:11).[1] She prefaces her request by calling Hashem by a phrase that was never used before, "*Hashem Tzevakot,*" "the God of Hosts."[2] Then she says that if only she be given the gift of a child, "I shall give him to Hashem all the

1. "Hashem, Master of Legions, if You take note of the suffering of Your maidservant, and You remember me, and do not forget Your maidservant, and give Your maidservant male offspring, I shall give him to Hashem all the days of his life, and a razor shall not come upon his head."
2. *Berakhot* 31b.

days of his life, and a razor shall not come upon his head" (I Samuel 1:11). A humble petition, perfectly structured.

Yet our Sages read into her words more than just a humble supplication. The phrase *Hashem Tzevakot* is taken to mean that Hashem created two hosts, a heavenly host and an earthly host. The heavenly host does not multiply, but the creation lives forever. In contrast, the earthly host does not live forever, but it multiplies. "Where do I belong?" she asks. "If I belong in the heavenly host, I should live forever. If I belong in the earthly host, I should have children." This interpretation of Hannah's words transforms her humble request into a demand.[3]

And it does not end there. "If You take note of the suffering of Your maidservant" (I Samuel 1:11) is interpreted to mean, if I have a child, fine. If not, I will closet myself with a man in the presence of my husband. He will warn me, and I will be forced to drink of the waters of the *sotah*. Hashem will not make the words of the Torah a farce. I will have children, since I am innocent. This interpretation transforms the humble request into a threat.[4]

The message that our Sages are conveying here, I submit, is that Hannah's request was not a *quid pro quo*, that if Hashem would grant her a child, in exchange, she would dedicate him to Hashem. Instead, she desired a child only as a vehicle to serve Hashem. And how do we know this? In her petition, she asks for *zera anashim*, "male offspring" (I Samuel 1:11). This means *zera ha-muvla bein anashim*, an ordinary child, one who would disappear in the crowd.[5] *Lo ḥakham, ve-lo tipesh*, "neither too wise nor a fool." And into this child she would pour every molecule of her being in order that he should realize his potential.

The next test of her sincerity comes at the time the child is born. When a prayer is answered, however unattainable it might have been before, it seems a natural right! And the desperate, hopeless plight of before is often forgotten.

In her prayer, Hannah used the phrase "if You take note of the suffering of Your maidservant" (I Samuel 1:11). This is almost identical

3. *Rashi* to I Samuel 1:11.
4. *Berakhot* 31b.
5. Ibid.

to what Leah said when Reuben was born.[6] So why did Hannah not name her child Reuben? The name Reuben would have fit so well into the phraseology of her prayer. But such a name might deflect Hannah from her high mission of "I shall give him to Hashem all the days of his life." She might feel that her primary purpose in having her child was to be free once and for all from the vicious taunts of Peninnah, and perhaps gain even more affection from her husband, although he says, "Am I not better to you than ten children?" (I Samuel 1:8). So that every time she would utter the name of her precious child, it would remind her of her vow in no uncertain terms, she called him *Shemuel*, "*ki me-Hashem she'iltiv*," "because from Hashem I requested him" (I Samuel 1:20).

The moment of truth comes when the child is weaned. Now we will see whether she keeps her vow. Does she project her fervor and idealism back in time to the fateful moment when she prayed in the Sanctuary for a child? If so, she will lend a maximal interpretation to her vow. But maybe she lost that enthusiasm and idealism, and will ascribe only a minimal interpretation to her vow.

Samuel was a Levite. Levites usually began their training at age twenty-five.[7] Hannah had promised that she would give her son to Hashem "all the days of his life." So her ambition for her child could very well have been limited to his taking his place in the rotation in the Temple. Until then, Elkanah's tutelage of Torah would have certainly sufficed as a minimal interpretation of "all the days of his life."

But no, she ascribes a maximal interpretation to this phrase and does nothing less than present Samuel to Eli, requesting that the child be his ward, his student. Incredible! Moreover, R. Nehorai interprets *morah* in the phrase "a *morah* shall not come upon his head" (I Samuel 1:11) as a razor, that Samuel would be a *nazir*.[8] Hannah apparently wanted to fulfill R. Yose's interpretation of *morah* as *mora basar va-dam*, "fear of

6. See Genesis 29:32 ("She called him Reuben, as she had declared, 'Because Hashem has seen my humiliation, for now my husband will love me.'").
7. Numbers 8:24.
8. Mishnah, *Nazir* 9:5; *Nazir* 66a. R. Nehorai draws a parallel between Samuel and Samson, who was a Nazarite, and with respect to whom it is said "a *morah* shall not come upon his head" (Judges 13:5).

human beings."[9] How? Let the child's first experience outside the home environment be *re'iyat panim ba-azarah*.[10] Let him imbibe the experience of fear of Heaven as his first experience and then build upon it.

Hannah was a woman who internalized the lesson of *le-David Hashem Ori* (Psalms 27) very well. David said only "one thing I ask of Hashem" (Psalms 27:4), but then proceeded to request a whole litany of things culminating in *ḥanneni ve-aneni*, "be gracious toward me and answer me" (Psalms 27:7), wanting a *mattenat ḥinnam*. But the explanation is that he desired only to be a servant of Hashem. He then had the right to ask that anything that would be an impediment to this should be removed.[11]

Hannah asked for only an ordinary son. But when Samuel was two years old, she already saw visions of his greatness. He would be no ordinary boy, lost in the crowd. Rather, he would be the very center of Jewish life. "May Hashem judge to the ends of the earth; may He give power to his King and raise the pride of his anointed one" (I Samuel 2:10).

Let our lot be of Hannah's, to aspire to high purpose. Then our *tefillot* will be answered beyond our wildest imagination!

---

9. Mishnah, *Nazir* 9:5; *Nazir* 66a. According to the *Maharsha*, R. Yose's interpretation of the word "*morah*" (מורה) should be understood as "authority" rather than "fear" because *morah* is written with the letter *heh* (ה) rather than with an *aleph* (i.e., מורא). R. Samuel Eliezer b. Judah ha-Levi Edels (*Maharsha*, Poland, 1555–1631), *Ḥiddushei Aggadot, Nazir* 66a. The *Malbim*, by contrast, understands R. Yose's interpretation of *morah* to be "fear" despite the spelling of *morah* with a *heh*. See R. Meir Loeb b. Jehiel Michel Weisser (*Malbim*, Poland, Romania, and Russia, 1809–1879), *Malbim* to I Samuel 1:11. See also *Radak* to I Samuel 1:11, s.v. "*u-morah* (understanding *Targum Yonatan*'s interpretation of *morah*, i.e., *marvat anash*, to mean fear of human beings, as if *morah* were written with an *aleph*).
10. In the time of the Temple, every Jewish male was required to appear in the Temple on the first day of each of the Three Festivals with a *korban olah* (Deuteronomy 16:16). The obligation to appear in the Temple is referred to as "*re'iyat panim ba-azarah*" (lit., "showing one's face in the Courtyard of the Temple"). See Maimonides, *Mishnah Torah, Ḥagigah* 1:1; R. Aaron b. Joseph ha-Levi (*Ra'ah*, Spain, ca. 1235–1300), *Sefer ha-Ḥinnukh*, eds. R. Yitzhak Yeshayah Weiss, R. David Zicherman, and R. Yitzhak Weinstein (Jerusalem: Mekhon Yerushalayim, 1992), mitzvah no. 452.
11. *Malbim* to Psalms 27:4.

Ignoring the Obvious

September 13, 1988

In the public readings on Rosh Ha-Shanah, we encounter four individuals who either do not recognize, or opt to ignore, the obvious. First we find a mother, Hagar. She is driven with her child Ishmael from Abraham's house. She is given the meager provision of a flask of water. When it runs out, the mother is made to watch her parched child pine away. But all along, the well was in front of her eyes, as we read that Hashem did not create a well for her. He merely opened her eyes.[1] The woman who was obsessed with "let me not see the death of the child" (Genesis 21:16) abandoned all sense of duty.

Would a Jewish woman, asks R. Samson Raphael Hirsch, conduct herself in the manner of Hagar, first casting her child under some brush, not caring if he would be injured thereby, and then separating herself from him "*ke-metaḥavei keshet*," "a distance of several bowshots" (Genesis 21:16)?[2] No. The Jewish mother would have clung to her child

1. Genesis 21:19.
2. R. Samson Raphael Hirsch (Germany, 1808–1888), Genesis 21:15–16.

and comforted him. She would have done as much as she could do. Yes, someone wrapped in self-pity does not see the obvious. Her salvation is staring her right in the face. And Hashem does not even listen to such anguish, the anguish of self-pity that is accompanied by an abandonment of a sense of duty. "God heard the cry of the youth" (Genesis 21:17), not the cry of Hagar.

The modern-day descendants of Hagar follow in the same tradition. They also screech "let me not see the death of the child." But they goad the Palestinian children and women to throw rocks and Molotov cocktails at the Israeli soldiers.[3] They conceal machine gun emplacement behind women and children.[4] And all along, those who finance the insurrection distance themselves safely *ke-metaḥavei keshet.*

And there were the two lads who accompanied Abraham to the fateful *Akedah.* On the third day, "they perceived the place from afar" (Genesis 22:4). Abraham sees the Divine Presence on Mount Moriah. He asks Isaac, "What do you see?" Isaac also sees the Divine Presence. But Eliezer and Ishmael see nothing.[5] What would Ishmael, the *metzaḥek,* "scorner," make of the *Akedah*? He would think that Abraham, an elderly man, had gone berserk and decided to murder his child. And Eliezer, "*ha-moshel be-khol asher lo,*" "who controlled all that belonged to Abraham" (Genesis 24:2), Abraham's spiritual heir,[6]

---

3. Islah Jad, "From the Salons to the Popular Committees: Palestinian Women, 1919–1989," in Jamal R. Nassar and Roger Heacock, eds., *Intifada: Palestine at the Crossroads* (New York: Praeger, 1990), 133; Don Peretz, *Intifada: The Palestinian Uprising* (Boulder, CO: Westview, 1990), 83–87, 97; Mare Tanenbaum, "PLO Inspired Violence," *Jewish Advocate,* December 31, 1987, 10.
4. Jillian Becker, *The PLO: The Rise and Fall of the Palestine Liberation Organization* (New York: St. Martin's Press, 1984), 204 ("PLO bases were defended with trenches and gun emplacements, many on top of schools and hospitals, and in the midst of houses.").
5. Genesis Rabbah 56:2.
6. Genesis Rabbah 59:8; *Yoma* 28b; *Maharsha, Ḥiddushei Aggadot, Yoma* 28b, s.v. "*ha-moshel*" and "*Damesek.*" The Talmud at *Yoma* 28b interprets the phrase that Eliezer had control over his master's household to mean that Eliezer had dominion over the teachings of his master. The Talmud derives this interpretation from the reference to Eliezer at Genesis 15:2 as "*Damesek Eliezer,*" an acronym for "*doleh u-mashkeh,*" he draws and gives others to drink, signifying that Eliezer drew from the Torah of his master Abraham and taught others Torah.

was, of course, a believer, but he would not see the episode behind the sacrifice of a child as God's orders. He would not see that the price of the *Akedah* was the whole future of the Jewish people. The price was a lost eternity – "*ani ve-ha-na'ar nelekhah ad koh,*" "I and the lad will go up to here" (Genesis 22:5). The promise "*koh yihiyeh zar'ekha*" (Genesis 15:5), that your offspring will be as numerous as the stars of the heaven, would not be fulfilled.[7]

And finally, Abraham did not react initially to the order "Do not stretch out your hand against the lad" (Genesis 22:12). He thought, what did I come here for? Surely I should at least draw some blood from Isaac?[8] Then the order came, "*al ta'as lo me'umah,*" "do not do anything to him" (Genesis 22:12).[9] Even then, as the *Rashbam* avers, Abraham was not sure if he should withdraw, if he should give credence to the order to withdraw, which contradicted the original instructions. His doubts were not resolved until he saw a ram caught in the thicket by its horns.[10] When he saw the ram, he then decided that it was meant to replace Isaac.[11]

If Abraham had not approached his mission with a full heart, with every molecule of his being, he surely would have grasped the straw that was cast his way and withdrawn happily when he heard "do not stretch out your hand against the lad." The stubbornness of spirit that Abraham displayed in his hesitation to withdraw showed perhaps an even greater loyalty to the mission than his initial acceptance of the mission.

---

7. Genesis Rabbah 56:2; *Midrash Tanḥuma, Va-Yera* 23; *Rashi* to Genesis 22:5, s.v. "*ad koh.*" Focusing on the word "*koh,*" the Midrash interprets the phrase "*ve-nelkhah ad koh*" to mean that Abraham said that he would see how Hashem would resolve the apparent conflict between His command to bring Isaac up as an offering and His promise "*koh yihiyeh zar'ekha,*" "so shall your offspring be, as numerous as the stars of the heavens" (Genesis 15:5).
8. Genesis Rabbah 56:7; *Rashi* to Genesis 22:12.
9. The Midrash explains that the word "*me'umah*" signifies that Abraham should not make a wound, "*mum,*" in Isaac. Genesis Rabbah 56:7; R. Zev Wolf Einhorn (*Maharzu,* Vilna, d. 1862), *Perush Maharzu* ad loc., s.v. "*al ta'as lo me'umah*" (noting that the word "*mum*" is spelled *me'um* at Daniel 1:4).
10. Genesis 22:13.
11. R. Samuel b. Meir (*Rashbam,* France, ca. 1080–1174), *Rashbam* to Genesis 22:13.

On this Rosh Ha-Shanah, may we resolve to not let ourselves be wrapped up in self-pity lest we, God forbid, become blinded to even the most obvious means of our survival. Let us have the vision to approach a mitzvah with the excitement that lets our imagination run wild. How many worlds are we creating with our mitzvot! How much merit are we conferring upon future generations! And finally, dare we desert from our service to our friend or the community by the slightest hint that we have done our job. No, we cannot walk away when we hear "do not stretch out your hand against the lad," and even when we hear "do not do anything to him."

The Yom Tov of Rosh Ha-Shanah

September 20, 1990

Rosh Ha-Shanah as a *yom tov* presents a glaring paradox. On the one hand, it is designated a day of judgment, when three books are opened.[1] But it is also a festival. In the words of Nehemiah, "Go, eat rich foods and drink sweet beverages, and send portions to those who have nothing prepared, for today is sacred to our Lord. Do not be sad; the enjoyment of Hashem is your strength!" (Nehemiah 8:10).

But there is a basic incompatibility here. As the Midrash puts it, if someone were on trial for his life, he would naturally be a nervous wreck. He would therefore neglect his physical appearance and would not even be able to think about food! Focusing of the festive mood of

1. *Rosh Ha-Shanah* 16b.

the day would seem to distract from the awesomeness of the day. It might even betray our belief that a day of judgment is really taking place.[2]

Permit me to suggest that the festive mood of the day is all for the purpose of reinforcing our resolve to make a spiritual leap on the Day of Judgment. Our thrust toward sweetness on the Day of Judgment focuses on two customs. One is the dipping of the *ḥallah* in honey, thus transforming the ordinary crust of bread into manna.[3] Here we make a graphic demonstration of our basic belief that the entire sustenance of man for the year is fixed for him from Rosh Ha-Shanah.[4]

Then there is the custom of dipping an apple in honey. Our tradition is very rich with symbolism, but possibly no object is more multifaceted in symbolism than the apple. "Like an apple tree among the trees of the forest, so is my Beloved among the sons" (Song of Songs 2:3). Why is Hashem compared to an apple? Just as an apple does not have an attractive appearance from afar, but when we come close, we realize that it has a nice fragrance, and when we taste it, we realize that it has a good taste, so, too, the demands that Hashem places upon us are at first blush onerous. But when we do the mitzvot, we find a sweetness in them.[5] Torah is also compared to an apple – "*rappeduni ba-tappuḥim*" (lit., "spread apples around me") (Song of Songs 2:5).[6]

But the resolve should be to react not only when we are thrust into a setting of Torah. "The orders of Hashem are upright, gladdening the heart" (Psalms 19:9). We reverse it and say that we must have Torah because "*ḥolat ahavah ani*," "I am lovesick" (Song of Songs 2:5). Without Torah, I am lovesick.

And finally, the Jewish people are compared to an apple – "He smelled the fragrance of his garments [*begadav*] and blessed him; he said, 'See, the fragrance of my son is like the fragrance of a field that Hashem

---

2. *Yalkut Shimoni, Va-Et'hanan* 825. See also Jerusalem Talmud, *Rosh Ha-Shanah* 1:3; R. Jacob b. Asher (*Tur*, Spain, 1270–1343), *Tur, Oraḥ Ḥayyim* 581 (citing midrash).
3. See Exodus 16:31 (stating that the manna "tasted like a cake fried in honey").
4. *Beitzah* 16a.
5. Exodus Rabbah 17:2; R. Enoch Zundel b. Joseph (Białystock, d. 1867), *Etz Yosef* ad loc., s.v. "*hada hu de-kesiv*" (explaining that the apple does not have many leaves, and thus does not appear attractive from afar).
6. Song of Songs Rabbah 2:14.

has blessed'" (Genesis 27:27).[7] Our Sages tell us, do not read the word as "*begadav*," "his garments," but rather as "*bogedav*," "his traitors." Even those Jews who appear to be traitors to the teachings of Judaism diffuse the fragrance of good deeds.[8] Hence the apple represents the eternity and mystique of the Jewish people – *Yisrael ve-Oraita ve-Kudesha Berikh Hu, ḥad hu*, "Israel, the Torah, and the Holy One, Blessed is He, are one,"[9] with the widest integration.

Yehi ratzon she-teḥadesh aleinu shanah tovah u-metukah![10]

7. *Ta'anit* 29b; *Rashi* to Genesis 27:27, s.v. "*ke-rei'aḥ sadeh asher berakho Hashem*."
8. *Sanhedrin* 37a; *Ba'al ha-Turim*, Genesis 8:21, s.v. "*va-yaraḥ*."
9. See Zohar, *Aḥarei Mot* 3:73a.
10. "May it be Your will that a good and sweet year will be renewed for us." This expression is said on Rosh Ha-Shanah when the apple is dipped in honey.

Making a Statement

September 9, 1991

The awesomeness of Rosh Ha-Shanah is succinctly expressed by our Sages in the dictum that three books are opened on this day: one for the absolutely righteous – they are immediately inscribed and sealed for life; one for the absolutely wicked – they are immediately inscribed for death; and one for those who are neither absolutely righteous nor absolutely wicked – their judgment is suspended until Yom Kippur. If they increase their merit in the interim, they will be inscribed for life. If not, God forbid, they will be inscribed for death.[1]

In recording this dictum, Maimonides departs from the talmudic text in a significant way. With respect to the one who is neither absolutely righteous nor absolutely wicked, the *beinoni,* Maimonides rules that if he does *teshuvah,* he will be inscribed for life; if not, for death.[2]

1. *Rosh Ha-Shanah* 16b.
2. Maimonides, *Mishneh Torah, Teshuvah* 3:3.

But why so stringent a requirement? It should suffice to do a single mitzvah to tip the scales. R. Yitzhak Hutner addresses himself to the contradiction and, in the process, enunciates a major Torah *hashkafah*.[3] "What is a *tzaddik* and what is a *rasha*?" he asks. He rejects the notion that there is an arithmetic accounting of mitzvot and *averot,* taking into consideration the quality of performance and the relative importance of the deed involved. That approach would lead to the peculiarity that one's spiritual station is constantly changing, even in a single day.

Instead, R. Hutner defines a *tzaddik* in terms of his attachment or attitude toward mitzvot. The *tzaddik* is committed to mitzvot, whereas the *rasha* is basically attracted to sin. The addition of one mitzvah or *averah* here and there will therefore make no difference.

A *beinoni,* on the other hand, is one with no identity. He vacillates between being attracted to good and being pulled by evil.

The only way a *beinoni* can leap to become a *tzaddik* is by demonstrating that he is attached to good, that he is committed. This requires nothing less than *teshuvah.* The performance of a single mitzvah will not do![4]

Permit me to suggest that the entire readings on Rosh Ha-Shanah are designed to give us the formula for how to leap from the book of the *beinoni* to the book of the *tzaddik.* It is by making a statement that we are indeed attached to mitzvot and repulsed by sin. One route is that we perform mitzvot that we would not otherwise perform on the basis of our own inclinations. Hence, we read that "Abraham circumcised his son Isaac at the age of eight days as God had commanded him" (Genesis 21:4). Abraham certainly would not have performed *milah* based on his own inclinations. And the greatest statement within the context of mitzvot is the *Akedah,* the ultimate submission of human will to Hashem.

But we are reminded that in the ordinary course of events of life, even in the lives of the great luminaries of the ages, certain things are done simply out of self-interest. Hence the reading of the apparently

3. R. Yitzhak Hutner (Brooklyn, 1907–1980), *Paḥad Yitzḥak, Rosh Ha-Shanah* (Brooklyn, NY: Mossad Gur Aryeh, 2008), *ma'amar* 18, pp. 136–138.
4. Ibid., 138.

irrelevant episode of Abimelech's covenant with Abraham.[5] This was a treaty based on self-interest.[6] So we need another route to leap from the *beinoni* to the *tzaddik,* and this is in the realm of human judgment and initiative. Here we can make a grand statement to show our attachment to good and repulsion toward evil.

It is the great women of Jewish history who provide us with the models here. One way to make a statement is to repudiate evil, even if the evil is of our own doing. Sarah tells Abraham, "Drive out this slavewoman with her son" (Genesis 21:10), even though Sarah had given Hagar to Abraham, saying, "Perhaps I will be built up through her" (Genesis 16:2).[7] Hannah made a statement with grand ambition, not to give in to natural limitations. The power of her prayer achieved for her a son. But she wanted only *zera anashim,* "male offspring," and promised "I shall give him to Hashem all the days of his life" (I Samuel 1:11).[8] Rachel made a statement by her supreme self-sacrifice to advance the welfare of her sister.[9] She gave Leah the signs "*she-lo teitze aḥoti le-ḥerpah,*" "that my sister not be put to shame."[10]

May we follow these grand models and be immediately inscribed in the Book of Life.

5. Genesis 21:22–32.
6. See R. Joseph Saul Nathanson (Galicia, 1810–1875), *Divrei Sha'ul al ha-Torah, Va-Yera,* Genesis 21:27, s.v. "*va-yikhretu sheneihem brit*" (explaining that Abraham did not violate the prohibition of "you shall not seal a covenant with them nor shall you show them favor" [Deuteronomy 7:2] by entering into a covenant with Abimelech because Abraham acted out of his own self-interest to recover the wells that Abimelech's servants had seized).
7. The Torah reading for the first day of Rosh Ha-Shanah is at Genesis 21:1–34.
8. The *haftarah* for the first day of Rosh Ha-Shanah is at I Samuel 1:1–2:10.
9. The *haftarah* for the second day of Rosh Ha-Shanah is at Jeremiah 31:1–19. There we read "Rachel weeps for her children" (Jeremiah 31:14).
10. Lamentations Rabbah, *petiḥta* 24. See also *Megillah* 13b; *Bava Batra* 123a; *Rashi* to Genesis 29:25; *Rashi* to Jeremiah 31:14; *Radak* to Jeremiah 31:14, s.v. "*ki einennu.*"

Abraham Called the Name of the Place *Hashem Yir'eh*

September 10, 1991

Our Forefather Abraham, who described himself as "I am but dust and ash" (Genesis 18:27), was regarded by our Sages as one of the most humble and meek people who ever lived.[1] Characteristically, a humble and meek person never regards his or her achievement as worthy of notice. Yet, when Abraham reached the pinnacle of his spiritual heights, at the triumph of the *Akedah,* he refused to remove Isaac from the *Akedah* until Hashem would promise him with an oath that He would consider the ashes of the ram as if they were the ashes of Isaac. Once the wish was granted, Abraham removed Isaac from the *Akedah.*[2]

Then, as an afterthought, Abraham demanded further that Hashem affix his stamp of *emet,* "truth," to the whole incident of the

1. See *Ḥullin* 89a.
2. *Midrash Tanḥuma, Va-Yera* 23; *Da'at Zekenim,* Genesis 22:14, s.v. "*asher ye'amer ha-yom.*"

Akedah. Hashem said, "Too late, but as a kindness, I will give *emet* to your descendant Jacob." "Grant truth to Jacob, kindness to Abraham" (Micah 7:20).[3]

Permit me to suggest that rather than reflecting a craving for recognition and immortality, Abraham's request reflects his generosity of spirit. If Abraham understood most profoundly that Hashem is the Master of All, and one must set aside his own feelings to be subservient to Hashem regardless of any conflict with his own inclinations, then this should be shared by his descendants. Why should it be invisible, known only to Hashem?

And, indeed, throughout the millennia of persecutions, each time a Jew lays down his life *al kiddush Hashem*, it is the product of the inspiration of Abraham at the *Akedah* because the sacrifice of the ram at the *Akedah* is considered as if Abraham sacrificed Isaac.

Eventually, everyone will understand what the *Akedah* was all about. They will pierce through the surface, what appears to be an old man bent on sacrificing his son, and understand that it represents the subservience of the self to Hashem. But this will only be later.

Abraham's inner aspiration regarding the *Akedah* can perhaps be read into the verse "Abraham called the name of that site '*Hashem Yir'eh*,' as it is said this day, on the mountain Hashem will be seen" (Genesis 22:14). The mountain suddenly appeared, to commemorate a great deed. This was a sign to Abraham that the *Akedah* would not be invisible to mankind, remaining only between him and Hashem, but would have its proper impact for all eternity.

Abraham called the place *Hashem Yir'eh*[4] but Melchizedek called it *Shalem*.[5] The combination of the names *Hashem Yir'eh* and *Shalem* produced the name *Yerushalayim*, "Jerusalem."[6]

---

3. *Da'at Zekenim*, loc. cit.
4. Genesis 22:14.
5. See Genesis 14:18.
6. Genesis Rabbah 56:10. Melchizedek is identified as Shem, the son of Noah. *Midrash Shoḥer Tov*, Psalms 76; *Perush Maharzu* to Genesis Rabbah ad loc., s.v. "*melekh Shalem*" (citing midrash).

Now, as we enter the new year and all eyes focus on the Middle East peace talks,[7] world Jewry can cry out and say to Hashem, we have captured the essence of Abraham of the *Akedah* in respect of Jerusalem. There is no issue that so inflames, that is so emotionally charged, where there is no compromise, as "Jerusalem united and indivisible." *Galui ve-yadu'a lefanekha Hashem,* "it is abundantly clear to you, Hashem," that the Jewish people will pay any price for this. And we do not have to request that the ram should be considered as if it were a human sacrifice because Jerusalem was captured with the blood of the valiant IDF and the tears of the Jewish people.

So we can at least expect that, with God's help, some aspect of Abraham's demand of *emet* should be realized. Most fundamentally, nothing should take place in the context of the negotiation for peace that would betray the name Jerusalem itself. Melchizedek's part was that he "brought out bread and wine" (Genesis 14:18). He accorded Abraham the right to intervene and stand against terrorism and tyranny. So, too, any advocacy of a Palestinian State would be tantamount to approval of terrorism, betraying the name *Yerushalayim* itself.

We have already seen a glorious chapter in the fulfillment of the blessing "I shall greatly increase your offspring like the stars of the heavens" (Genesis 22:17) with one million Russian immigrants coming to Israel.[8] May they come in peace, and may the transition be as smooth as possible. May Hashem give Congress the discernment to reject President Bush's plea for a three-month hiatus in the consideration of the ten billion dollars of housing loan guarantees until the Middle East Conference is over.[9] This is blackmail, to make humanitarian aid a lever for

7. David Makovsky, "Provided Israel's Terms for Palestinian Team Are Accepted, Shamir 'Yes' to Talks," *Jerusalem Post*, August 2, 1991, 1; Michel Zlotowski, "Shamir Says, 'We Will Still Go to Peace Talks,'" *Jerusalem Post*, September 13, 1991, 1. The conference was held in Madrid from October 30, 1991, to November 1, 1991, hosted by Spain and co-sponsored by the United States and the Soviet Union. Paul G. Peirpaoli Jr., "Madrid Conference," in Spencer C. Tucker, ed., *Encyclopedia of the Arab-Israeli Conflict: A Political, Social and Military History* (Santa Barbara, CA: ABC-CLIO, 2008), 657.
8. Abraham Rabinovich, "Planning for One Million New Israelis: Between a Vision and a Nightmare," *Jerusalem Post*, August 16, 1991, 5.
9. Clyde Haberman, "Israel Dismayed by Bush Delay on Loans," *New York Times*, September 8, 1991, 3.

political gain for the Arabs. This is not *emet*. This betrays a principle that humanitarian aid should not be mixed into politics.[10]

And, yes, we dare imagine beyond this for the final fulfillment of the blessing "your offspring shall inherit the gate of its enemies" (Genesis 22:17), which is not military conquest but rather the supremacy of the Torah to the other branches of wisdom and the submission of the entire world to *da'at Torah*.[11]

10. See, e.g., International Federation of Red Cross and Red Crescent Societies, "Code of Conduct; Principles of Conduct for the International Red Cross and Red Crescent Movement and NGOs in Disaster Response Programmes" (1994), no. 3 ("Aid will not be used to further a particular political or religious standpoint.").
11. See R. Samson Raphael Hirsch, Genesis 22:17.

Tashlikh – The Unifying Mitzvah

September 21, 1998

Perhaps there is no custom in our tradition that is more widely practiced than *Tashlikh*. Observance of this ritual runs the entire gamut, from the minimalist who says, "Sure, it's ideal to do *Tashlikh* on the first day of Rosh Ha-Shanah, but if not, performing *Tashlikh* during the Ten Days of Repentance is fine.[1] Hoshana Rabbah is a good time,[2] and if not, any time before Ḥanukkah."[3] With respect to place, "Sure, it's ideal to be physically

1. R. Joseph Hayyim b. Elijah al-Hakam (*Ben Ish Ḥai*, Baghdad, 1833 or 1835–1909), *Torah le-Shemah, Oraḥ Ḥayyim* no. 145; R. Israel Hayyim Friedman (Hungary, 1852–1922), *Likkutei Maharih*, vol. 3 (Hungary: Sziget, 1900–1911), *Seder Rosh Ha-Shanah*, p. 77.
2. See Dr. Yom Tov Levinsky, *Sefer ha-Mo'adim: Sukkot*, vol. 4 (Tel Aviv: Devir, 1951), 385–386 (recording the custom of certain communities to perform *Tashlikh* on Hoshana Rabbah, and noting that in Galicia, it was customary on that day to escort those who were unable to perform *Tashlikh* on Rosh Ha-Shanah to a river so they could recite *Tashlikh*).
3. From the first day of Elul until Ḥanukkah, the form of an outstretched arm appears in the sky as a sign that those who were unable to repent during the Ten Days of

near a body of water, but if not, just swivel toward the oceanside view in your office and recite *'mi Kel kamokha'* (Micah 7:18).[4] And why not say *Tashlikh* on the way home on the subway as you are passing the East River?"

But then there are the maximalists, satisfied only with *mehadrin min ha-mehadrin*. For them, *Tashlikh* must be performed only on the first day of Rosh Ha-Shanah before *Minḥah* – it is a *mitzvah be-zemano* (lit., "in its time").[5] And one must be physically present near a body of water and make sure that the water contains fish. That way, you can also enjoy a symbolic advantage – just as a fish's eyes are open all the time and it has no eyelids, Hashem watches us always.[6] And just as fish are not visible, so, too, we are impervious to the Evil Eye.[7] And don't forget to shake your pockets, symbolizing that we are getting rid of our sins.[8]

Then there are people who say that the crowds and the socializing distract them from the holiness of the day, and skip *Tashlikh* altogether.

The custom of *Tashlikh*, however, touches the religious bone of almost every Jew.

Repentance may repent and be accepted before the last day of Ḥanukkah. See R. Joseph Benjamin Reich (Halych, Galicia, ca. 1840–1911), *Benei Binyamin, Ḥanukkah*, s.v. "*shamati mi-peh kadosh*" (quoting R. Zevi Elimelech Dynow).

4. R. Moses Sofer (*Ḥatam Sofer*, Hungary, 1762–1839) would recite *Tashlikh* on a hill behind his house from where he could see a river at a distance. R. Hezekiah Feivel Plaut (Hungary, 1818–1895), *Likkutei Ḥever ben Ḥayyim*, vol. 3, Introduction, *Minhagei Mori ha-Gaon Ḥatam Sofer*; R. Isaac Zvi Bernfeld, *Siddur Tefillah Ḥatam Sofer*, vol. 2 (New York: Gross Bros., 1966), *Seder Tashlikh*.
5. R. Shneur Zalman of Liadi (Russia, 1745–1812), *Shulḥan Arukh ha-Rav, Oraḥ Ḥayyim* 583:7; R. Israel Meir ha-Kohen Kagan (*Ḥafetz Ḥayyim*, Radin, 1838–1933), *Mishnah Berurah* 583:8.
6. R. Isaiah ha-Levi Horowitz (*Shelah ha-Kadosh*, Prague, ca. 1565–1630), *Shenei Luḥot ha-Berit, Masekhet Rosh Ha-Shanah Ammud ha-Din, Ner Mitzvah* ¶ 25, *hag'hah*, s.v. "*u-matzati kavvanah nekhonah*"; R. Elijah Shapira (Prague, 1660–1712), *Eliyahu Rabbah, Shulḥan Arukh, Oraḥ Ḥayyim* 596.
7. R. Moses Isserles, *Darkhei Mosheh* to *Tur, Oraḥ Ḥayyim* 583, n. 2; R. Shneur Zalman of Liadi, *Shulḥan Arukh ha-Rav, Oraḥ Ḥayyim* 583:7; *Ḥafetz Ḥayyim, Mishnah Berurah* 583:8. See also *Berakhot* 20a (noting that fish are protected from the Evil Eye by the waters that cover them). The Evil Eye is a destructive spiritual force engendered by jealous attention. See R. Judah Loew b. Bezalel (*Maharal*, Prague, ca. 1525–1609), *Netivot Olam, Netiv Ayin Tov*.
8. R. Hayyim b. Joseph Vital (Safed, 1542–1620), *Peri Etz Ḥayyim, Sha'ar ha-Shofar*, ch. 5; R. Ephraim Zalman Margolioth (Ukraine, 1762–1828), *Matteh Ephraim* 598; R. Joseph Kosman (Germany, 18th cent.), *Noheg ka-Tzon Yosef, Rosh Ha-Shanah* 19.

But what is *Tashlikh* really about? The *Rema* says that is about repentance, on the basis of the verse *"ve-tashlikh be-metzulot yam kol ḥattotam,"* "You will cast all their sins into the depths of the sea" (Micah 7:19).[9] The origins of *Tashlikh* are very obscure. The *Maharil* offers that it commemorates the *Akedah.*[10] The *Kitzur Shulḥan Arukh* says that it connotes the coronation of a king, which was done near springs, symbolizing that his reign should endure.[11]

Don't these various understandings of *Tashlikh* dilute its purpose and detract from the aspect of repentance?

Permit me to suggest that the explanation of the *Ḥiddushei ha-Rim* offers a reconciliation of the various *ta'amim* (reasons). He told his Hasidim to de-emphasize the *ḥaratah,* "remorse," aspect of *teshuvah* and put the lion's share of one's energies into *kabbalah al ha-atid,* "resolutions for the future." Remorse makes us focus on the sin that we committed, so we get mired down, even beaten. We become broken. We wallow in mud. It is better to concentrate on *kabbalah al ha-atid.*[12]

Tashlikh is all about repentance. The role of the *ta'amim* then is to present us with a model for the elements to make *kabbalah al ha-atid* successful. We need the iron determination of Abraham and Isaac to overcome the obstacles of a river that the Satan put in their path.[13] But we also need a sense of exaltation and excitement that accompanies a coronation. And we should concentrate on the future because "if one comes to purify himself, he is helped."[14] Hashem will surely help us if we set our sights on a grand *kabbalah al ha-atid.*

Tashlikh demonstrates that even when Jews are seemingly very far apart, we are nevertheless very close to achieving reconciliation and unity.

---

9. *Rema* to *Shulḥan Arukh, Oraḥ Ḥayyim* 583:2.
10. R. Jacob b. Moses Moellin (*Maharil,* Germany, ca. 1360–1427), *Sefer Maharil: Minhagim,* ed. Shlomo Spitzer (Jerusalem: Mekhon Yerushalayim, 1989), 277, ¶ 9. See also *Darkhei Mosheh* to *Tur, Oraḥ Ḥayyim* 583, n. 2 (citing *Maharil*).
11. R. Solomon Ganzfried (Hungary, 1804–1886), *Kitzur Shulḥan Arukh* 129:21.
12. R. Yitzhak Meir Alter (*Ḥiddushei ha-Rim,* Poland, 1799–1866), *Ḥiddushei ha-Rim al ha-Torah, Mo'adim ve-Likkutim* (Jerusalem: Mossad ha-Rim Levine, 1992), *Yom Kippur,* p. 261.
13. *Yalkut Shimoni, Va-Yera* 99; *Midrash Tanḥuma, Va-Yera* 22.
14. *Yoma* 38b.

The Eternity of the *Akedah*

September 22, 1998

A humorist once said that for a speech to be immortal, it need not be eternal.[1] So much for a speech. But if an event in Jewish history is to be immortal, it must have the power to inspire for all eternity. So it was with the *Akedah*. The ram that suddenly appeared tangled in the brush and became the substitute for Isaac reappeared again and again in Jewish history. No part of it was wasted. The shofar that we heard at Sinai was produced from the left horn of the ram. The shofar that will be used to announce the Messiah will be produced from the right horn of the ram. Moreover, the strings for the harp of King David came from the sinews of the ram, and the belt of Elijah came from the skin of the ram.[2]

What is the Midrash telling us? There can be no doubt that the essence of the *Akedah* is the triumph of blind faith. Satan had argued to Abraham, your piety is your hypocrisy – you yourself have preached that

1. The saying is attributed to Muriel Humphrey, the wife of Hubert Humphrey. David Young, *Great Funny Quotes* (Round Rock, TX: Wind Runner Press, 2012), 232.
2. *Pirkei de-Rabbi Eliezer* 31; *Midrash ha-Gadol*, Genesis 22:13.

human sacrifice is abhorrent to God. Your piety is your insanity – people will say that an old man has gone berserk. Your piety is your irrationality – you, Abraham, have led the world out of *tohu va-vohu* into the era of Torah by preaching that there is but one God and that God is an *ohev ḥesed*, a "lover of kindness."[3] Who will be your spiritual heir to carry forward your mission? If you sacrifice Isaac, your life's work will go up in a puff of smoke! And you could not have heard correctly because the instruction "Please take your son … and bring him up there as an offering" (Genesis 22:2) amounts to Hashem reneging on His promise "through Isaac offspring will be considered yours" (Genesis 21:12), that from Isaac will proceed a multitude, and your descendants will be as numerous as the stars of the firmament.[4]

Faith triumphed over everything. At Sinai, we achieved the level of faith as a collective. We said *na'aseh ve-nishma*, "we will do and we will listen" (Exodus 24:7). We made a commitment to do, before we knew what was entailed.

But the Midrash says much more. The harp of David was produced from the sinews of the ram. How could the harp have produced the sweetest music possible, catapulting David to the highest level of happiness, bliss, and ecstasy? Is this not the opposite of the emotions that Abraham experienced as he went about his instructions to offer his son as a sacrifice – I will proceed but with a broken heart? No. Abraham was completely at peace with himself. We can see that from the resistance that he mounted when he was given the order to withdraw, "Do not stretch out your hand against the lad and do not do anything to him" (Genesis 22:12).

The lesson is that faith produces happiness. We do not have to look elsewhere for stimulation.

The Midrash says more. The belt of Elijah was made from the skin of the ram. Elijah produced clarity in the belief in Hashem – *Hashem hu ha-Elokim*, "Hashem, He is the God" (I Kings 18:39). But Abraham's trial was that even though he should have been confused, he still proceeded and did the will of Hashem. It was only because Elijah was a

3. See *Avodah Zarah* 9a.

4. Genesis 15:5.

man of perfect faith that God gave him the gift of producing certainty. Certainty is a gift.

And then there is a higher certainty, the blast of the shofar that will announce the Messiah, the shofar that will be made from the right horn of the ram. "For then I will change the nations [to speak] a pure language so that they all will proclaim the Name of Hashem, to worship Him with a united resolve" (Zephaniah 3:9).

Now, as the *Malbim* points out, in the Messianic era, the nations of the world will have achieved enlightenment and refinement, great knowledge and humanitarianism.[5] Then we will become the *or la-ammim*, "the light unto the nations."[6] We will speak to them *be-safah verurah*, "with a pure language," that they should recognize our leadership and that we are the authorities, that we are the light. Here again, the clarity is a gift from Hashem, because its source again is *emunah peshutah* of a prodigious amount.

The modern man finds this alien. According to secular thinking, we are compartmentalized; faith, logic, and emotion are three different dimensions and have different sources. We are told that our job is to harmonize them. But that is not so! All derive from a single source, *emunah*.

Permit me an analogy in Coca Cola. The secret is in the sequence and the intervals of adding ingredients because reverse engineering can reveal all the ingredients and their proportions.[7]

If we feel that in our lives, the harp of David is not what we would like it to be, and if we feel that the certainty we would like to find in our lives as we move forward is not there, and in our national existence, we are not the light for the nations of the world, perhaps the answer is less harmonizing and more searching for the source, *emunah peshutah*.

---

5. *Malbim* to Zephaniah 3:9.
6. See Isaiah 42:6 and 49:6 (using the term "*or goyim*," "a light unto the nations").
7. See Mark Pendergast, *For God, Country, and Coca-Cola: The Definitive History of the Great American Soft Drink and the Company That Makes It*, 3rd ed. (New York: Basic Books, 2013), 489.

Malkhut on Rosh Ha-Shanah

September 27, 2003

In the teaching of our Sages, the central theme of Rosh Ha-Shanah is *malkhut*. On this day, we coronate Hashem and we must accept His sovereignty over us. The theme of *malkhut* is crafted with ten carefully selected verses in the *Shemoneh Esreh*.

The model for a qualifying verse is *Shema Yisrael*. In this verse, we express the unity of Hashem, His Oneness, and the yearning that someday, He will be universally recognized.[1] It is therefore a surprise to find in the *malkhuyyot* mosaic the verse "He [Hashem] perceived no iniquity in Jacob; He saw no perversity in Israel" (Numbers 23:21). These are words that the angel put into Balaam's mouth. And "Hashem, his God, is with him" (Numbers 23:21). Even if, as *Rashi* says, we make Hashem angry or rebel against Him, the Divine Presence does not

1. Deuteronomy 6:4; *Rashi* ad loc.

depart from us.[2] And "*teruat Melekh bo,*" "the friendship of the King is in him" (Numbers 23:21). Deep down, no matter what, the Jew feels the friendship of the King.

I would ask you, where is the intensity and totality of our commitment to Hashem in this verse? The verse seems to validate us regardless of our level of commitment.

Far from undermining the theme of *malkhuyyot,* this verse provides a powerful motivational force for us to accept Hashem's sovereignty. The story of Onkelos the Convert shows how.

One of the most wicked and abhorrent enemies of the Jewish people was Titus *ha-Rasha.* He destroyed the Second Temple. The wicked Emperor heard that his nephew, Onkelos, became a convert to Judaism, so he sent a troop to bring him back to Rome and remove him from his new religion. The trip of the first troop was unsuccessful. Onkelos engaged the soldiers in theological discussions, and the troop converted to Judaism. Titus sent a second troop. The same thing happened; the troop converted. Titus then sent a third troop with instructions not to engage Onkelos in any conversation whatsoever. As they departed for Rome, he caused the soldiers to focus on the *mezuzah.* Onkelos' explanation of the *mezuzah* proved a sound bite for the troops to convert.[3]

Onkelos drew a contrast between a mortal king and Hashem. A mortal king sits inside and his guards watch him from the outside. But Hashem acts differently with His people. We, His people, are inside, and Hashem watches us as we depart and enter our home. "Hashem will guard your departure and your arrival" (Psalms 121:8).

How did the succinct explanation of the *mezuzah* make the troop convert? The answer is that it was a rude awakening for them. The point was now driven home to them that they were merely cogs in a wheel to preserve the power of Titus. Titus' rule was for self-glorification. Not so Hashem's rule over us. Hashem's rule is designed to benefit us, so Hashem is watching us.

The verse "He perceived no iniquity in Jacob" takes this theme one important step further. How can we tell what the real agenda of the

2. *Rashi* to Numbers 23:21, s.v. "*Hashem Elokav immo.*"
3. *Avodah Zarah* 11a.

King is, if he rules for himself or for the people? To find the answer, just look at how he treats someone whom he suspects of disloyalty and how he defines disloyalty. To get an idea of this, see if the King employs a spy network. Look in the prisons. Are they filled with political prisoners?

The rule of Hashem is dramatically different. Hashem always gives us the benefit of the doubt – "Hashem, his God, is with him, and the friendship of the King is in him" (Numbers 23:21) – because His reign is for our benefit.

It is only the Jew who is suffused with ebullience over Hashem's love for him and the knowledge that Hashem never gives up on him who can accept *ol malkhut Shamayim* with great enthusiasm and total commitment. It is only such a Jew who can say with integrity and sincerity *al ken nekavveh*, "therefore we put our hope in You, Hashem, our God, that we may see very soon the splendor of Your might."[4] This Jew will not only say these words with purity and enthusiasm, but will identify with the author of the words, Achan.[5]

Achan was guilty of a terrible sin of veiled misconduct. As a people, we were moving inexorably toward our destiny. Joshua entered the Land of Israel. The waters of the Jordan split.[6] We conquered Jericho.[7] The shofar caused the walls to crumble.[8] We seemed so near to the conquest of the entire Land and the building of the Temple, the unfolding of the Kingdom of Heaven in its fullness.

But then the momentum came to an abrupt halt. In the attempted conquest of Ai, thirty-six Jews fell. What seemed so easy to conquer turned into an ignominious defeat.[9]

Hashem tells Joshua that there is a sinner among the Jewish people who is the cause of their reversal. Through the casting of lots, Joshua finds out that it is Achan. Achan confesses that he was guilty of

---

4. *Aleinu* Prayer.
5. R. Nosson Nota Shapira (Krakow, 1585–1633), *Megaleh Amukot* § 133; R. Moses b. Judah Makhir (Safed, 16th cent.), *Seder ha-Yom* (*kavvanat Aleinu*). The first letters of *al ken nekavveh* (על כן נקוה) form the name Achan (עכן).
6. Joshua 3:16.
7. Joshua 6:1–27.
8. Joshua 6:20
9. Joshua 7:4–6.

veiled misconduct. He violated the ban against taking spoils from Jericho. He hid a bar of gold, silver coins, and a beautiful garment underground in his tent.[10]

What a rude awakening for Achan. Did he think that he could unilaterally stop the momentum of the Jewish people? It was misconduct that only he knew about. And the gold bar and silver coins were the property of the Sanctuary. He did not benefit from them or damage them. The greatness of Achan was that he repented and said "*al ken nikavveh.*" He yearned that with his confession, the Jewish people would go forward and the drive toward *malkhut Shamayim* could proceed to a climax.[11]

We are Achan because we imagine that whatever we do wrong cannot possibly disrupt the momentum of the Jewish people toward our destiny. On Rosh Ha-Shanah, we are challenged to relate to the repentance of Achan and acknowledge that our shortcomings are holding up *malkhut Shamayim* in its full glory. And we should do our best to move the Jewish people forward.

It is only the Jew who comes with the firm knowledge that Hashem regards him as a friend, that no matter what, His loyalty is near, the *teruat Melekh bo* Jew, who is capable of making the commitment to leap with deeds so we can move forward and say "therefore we put our hope in You, Hashem, our God, that we may see very soon the splendor of Your might."

---

10. Joshua 7:10-21; *Sanhedrin* 43b–44a.
11. *Seder ha-Yom*, loc. cit.

One Hundred Blasts

September 28, 2003

In the thinking of our Sages, the *shevarim-teruah* sound of the shofar mimics the wailing of the suffering of human beings.[1] But what is the context of the whimpering and sighs that we are mimicking?

Our Sages tell us that the hundred blasts of the shofar counteract and nullify the hundred tears of Sisera's mother.[2] Sisera was late from the battlefield. His mother worries. She goes to the window. She begins to wail as she peeks through the latticework, "Why do his chariots tarry?" (Judges 5:28). One hundred letters encompass her words until she begins to console herself with *"ha'lo yimtze'u ye'ḥalleku shalal,"* "he is probably looking for more spoils" (Judges 5:30).

The tears of Sisera's mother were wicked tears with no redeeming value. Why? We can place them in the framework of the law that every

1. *Rosh Ha-Shanah* 33b.
2. *Tosafot* to *Rosh Ha-Shanah* 33b.

teruah – broken, doleful sound – must be preceded and followed by a *tekiah*.[3] If the *teruah* is not preceded and followed by a *tekiah*, it is not a *teruah*.

In our tradition, the *tekiah*, the straight blast, is associated with high purpose and high mission. At Sinai, there was the blast of the *tekiah*.[4] And the Messiah will be heralded with the sound of the *tekiah*.[5]

The *teruah* of Sisera's mother was not sandwiched between two *tekiot*. She had no noble purpose in life. She raised and was the cheerleader of an evil monster whose motto probably was "might makes right." And after she cried, there was no *tekiah*, no rethinking or repudiation. Instead, she consoles herself that Sisera is late because he is busy with spoils and ravishing Jewish girls.

The mother of Sisera is not a relic of the past. She is truly revived in the Arab world, the European Union, the United Nations. She has taken up the causes of the Palestinians and become their mother, empathizing with their suffering.

Our bottle of tears is overflowing with the suffering of our brethren. But we do have one tear for them. The wailing of the mother of Sisera actually takes up 101 letters, and the hundred blasts of the shofar counteract only one hundred tears. One tear is left, the tear of a mother for the loss of her child. We regret that in pursuing the murderers and terrorists, and dismantling the terrorist infrastructure, there is collateral damage of innocent lives. We regret it, but it is inevitable because we are only human, and the Palestinian Authority refuses to live up to its responsibility to dismantle terror.

But to the sympathizers with the Palestinians we say, where is the *ekiah* – high moral purpose – before and after the whimpering of the murderers and the victims? There is no *tekiah* before. Instead, there is the death culture and hatred toward us fostered from the cradle – incitement, constant incitement. And after the death of the terrorists and innocent

3. *Rosh Ha-Shanah* 34a.
4. See Exodus 19:16 ("the sound of the shofar [*kol shofar*] was very powerful"); Exodus 19:19 ("the sound of the shofar [*kol shofar*] grew continually much stronger"); R. Zevi Elimelech Dynow (*Benei Yissaskhar*, Poland, 1785–1841), *Benei Yissaskhar*, *Ma'amerei Ḥodesh Tishrei*, *ma'amar* 3, *derush* 1 (noting that the phrase "*kol shofar*" in the Torah indicates the sound of a *tekiah*).
5. See Isaiah 27:13.

civilians, there is no *tekiah*, no resolve to repudiate terrorism and do something about it. Instead, there is more of the same.

Whose tears are coming out of the shofar? Are they the tears of the Generation of the Wilderness? No. When they heard the report of the Spies, "the people wept that night" (Numbers 14:1). They were demoralized. They were hearing the *tekiah* of Sinai, but could not hear the voice of Caleb, "We shall surely ascend and conquer it, for we can surely do it!" (Numbers 13:30). They could not produce the *tekiah aḥaronah*. Instead, they were stopped in their tracks with tears of self-pity and paralysis.

So whose tears are coming out of the shofar? I would say they are Hannah's. She describes herself as "a woman of aggrieved spirit" (I Samuel 1:15). She is the human manifestation of the *teruah*, a woman who is bitter and doleful. Yes, she was a living *teruah* and desperately wanted a child. But when she cried for her child, before she told Eli that she was a bitter woman – a *teruah* – she prayed to Hashem. And her prayer that precedes her self-identification as a living *teruah* was a powerful *tekiah*. She took up high mission and purpose. She seized nobility. "I will give him to Hashem all the days of his life" (I Samuel 1:11). If Hashem granted her a child, she would raise him as a servant of Hashem. She would dedicate his life to Torah and mitzvot.

When her request became a reality, Hannah did not recall her *tekiah* with a minimalist interpretation of her commitment. She could have decided that she would bask in the pleasure of having a son and keep him at home until he was twenty-five. That is when Levites first began their service in the Temple.[6] In the meantime, a *ḥavruta* with Elkanah would suffice.

No, instead she produces a *tekiah gedolah* and reads into her original words the highest commitment. She brings her child to Eli after she weans him and tells Eli, "This is the child of your blessing, 'The God of Israel will grant the request you have made of Him'" (I Samuel 1:17). You take him under your wing. He will be your *talmid* and constant companion. "I have dedicated him to Hashem; all the days of his life he is dedicated to Hashem" (I Samuel 1:28).

6. Numbers 8:24.

There is a cry that does not need a *tekiah* before it or after it, that needs no framework of the shofar. It is the cry that represents heroic action of a far superior nature – "Rachel weeps for her children" (Jeremiah 31:14). It is always a merit, even after her death. Our mother Rachel loved Jacob, and Jacob loved her, but she helped her father pull off the charade *she-lo teitze aḥoti le-ḥerpah,* "that my sister should not be disgraced."[7] Alas, we are not Rachel, only Hannah. But the better the *tekiot* of Hannah, the more Hannah merges with Rachel.

---

7. Lamentations Rabbah, *petiḥta* 24. See also *Megillah* 13b; *Bava Batra* 123a; *Rashi* to Genesis 29:25; *Rashi* to Jeremiah 31:14; *Radak* to Jeremiah 31:14, s.v. "*ki einennu.*"

Zikhronot

September 16, 2004

There is no day in the year when the *Akedah* is more prominent in our prayers than the second day of Rosh Ha-Shanah. We get four doses of it: *korbanot*,[1] the Torah reading,[2] shofar,[3] and *zikhronot*.[4] The crescendo is "May You mercifully remember the *Akedah* of Isaac for the sake of his offering."[5]

As an act of pure faith, requiring the maximum possible self-denial and self-sacrifice, there is nothing comparable to it in the entire history of the world. In human society, if someone were to save our lives and catapult us to an unimaginable quality of life, we would be very careful not to slight our benefactor with the mention that other people also did favors for us

---

1. This refers to the portion of the Morning Prayer during which the biblical passages recording the *Akedah* are recited.
2. The Torah reading for the second day of Rosh Ha-Shanah is at Genesis 22:1–24.
3. The horn of a ram is used as the shofar because it evokes the *Akedah*, when a ram was substituted for Isaac as a sacrifice. See *Rosh Ha-Shanah* 16a.
4. *Zikhronot*, "remembrances," is a portion of the *Musaf* Prayer for Rosh Ha-Shanah.
5. *Musaf* Prayer, Rosh Ha-Shanah.

when those favors pale in comparison. Also, as the recipient of an overwhelming favor, we are more likely to fail to appreciate lesser acts of kindness and even to take them for granted because they do not measure up.

Hashem is not like that at all. Hashem remembers the events of the past with the Thirteen Attributes of Mercy. "You lovingly remembered Noah."[6]

Noah was a righteous person. He was righteous enough to save himself, but he could not save the world. And we are the sons of Abraham, not the sons of Noah. So why is Noah mentioned at all in connection with the *Akedah*? Also, Hashem blessed Noah with "*peru u-revu*," "be fruitful and multiply" (Genesis 9:1), not with "his remembrance comes before You, Hashem, our God, to make his offspring as abundant as the dust of the earth and his descendants as the sand by the sea."[7] This paraphrases the blessing that Abraham received at the *Akedah*.

But Hashem knew that there was some connection between the moral climate that Noah set by "for it is you whom I have seen to be righteous before Me in this generation" (Genesis 7:1) and the later coming of Abraham, who ends *tohu va-vohu* and begins an era of Torah.[8] So it is with Thirteen Attributes of Mercy that Hashem remembers Noah.

And "I recall for you the kindness of your youth, the love of your nuptials, your following Me into the Wilderness, into an unsown land" (Jeremiah 2:2). We could ask, was it not a matter of self-interest for us to follow Hashem in the Wilderness, as we were afflicted and persecuted by the Egyptians? And we may ask, what of the retrospection of "with ten trials did our ancestors test the Holy One, Blessed is He, in the Wilderness"?[9] We said, "Let us appoint a leader and let us return to Egypt!" (Numbers 14:4). But Hashem remembers with the Thirteen Attributes of Mercy the *devekut* element in the spontaneous agreement to go to an "unsown land" (Jeremiah 2:2). This sentiment was there, and it stands out and cancels all the negatives.

---

6. Ibid.
7. Ibid.
8. *Avodah Zarah* 9a.
9. Mishnah, *Avot* 5:4.

Finally, "Is Ephraim My favorite son or a delightful child, that whenever I speak of him I remember him more and more?" (Jeremiah 31:19). This is a three- or four-year-old child, when he begins to talk. It is when the babble turns into intelligent speech. Abraham made a party for Isaac, not when he was born but only when he was weaned because this is when the delight of parents comes to fruition and blossoms.[10] We are all called Ephraim. Hashem yearns for our first gropings to establish a dialogue with us because Hashem sees the beginnings of purity and goodness. This tells us that when "the remembrance of everything fashioned comes before You,"[11] it is the same way, with the Thirteen Attributes of Mercy. So, too, is our duty to emulate Hashem in our interpersonal relationships with the Thirteen Attributes of Mercy, and to remember our fellow Jew with the Thirteen Attributes of Mercy.

Why do we pray that Hashem should "mercifully" remember the *Akedah* of Isaac?[12] Is there any way to remember the *Akedah* other than with mercy? The answer is yes, because everything else just pales in comparison. So we pray that Hashem give maximum remembrance with mercy to everything else too.

10. Genesis 21:8; R. Bahya b. Asher (*Rabbenu Beḥaye*, Saragossa, 1255–1340), *Rabbenu Beḥaye al ha-Torah*, Genesis 21:8, s.v. "*be-yom higgamel et Yitzḥak.*"
11. *Musaf* Prayer for Rosh Ha-Shanah, *Zikhronot*.
12. Ibid.

Yom Kippur

The Crimson Cloth

October 2, 1987

In olden times, the ritual of Yom Kippur contained an element of high drama. A goat, called the *sa'ir ha-mishtale'aḥ*, was led outside Jerusalem to a desolate and forsaken place. The animal was made to scale a mountainous terrain. When it reached the cliff, half of a crimson cloth was tied to a nearby rock and the other half around the horns of the animal. Everyone watched with baited breath to see if the crimson cloth would miraculously turn white as the *sa'ir* was hurled off the cliff. If it did, spontaneous jubilation would be observed. If not, sadness, depression, and anxiety would set in.[1]

Historically, this ritual of the crimson cloth went through three stages. In the first stage, it was a family ritual. Each family would affix a crimson cloth to its window sill. Some cloths would miraculously turn white, while others would remain red. But the practice was discontinued.[2] The modern cynic would be tempted to theorize

1. *Yoma* 67a.
2. Jerusalem Talmud, *Yoma* 6:5, *Shabbat* 9:3.

that the practice came into disuse on account of the hypocrites and charlatans; they would undoubtedly coat the crimson material with invisible white ink that would later become visible, and perpetrate a fraud that they were pure.

But our Sages tell us differently. The practice was discontinued because the people were embarrassed from one another. Those who were not subject to the divine favor were embarrassed, but so were the people who witnessed the miracle of the red cloth turning white.[3] Surely, the righteous saw the benefit of subjecting themselves to a rigorous standard, as the humiliation and pain that they would experience if the red cloth would not change color would spur them on to the very heights. But all this would be at the expense of humiliating those whose cloth did not turn white, *mitkabbed be-kalon shel ḥavero*.[4] Yes, the clamor for the removal of the practice came, as it appears, from the righteous.

The form of the ritual then turns from a family rite to a communal practice. One red cloth is strategically placed at the entrance of the Sanctuary. Now it is the community, not the individual, who is in the spotlight. Notwithstanding this change in focus from the individual to the community and the additional advantage that this procedure served to inform the *Kohen Gadol* when to continue the service,[5] the procedure also fell into disuse. We can only speculate that the switch to tying the red cloth on the *sa'ir* was to soften the shock and blow if the cloth did not turn white. Whereas throngs of people were outside the Sanctuary, only a few accompanied the *sa'ir ha-mishtale'aḥ*. The latter system allowed the news to merely filter down rather than to expose everyone to the shock at the same time.

It appears that we have a remarkable capacity to adjust to increasingly lower levels of relationship with Hashem. Forty years before the destruction of the Second Temple, the red cloth no longer turned white, the Western Light went out, and the doors of the Temple opened miraculously

---

3. Jerusalem Talmud, *Yoma* 6:5, *Shabbat* 9:3.
4. One who elevates himself through the degradation of another person is said to lose his share in the World to Come. Jerusalem Talmud, *Ḥagigah* 2:1; Genesis Rabbah 1:5; Maimonides (*Rambam*, Egypt, 1135–1204), *Mishneh Torah*, *De'ot* 6:3.
5. See R. Solomon b. Isaac (*Rashi*, France, 1040–1105), *Rashi* to *Yoma* 68b, s.v. "*na'aseit mitzvato.*"

by themselves, so as to invite, God forbid, our enemies to enter.[6] All these bad omens for such a long period of time, which amounted to a reproof of the community, did nothing to spur the community to greater heights.

At the same time, an opposite disturbing trend is also discernible. The Second Temple was destroyed because of *sinat ḥinnam,* which manifested itself as in the incident of Kamtza and Bar Kamtza, when people purposely embarrassed others on the principle of the matter.[7] We return to the notion that the crimson cloth ritual should be performed on an individual or family basis.

We have the unique opportunity tonight to bury all sense of individual pride, channel our sense of pride to the community, and direct our efforts so that the glory of the community can be magnified, as if we are saying to Hashem: Let us restore the crimson cloth on a communal basis. "Display for us a sign for good, so that our enemies may see it and be ashamed."[8]

Let us make a sign that we want to move higher, that we want to come a little closer to the genius of Torah, to R. Akiva, *oker harim ve-toḥanan zu ba-zu be-sevarah,* "who would uproot mountains of halakhic problems and grind them one against the other by thorough analysis."[9]

A little closer to R. Hutzpit Meturgeman, who was a great popularizer of Torah but did not dilute it in the process. A bird was singed when it passed through his air space because of the holiness of his Torah.[10]

And let's get a little closer to the charity of R. Yeshevav, who had to be restrained in his giving because he was overgenerous.[11]

---

6. *Yoma* 39b.
7. *Gittin* 55b–56a; Lamentations Rabbah 4:3.
8. *Seliḥot, Elokeinu she-ba-Shamayim*; *Shema Kolenu* Prayer on Yom Kippur. Cf. Psalms 86:17.
9. R. Meir b. Jehiel (13th cent.), "*Arzei ha-Levanon*" (*kinah* recited on Tish'ah be-Av), reprinted in Alter Wilner, *Aseret Harugei Malkhut ba-Midrash u-be-Piyyut* (Jerusalem: Mossad HaRav Kook, 2005), 346.
10. R. Meir b. Jehiel, "*Arzei ha-Levanon,*" op. cit., 347; R. Isaac b. Moses (*Or Zaru'a,* Vienna, ca. 1180–1250), *Or Zaru'a, Hilkhot Bekhorot, siman* 510. R. Hutzpit was considered equivalent to Jonathan b. Uzziel, whose fiery breadth of Torah would singe a passing bird. *Sukkah* 28a; *Bava Batra* 134a.
11. *Ketubbot* 50a.

And let's get a little closer to R. Judah b. Bava, who was the exemplar of concern for the continuity of Torah, who endangered his life to give *semikhah* to Torah scholars![12]

And let's get a little closer to the ideal bond of love between two friends, R. Shimon b. Gamliel and R. Yishmael *Kohen Gadol*.[13] Let's make out of the intensity of goodness the sign of: "Display for us a sign for good, so that our enemies may see it and be ashamed."

---

12. *Sanhedrin* 14a. The Romans had decreed that anyone who gave or received rabbinic ordination would be put to death, the city in which the ordination took place would be demolished, and the boundaries in which it had been performed would be uprooted. Undeterred by the decree, R. Judah b. Bava went and sat between two great mountains that lay between two large cities and ordained five elders: R. Meir, R. Judah, R. Shimon, R. Jose, and R. Eleazar b. Shammua.
13. *Arzei ha-Levanon*, op. cit., 345. R. Shimon b. Gamliel and R. Yishmael each did not want to see the suffering of his friend and therefore begged to be killed first. The executioner then cast lots, which fell upon R. Shimon b. Gamliel. When R. Yishmael took sight of the decapitated head of R. Shimon b. Gamliel, "he placed his eyes upon his eyes and his mouth upon his mouth with absolute love."

Barukh Shem Kevod Malkhuto le-Olam va-Ed

October 3, 1987

One aspect of the singularity of the holiness of Yom Kippur is that on this day, we have the privilege of reciting the phrase *barukh Shem kevod* out loud.[1] Lest we take this privilege lightly, we need only recall the analogy that our Sages make in this respect. It is likened to one who steals jewelry from the royal palace for his wife and forewarns her that she should not dare wear it publicly, only in the privacy of their home.[2] This statement of our Sages transforms the whisper utterance of *barukh Shem* during the entire year into the unarticulated fear of being discovered saying this phrase.

1. R. Jacob b. Asher (*Tur*, Spain, 1270–1343), *Tur, Oraḥ Ḥayyim* 619; R. Joseph Caro (Safed, 1488–1575), *Shulḥan Arukh, Oraḥ Ḥayyim* 619:2. The entire phrase is *Barukh Shem kevod malkhuto le-olam va-ed*, "Blessed is the Name of His glorious kingdom for all eternity."
2. Deuteronomy Rabbah 2:36, quoted by *Tur, Oraḥ Ḥayyim* 619.

What transforms the utterance of the phrase from a stolen expression to one that we so proudly and exultantly recite? Perhaps the key here is the comment by our Sages that *barukh Shem* is equivalent to *amen,* except that in the Sanctuary, the more elaborate phrase *barukh Shem* was recited.[3]

Now, we know that *amen* is an expression of affirmation. Then so is *barukh Shem*. We can well understand why we whisper *barukh Shem* during the course of the year after we proclaim "Hear O Israel." We are saying that Hashem is now *our* God, but we fervently look to the day when He will be universally recognized.

Honest self-appraisal will challenge the authenticity of that sentiment for us. Have we really accepted the yoke of Heaven in our personal lives in the form of the meticulous observance of the Torah? And do we really desire the expansion of *kedushah* to every corner of the world, which, as the *Ḥayyei Adam* understands, is the *kavvanah* that we must have when reciting *Shema* and *barukh Shem*?[4] If there is such a thing as an *amen yesomah* (lit., "an orphaned *amen*")[5] and an *amen ḥatufah* (lit., "a snatched *amen*"),[6] we can say this in regard to our lofty declaration. How dare we affirm what we said with *barukh Shem*?

On Yom Kippur, the *Shema* is suffused with *teshuvah,* which entails both *ḥaratah,* "remorse," and *kabbalah al ha-atid,* "resolutions for the future." Our *kabbalat ol malkhut Shamayim* is indeed different. It is a new one filled with resolutions for the new year. So we can affirm this with an exultant *barukh Shem.*

But there is another tradition here. When Jacob was on his deathbed and wanted to reveal to his sons the date of the coming of the Messiah, suddenly the Divine Presence departed from him and

---

3. *Ta'anit* 16b; *Rashi* to Deuteronomy 32:3.
4. R. Abraham Danzig (Prague, 1748–1820), *Ḥayyei Adam* 21:11.
5. An *amen yesomah* is an *amen* that is said in response to a blessing when the person answering *amen* is not aware of which blessing was said. *Berakhot* 47a; *Rashi* and *Tosafot* ad loc.; *Shulḥan Arukh, Oraḥ Ḥayyim* 124:8.
6. An *amen ḥatufah* occurs when the *aleph* of *amen* is pronounced with a *ḥataf* instead of a *kamatz,* or the *amen* is said before recitation of the blessing is completed. *Berakhot* 47a; *Rashi* ad loc., s.v. "*ḥatufah*"; *Shulḥan Arukh, Oraḥ Ḥayyim* 124:8.

the message was blocked. Jacob then feared that some of his children were not worthy, and he expressed this fear. Whereupon, all his sons proclaimed, "Hear O Israel, Hashem is our God, Hashem is the One and Only" (Deuteronomy 6:4). When Jacob heard this declaration, he responded with *barukh Shem.*[7]

When Moses gave us the Torah, he did not insert *barukh Shem* after *Shema*. That is why we recite *barukh Shem* only in a whisper during the rest of the year. The reason that Jacob recited *barukh Shem* and Moses did not can be explained with the general rules of *amen*. One rule is that "greater is the one who answers *amen* than the one who says the blessing,"[8] and the other is that if one answers *amen* after his own blessing, it is *megunneh*, "reprehensible."[9]

Now, Jacob was affirming what he heard from his sons. But Moses could not say *barukh Shem* because he would be affirming his own statement, and this is *megunneh*. We can well understand this, as Moses said, "What does Hashem, your God, ask of you? Only to fear Hashem" (Deuteronomy 10:12). This implied that fear of Heaven was a small matter. And our Sages say, yes, for Moses it was indeed a small matter.[10] Now, when a leader who preaches a standard of fear of Heaven that is perhaps considerable for the great masses affirms his own statement, the chasm between him and his flock widens even more. But, if someone else would affirm Moses' lofty pronouncement, the affirmation would bring the ideal closer to the people.

During the course of the year, we dare not affirm our own blessing, as this is *megunneh*. On Yom Kippur, a day suffused with *teshuvah*, our intent in reciting *barukh Shem* is to reinforce and invigorate the *Shema* that we hear from others.

As *Rabbenu Beḥaye* explains it, why is the one who answers *amen* greater than the one who recites the blessing? It is because the one who recites the blessing merely pronounces something. But the one who

7. *Pesaḥim* 56a.
8. *Berakhot* 53b.
9. *Berakhot* 45b.
10. *Berakhot* 33b.

answers *amen* brings the statement to the level of truth, giving it the character of *edut,* the testimony of two witnesses.[11]

This is what we are offering on Yom Kippur. We will not allow any spark of *kedushah* that we encounter to flicker and dim. We will reinforce it by joining it and giving it encouragement. If we see a learning group, we will go there. If we see a person or group involved in *ḥesed* or communal benefaction, we will not, God forbid, demoralize them, but instead we will reinforce the good and lend support to it.

Perhaps the grandest *barukh Shem* that we can accomplish is to recite *barukh Shem* after the *Shema* that is silent because it is in the form of a legacy. This is the *yir'at Shamayim* that our parents and teachers implanted in us. We dare not allow this ember to be extinguished. We must embrace it and advance it as much as we can. And there is also the *Shema* of the six million *kedoshim* recited on the way to martyrdom. Dare we allow it to fade into oblivion? No. We must affirm it and commit ourselves to sanctify the Name of Heaven, to extend *malkhut Shamayim* to the very four corners of the earth. No less!

11. R. Bahya b. Asher (*Rabbenu Beḥaye,* Saragossa, 1255–1340), *Rabbenu Beḥaye al ha-Torah,* Exodus 14:31, s.v. "*va-yir'u ha-am va-ya'aminu.*"

The Second Tablets

October 9, 1989

Historically, two events occurred on Yom Kippur. First, *yom seliḥah u-meḥilah,* "a day of forgiveness" – Hashem reconciled Himself and His people, and forgave us for the Sin of the Golden Calf. Second, *yom she-nittenu luḥot ha-sheniyyot* – the Second Tablets were given to us.[1]

An elaborate superstructure is built around *yom seliḥah u-meḥilah,* as the major obligation and theme of Yom Kippur is repentance. With respect to the giving of the Second Tablets, development of this theme is deferred until Simḥat Torah.

Permit me to suggest, however, that the giving of the Second Tablets is a theme that is much integrated with *yom seliḥah u-meḥilah,* specifically in relation to reconciliation between man and his fellow. Yom Kippur is a commemoration of the second acceptance of the Torah because the first one failed. And why?

---

1. *Ta'anit* 30b; *Rashi* ad loc., s.v. "*she-nit'nu bo luḥot aḥaronot*"; *Bava Batra* 121a; *Rashi* ad loc., s.v. "*yom she-nit'nu bo luḥot ha-aḥaronot*" (citing *Seder Olam* 6); *Midrash Tanḥuma, Ki Tissa* 31.

The *Mikhtav me-Eliyahu* suggests that in a very short time of seven weeks, we were catapulted to the forty-ninth degree of purity. This element of divine grace in our acceptance of the Torah is capsulated, according to the *Mikhtav me-Eliyahu,* in noting that as far as the First Tablets were concerned, "the Tablets were God's handiwork, and the script was the script of God, engraved on the Tablets" (Exodus 32:16). The Tablets represented the heart of man. Hashem gave us the heart to accept the Tablets, but without any struggle or painful striving on our part.[2]

Like anything in life, something easily acquired is viewed lightly and is taken for granted. So we were very vulnerable to a fall, the Sin of the Golden Calf.

Despite our precipitous fall, Hashem tells Moses, "Carve for yourself two stone tablets like the first ones" (Exodus 34:1). They will not be made by Hashem. They will be made by you; you will supply the heart this time. But you can reach the level of the First Tablets. And how? I would suggest that this was possible by emulating that part of the first acceptance of the Torah that was not a failure. That was Moses' acceptance of the Torah, when a life-and-death struggle took place in heaven. The angels said, "What is man that You are mindful of him, and the son of man that You visit him?"[3] "Hashem, our Master, how mighty is Your Name throughout the earth, Who places Your majesty upon the heavens!"[4] Hashem told Moses that he must give the answer himself – Moses, you're on your own.

Moses summoned his creativity and came up with a powerful, irrefutable answer. He proceeded to go through the Ten Commandments and asked, "Is the Torah relevant to you angels?" The angels then realized that Moses was not a competitor, taking the Torah from the heaven and bringing it down to earth. He was not subtracting from the Divine Glory. Quite to the contrary, he was adding to the Divine Glory

2. R. Eliyahu Eliezer Dessler (Lithuania, England, and Benei Berak, 1892–1953), *Mikhtav me-Eliyahu,* eds. R. Aryeh Carmell and R. Alter Halperin, 5th ed., vol. 2 (Benei Berak: Hever Talmidav, 1964), pt. 1, *Shavuot, Shenei Ofanei Kabbalat ha-Torah,* pp. 26–30.
3. Psalms 8:5.
4. Psalms 8:2.

because the Torah was then transformed from an abstract doctrine into one that had an impact on human life. It was relevant to human society.[5]

This celestial struggle between Moses and the angels is going on today, bringing much dismay to the Orthodox Jewish community and generating much *sinat ḥinnam*. There is one camp that is taking up the position of the angels and saying, "Place Your Majesty upon the heavens." This camp is looking cynically and critically at the college campuses, the professional world, the political scene, and saying that the Orthodox Jew does not belong there. But then there are those who want to expand the sphere of the Torah to ever-increasing places and sanctify them.

How is reconciliation and respect to be reached between these competing ideologies so that a semblance of unity can prevail among the Jewish people? Well, I would say that even within the framework of an insular world, we must engage in self-examination and retrospection, that we should not, God forbid, be giving up, gradually retreating and withdrawing.

The sphere of heaven today is not just *limmud ha-Torah* and *tefillah*. There is the whole sphere of the relationship between oneself and one's family, one's friends, and society at large, *bein adam le-ḥavero*. Each sphere must be suffused with Torah. We cannot live a compartmentalized life.

But those who want to expand the sphere of Torah to the ever-increasing societal institutions must be honest to realize that penetration into these areas requires more than just *Shabbat* and *kashrut*. We must realize that to penetrate into the college campuses, the professional world, and the political stage requires at the very least rejection of some of the values and practices of these institutions. It requires repudiation and the setting up of counteractions. And on the positive side, it requires *kiddush Hashem*.

When the college students protested at Auschwitz, they used the political activities of the college campus as a vehicle for *kiddush Hashem*.[6]

---

5. *Shabbat* 88b–89a. The recognition of the angels that Moses was not a competitor can be seen in the gift of *ketoret* that the angels presented to Moses at the conclusion of the struggle. See *Shabbat* 89a.

6. On July 23, 1989, Jewish students from across Europe demonstrated amid a crowd of hostile Poles to demand the removal of a Catholic convent from the former Nazi death camp at Auschwitz. Members of the convent had erected a twenty-four-foot cross atop a mass grave where many Jews were buried. See "Poles Jeer at Jews Protesting at Auschwitz Convent," *Jerusalem Post*, July 24, 1989, 2; Jacob Davidson, "Carmelite

In the business world, corporate operations should be suffused with Jewish values of truth in advertising, decency in labor relations, and fairness in competitive tactics. The medical profession must also get a full dosage of the Jewish ideal with respect to various medical ethics issues of the day, including genetic engineering. And finally, the political stage, whether it is local, state, national, or international, must be suffused with the Jewish ideal of *tikkun olam* and be a platform for us for promoting and defending the interests of our beloved State.

We fulfill the second acceptance of the Torah by making the Torah ever more relevant and drawing out from it approaches and directions for the modern man. Most fundamentally, relevance must demonstrate itself in centrality of purpose.

Hypocrisy at Auschwitz," *Jerusalem Post*, July 25, 1989, 4; John Tagliabue, "Strife Returns to a Convent at Auschwitz," *New York Times*, July 27, 1989. See also Ron Kampeas, "Students: 'No' to Convent," *Jerusalem Post*, July 28, 1989, C5 (describing demonstration held by Israeli students in front of the Apostolic Delegation on the Mount of Olives to protest convent at Auschwitz).

Sabbath of Sabbaths

September 28, 1990

Our Sages make a curious statement. If we would only meticulously observe two Sabbaths, we would merit immediate redemption.[1] Now, if the Sabbath has the power to bring redemption, why would the observance of two Sabbaths suffice? In interpreting this enigmatic statement of our Sages, R. Tzvi Elimelech of Dinov observes that Yom Kippur is also called the Sabbath – *Shabbat Shabbaton* (Leviticus 23:32).[2] If we would learn how to celebrate the double Sabbath, we would merit immediate redemption. The challenge is that the Sabbath and Yom Kippur are opposites. The essence of Yom Kippur is *innui*, "deprivation of sensual pleasures,"[3] whereas the essence of the Sabbath is *oneg*, "indulgence."[4]

1. *Shabbat* 118b.
2. R. Zevi Elimelech Dynow (*Benei Yissaskhar*, Poland, ca. 1783–1841), *Benei Yissaskhar, Ma'amrei Ḥodesh Tishrei*, no. 7.
3. Leviticus 23:32.
4. Isaiah 58:13; R. David Kimhi (*Radak*, Provence, ca. 1160–ca. 1235), *Radak* ad loc., s.v. "*ve-karata la-Shabbat oneg*"; *Shabbat* 118a–b; Maimonides, *Mishneh Torah, Shabbat* 30:1, 7.

Permit me to suggest that the paradox runs deeper. On Yom Kippur, we undergo catharsis. We purge our souls. We engage in repentance, self-accusation, self-condescension. We make ourselves into nothing, *ke-ḥeres ha-nishbar*, "like a broken shard."[5] But at the same time, on the Sabbath, we have the *neshamah yeterah*, which is an extra measure of spiritual energy for grand action on a cosmic level.[6]

Perhaps the key to reconciling the paradox is the recognition that we have two identities, as individuals and as members of the Jewish community. This distinction plays a central role in the thinking of R. Joseph B. Soloveitchik.[7] On Yom Kippur, we seek two atonements: one as individuals and one as members of the Jewish community. A striking contrast appears between the confession of the individual and that of the community.[8] The individual makes his confession at the conclusion of the prayer while the *ḥazan* recites the communal confession in the middle of the service. In addition, the individual's confession is recited without any introductions whereas the communal confession is preceded by the *seliḥot*, which include a declamation of the Thirteen Attributes of Mercy.

In our personal lives, we should lean toward humility. But for the community, we must exude pride bordering on arrogance.

In our personal lives, we should lean toward self-denial. But for the community, we should lavish abundant resources on it – *Zeh Keli ve-anvehu*, "This is my God and I will adorn Him" (Exodus 15:2). Nothing is too good for the community.

In our personal lives, we should be trusting, always giving our friend the benefit of the doubt. But in our communal identity, we must be mistrusting and suspicious.

5. *U-netanneh Tokef* Prayer, Rosh Ha-Shanah and Yom Kippur Liturgy.
6. On the eve of the Sabbath, Hashem gives man a *neshamah yeterah*, an "additional soul," which departs at the conclusion of the Sabbath. *Beitzah* 16a; *Ta'anit* 27b.
7. Pinchas H. Peli, *On Repentance: In the Thought and Oral Discourses of Rabbi Joseph B. Soloveitchik* (Jerusalem: Oroth, 1980), 116–121.
8. Ibid., 127–132.

The Reading of the Torah by the High Priest

October 4, 1995

We are all familiar with the concept of *tirḥa de-tzibbura.*[1] Its most popular timely application is the admonition to rabbis not to prolong their sermons. A surprising application is found in connection with the reading of the Torah in the time of the Temple. The *Kohen Gadol* was the *ba'al ko're.* He read *Parashat Aḥarei Mot.* When it came to the *maftir,* our Sages tried to figure out how to proceed. To take out another *sefer Torah* is rejected. People might think that the one there is defective.[2]

1. See, e.g., *Berakhot* 12b (stating that the Sages desired to establish *Parashat Balak* [Numbers 22:2–25:9] in the reading of *Shema,* but did not do so to avoid burdening the congregation with a lengthy reading); *Shulḥan Arukh, Oraḥ Ḥayyim* 126:4 (stating that if the *sheli'aḥ tzibbur* made a mistake when reciting his private prayer other than in the first three blessings of the *Shemoneh Esreh,* he does not repeat his prayer so that he does not burden the congregation by making them wait; instead, he can rely on the prayer that he will recite out loud for the congregation).
2. *Yoma* 70a (opinion of R. Huna b. Judah).

This scroll was used to authenticate all the *sifrei Torah* of the Jewish people.[3] The *Kohen Gadol* put away the *sefer Torah* and proceeded to read the *maftir* by heart. Before doing so, he said, "More than what I have read before you is written here."[4]

But why not roll the *sefer Torah* from *Parashat Aḥarei Mot* to *Parashat Pinḥas*? No. Because of *tirḥa de-tzibbura*. Now, reading the Torah by heart within the context of the mitzvah of *Keri'at ha-Torah* is an absolute prohibition.[5] If it were done here, there would surely be a commotion. Yet, the prohibition was suspended on account of *tirḥa de-tzibbura*.[6]

But I ask you, where is the *tirḥa de-tzibbura*? How long does it take to roll the *sefer Torah* from *Aḥarei Mot* to *Pinḥas*? About three minutes. It is Yom Kippur. There is no drink, no food. There is nowhere to go. And I would propose that 95 percent of those assembled would regard it as a great privilege to get a glimpse of the *Kohen Gadol* being *golel* the *sefer Torah* in all his splendor.[7] So, *tirḥa de-tzibbura*? For whom?

Because it is a large crowd, there must be someone who we cannot identify in advance, to whom we cannot point our finger, who is annoyed and will think that the action shows no respect for his or her time.

Requiring the *Kohen Gadol* to read the Torah by heart demonstrates that *tirḥa de-tzibbura* is a very delicate concept. It prohibits not only an action that will clearly demonstrate a contempt for the community, but also an action that will in a tolerable manner slightly cause some annoyance to one who is just a statistic for us at this point.

What a powerful lesson in *kevod ha-beri'ot*. If we must be concerned with the discomfiture of the abstract, anonymous man, *a fortiori* we must be concerned with the feelings of the real man with whom we interact.

---

3. See *Rashi* to *Bava Batra* 14b, s.v. "*sefer Azarah*," and *Mo'ed Katan* 18b, s.v. "*afilu be-sefer Ezra*."
4. *Yoma* 68b, 70a.
5. *Gittin* 60b; *Temurah* 14b; Maimonides, *Mishneh Torah, Tefillah* 12:8.
6. *Yoma* 70a; *Rashi* ad loc., s.v. "*mipnei kevod tzibbur*"; Maimonides, *Mishneh Torah, Tefillah* 12:23.
7. See *Mar'eh Kohen, Musaf* Prayer on Yom Kippur (describing the splendor of the *Kohen Gadol* on Yom Kippur).

The reading of the Torah by the *Kohen Gadol* is somewhat of an anti-climax in the events of the day. It is not begun until the *sa'ir la-azazel* is taken care of. The *sa'ir* is heaved off a precipice with a crimson cord tied to its horns. It is a tense moment because the Jewish nation is watching with baited breath – will the crimson cord turn white?[8] If it does, the whole Jewish nation spontaneously breaks out in jubilation. It is a divine sign that Hashem has forgiven us. What an anti-climax to proceed now with the reading of the Torah.

But wait a minute. One partakes in the atonement of the *sa'ir la-azazel* for *kalot ve-ḥamurot,* "lesser sins and severe sins," only if he has pacified his friend and is not guilty of sins *bein adam le-ḥavero.*[9] What a chilling thought for the reflective man. He sees the *Kohen Gadol* in all his pomp and splendor. The *Ḥazan ha-Knesset,* "Attendant of the Synagogue," passes the Torah to the *Rosh ha-Knesset,* the "Head of the Synagogue," who hands it to the *Segan,* the "Deputy High Priest," and the *Segan* hands it to the *Kohen Gadol.* A whole hierarchy of officials is beneath the *Kohen Gadol.*[10] If the most important man among the Jewish people shows such deference, not causing an annoyance or some discomfiture, *kal ve-ḥomer* for the real man with whom we interact. So the regular man thinks, maybe I was excluded from the atonement of the *sa'ir ha-mishtale'aḥ* because I did not give the *tzibbur* or my fellow their due.

Let it be our lot, as we stand before *Yizkor,* to give the *tzibbur* and our fellow man their due.

8. *Yoma* 67a.
9. Mishnah, *Yoma* 8:9; *Yoma* 85b; Maimonides, *Mishneh Torah, Teshuvah* 1:2.
10. *Yoma* 68b.

The Day the Satan Is Not Permitted to Accuse

October 13, 2005

One aspect of the uniqueness of Yom Kippur is that on this day, Hashem removes from the Satan the power and license to accuse us. The year has 365 days. "*Ha-Satan*" in *gematria* is 364, intimating that there is one day in the year when the Satan has no license to accuse us.[1]

Instead, on Yom Kippur, the Satan becomes our friend and advocate, singing our praises to the *Ribbono shel Olam*. As the Midrash puts it, on Yom Kippur, the Satan tells Hashem, "I have scanned all the houses of worship of the Jewish people and I have found Your children to be like angels. They fast and are donned in white. And they are the real thing because I know that angels are naturally always in a standing position, as You have created them without joints. So, too, the Jewish people are in a standing position the entire day."[2]

1. *Yoma* 20a.
2. *Pirkei de-Rabbi Eliezer* 46.

When the Satan becomes our friend and advocate, I, for one, begin to worry. The power to accuse is not the same as the power to ensnare.

Permit me to suggest that on this day, *yom ha-kadosh,* Hashem in his abundant mercy reveals to us the secret of the dominant modus operandi of the Satan. It consists of heaping praise on us. Because we are protected by the *yetzer tov,* a frontal, brutal demand to do evil will often not work. If it entails hurting our fellow, the demand assaults our basic sense of decency. If it involves defying Hashem's commandments, it offends our basic sense of *emunah.*

So the way to succeed for the Satan is to engage us by use of the words *tov me'od,* "very good." This is explicitly stated in the Midrash. "And God saw all that He had made, and behold it was *tov me'od*" (Genesis 1:31). "*Tov me'od, zu yetzer ha-ra,*" "very good" refers to the Evil Inclination.[3]

But how can the very incarnate of evil be *tov me'od*? The answer is that the *yetzer ha-ra* accomplishes his best work by being the cheerleader of all our mediocre and inferior efforts. Suppose we encounter a mitzvah or duty that we must perform, but we become a victim of *ones* (i.e., uncontrollable circumstances that make the execution of the mitzvah impossible). Hashem says you are not culpable of failing to perform the mitzvah. The Satan chimes in and becomes the cheerleader of failure by adding, "Don't feel guilty. In fact, feel good, *tov me'od,* because you tried hard, and trying hard is what counts." Next time, you can even try less and it will also be cheered on by the Satan. *Tov me'od.*

Then suppose you observe a friend do a glistening act of *ḥesed* and some fabulous good deed for the community. The Satan will compel you to go over to that person and say "*tov me'od,*" and say so very sincerely. But in a moment, the inspiration will dissipate, and one will not be moved to emulate the selfless good deed.

The Satan is engaged in a relentless campaign to praise mediocrity and make us quickly fall down the slippery slope of hearing his praise even when we step into the most passable form of goodness. It is then that we really fall into the clutches of the Satan because then there is

3. Genesis Rabbah 9:7.

very little difference between what is barely good and what is actually evil. We are then set up for virulent forms of evil.

On Yom Kippur, Hashem shows us what the Satan is all about, how he does his best work. Look at what he praises us for, that on Yom Kippur we look like angels.

There was another time in Jewish history when we as a people were praised for looking like angels. It was when we pronounced at Sinai "*na'aseh ve-nishma,*" "we will do and we will listen" (Exodus 24:7). Six hundred thousand angels came down and placed two crowns on each of our heads, one corresponding to *na'aseh,* and one corresponding to *nishma,* because we behaved like angels, suppressing our free will and showing blind obedience to Hashem.[4]

What a difference between the two episodes. On Yom Kippur, the praise of the Satan is but superficial and shallow. It all relates to materialistic pleasures that we deny ourselves. We seem not to be in need of food and we are dressed in white. And, yes, we stand all day. That is certainly nothing but an exaggeration because we do not literally stand all day. And we bend our knees at *kor'im,* so we do have joints.

But *na'aseh ve-nishma* is the real McCoy of *tov me'od*. It was in that glorious moment that we truly transcended our human limitations and showed that we were angels, demonstrating blind obedience to Hashem, suspending our autonomy and independence.

We are now standing at the threshold of *Yizkor*. We are paying homage to the memory of our parents and the six million martyrs. We can pay homage to their memory only by building on the *tov* that we received from them, building on it with a perfectionist drive. So we must reject the *tov me'od* of the Satan on Yom Kippur and embrace the *tov me'od* of the two crowns that we received at Sinai.

4. *Shabbat* 88a.

Thou Shall Not Covet

September 28, 2009

In a fascinating teaching, *Tanna de-vei Eliyahu* tells us that the Ten Days of Repentance correspond to the Ten Commandments.[1] Proceeding from this teaching is that Yom Kippur corresponds to the Tenth Commandment, *lo taḥmod,* "thou shall not covet" (Exodus 20:14).

This pairing may seem odd. But permit me to suggest that it captures the very essence of the holiness of the day.

Our Sages teach that our norm as a people is never mediocrity. No. When we are at our best, we scale the highest mountains. We are *rokhev aravot,* "riding upon the highest heavens."[2] But when we fall, God forbid, we fall all the way to the lowest depths.

This is all captured by focusing on *lo taḥmod.* If we are guilty of prohibited desires, *ḥimmud ha-lev,* we are vulnerable to falling down the slippery slope right into the lap of the Torah reading for *Minḥah,*[3] which

1. *Tanna de-vei Eliyahu, Seder Eliyahu Zuta* 22.
2. Cf. Psalms 68:5.
3. Leviticus 18:1–30.

deals with the prohibition of incest and bestiality, what is called *tevel*, a "perversion."[4] And we also read the warning not to adopt the ways of the Amoraim. If we do that, the land will vomit us out.[5]

I would ask you, in the entire Torah, is there a more harsh reading than the reading of *Minḥah* on Yom Kippur? And why? Because Yom Kippur corresponds to *lo taḥmod*. If we do not control prohibited desire, then we are vulnerable to leading a life without control whatsoever, the ways of the Canaanites.

But there is a flip side to *lo taḥmod*. *Kol de-asar lan Raḥmana shara lan kevvaseih*, "whatever Hashem prohibited, He permitted in a different form."[6] And it applies to *lo taḥmod*. Also, "One is obligated to say: 'When will my deeds reach the level of the deeds of Abraham, Isaac, and Jacob?'"[7] Not to the level of parents, grandparents, or even great grandparents, but all the way back to the Patriarchs. In the words of the poet Emerson, we are asked to hitch our wagon to a star![8]

What Hashem wants of us is capsulated in the well-known phrase *Raḥmana libba ba'i*, "God wants our hearts."[9] All the prohibitions of the Torah are, however, violated with specific actions.[10] *Lo taḥmod* is no exception. However, unique is the prohibition of *lo taḥmod* in that the action required is only a technicality. The essence of the sin is prohibited desire.[11]

Let's look at how Maimonides formulates the prohibition. Suppose Feivel is a frequent visitor to the home of Simon and Rachel. He sees that they have a beautiful candelabrum. It is a family heirloom. Feivel is infatuated with the candelabrum. On one visit, he gathers up

---

4. Leviticus 18:23.
5. Leviticus 18:28.
6. *Ḥullin* 109b.
7. *Tanna de-vei Eliyahu, Seder Eliyahu Rabba* 25.
8. Ralph Waldo Emerson, *Society and Solitude* (Boston: Osgood, 1875), "Civilization," 25.
9. Zohar, *Terumah* 2:162b; Zohar, *Ki Tetze* 3:281b; *Sanhedrin* 106b; *Rashi* ad loc., s.v. "*revusa le-mibba'ei be-ayyei*"; Abraham b. Meir ibn Ezra (Ibn Ezra, Spain, 1089–1164), *Yesod Mora, sha'ar* 7.
10. See *Kiddushin* 40a.
11. Maimonides, *Sefer ha-Mitzvot, mitzvat lo ta'aseh* no. 266; Maimonides, *Mishneh Torah, Gezeilah* 1:9; R. Vidal Yom Tov of Tolosa (*Maggid Mishneh*, Spain, ca. 1300–1370), *Maggid Mishneh* ad loc., s.v. "*ve-ein lokin al lav zeh.*"

enough gumption to say, "I love your candelabrum. I would like to buy it from you."

Simon and Rachel blush. They are taken aback. They are embarrassed by the offer. They never viewed their home as a store displaying items with invisible prices. So they are dismissive and say it is not for sale. But Feivel does not give up. He persists. On subsequent visits, he brings the matter up again and offers a higher price, to no avail. Feivel even sends Shrage to tell Simon and Rachel that Feivel cannot live without the candelabrum. Finally, Feivel succeeds in getting the candelabrum for a hefty price.

Maimonides tells us that Feivel violates *lo taḥmod*. It consists of his pestering and harassing to get the item. But there is no flogging as a punishment. Is this not astonishing? Maimonides says that without actually acquiring the item, there is no violation of *lo taḥmod*. The answer is that the prohibition consists of the nagging, badgering, and harassing. The role that acquisition plays is that it is only a measure of the amount of nagging that it takes to violate the prohibition. If you are not willing to accept failure and you do as much nagging as necessary to acquire the item, you violate *lo taḥmod*.

Violation of *lo taḥmod* is the direction in which Hashem does not want the heart to go. *Lo taḥmod* is where the heart should not go, but "when will my deeds reach the level of the deeds of Abraham, Isaac, and Jacob" is the direction in which the heart should go. And going in that direction catapults us to the highest level of virtue.

May it be a *shenat taf, shin, ayin – tehei shenat aliyyah*, "may it be a year of ascendancy,"[12] to scale the mountainous heights and be *rokhev aravot* in Torah, *avodah*, and *gemilut ḥasadim*.

---

12. The first letters of *tehei shenat aliyyah* (תהי שנת עליה) are the same as the Hebrew year 5770 (תש"ע).

Sukkot – First Days

The Key to the Future Redemption

September 26, 1988

For many, it is a matter of puzzlement that we celebrate the Exodus from Egypt with two festivals, Passover and Sukkot. Why would not one festival suffice?

Perhaps the following contrast provides us with the answer. On Passover, we recognize that *ge'ullah* is a process, and we focus on the critical stages of that process, the milestones of the four redemptions: *Ve-hotzeti,* "I shall take you out from under the burdens of Egypt." *Ve-hitzalti,* "I shall rescue you from their service," which is the cessation of slavery. Then, *ve-ga'alti,* "I shall redeem you with an outstretched arm." And finally, *ve-lakaḥti,* "I shall take you as a people," denoting spiritual redemption.[1]

In contrast, on Sukkot, we celebrate a slice of time, forty years, when we as a people experienced a special feeling of divine providence.

1. Exodus 6:6–7.

"I caused the Children of Israel to dwell in booths when I took them out of the land of Egypt" (Leviticus 23:43). Encapsulating the essence of the divine providence that we experienced during this period were the Clouds of Glory that enveloped the Jewish people throughout their forty-two sojourns in the Wilderness.

Pointing out that Ezekiel calls our present Exile the *midbar ha-ammim*, "the wilderness of the nations,"[2] *Rabbenu Beḥaye* posits that the key to our future redemption can be found in a study of the forty-two sojourns of the Children of Israel in the Wilderness.[3] What an astonishing proposition! During our stay in the Wilderness, it says "*va-yis'u*," and "*va-yaḥanu*," we journeyed and we encamped.[4] But everything was according to divine instruction. It was the lifting of the Clouds of Glory over the Tabernacle that gave us our cue to journey, and it was the settling of the Clouds of Glory over the Tabernacle that gave us our cue to encamp.[5] In contrast, as we find ourselves in our present wanderings, we do not have the advantage of divine cues. We do not even know if we are coming or going!

If we study the account of the forty-two sojourns, we will note that it is mostly a recording of names of places. But in three instances, something more is mentioned; there is some elaboration. I would submit that in focusing on these three elaborations, we can find our mission in the Diaspora, we can regain our bearings if they are lost, and finally find the secret of how we can seize the initiative and end our meanderings, getting a good sense of direction.

If we had to select a single journey that describes succinctly the very essence of our condition in the Diaspora, it would be "they journeyed from Marah and arrived at Elim" (Numbers 33:9). Here it does not say "they journeyed… and they encamped," but rather "they journeyed… and arrived," and only later "they encamped" (Numbers 33:9).

2. Ezekiel 20:35.
3. R. Bahya b. Asher (*Rabbenu Beḥaye*, Saragossa, 1255–1340), *Rabbenu Beḥaye al ha-Torah*, Numbers 33:2, s.v. "*le-mas'eihem al pi Hashem.*"
4. Numbers 33:5–37, 33:41–48.
5. Exodus 40:36–38; R. Solomon b. Isaac (*Rashi*, France, 1040–1105), *Rashi* to Exodus 40:38.

In the long, bitter *galut* of the Diaspora, we have always been driven from host countries by means of persecutions, pogroms, and holocausts. We had no plan of action for where we would go. There were no hospitable countries waiting with open arms to receive us. No. We were driven. We journeyed and we stumbled upon a place – "They arrived at Elim."

But what did we find? This is our mission. We must rebuild Torah in the Diaspora. We must find there *shiv'im temarim*, seventy date palms (Numbers 33:9). The date palm is symbolic of the *tzaddik*. "*Tzaddik ka-tamar yifraḥ*," "a righteous man will flourish like a date palm" (Psalms 92:13). We must build a city that has seventy elders. This evokes the image of the Great Sanhedrin, which was located in Jerusalem, or the seventy elders appointed by Moses to replace him.[6] The number is not seventy-one because no matter how much we achieve in *galut*, we will still fall short of the spiritual heights that we can achieve in the Land of Israel where a *beit din* of seventy-one sits.

And we also found there twelve wells,[7] signifying the diversity of the Jewish people. In rebuilding Torah in the Diaspora, each Jew can make a contribution of his own.[8]

Just as it is true of our people as a collective, so is it true for us as individuals. Our opportunities for greatest accomplishment in the spiritual domain will come in the moments of distraction or deflection from the path that we may regard as very sweet but the Torah considers bitter. It is that moment when a friend will drag us into a *shul*, into a yeshivah, get us interested in a cause, draw us into the building of seventy date palms. We should be particularly sensitized to these moments because the holy work will be accomplished by twelve wells. Each Jew will have something to contribute.

There will be moments of triumph on both a personal and national level in *galut*. We will be particularly vulnerable at these moments to lose our bearings. We will be vulnerable to fall into the trap

6. *Rashi* to Exodus 15:27; *Mekhilta* to Exodus 15:27.
7. Numbers 33:9.
8. *Rashi* to Exodus 15:27; *Mekhilta* to Exodus 15:27. The twelve wells correspond to the Twelve Tribes.

of proclaiming "my strength and the might of my hand made me all this wealth" (Deuteronomy 8:17).

How can we get back on track and see the element of divine providence in our success? It is by noting that "they journeyed from Rameses in the first month, on the fifteen day of the first month, on the day after the *pesaḥ* offering; the Children of Israel went forth with an upraised hand, before the eyes of all Egypt" (Numbers 33:3). We identify with the exuberant triumph of leaving Egypt, the house of slaves, with a *yad ramah*, an "upraised hand."

But the Torah elaborates, "The Egyptians were burying those among them whom Hashem had struck, every firstborn; and on their gods Hashem had inflicted punishments" (Numbers 33:4). We realize that our triumph was impossible to achieve on our own. Would the Egyptians have allowed us to leave without pouring their fury on us, observing that the very cause of their misery was passing through? We could leave with an upraised hand only because Hashem arranged things such that the Egyptians would be preoccupied with burying their dead. They would be busy with their own *tzarot* and therefore they would leave us alone!

So, too, in every personal or national triumph, it is incumbent upon us to look for the element of "the Egyptians were burying those among them whom Hashem had struck." Hashem is always staging and arranging events so that we can realize success and triumphs. This brings us back on course in the *midbar ha-ammim*. We perceive the element of divine providence in our success.

But the modern Jew wants to know how he can seize the initiative. What action can he take to end the futile wanderings in the *midbar ha-ammim*? The answer, I submit, lies in focusing on the third instance of elaboration in the account of the sojourns in the Wilderness, the statement that Aaron died at Mount Hor, and precisely during the fifth month and on the first day of the month.[9] But the precise timing when Moses and Miriam died is not recorded in the Torah. Why?

I would submit that when the great teacher of Torah dies, it is possible for the community to continue on a high plane for just a little

9. Numbers 33:38.

while. Therefore, his or her death would not be felt immediately. But when the great peacemaker dies, his death is immediately felt. To make peace, one must engage in much machinations and maneuverings. How many white lies must be told! Peacemaking requires constant orchestration. The minute we cease to make peace, what was already accomplished collapses.

Aaron's death, therefore, could not be hidden. As soon as he died, a void was felt. And it was in the fifth month and on the first day. *Shalom* is the vessel that holds blessing for society.[10] It is the most fundamental building block. When peace and harmony prevail, Torah, *yir'at Shamayim*, and *ḥesed* can accomplish extraordinary things. As soon as Aaron died and the climate of peace began to dissipate, an opening was found by our enemies to attack. "The Canaanite King of Arad, who dwelled in the south, heard that Israel had come by the route of the spies, and he warred against Israel and took a captive from it" (Numbers 21:1).

If we take up the work of Aaron, the impediments along our path fall to the wayside and the path before us becomes crystal clear. We see where we are going, and the triumph of *yad ramah* is near at hand.

---

10. Mishnah, *Uktzin* 3:12 ("The Holy One, Blessed is He, did not find any vessel to hold blessing for Israel other than peace.").

A New Form of Anti-Semitism

September 27, 1988

The Festivals of Passover and Sukkot project a stark contrast concerning our attitude toward the nations of the world.

On Sukkot, in the time of the Temple, we offered seventy bulls, beginning with thirteen on the first day of the Festival, and culminating with seven on the last day.[1] This constitutes our intercession on the part of the nations of the world, and our concern for their welfare.[2] Hidden in our importuning for the welfare of the nations is our hope that wickedness will dissipate. This hope is expressed in the symbolism of *mitma'atim ve-holkhim*, that the number of bulls offered on each day

1. Numbers 29:13–33.
2. *Sukkah* 55b; *Rashi* ad loc., s.v. "*shiv'im parim*" (noting that the offerings of the bulls atoned for the seventy nations so that they would receive rain, as the nations are judged on Sukkot whether they are worthy to receive rain); *Rashi* to Numbers 29:18 (explaining that the offerings of the bulls protected the seventy nations from punishment).

is less than the number offered on the preceding day.[3] This is therefore quite a positive approach to the nations of the world.

In sharp contrast, on Passover, we importune Hashem, "*Shefokh ḥamat'kha el ha-goyim asher lo yeda'ukha*," "Pour Your wrath upon the nations that do not recognize You" (Psalms 79:6). Our approach to wickedness is direct and negative. Quite explosive!

Perhaps the insight of the *Sefat Emet* provides us with the explanation of this contrast. He points out that while Halakhah treats each of the Three Festivals the same with respect to the obligation of *simḥah*, the word "*ve-samaḥta*" does not appear at all with respect to Passover, only once with respect to Shavuot,[4] and thrice with respect to Sukkot.[5] Why? The answer is that historically, Passover meant only physical freedom, the birth of a nation. But this is nothing in itself to rejoice about. It was only when we assumed our mission at Sinai on Shavuot that we could reach *ve-samaḥta* once. And then as we truly assumed our mission in the fullest sense, the ingathering, the harvest, could we really rejoice, thrice rejoicing![6]

On Passover, we are an infant; on Sukkot, a giant. Well, the infant is fragile and delicate. An attack on him threatens his very existence. But the giant can respond with a measured attack, and even turn the other cheek, sometimes.

The challenge that we face today is whether we have the wisdom, sensitivity, and perspective to detect incipient forms of threats to our very existence.

In the past week, our community was shaken by the shocking arson attack on a local synagogue. Five *sifrei Torah* were burned and the synagogue was laid ruin.[7]

---

3. In general, the practice is to increase rather than decrease in number in matters of sanctity. *Shabbat* 21b.
4. Deuteronomy 16:11.
5. Leviticus 23:40 ("you shall rejoice before Hashem, your God, for a seven-day period"); Deuteronomy 16:14 ("you shall rejoice on your festival"); Deuteronomy 16:15 ("you will be completely joyous").
6. *Sefat Emet, Sukkot* (5658/October 1897). Cf. *Yalkut Shimoni, Emor* 654.
7. Ari L. Goldman, "2 Boys Held in Synagogue Fire and 10,000 Mourn 5 Torahs," *New York Times*, September 19, 1988, B1.

This incident points up, I would submit, a new form of anti-Semitism. The perpetrators were found to be juveniles, beyond the reach of the law. The law is so compassionate toward the perpetrators that even their names were not disclosed.[8] This raises the specter of vile people committing the most abominable acts of anti-Semitism through the agency of children, all along disavowing knowledge and responsibility.

This is quite an alarming development. It is only now that social scientists are coming up with new theories of how Hitler was able to attract so much support.[9] In 1933, he commanded only 37 percent of popular support.[10] Ten years later, the whole populace was enthusiastically carrying out his plan of genocide. Attributing the phenomenon to a threat of recrimination is nothing less than a travesty. What explains it is that when people are exposed to Nazi newspapers, Nazi propaganda, and Nazi policies, and they respect Nazis for ten years, then attitude follows behavior, to reduce cognitive dissonance.

We must press ahead to make sure that every avenue of punishing the perpetrators be found. The incident can be viewed as a crime directed by an adult because it happened in Flatbush on *yom tov* when people congregate in the synagogue to learn Torah even late in the evening. It is a densely populated area! A definite threat to life. The parents of the perpetrators should be held responsible. Legislation is necessary. And finally, we must insist upon a massive educational effort by our highest city officials to condemn these acts and set into motion a force to counter the prevailing attitude.

There is much truth in the popular metaphor that anti-Semitism is a disease of the body politic, sometimes ravaging the organism, and at other times in remission, but always looking for the conditions to re-emerge.

R. Samson Raphael Hirsch's interpretation of *shefokh ḥamat'kha* is similar to the sentiment behind the offering of seventy bulls, the concern for the welfare of the nations, because, he notes, it is only ***el ha-goyim,***

8. Ibid.

9. See, e.g., Ervin Staub, *The Roots of Evil: The Origins of Genocide and Other Group Violence* (Cambridge: Cambridge University Press, 1989), 91–127.

10. Joseph W. Bendersky, *A History of Nazi Germany: 1919–1945*, 2nd ed. (Chicago: Burnham, 2000), 91.

a warning *toward* the nations. It is not wrath *upon* the nations, which is the meaning of the end of the verse "*al mamlakhot asher be-Shimkha lo kara'u,*" "upon the kingdoms that do not invoke Your Name."[11] Please God, let our intense efforts toward education, dialogue, and legislation obviate any need for us to go further to *al mamlakhot*.

11. R. Samson Raphael Hirsch to Psalms 79:6.

May He Erect for Us the Booth of David that Has Fallen

October 14, 1989

We are all familiar with the tradition that the Festival of Sukkot commemorates the Clouds of Glory that enveloped the Children of Israel in the Wilderness.[1] Yet, in the special insertion in *Birkat ha-Mazon* on Sukkot, no mention is made of this historical event. Instead, we beseech Hashem, "May He, the Compassionate One, erect for us the booth of David that has fallen."[2]

If the latter phrase was chosen, it must be that it focuses on a particular aspect of the miracle of the Clouds of Glory and builds on this to capture for us the message of the Festival.

---

1. Leviticus 23:43.
2. Grace after Meals for Sukkot. Cf. Amos 9:11.

The Jewish ideal, as R. Samson Raphael Hirsch puts it, can be expressed as the achievement of the proper blending of the roof and the walls of the sukkah.[3] Naturally, the roof and the walls are in basic conflict. The roof cannot be made of material that is still connected to the terrestrial world or from a vessel, anything that has the imprint of man's dominance.[4] The roof of the sukkah hence conveys the message that we may not rely on the forces of nature or our own ingenuity for our security. We must rely only on Hashem! But, as far as the walls are concerned, they may be made from natural materials or a vessel.[5]

In the Generation of the Wilderness, we had no ability to build walls because we were in a desolate desert; we had no raw material to draw upon. Moreover, it was a society without material striving. In addition, only the fool could delude himself into thinking that his own ingenuity could extricate himself from the perils that he faced. The *tzila de-meheimenuta*, "shelter of faith," was self-evident.[6]

But what could man do to show that he did not take the *tzila de-meheimenuta* for granted? The only thing to do was to build a sukkah, in accordance with R. Akiva's opinion that the sukkot in the Wilderness were actual huts,[7] to show by human action that we are not worthy of the miracle. We built walls as a statement that we appreciated the *tzila de-meheimenuta*.

According to Tradition, the holiness of the sukkah is rooted in the action that Jacob took – "he built for himself a house, and for his livestock he made *sukkot* [shelters]; he therefore called the place Sukkot" (Genesis 33:17).

---

3. R. Samson Raphael Hirsch (Germany, 1808–1888), Leviticus 23:43.
4. Mishnah, *Sukkah* 1:4; *Sukkah* 11a; *Rashi* ad loc., s.v. "*pesulah*"; *Sukkah* 12a; Maimonides (*Rambam*, Egypt, 1135–1204), *Mishneh Torah, Sukkah* 5:1–2; R. Jacob b. Asher (*Tur*, Spain, 1270–1343), *Tur, Oraḥ Ḥayyim* 629; R. Joseph Caro (Safed, 1488–1575), *Shulḥan Arukh, Oraḥ Ḥayyim* 629:1–2, 13.
5. Mishnah, *Sukkah* 1:5; *Sukkah* 12a; *Mishneh Torah, Sukkah* 4:16; *Tur, Oraḥ Ḥayyim* 630; *Shulḥan Arukh, Oraḥ Ḥayyim* 630:1.
6. Zohar, *Emor* 103b.
7. *Sukkah* 11b.

R. Aharon Kotler asks, what difference does it make that Jacob built sukkot? Also, since the verse states "*va-yiven lo bayit*," "he built for himself a house," why did Jacob call the place Sukkot? The answer is that Jacob was making a statement that he believed in the promise made to Abraham, "Arise, walk about the land through its length and breadth, for to you I will give it" (Genesis 13:17). Since the land was suitable for grazing, Jacob staked a claim for settlement of the land. What Jacob did is the root of the holiness of Sukkot. We must take the roof, which represents faith in Hashem, and build walls, to show that we do not just pay lip service to our articles of faith, but we take action on them.[8]

But what of the Jew who really believes that he builds the walls on the blueprint of the roof, that the *sekhakh* is the motivating force behind his actions, but is complacent, feeling that enough of his actions are connected to the roof? He has no yearning that more of his actions should be motivated by the roof. For the complacent Jew, it is necessary to relate to the sukkah of the Leviathan.[9] This refers to the day when the ultimate perversion of the relationship between the walls and the *sekhakh* will end.

Isaiah speaks of two types of Leviathans. One is called "*naḥash bari'aḥ*," the strongest serpent, and the other is "*naḥash akallason*," the crooked one.[10] Both will be slain by Hashem.[11] They represent brute force and the cunning nature in the ultimate perversion of the *sekhakh*. Man deifies himself and imagines that Hashem acquiesces.

The Leviathan will perish and a new era will be ushered in. This is the *livyatan*, from the root ל-ו-ה, which means some form of association.[12] Either it is equal, as when Leah says "*ha-pa'am yillaveh ishi elai*," "this time my husband will become attached to me" (Genesis 29:34), or

---

8. R. Aharon Kotler (Lakewood, 1891–1962), cited in Irving M. Bunim, *Ever Since Sinai: Essays on the Valued, the Vanishing, and the Everlasting in American Jewish Life* (Jerusalem: Feldheim, 1977), 236–241.
9. See *Bava Batra* 75a (stating that Hashem will make a sukkah for the righteous from the hide of the Leviathan).
10. Isaiah 27:1.
11. Ibid.
12. R. David Kimhi (*Radak*, Provence, ca. 1160–ca. 1235), *Sefer ha-Sharashim*, s.v. "*lamed-vav-heh*."

subordinate, as in the word "*loveh*," "debtor." Hence the sukkah of the Leviathan represents the sukkah of the whole of mankind. It represents the realization of our cosmic mission when the Torah will be the blueprint for *tikkun olam*. And this is a heavy burden. It represents the ultimate striving by us to construct walls that have the blueprint of the *sekhakh*.

Who epitomized both of these aspects of the sukkah? Who was the one who was driven to construct walls from the materials of the *sekhakh* but was also restless, feeling that there was an imbalance in his life, that the *sekhakh* was weaker than the walls, and wanted to counteract it? It was David.

David wanted to be hidden in the sukkah – "He will conceal me in the concealment of His Tent" (Psalms 27:5). And he says, "Teach me Your way, Hashem, and lead me on the path of integrity because of my watchful foes" (Psalms 27:11). Let the *sekhakh* be a blueprint for me to such an extent that even the onlookers, the worst type of enemies who are waiting to pounce upon me and are waiting for me to make a mistake, will find my conduct so perfect that no mistake will be found.[13]

And it was David who was restless, who yearned for a larger role for *malkhut Shamayim*, who captured the spirit of the sukkah of the Leviathan. He proclaimed to Nathan, "I am living in a house of cedar while the Ark of God dwells within the curtain" (II Samuel 7:2).

It is the spirit of Jacob of "he therefore called the place Sukkot" (Genesis 33:17) and the spirit of the *sukkat Livyatan* that are embedded in our yearning "May He, the Compassionate One, erect for us the booth of David that has fallen."

13. See *Radak* to Psalms 27:11, s.v. "*le-ma'an shorerei*." See also *Rashi* to Psalms 5:9, s.v. "*shorerei*"; Abraham b. Meir ibn Ezra (Ibn Ezra, Spain, 1089–1164), Ibn Ezra to Psalms 5:9, s.v. "*le-ma'an shorerei*."

The Radish and the Honey

October 5, 1990

In the spirit of the old Yiddish saying "*oyf a mayseh* [concerning a story], you do not ask questions, you just listen,"[1] permit me to relate a parable of a *maggid* of yore.[2]

It once happened that a radish wanted to get married. He took a great liking to a fine mass of honey in a beehive. The honey was to be his bride, he decided. But first the radish had to ask permission of the bee, the father of the honey. Upon one look at the radish, the papa bee cringed in disdain. "Look at yourself! How dirty you are, all covered with earth. I will never allow you into my family. And my honey, she is so sweet and lovely. Go away!"

1. See Rachel Rosmarin, *Mamma Used to Say: Pearls of Wisdom from the World of Yiddish* (Jerusalem: Feldheim, 2000), 165.
2. The story is retold in Irving M. Bunim, *Ever Since Sinai: Essays on the Valued, the Vanishing, and the Everlasting in American Jewish Life* (Jerusalem: Feldheim, 1977), 196–197.

Without a word, the radish left. But he cleaned, scrubbed, and polished himself, and returned for a second audience. The father bee was still very displeased with the radish, as he found his red skin repulsive. Undaunted, the radish peeled off his red skin and returned for another audience, a clean, gleaming white. Now, the father bee could not refuse and reluctantly agreed to the match.

The wedding was made by cutting the radish into thin slices and cooking it in the honey. So then the question arose, what blessing should be recited on the mixture, an integrated mass? The blessing on the radish is *ha-adamah,* but the blessing on the honey is *she-ha-kol.* The answer is that the appropriate blessing is *ha-adamah* because the radish is the *ikkar,* the main ingredient, and the honey provides flavor and is therefore *tafel,* only the secondary ingredient.[3]

The father bee was livid! "I never wanted this lump of a vegetable for a son-in-law, and now he has managed to turn the tables on me and become the *ikkar* while my honey is the *tafel.*"

We are all familiar with the midrash that the Four Species that we take on Sukkot represent four different kinds of Jews. Standing at the peak of perfection is the *etrog.* It has both taste and fragrance, representing Torah and good deeds. Hence, the *etrog* embodies all the *ma'alot* (positive attributes). Then there is the *lulav,* which has taste but no fragrance, representing the Jew who has Torah but not good deeds. Then there is the *hadas,* which has fragrance but not taste, representing the Jew who has good deeds but not Torah. And finally, there is the *aravah,* which has neither taste nor fragrance, representing the Jew without either Torah or good deeds. Hashem says that one union, an *aguddah aḥat,* should be made out of all these different types of Jews.[4]

Now, if the *etrog* could only talk, it would protest, "It is patently unfair that the blessing is recited on the *lulav.* It should be recited on the *etrog* since I have all the *ma'alot* and therefore am the *ikkar* and the other species are *tefalim.*"

But, permit me to suggest that the question is itself the answer. The role of the *etrog* in the *aguddah aḥat* is clearly outreach. It must

3. *Shulḥan Arukh, Oraḥ Ḥayyim* 212:1.
4. Leviticus Rabbah 30:12.

influence the other Jews with its abundant goodness in Torah and *ma'asim tovim*. If the *etrog* is preoccupied with recognition, it will fail in its mission. On a wider level, the *aguddah aḥat* perhaps fails to achieve its potential precisely because we are all fighting about the blessing, the blessing that we begrudge that is recited over the achievement of others.

If the *aguddah aḥat* is to achieve its maximum potential, the *etrog* must look upon itself and its fellow species as live species. The Midrash depicts the *etrog* as the heart of the human organism.[5] But it must be a wise, discerning, and sensitive heart, and not regard the other Species as inferior, hapless unfortunates that it must help. No, the other Species must be regarded as having inherent worth as well.

The *aravah* might be devoid of Torah and *ma'asim tovim*, but it is in the shape of a mouth.[6] The mouth that today is silent or utters nonsense, or even profanities, is capable of being transformed into a mouth that sings the praises of Hashem and expresses the most noble of human sentiments. And the *hadas*, which has good deeds but no Torah, also has inherent worth because it is in the shape of an eye.[7] It has perspective from which the *etrog* can deeply benefit. And the *lulav*, which is the insular *talmid ḥakham*, is the spinal column, the nervous system that communicates to the entire body.[8] Torah provides meaning to every sphere of our existence in the microcosm of our personal lives, and in the wider world is the light of the universe, the *or la-ammim*.[9]

When the Four Species view each other as sensitive and caring, and their relationship as symbiotic and cooperative, the *aguddah* splits the very heavens!

---

5. Ibid., 30:14.
6. Ibid.
7. Ibid.
8. Ibid.
9. Cf. Isaiah 42:6, 49:6.

For His Livestock He Made Shelters

September 23, 1991

The holiness of Sukkot, according to our Sages, finds its roots in the dramatic and bold action of our Patriarch Jacob. After pacifying his brother Esau, Jacob journeyed to Sukkot. "He built for himself a house, and for his livestock he made sukkot [shelters]; he therefore called the place Sukkot" (Genesis 33:17).

R. Aharon Kotler finds Jacob's choice of the name Sukkot curious.[1] If someone would acquire a large tract of land and build on it a home and also a garage, should he call the place "Garageland"? The home is obviously the *ikkar*, and the shack for the cattle *tafel*. Why, then, call the place Sukkot?

---

1. R. Aharon Kotler, cited in Irving M. Bunim, *Ever Since Sinai: Essays on the Valued, the Vanishing, and the Everlasting in American Jewish Life* (Jerusalem: Feldheim, 1977), 236–241.

R. Aharon answers that Jacob's intent here was to demonstrate that he gives more than just lip service to the promise to Abraham, "Arise, walk about the land through its length and breadth, for to you I will give it" (Genesis 13:17). Jacob surveyed the land and made a statement that it was suited for grazing. He stayed therefore for eighteen months – two summers sandwiched by winter.[2] He showed thereby that he really believed the promise of "to you I will give it."

Well, permit me to suggest that if the great *tzaddik* and intercessor of the Jewish people R. Levi Yitzhak of Berdichev (*Berdichever Rav*, Ukraine, 1740–1809) would come down now, he would find a great merit for the Jewish people. *Ma'aseh avot siman le-banim*. Jacob showed the way, but many thousands of years later, we followed his example and went further.

The government in Israel has set up settlements in the West Bank. Jacob made his statement of love of *Eretz Yisrael* and acknowledged the divine gift after he pacified Esau and his relationship with him was at a peak of friendliness. But the successive Israeli governments and the courageous settlors settled the West Bank when a state of war still existed between Israel and Arab countries,[3] and the United States, Western Europe, and Russia hammered away that the settlements were illegal and an obstacle to peace![4] So, too, the world press drummed away.[5] Also, whereas Jacob made his dramatic initiative for an eighteen-month period, the settlement of the West Bank stretches almost twenty-four years. Finally, Jacob took his initiative in relation to what embellishes physical and material life, but we have made the statement that the Land

2. *Megillah* 17a; *Rashi* to Genesis 33:17.
3. William W. Harris, *Taking Root: Israeli Settlement in the West Bank, the Golan and Gaza-Sinai, 1967–1980* (Chichester, NY: Research Studies Press, 1980), chs. 2 & 5; Don Peretz, *The West Bank: History, Politics, Society, and Economy* (Boulder, CO: Westview Press, 1986), 45–54.
4. "Reagan Assails New W. Bank Settlements," *Boston Globe*, August 28, 1983, 1; "Israeli Settlements Criticized by Common Market Leaders," *New York Times*, March 23, 1983, A2; Wolf Blitzer, "West Bank Decision Angers U.S.; State Dept. Calls Decision 'An Obstacle to Peace,'" *Jerusalem Post*, July 27, 1977, 1; "An Obstacle to a Negotiated Peace: West Bank Settlements 'Illegal,' Scranton Tells Security Council," *Jerusalem Post*, March 25, 1976, 4.
5. Moshe Sharon, "Concepts of Peace," *Jerusalem Post*, February 18, 1983, 6.

of Israel is suitable for settlement by people. It is therefore a statement of "he built for himself a house."

Our resolve is now being severely threatened with the suspension of Israel's request for ten billion dollars of loan guarantees. And as Leslie Gelb reveals in his column, it is part of a secret, wider plan to be at once more demanding and more generous toward Israel.[6]

Last year, we prayed "*tehei shenat ve-ar'ennu niflaot*," "may it be a year of 'I will show it wonders' (Micah 7:15)."[7] We have witnessed a fulfillment of this in the emergence of our beloved State and people almost unscathed by the cataclysmic turmoil that embroiled the Middle East last year.[8]

Let us work and pray so that we proceed from the hidden miracle to the open miracle and witness *haramat keren ha-Torah u-Klal Yisrael.*

---

6. Leslie H. Gelb, "A Secret Plan for Israel," *New York Times*, September 22, 1991, E17.
7. The first letters of "*tehei shenat ve-ar'ennu niflaot*" are the same as the Hebrew year 5756 (תשנ"ו). The phrase "*ve-ar'ennu niflaot*" refers to the description of the Future Redemption at Micah 7:15 ("As in the days when you left the land of Egypt, I will show it wonders.").
8. The reference is to the Persian Gulf War that spanned August 2, 1990, to February 28, 1991. See generally Lawrence Freedman and Efraim Karsh, *The Gulf Conflict 1990–1991: Diplomacy and War in the New World Order* (Princeton, NJ: Princeton University Press, 1993).

Season of Our Rejoicing

October 12, 1992

Each of the Three Festivals has its own distinctive character, but the common denominator is the mandate of "*ve-samaḥta be-ḥaggekha,*" "you shall rejoice on your festival" (Deuteronomy 16:14).[1] With respect to Halakhah's specifications here, there is no difference among the Three Festivals. Why then is Sukkot, and only Sukkot, officially designated as *zeman simḥatenu,* "the season of our rejoicing"?[2]

Permit me to suggest an approach. Our Sages make a very emphatic statement regarding *simḥah*: *Ein simḥah ke-hattarat ha-sefekot,* there is no joy like the resolution of doubts.[3] The ecstasy proceeding

1. *Pesaḥim* 109a; Maimonides, *Mishneh Torah, Yom Tov* 6:17; R. Jacob b. Asher (*Tur,* Spain, 1270–1343), *Tur, Oraḥ Ḥayyim* 529; *Shulḥan Arukh, Oraḥ Ḥayyim* 529:2.
2. *Shemoneh Esreh* Prayer for Sukkot, *Atah Beḥartanu*; Kiddush for Sukkot.
3. R. Joseph b. Meir Teomim (Galicia, ca. 1727–1792), *Peri Megadim, Oraḥ Ḥayyim, Mishbetzot Zahav* 682:1. For similar formulations of this statement, see R. Moses Isserles (*Rema,* Poland, 1525 or 1530–1572), *She'elot u-Teshuvot ha-Rema, siman* 5 ("*lo ta'am ta'am simḥah mi she-lo ta'am simḥat sefekot ve-hattaratam*"), and R. Jehiel Hillel b.

from the resolution of doubts plays a vital role in the Festival of Sukkot on different levels.

In the thinking of the *Gra*, the verse "I caused the Children of Israel to dwell in booths when I took them out of the land of Egypt" (Leviticus 23:43) does not refer to the initial gift of the Clouds of Glory but rather to their restoration.[4] They were removed after the Sin of the Golden Calf. For the almost three months of their disappearance, we had grave doubts regarding our physical survival and our relationship with Hashem. Well, all these doubts were removed with the restoration of the Clouds of Glory, as it was a sign of divine favor. Hence the designation of *zeman simḥatenu*.

But there is a different reason as well. The mitzvot of Sukkot – the Four Species and the sukkah – represent the formula par excellence for the resolution of doubts in the realm of *emunah*. It is the formula to acquire *simḥah* in the realm of our belief system and trust in Hashem.

The sukkah represents true trust in Hashem.[5] If one misses this point, the mitzvah of sukkah becomes meaningless. But how can *bittaḥon* be legislated? Only actions, not emotions, can be legislated. The answer is the inter-relationship between the Four Species and the sukkah. Meticulous performance of mitzvot produces *emunah* as a byproduct. This is a recurring theme in the *Ḥinnukh*.[6]

David Altschuler (Galicia, 18th cent.), *Metzudat David*, Proverbs 15:30 ("*ein ba-alom simḥah ke-hattarat he-sefekot*").

4. R. Elijah b. Solomon Zalman (Vilna Gaon or *Gra*, Vilna, 1720–1797), *Be'ur ha-Gra*, Song of Songs 1:4.
5. See Zohar, *Emor* 103b (describing the sukkah as the *tzila de-meheimenuta*, "shelter of faith").
6. *Sefer ha-Ḥinnukh* teaches "*ha-adam nif'al aḥar pe'ulotav*" (lit., "a person is made according to his deeds"). See R. Aaron b. Joseph ha-Levi (*Ra'ah*, Spain, ca. 1235–1300), *Sefer ha-Ḥinnukh*, eds. R. Yitzhak Yeshayah Weiss, R. David Zicherman, and R. Yitzhak Weinstein (Jerusalem: Mekhon Yerushalayim, 1992), mitzvah no. 16 (prohibition against breaking a bone of the paschal offering). See also ibid., mitzvah no. 40 (prohibition against building an altar from hewn stone); mitzvah no. 99 (commandment that Priests wear the Priestly Vestments); mitzvah no. 264 (obligation for a Priest to become impure for a close relative); mitzvah no. 299 (commandment to bring a *Musaf* offering on each of the seven days of Passover); mitzvah no. 324 (commandment to take a *lulav* on Sukkot); mitzvah no. 401 (commandment to bring two lambs as a burnt offering daily).

Also, on a symbolic level, the Four Species represent different kinds of Jews.[7] It is by means of *aḥdut* that *emunah* is produced as a byproduct, through the collective sharing of a religious experience.[8]

But it would seem that the answer to our original question is quite simple. Sukkot is designated as *zeman simḥatenu* because it coincides with the harvest.[9] Sukkot is called "*Ḥag ha-Asif*," the "Festival of the Ingathering" (Exodus 23:16). But here is the challenge: What is our standard for considering the Festival of the Ingathering a *zeman simḥatenu*? If the harvest is less than last year, do we feel that it is *zeman simḥatenu*? If the economy is in a recession, not only are the unemployed adversely affected, but even those employed in good, high-paying jobs are anxious and fearful. They are concerned that they might lose their jobs, not get a raise, be required to pay higher taxes, and not be able to find another job if they want to change employment. We hence have a very high standard for *zeman simḥatenu* for our material harvest. We are challenged to match this standard for the natural *zeman simḥatenu* with our standard for spiritual harvest!

On the fifteenth day of Tishrei, we had *hattarat ha-sefekot*, the *zeman simḥatenu* as far as our relationship with Hashem. But for some elements of society, *zeman simḥatenu* in the spiritual realm occurred much earlier. For them, there was no need for the Clouds of Glory. As soon as they heard that they would not be annihilated for committing idolatry, that was enough. For others, the restoration of their relationship with Hashem happened when Hashem said to Moses "release Me, and I shall destroy them" (Deuteronomy 9:14), but allowed him to pray forty days. That is enough for restoration. *Zeman simḥatenu*. Prayer by proxy is good enough.

Then we have forty days of restoration to Torah, when Moses ascends to the heavens for the second time. That is enough for others. For them, it is *zeman simḥatenu* when the relationship with Hashem

---

7. Leviticus Rabbah 30:12.
8. See R. Aaron b. Joseph ha-Levi, *Sefer ha-Ḥinnukh*, mitzvah no. 612 (*hak'hel*).
9. See R. Samuel b. Meir (*Rashbam*, France, ca. 1080–1174), *Rashbam* to Leviticus 23:39; Ibn Ezra to Deuteronomy 16:15; *Rashi* to *Pesaḥim* 36b, s.v. "*zeman simḥah*"; *Yalkut Shimoni, Emor* 654; R. Aaron b. Joseph ha-Levi, *Sefer ha-Ḥinnukh*, mitzvah no. 324 (commandment to take a *lulav* on Sukkot).

consists of the spiritual elite occupying themselves with Torah, but not the general masses. For still others, *zeman simḥatenu* came when the Second Tablets were given. That democratized the Torah and restored the relationship with Hashem. But they gloss over the difference in the spiritual level between the first Tablets and the second Tablets.[10]

And then comes the call to construct the Tabernacle. For some, it is *zeman simḥatenu*, rejoicing in the knowledge that the Tabernacle will be built. But for others, it is not yet enough, since they see new challenges of participating. Two days of collections are necessary.[11] Then there is an inventory of what was donated. That is sufficient for some people.[12] The contribution of materials for the construction of the Tabernacle is *zeman simḥatenu*, but the holiness of being in the Tabernacle is for others.

What should we consider our *zeman simḥatenu*? We are challenged to match our concept of *zeman simḥatenu* in the material realm with *zeman simḥatenu* in the spiritual realm. The ideal is that "when last seen, they were still climbing."[13]

---

10. See R. Eliyahu Eliezer Dessler (Lithuania, England, and Benei Berak, 1892–1953), *Mikhtav me-Eliyahu*, eds. R. Aryeh Carmell and R. Alter Halperin, vol. 1, 222–223; vol. 2, pt. 1, *Shavuot, Shenei Ofanei Kabbalat ha-Torah* (Benei Berak: Hever Talmidav, 1964), 26–30.
11. Exodus 36:3.
12. Exodus 36:7.
13. The expression refers to George Mallory and Andrew Irvine, who attempted to climb Mount Everest. They were last seen by a fellow climber, Noel Odell, on June 8, 1924, still climbing to the summit. Wade Davis, *Into the Silence: The Great War, Mallory, and the Conquest of Everest* (New York: Vintage Books, 2012), xiv.

The Prominence of the *Aravah*

October 18, 2005

Perhaps the most paradoxical symbol in Jewish ritual is the *aravah*. Today, the *aravah* joins with the *etrog*, *lulav*, and *hadasim* to form the mitzvah of the Four Species.

The Four Species represent different types of Jews.[1] The companions of the *aravah* represent Jews who have Torah and good deeds, or both. But the poor *aravah* represents the Jew without Torah or good deeds. We would call him the nondescript Jew. If we wanted to be harsh, we would say he is the lackluster Jew, or the Jew who is useless.

But is the *aravah* really the symbol of uselessness? Consider that in the time of the Temple, we had the ceremony of *mitzvat aravah*. Every day, the Priests would go down to the Valley of Motza and retrieve giant *aravot* and bedeck the Altar with them. Every day, the

1. Leviticus Rabbah 30:12.

Priests would circuit the Altar and pronounce, "Please Hashem, save now!" (Psalms 118:25).[2]

So here the ritual item of choice is the *aravah*. The *aravah* jumps into prominence ahead of the other three of the Four Species.

We reconcile the two rituals by simply noting that the *aravah* must assume prominence, whether it is alone or in the company of the other Species. If the *aravah* feels isolated, alone, and neglected, it is not getting its due. It must feel comfortable, accepted, and, yes, exuberant in the company of the other three Species.

The Talmud tells us that the Golden Age of Jewish spiritual accomplishment was in the days of King Hezekiah. "They searched from Dan until Beer Sheba, and no ignoramus was found."[3] R. Ahron Soloveichik derives from this that the greatness of a generation is measured not by the spiritual stature of its leaders, but rather by that of the masses.[4]

If there is one thing certain in Jewish life, it is that unity is not a constant. It never remains stationary. It is either rising or falling. If the *aravah* gets its due, we can be sure that Jewish unity is rising.

In the Torah educational enterprise and in society at large, the issue will always arise, to whom should we devote additional energy? Should it be to boost the brightest students or the weakest students, the spiritually thriving or those who are groping? The answer is always: Favor the weaker vessel. The quality of life will always rise the most when we give them emphasis.

The choice of the *aravah* for *mitzvat aravah* is not happenstance. The *aravah* has the shape of the mouth.[5] When the *aravah* exuberates in the company of the other Species, the prayer of the Jewish people rises to the highest purity and reaches the seventh heaven, *aravot*.[6]

2. Mishnah, *Sukkah* 4:5; *Sukkah* 45a.
3. *Sanhedrin* 94b.
4. R. Ahron Soloveichik (Chicago, 1917–2001), *Logic of the Heart, Logic of the Mind: Wisdom and Reflections on Topics of Our Times* (Jerusalem: Genesis Jerusalem Press, 1991), 29.
5. Leviticus Rabbah 30:14.
6. See *Ḥagigah* 12b (noting that the seventh heaven is called *aravot*); R. Elijah b. Solomon Zalman, *Siddur Me'orei ha-Gra* (Jerusalem, 1999), 90, s.v. "*ve-yippaked ve-yizzakher*" (citing *Ḥagigah* 12b).

Sukkot – Shabbat Ḥol ha-Mo'ed

Kohelet on Sukkot

October 10, 1987

One of the mysteries of the Festival of Sukkot is the reading of *Kohelet*. After all, Sukkot is officially designated as *zeman simḥatenu*, the season of our rejoicing,[1] while the mood of *Kohelet* is decidedly morose. We get the impression that everything in life is "futile and a vexation of the spirit" (Ecclesiastes 1:14).

Rather than viewing *Kohelet* as depressing, I would propose that its message actually enhances our joy and directs it toward high mission and purpose.

The Festival of Sukkot is called *rishon le-ḥeshbon avonot*, "the beginning of the accounting period for sins."[2] We therefore need a battle plan for the new year.

What is the battle plan? One should always incite the Good Inclination to fight against the Evil Inclination. If he succeeds, fine and well. If not, he should occupy himself with Torah. If he succeeds, fine. If not,

---

1. *Shemoneh Esreh* Prayer for Sukkot, *Atah Beḥartanu*; Kiddush for Sukkot.
2. *Midrash Tanḥuma, Emor* 22.

he should accept the yoke of Heaven. If that does not work, he should remember the day of death.[3]

Now, *Kohelet* is a master of knowing how to incite the Good Inclination against the Evil Inclination. After we are duly introduced to *Kohelet* as the wisest of all men,[4] and our expectations are built up for a scintillating and profound insight, we are shocked with an insult. We are told, "*motar ha-adam min ha-behemah ayin*," "the difference between man and beast is naught" (Ecclesiastes 3:19). But how can this be? Man is endowed with speech, intellect, and a higher spirit. *Kohelet*'s statement, we say to ourselves, is dead wrong!

But then, we contemplate that *ayin* (אין) is the *roshei tevot* of *amirah* (אמירה), *yediah* (ידיעה), and *neshamah* (נשמה), speech, intellect, and soul.[5] So we are calmed down.

But man is constantly tossed about between the world of *remez* and the world of *peshat*. And we realize that while, if we look at the totality of our life, we might be convinced that we are superior to an animal, what if we take a small slice of time, an hour, a day, a week? What of this? Can we also say with conviction "the difference between man and beast is naught"?

Kohelet enhances our *simḥat yom tov* by converting what we regard as a disability into an advantage. There are so many things that we do not understand about the divine governance of the world. This ignorance has led many people astray, causing them to turn to agnosticism and atheism. *Kohelet* shows us that our ignorance of certain things works to our great benefit.

"He has also put an enigma into their minds so that man cannot comprehend what God has done from beginning to end" (Ecclesiastes 3:11). And all this is for the good. If man were obsessed with his mortality, who would plant? Who would build? Who would marry? Who would conduct scientific research? So death is hidden.

---

3. *Berakhot* 5a (R. Levi b. Hama in the name of R. Simeon b. Lakish).
4. See Ecclesiastes 1:16. See also I Kings 5:11.
5. R. Hayyim Joseph David Azulai (*Ḥida*, Jerusalem, 1724–1806), *Ḥomat Anakh, Kohelet* 14; *Ḥadrei Vaten: Derushei Musar al Seder ha-Parshiyyot, Va-Yera* II, ¶ 4.

And not only this, but we never think about it either, all to our benefit, as this is certainly against logic. So we see a divine imprint in man.

So, too, we do not see justice in the world. We have the age-old question of *tzaddik ve-ra lo* and *rasha ve-tov lo*, "why do the righteous suffer and the wicked prosper?"[6]

But the lack of comprehension of the divine plan is quite necessary. If our perception of justice were keen, if we would always see how sin is punished and virtue is rewarded, virtue would be compelling, and we could never claim reward for our virtue.[7] So our lack of perception of justice creates a trial for us, and this magnifies our virtue. Then we can expect a great reward for it. Ah! Is our *simḥat yom tov* enhanced!

And life, *Kohelet* tells us, is full of surprises. The race is not always won by the swift. The battle is not always won by the strong. The wise even lack bread. The genius is not wealthy, and the advice of people of practical wisdom is not always taken.[8]

So what does this show? It shows that there is divine intervention in our lives. Outcomes occur that are not the product of natural forces.

Kohelet never gives us *musar*. It is a soft sell. He does not directly tell us to accept *ol malkhut Shamayim* except in the very last verse. Torah and good deeds are couched in terms of eating and drinking.[9] We need to make a distinction that only "beneath the sun" is *hevel havalim*, "futility of futilities," but not what preceded the sun, i.e., the Torah.[10] But his genius surely plants the seeds of *emunah*. He gets us thinking.

If our ego is piqued on Sukkot, *Kohelet* plays on it and asks us, do we want immortality? And he shows us the way. He tells us that "a good name is better than good oil" (Ecclesiastes 7:1). The reputation acquired

6. *Berakhot* 7a.
7. Maimonides, *Mishneh Torah, Teshuvah* 5:4.
8. Ecclesiastes 9:11.
9. Ecclesiastes 8:15; Ecclesiastes Rabbah 8:16; R. Baruch ha-Levi Epstein (*Torah Temimah*, Belarus, 1860–1941), *Torah Temimah* to Ecclesiastes 8:15. Just as eating and drinking sustain the body, Torah and good deeds sustain the soul. See Zohar, *Tzav* 3:29b.
10. *Shabbat* 30b.

through learning Torah and performing good deeds lives forever, longer than the embalming oil that preserves the dead.[11]

And *Kohelet* speaks of the day of death. He describes man as a pitiful fish that is suddenly ensnared by an evil net.[12] Life, with no warning, abruptly ends. But the realization of this cannot but be put to our advantage – "let your garments always be white" (Ecclesiastes 9:8). We imagine each day to be our last and make the best use of it by learning Torah and performing good deeds.[13]

But the image of life and death changes quite dramatically at the very end of *Kohelet*. There we are presented with an image of life as a majestic machine. We are urged to repent before the silver cord snaps, before the golden bow shatters.[14] And then dust returns to the earth, and the spirit to Hashem Who gave it.[15]

Our overwhelming sentiment at this point is a desperation to keep the machine going, this thing of beauty from disintegrating. How can we accomplish this? The message of the last verse rings out with clarity – "The sum of the matter, when all has been considered: Fear God and keep His commandments, for that is man's whole duty" (Ecclesiastes 12:13).

---

11. R. Moses Alshekh (*Alshekh*, Safed, 1508–1593), *Devarim Tovim*, Ecclesiastes 7:1.
12. Ecclesiastes 9:12.
13. *Rashi* to Ecclesiastes 9:8.
14. Ecclesiastes 12:6.
15. Ecclesiastes 12:7.

The Ultimate Renunciation of the *Gag* Mentality

October 1, 1988

We often strengthen our belief in a principle by fostering a negative attitude toward what stands diametrically opposed to it. A case in point is the mitzvah of sukkah. We are ordered to abandon the security and comfort of our homes and repair to a frail hut for seven days. The essence of the sukkah is its *sekhakh*. Halakhah's technical requirement is that the *sekhakh* must be made of unstable and delicate materials, to allow the elements to penetrate.[1] The lesson is the futility of self-reliance and the need to put our faith in the *Ribbono shel Olam*.[2]

On *Shabbat Ḥol ha-Mo'ed,* we read a portion in Ezekiel that describes the devastating defeat of Gog and Magog in the days of the

1. *Tosafot* to *Sukkah* 2a, s.v. "*ki avid*"; R. Jacob b. Asher (*Tur*, Spain, 1270–1343), *Tur, Oraḥ Ḥayyim* 631; R. Abraham Abele Gombiner (*Magen Avraham*, Poland, ca. 1635–1682), *Magen Avraham* to *Shulḥan Arukh, Oraḥ Ḥayyim* 631, n. 2; R. Israel Meir ha-Kohen Kagan (*Ḥafetz Ḥayyim*, Radin, 1838–1933), *Mishnah Berurah* 631:6.
2. R. Samson Raphael Hirsch (Germany, 1808–1888), Numbers 29:13.

Messiah.[3] Correction – Gog to *gag* (i.e., roof). R. Samson Raphael Hirsch found in *gag* the diametrically opposed philosophy of sukkah.[4] What the *gag* philosophy entails is man's delusion that just as he can wall himself in from his fellow man, he can also build an impervious roof and separate himself from God. The extreme variety of this philosophy takes the form of an obsessive belief in one's own power – self-deification.

Now, Ezekiel describes the cataclysmic defeat of Gog and Magog. The manner of the defeat leaves no doubt that God vanquished them. Not only are they defeated with the sword and pestilence, but the enemy in its panic turns on itself, and is pelted with hail and torrential rains.[5] "I will be exalted, and I will be sanctified, and I will make Myself known before the eyes of many nations; they will know that I am Hashem" (Ezekiel 38:23).

But then something that would strike the contemporary man as astonishing happens. In the pandemonium of defeat, an arsenal of all sorts of weapons is strewn on the mountains of Jerusalem. We find a total of seven types of weapons, defensive weapons and offensive weapons, of the short- and long-range varieties. Jews come out of their inhabited areas and draw upon these weapons, using the wooden components for fuel. For seven years, there is no need to draw wood from the fields or to cut down trees in the forest.[6]

How astonishing. The enemy is humbled and decimated, but his weapons are left intact. Which modern nation would resist the temptation to collect the weapons and store them in case the enemy rises up again for another attack? Which nation would resist the temptation to study the technology embedded in the weapons for the purpose of reproducing them to be used against the enemy if need be? Does this not constitute prudent action?

What we are seeing here, I would submit, is the ultimate renunciation of the *gag* philosophy and the ultimate affirmation of the sukkah

3. Ezekiel 38:18–39:16.
4. R. Samson Raphael Hirsch, Numbers 29:13 and *Haftarah le-Shabbat Ḥol ha-Mo'ed Sukkot.*
5. Ezekiel 38:22.
6. Ezekiel 39:9–10.

philosophy. On that crossroad in our history, when we see a devastated enemy, we will make the ultimate gesture of faith in Hashem – we will unilaterally disarm!

Perhaps there is no phenomenon today that demonstrates the dual potential of man in respect of the *gag* and sukkah philosophies more than the satellite. A country can orbit its satellite to let it get caught up in the *gag* mentality, but at the same time, it can lead to an increased awareness of Hashem. "How abundant are Your works, Hashem; with wisdom You made them!" (Psalms 104:24).

This past week, our beloved State, the State of Israel, achieved a spectacular feat. It became only the eighth nation to launch a satellite, the Ofek.[7] The feat was universally acclaimed in both the international scientific and political communities.[8]

I dare say, if the newest entrant into space would have been one of many other countries, the reaction would have been entirely different. Instead of jubilation, it would have been trepidation. Just imagine if Libya had been the new entrant. In the hands of a megalomaniac dictator, the satellite would have been a new vehicle to exploit and extort humanity, a means of controlling world events, in short, a vehicle to unleash the *gag* mentality.

But Israel's success evoked the sentiment of hope! The satellite represents the prospect of the inauguration of a new era of peace and stability in the region.

The ability to launch a satellite implies an ability to launch a ballistic missile. Now Israel will be able to intercept nuclear and chemical warheads at high altitude before they contaminate the environment. Also, the potential for a spy satellite is enormous. The lead time is only

---

7. John Kifner, "Israel Launches Space Program and a Satellite: Spy Craft Are Expected to Be Main Emphasis," *New York Times*, September 20, 1988, A1.
8. Glenn Frankel, "Israel Launches Its First Satellite into Orbit; Major Step Seen toward Ability to Spy on Arabs from Space," *Washington Post*, September 20, 1988, A1; Daniel Williams, "Israel Fires 1st Satellite into Space; Denies It's for Spying: Impact on Mideast Arms Race Possible," *Los Angeles Times*, September 20, 1988, 1; "Jordan: Offeq-I Has 'Military Role,'" *Jerusalem Post*, September 20, 1988, 2; Lisa Perlman, "Satellite Launch Marks Israel's Calling Card to the Space Age," *Nature* 335, no. 6189 (September 29, 1988): 387; Jeffrey Richelson, "Military Intelligence: SPOT Is Not Enough," *Bulletin of the Atomic Scientists* 45, no. 7 (September 1989): 26–27.

five to seven minutes.[9] Think of what it would have meant in the Yom Kippur War. Finally, the satellite acts as another means of reinforcing demilitarization.

A peculiarity of the Ofek that I see is that it travels from East to West, instead of from West to East,[10] that is, Providentially![11]

May Israel's entry into the Space Age spell a difference, one step closer to the sukkah mentality and one step further away from the *gag* mentality.

---

9. Dore Gold, "Launching of Israeli Satellite Sends a Message to Other Mideast States," *Jewish Exponent*, September 30, 1988, 3.
10. "Israeli Satellite Functioning Well after First Day of Orbit," *Jewish Telegraphic Agency*, September 21, 1988. Typically, spacecraft are launched eastward, in the same direction as the Earth's rotation, because the Earth's rotation provides additional velocity for the spacecraft. The direction of the launch, however, may be restricted by safety considerations, such as preventing first rocket stages or a malfunctioning rocket from falling on populated areas. Political considerations do not allow Israel to launch its spacecraft eastward. Consequently, Israel is required to launch satellites westward, over the Mediterranean Sea. Mike Gruntman, *Blazing the Trail: The Early History of Spacecraft and Rocketry* (Reston, VA: American Institute of Aeronautics and Astronautics, 2004), 451.
11. See *Bava Batra* 25a (opinion of R. Abbahu that that the Divine Presence is in the West); R. Bahya b. Asher, *Rabbenu Beḥaye al ha-Torah*, Deuteronomy 3:27 (stating that it is known that the Divine Presence is in the West); R. Judah Loew b. Bezalel (*Maharal*, Prague, ca. 1525–1609), *Gevurot Hashem*, ch. 62.

The Hero of Sukkot

September 24, 1994

The biblical figure who is most intimately associated with Sukkot is Aaron. The Festival of Sukkot commemorates the Clouds of Glory.[1] Our Sages inform us that the Clouds of Glory, which enveloped the Jewish people in the Wilderness, were conferred in the merit of Aaron.[2]

I hate to be a spoiler, especially with respect to my namesake, and especially today, on the fifth day of Sukkot, on which Aaron is the main *ushpizin*, but other brilliant figures put in a claim for association with Sukkot – Abraham[3] and Jacob.[4]

We can reconcile these conflicting claims by looking more closely into the nature of the *ḥesed* of the Clouds of Glory. The question is often asked, just as we have the Festival of Sukkot to commemorate the

1. *Sukkah* 11b.
2. *Ta'anit* 9a.
3. The Midrash records that Hashem gave Abraham's descendants the mitzvah of sukkah in reward for Abraham telling the angels "recline beneath the tree" (Genesis 18:4). *Midrash Tanḥuma, Va-Yera* 4. See also Numbers Rabbah 14:2.
4. *Tur, Oraḥ Ḥayyim* 417.

Clouds of Glory, why do we not have a special festival to commemorate the manna and the Well of Miriam? The *Benei Yissaskhar* answers that if Hashem took us out of Egypt, He was obligated to provide us with basic necessities in the form of food and water. But as far as shelter was concerned, He could have left us to our own devices, and we could have been made to do with makeshift shacks.[5] But, in the opinion of R. Eliezer, we were provided with the Clouds of Glory,[6] a *ḥesed* beyond our wildest imagination. We were protected from the elements. Also, "your garment did not wear out upon you" (Deuteronomy 8:4), as the Clouds of Glory pressed the clothing, making them like new.[7] In addition, we were conferred these benefits even though we never asked for them.

For the Jewish people to be conferred *ḥesed* of the magnitude of the Clouds of Glory, then *ḥesed* had to have already been the character trait of the progenitor of the Jewish people. And indeed it was! Each of the biblical figures associated with Sukkot displayed the character trait of performing unexpected *ḥesed*. It begins with Abraham, but it was taken a step further with Jacob, and even higher by Aaron.

The essence of Abraham was *ḥesed*. Often, *Raḥmana le-tzlan*, when you are in excruciating pain and it is "the heat of the day" (Genesis 18:1), you are excused. But Abraham does the unexpected. He tells the angels, "Recline beneath the tree" (Genesis 18:4), as if to say, Don't worry; stay as long as you want. And "he stood over them beneath the tree and they ate" (Genesis 18:8). An act of unexpected *ḥesed* made an impression and creates inspirational energy, affecting the behavior of future generations and inspiring them to climb higher than otherwise possible.

It set the stage for Jacob. He also did the astonishingly unexpected *ḥesed*. He wanted to implant *emunah* in a yet unborn generation. He did this by demonstrating that he really believed in Hashem's promise to Abraham, "Arise, walk about the land through its length and breadth, for to you I will give it" (Genesis 13:17). Jacob surveyed the entire land and

---

5. R. Zevi Elimelech Dynow (*Benei Yissaskhar*, Poland, ca. 1785–1841), *Benei Yissaskhar*, vol. 2, *Ma'amerei Ḥodesh Tishrei, ma'amar* 10 (citing R. Hayyim Joseph David Azulai, *Rosh David*, beginning of *Parashat Emor*).
6. *Sukkah* 11b.
7. *Rashi* to Deuteronomy 8:4, s.v. "*simlatekha lo baltah*"; *Midrash ha-Gadol*, Deuteronomy 8:4.

decided that Sukkot was good for pasture. He wanted the yet unborn generation to know this, so he made a statement of this by staying there eighteen months.[8]

This sets the stage for Aaron. "Of Levi he said, 'Your Tumim and Your Urim befit Your devout one [*ish ḥasidekha*]'" (Deuteronomy 33:8). The only one called "*ḥasid*" in the entire *Tanakh* is Aaron because with respect to the Golden Calf, Aaron committed an *averah le-shemah,* a sin for the sake of Heaven.[9] He does the unexpected. So this is the merit for us to be conferred unexpected *ḥesed.*

What we have here is a demonstration of the principle of "*notzer ḥesed la-alafim,*" "preserver of kindness for thousands of generations" (Exodus 34:7). If someone does a *ḥesed,* it is not an isolated action. It sets into motion inspirational energy that catapults others to new heights, which, in turn, catapults others to even greater heights. A *ḥesed,* hence, rises from the microcosm of a Jewish home to an act that eventually affects a whole nation.

8. *Megillah* 17a; *Rashi* to Genesis 33:17.
9. Ibn Ezra to Deuteronomy 33:8, s.v. "*asher nissito be-Massah.*"

The Battle of Gog and Magog

October 2, 2004

The final defeat of Gog and Magog, according to Tradition, will occur in the month of Tishrei. It is for this reason that we read today the story of their defeat in the *haftarah*.

The *Shem mi-Shemuel*, quoting the *Arizal*, identifies Gog and Magog as the spiritual heirs of Amalek.[1] The *Rav*'s teaching gives us a poignancy and immediacy to the battle of Gog and Magog. It is in progress right now.

The most pernicious evil the world faces today is terrorists in the form of suicide bombers. This phenomenon is the scourge of the earth. We suffer horrifically from it.

The terrorists resemble the ancestors of Amalek in three important ways. First, they pierce the aura of invincibility. Hashem liberated us from Egypt with the Ten Plagues and the Splitting of the Sea of Reeds.

1. R. Shmuel Bornsztain (*Shem mi-Shemuel*, Poland, 1855–1926), *Shem mi-Shemuel, Ḥol ha-Mo'ed Sukkot* (5673/September 1912), p. 187.

We exuded an aura of invincibility. Amalek knew this when they attacked us, but their hatred for us made them come after us. "*Asher kar'kha ba-derekh*" (lit., "they happened upon you on the way") (Deuteronomy 25:18). *Kar'kha* is an expression of "*kar*" (cold) – they put a chill in the fear of others.[2] The children commit a horrific suicide but embolden the next person. The first suicide bombers were Amalek.

Second, they attack the weak and defenseless. The modus operandi of Amalek is "he killed among you all the weaklings at your rear" (Deuteronomy 25:18).

Lastly, "*lo ya're Elokim*," "he did not fear God" (Deuteronomy 25:18). Nothing new – in the past, people have killed in the name of God. But the modern-day terrorists say that God's will is the death culture. This should arouse the entire civilization to cry out to Hashem what we alone cry out in desperation, "Why should the nations say, 'Where now is their God?'" (Psalms 115:2).

The battle against terrorism is all-encompassing. It is a massive military operation and an effort to stop the financing of terrorism. But it must also involve the eradication of the death culture. This is intimated in today's *haftarah* in the seven-month cleansing of the land.[3] It is not enough that the enemy is dead. Every molecule evidencing its former physical existence must be eradicated.

There is a unique expression of "*anshei tamid*," "permanent officials" (Ezekiel 39:14). They establish Zion, and also weapons are converted to fuel.[4] It is not enough to eradicate the death culture. The culture must also be converted to one that affirms "*u-vaḥarta ba-ḥayyim*," "you shall choose life" (Deuteronomy 30:19).

Aaron is the antidote to Amalek. Why? Because what counteracts brazen wickedness is humility – "*hatzne'a lekhet im Elokekha*," "walk humbly with your God" (Micah 6:8). Aaron would not have succeeded in making peace unless he was exceedingly humble. Moses had to tell Aaron "come near the Altar" (Leviticus 9:7) to perform the service for which Aaron was chosen because Aaron was embarrassed and afraid

---

2. *Rashi* to Deuteronomy 25:18, s.v. "*asher karekha ba-derekh*" (third interpretation).
3. Ezekiel 39:12.
4. Ezekiel 39:9-10.

to approach. Moses tells Aaron, "Why are you embarrassed? For this you were selected."[5] The proof that Aaron is the antidote to Amalek is that as soon as Aaron died, the Canaanite King of Arad instigated a war against Israel and took a captive from it.[6] Arad is Amalek.[7]

5. *Rashi* to Leviticus 9:7, s.v. "*kerav el ha-mizbe'aḥ.*"
6. Numbers 21:1.
7. *Midrash Tanḥuma, Ḥukkat* 18; *Rashi* to Numbers 21:1, s.v. "*yoshev ha-Negev.*"

Nobel Laureate in Economics: Robert J. Aumann

October 22, 2005

This year, the Nobel Prize in Economics was awarded to Robert J. Aumann of Hebrew University. Since the inception of this award in 1969, it marks the first time that the award was given to a person who is a deeply religious Jew and a first-rate Talmudist.[1]

In an interview conducted about a year ago, published in a prestigious economics journal and now widely referred to, Aumann was asked to identify the people who had most influenced his life. Prominently included in his response was his *rebbe* of fifty years ago, R. Shmuel Dovid

1. Louis Uchitelle, "American and Israeli Share Nobel Prize in Economics," *New York Times*, October 11, 2005, C2.

Warshavchik, *zt"l*, at the Rabbi Jacob Joseph School – my yeshivah, and my father-in-law.[2]

I think *Kohelet* would very much approve of this year's awardee. Yes, Aumann is a singular genius and a world-renowned scholar. But, "The sum of the matter, when all has been considered: Fear God and keep His commandments, for that is man's whole duty" (Ecclesiastes 12:13).

Aumann won the Nobel Prize for enhancing our understanding of conflict and cooperation through game theory analysis.[3] Aumann's work is therefore a commentary on one of the major themes of *Kohelet* – cooperation and competition. *Kohelet* devalues and denigrates competition. "I have seen all man's labor and skillful enterprise, and it is all the product of jealousy" (Ecclesiastes 4:4). As Ibn Ezra explains, it is all the product of man's competitive drive to outdo his neighbor in the acquisition of material goods and reputation.[4]

But *Kohelet* praises cooperation – "two are better than one" (Ecclesiastes 4:9). Two in cooperative effort are always greater than one. If both fall down, each can help the other get up. If only one is attacked, he can be overwhelmed, but two can resist the attack. Two can warn each other, in the sense of reinforcing each other's spiritual stature. And three acting in cooperation are especially strong – "a three-ply cord is not easily severed" (Ecclesiastes 4:12).

Those who took up Aumann's models said that if we start out with conflict, whatever it is – between firms in the marketplace or between superpowers in the Cold War – if the relationship is an ongoing one, each participant will adopt strategic behavior and will realize that he or she can anticipate and affect what the rival will do. So you learn very quickly that nasty conduct invites retaliation. And if you do not keep your promises, you will not be trusted in the future. Aumann's point is that conflict eventually gives way to cooperation! "The end of the matter is better than its beginning" (Ecclesiastes 7:8).

2. Sergiu Hart, "An Interview with Robert Aumann," *Macroeconomic Dynamics* 9, no. 5 (2005): 729.
3. Uchitelle, "American and Israeli Share Nobel Prize," C2.
4. Ibn Ezra to Ecclesiastes 4:4.

Our Sages tell us that the *ge'ullah* will occur only in the mindset of *yi'ush*, "despair," and total lack of expectation, *heseḥ ha-da'at* (lit., "removal of thought").[5] I find in Robert Aumann, whose Hebrew name is *Yisrael*, a microcosm of the Jewish people.

Aumann's winning of the Nobel Prize was totally unexpected from three different standpoints. One, from the public standpoint. The conventional wisdom is that only an economist in the public glare will win the Nobel Prize, as, for example, Friedman and Samuelson.[6] But Aumann is the least likely economist to show up on the nightly news. His scholarship is so abstract and theoretical, it is twice removed from practicality. He is a theoretical mathematician concerned with the purest of the pure of math. His work was then taken up in theoretical economics.[7] And you know, prominent people command a very high fee for speaking. They are completely inaccessible. You need to deal with an agent. But Professor Aumann came to our *shul* this past summer on short notice and without fanfare.

Second, Aumann himself did not think that he would win. Complete surprise. In 1994, three of his colleagues won: Nash, Harsanyi, and Selten.[8] Would the Nobel Committee revisit the same field?

Third, and most important, the political environment today would predict that it was impossible for Aumann to win the Nobel Prize. Academia is permeated with left-thinking scholars, and there is incredible anti-Israel and anti-Jewish sentiment throughout academia.[9] Many Israelis have been ousted from editorial boards of scholarly journals.[10]

5. *Sanhedrin* 97a.
6. The references are to the American economists Milton Friedman (1912–2006) and Paul A. Samuelson (1915–2009).
7. See Royal Swedish Academy of Sciences, "Robert Aumann's and Thomas Schelling's Contributions to Game Theory: Analyses of Conflict and Cooperation," October 10, 2005, 12–22.
8. Peter Passell, "Game Theory Captures a Nobel," *New York Times*, October 12, 1994, D1. The 1994 Nobel Memorial Prize in Economic Science was awarded to John F. Nash of Princeton University, John C. Harsanyi of the University of California at Berkeley, and Reinhard Selten of the University of Bonn.
9. See generally Kenneth Lasson, "Scholarly and Scientific Boycotts of Israel: Abusing the Academic Enterprise," *Touro Law Review* 21, no. 4 (2006): 989–1076.
10. In June 2002, Professor Mona Baker of the University of Manchester's Institute of Science and Technology removed Professor Miriam Slesinger of Bar-Ilan University

Aumann is an Israeli Jew who could not be more to the right on the political map. Yet, he won. How amazing, leaping from obscurity to fame, *ke-heref ayin* (lit., "like the blink of an eye").[11]

Let Aumann's example be an *ot*, a sign of what Hashem has in mind for us. Hashem puts in his *tefillin* the statement "*mi ke-amm'kha Yisrael?*," "Who is like Your people Israel?" (I Chronicles 17:21).[12] May we witness *haramat keren Yisrael ke-heref ayin* and see *bi'at go'el tzedek* speedily in our days.

---

and Professor Gideon Toury of Tel Aviv University from the boards of two journals that she owned and edited. See Lasson, "Scholarly and Scientific Boycotts," 1000; Edward Alexander, "The Academic Boycott of Israel: Back to 1933?" *Jerusalem Post*, January 3, 2003, B9.

11. The expression "*yeshuat Hashem ke-heref ayin*" is found in the portion of the *seliḥot* that begins "*Ezri Yavo*." See *Ezri Yavo, Seliḥot* of Zadok b. Aaron ibn Alamani (Alexandria, 12th cent.), printed in *Siftei Renanot* (Venice, 1648). See also R. Obadiah b. Jacob Sforno (*Sforno*, Italy, ca. 1470–1550), *Sforno* to Genesis 41:14.
12. *Berakhot* 6a.

Shemini Atzeret

You Are Children to Hashem

October 7, 1985

Each Festival has its own mystique and splendor. And so, too, Shemini Atzeret. Our Sages understood it to represent the tender call of Hashem to us, His people, *kasheh alai peredatekhem*, "your departure is difficult for Me." You have celebrated with Me for seven days. Please stay another day.[1]

Well, if we stay another day, why do not all the mitzvot enjoy a continuity on an equal basis? Only the mitzvah of sukkah remains, but not the Four Species.

I would propose that the question is itself the answer. Hashem is telling us that His invitation is not based on His satisfaction with our performance and loyalty, on our *etrogim* or *hadasim*, or even our *aravot*,

1. R. Solomon b. Isaac (*Rashi*, France, 1040–1105), *Rashi* to Leviticus 23:36, s.v. "*atzeret hi.*"

which have the merit of their willingness to be part of an *aguddah aḥat.*[2] No. Instead it is *Avinu,* "our Father," Who is reaching out. It is the Clouds of Glory that are talking to us, the protective element, enveloping us in each direction. It is the father image. Hashem is not speaking to us as *Malkenu,* "our King," or *Bor'enu,* "our Creator," or *Yotzrenu,* "the One Who fashioned us," or *Ro'enu,* "our Shepherd," but as *Avinu,* "our Father."

"*Elleh mo'adei Hashem mikra'ei kodesh asher tikre'u otam be-mo'adam,*" "these are the appointed festivals of Hashem, the holy convocations, which you shall designate in their appropriate time" (Leviticus 23:4). Our Sages tell us: Do not read the word "*otam,*" "them," but rather "*atem,*" "you."[3] Even if you err inadvertently, even if you err deliberately, even if you are misled in designating the New Moon, the Festivals that are set according to the designation of the New Moon are the official Festivals.[4] Then, as the *Maggid mi-Kozhnitz* explains, *kal ve-ḥomer* when it says "*banim atem la-Hashem Elokeikhem,*" "you are children to Hashem, your God" (Deuteronomy 14:1), even if you err inadvertently, even if you err deliberately, even if you are misled, you are still the children of Hashem.[5]

We thus go full circle on Sukkot from an anxiety that we will be rejected to Shemini Atzeret, when Hashem invites us to stay because we are His children.

---

2. See Leviticus Rabbah 30:12.
3. *Rosh Ha-Shanah* 24a.
4. *Rosh Ha-Shanah* 25a.
5. R. Yisrael Hopsztajn (*Maggid mi-Kozhnitz,* Poland, ca. 1733–1814), cited in R. Yo'etz Kayam Kaddish, *Si'aḥ Sarphei Kodesh,* vol. 2 (Warsaw: Lewin-Epstein, 1923), 75–76.

The Response to *Kasheh Alai Peredatekhem*

October 3, 1988

The essence of the character of the Festival of Shemini Atzeret is encapsulated in Hashem's tender call to the Jewish people, *kasheh alai peredatekhem*, "your departure is difficult for Me." You have already been here with me for seven days. Remain another day.[1]

Our response to Hashem's gesture of *ḥibbah yeterah* is found in today's Torah reading.[2] For the ordinary person, one who has stayed behind and not advanced to Shemini Atzeret, a series of demands evokes at least a tinge of irritation, annoyance, and sense of burden. But for the man who is ready to reciprocate Hashem's call of *kasheh alai peredatekhem* with a measure of *ḥibbah yeterah*, all the demands can be met with cheerful delight.

1. *Rashi* to Leviticus 23:36, s.v. "*atzeret hi.*"
2. Deuteronomy 14:22–16:17.

First we encounter the obligation of *ma'aser sheni*. On the surface, it appears that Hashem is treating us here to a family outing. It also appears that the Torah is weaning us with the mitzvah of *tzedakah*. Charity begins at home, and it is not even until the third year of the *Shemittah* cycle that *ma'aser ani* displaces *ma'aser sheni*.[3] But a more careful look reveals an element of surprise. As the *Netziv* points out, taking one-tenth of the produce of our field to Jerusalem to be eaten there, or consuming the food that we purchase with the money that we bring there instead of the produce, entailed a very long stay in Jerusalem. The ordinary man would not be able to stay long, so the tithe would end up as *tzedakah* for *talmidei ḥakhamim* or support for *talmud Torah* of the owner of the *ma'aser sheni*.[4]

Then we encounter the difficult mitzvah of extending a loan near the approach of the Sabbatical year. The Torah considers it a *davar beliyya'al*, a "lawless thing," not to give the loan.[5] But is this not a mischaracterization of what is happening? It is really not a loan. It is really *tzedakah* because the loan will be released by the Sabbatical year.[6] The man of faith, the man suffused with the Shemini Atzeret spirit, focuses on the phrase "for in return for this matter, Hashem, your God, will bless you" (Deuteronomy 15:10), and truly believes that Hashem will give him back the money that was extended as a loan.

---

3. During the time of the Temple, *terumah* and *ma'aser* were required to be taken from agricultural produce to render it fit for ordinary consumption. First, *terumah* was set aside for the Priests. Next, *ma'aser rishon*, the first tithe, consisting of one tenth of the remainder, was given to the Levites. Numbers 18:21–24. A second tithe was then given. In the first, second, fourth, and fifth years of the sabbatical cycle, the second tithe was called "*ma'aser sheni*." Deuteronomy 14:22–26. In the third and sixth years, the second tithe was called "*ma'aser ani*," which was given to the poor. 14:28–29, 26:12. *Ma'aser sheni* was required to be eaten in Jerusalem. If it was too difficult to carry the produce to Jerusalem, *ma'aser sheni* could be redeemed for money, consisting of the value of the produce plus one-fifth. The money would then be taken to Jerusalem, where the owner would spend it on food or *shelamim* offerings. Leviticus 27:31; Deuteronomy 14:25–26; Mishnah, *Ma'aser Sheni* 1:3, 2:1; Jerusalem Talmud, *Ma'aser Sheni* 1:2, 2:1.
4. R. Naphtali Tzvi Yehudah Berlin (*Netziv*, Russia, 1816–1893), *Ha'amek Davar*, Deuteronomy 14:23, s.v. "*le-ma'an tilmad le-yir'ah*."
5. Deuteronomy 15:9.
6. Deuteronomy 15:1-2.

Then we read the obligation of setting up the freed *eved Ivri* with a liberal severance. The Torah records the obligation as if we had not been doing *ḥesed* with the *eved Ivri* until now: "It shall not be difficult in your eyes when you send him away free from you, for double the earnings of a hired worker he has labored for you, six years" (Deuteronomy 15:18). We have to be mollified that the *eved* should be given the liberal severance.

Is this not a misrepresentation of our treatment of the *eved Ivri* until now: "Whoever acquires an Israelite bondsman acquires a master for himself."[7] But the man who has abandoned the Shemini Atzeret level takes this as *musar*. We speak to this man and tell him that he must refine his concept of *ḥesed*. It is just beginning now. What you did until now was only justice and decency. And to highlight this, the Torah purposely describes *ha'anakah*, the obligations of the master to his servant upon freeing him, in *Parashat Re'eh*,[8] while presenting the basic master-servant relationship in *Parashat Mishpatim*,[9] in two separate *sidrot*.

Finally, we encounter the mitzvah of *bekhor*.[10] The benevolent man may readily agree to accept obligations of charity, but he stubbornly clings to the notion that he has a private domain that cannot be invaded. But *bekhor* is the first fruit, which man naturally regards as his private domain, and this, too, is part of the Priestly Gifts.

On Hoshana Rabbah, a ring of the *lulav* is removed.[11] Hoshana Rabbah is the bridge between Sukkot and Shemini Atzeret. On Sukkot, the unit of the Jewish people is held together with rings. But on Shemini Atzeret, the unit need not be held together with cords or rings. The love between Jews becomes unbounded on Shemini Atzeret!

---

7. *Kiddushin* 20a.
8. Deuteronomy 15:13–15.
9. Exodus 21:1–6.
10. Deuteronomy 15:19–23.
11. R. Joseph Caro (Safed, 1488–1575), *Shulḥan Arukh, Oraḥ Ḥayyim* 664:1.

Reciprocating *Kasheh Alai Peredatekhem*

October 21, 1989

The essence of the Festival of Shemini Atzeret is capsulated by the tender call of Hashem to the Jewish people, *kasheh alai peredatekhem* (lit., "your departure is difficult for Me"). You have been celebrating with Me for seven days; please stay one more day![1]

Permit me to suggest that the various special mitzvot that we perform on Shemini Atzeret represent a reciprocation of this sentiment on our part.

When we finish reciting the Torah, we immediately begin again with *Bereshit,* as if to say, we cannot tear ourselves away from the Torah. As soon as we finish, we begin again!

But the unity of the Jewish people is expressed as *Yisrael ve-Oraita ve-Kudesha berikh Hu, ḥad hu,* "Israel, the Torah, and the Holy One, Blessed is He, are one."[2] So there is the attachment of the Jew to

1. *Rashi* to Leviticus 23:36, s.v. "*atzeret hi.*"
2. See Zohar, *Aḥarei Mot* 3:73a.

Hashem, but also the attachment of the Jew to *Klal Yisrael*. And we get a glimpse into how magnificent the bond can be between Hashem and the individual Jew and the *klal*.

We read of the death of Moses on Shemini Atzeret.[3] Yes, he was a miracle man, bringing down to the earth "signs and wonders" on Egypt.[4] But also "*u-le-khol ha-yad ha-ḥazakah*," "by all the strong hand" (Deuteronomy 34:12). We are surprised by the interpretation of the Midrash. The Midrash tells us that Hashem said, "Go, descend, for your people that you brought up from the land of Egypt has become corrupt" (Exodus 32:7). Moses is holding the *luḥot* and he refuses to let them go. A tug of war ensues between Hashem and Moses. In the desperate struggle, Moses prevails.[5]

This is not a story of how a mortal prevails against Hashem, God forbid. Rather, it is testimony by Hashem that every molecule of Moses' being believed in *Klal Yisrael* and had faith in them that they could not fail. Until he would see with his own eyes the wild abandon at the foot of the mountain, he would not stop believing. And the *yad ha-ḥazakah*, "the mighty hand" – whose hand is it? The reference is not to Hashem's hand. No. It is Moses' hand![6] Moses held on to the Tablets. And finally, "the awesome power that Moses performed before the eyes of all Israel" (Deuteronomy 34:12). *Rashi* says that this refers to the breaking of the *luḥot*.[7] This is how Moses showed that he believed in *Klal Yisrael*.

I would submit that at no moment in Moses' career was the gap between Moses and *Klal Yisrael* larger. The *ish ha-Elokim* who refrained from eating and drinking for forty days – "I remained on the mountain for forty days and forty nights; bread I did not eat, and water I did not drink" (Deuteronomy 9:9) – returns and finds idolatry, the Sin of the Golden Calf.

But his love for the *klal* knows no bounds. It is unshakable. He seeks a way in the desperate moment to embrace the *klal*. The act of

---

3. Deuteronomy 34:1–8.
4. Deuteronomy 34:11.
5. Exodus Rabbah 43:1.
6. Ibid., 46:3; R. Zev Wolf Einhorn (*Maharzu*, Vilna, d. 1862), *Perush Maharzu* ad loc., s.v. "*le-khol ha-osot*."
7. *Rashi* to Deuteronomy 34:12, s.v. "*le-einei kol Yisrael*."

anger would shame *Klal Yisrael,* as if to tell them they do not merit the Torah. It would be very effective, but at the same time, Moses would lose some of his stature as an *ish ha-Elokim:* "Every man who becomes angry, if he is a Sage, his wisdom departs from him; if he is a prophet, his prophecy departs from him."[8] But he was ready to descend in order to elevate the *klal.* It was a *yeridah le-tzorekh aliyyah,* a descent for the sake of elevating the *klal.*[9]

And the breaking of the Tablets assumes an important role in Jewish history. In the Wilderness, we were led by the broken Tablets. Why? Would it not have been more appropriate to be led by a symbol of triumph rather than a symbol of failure? No! If we had been led by a symbol of glorious triumph, we could have been inveigled into a self-congratulatory complacency. Better that we be led by a symbol of failure, the broken Tablets. Yes, it is a symbol of failure because of the Sin of the Golden Calf, but it is also the symbol of glorious triumph, the unsurpassed heights of *na'aseh ve-nishma,* "we will do and we will listen" (Exodus 24:7). The broken Tablets are at once a symbol of both triumph and failure, all wrapped together. There can be no better symbol to follow. Better that we adopt lofty goals and fall short than adopt limited goals and succeed.

8. *Pesaḥim* 66b.
9. See R. Dov Baer Friedman of Leova (Romania, 1827–1876), cited in R. Aharon Yaakov Greenberg (Israel, 1900–1963), *Iturei Torah: Likkut, Nisaḥ u-Biur,* vol. 3 (Tel Aviv: Yavneh, 1970), 261, s.v. "*va-yishlaḥ mi-yado.*"

The Reading of the Death of Moses on Shemini Atzeret

September 30, 1991

In the insight of the Gaon of Vilna, the essence of the Festival of Shemini Atzeret is encapsulated in a verse from today's reading, "*ve-hayyita akh same'aḥ*," "you will be completely joyous" (Deuteronomy 16:15).[1] And why? Because as Sukkot fades into Shemini Atzeret, all the mitzvot of Sukkot, the sukkah and the Four Species, disappear. The only thing that remains is the mitzvah of *simḥat yom tov*.

Indeed, the usual mitzvah of *simḥat yom tov*, which consists of a festive meal in the company of family and friends,[2] is built up and expands to the *simḥah* of accomplishment when we experience *siyyum*

1. *Ḥiddushei ha-Gra, Sukkah* 48a; *Kol Eliyahu, Re'eh.*
2. Maimonides (*Rambam*, Egypt, 1135–1204), *Mishneh Torah, Yom Tov* 6:17–18.

ha-Torah. Then we jubilate with the gift of the Torah from Hashem with *hakkafot.*

It is therefore striking that in the midst of *ve-hayyita akh same'aḥ,* and in fact, in no less a place than the dramatic moment of *siyyum ha-Torah,* our *simḥat yom tov* is marred with the reading of the death of Moses. This represents an irretrievable loss, as we read "never again has there arisen in Israel a prophet like Moses" (Deuteronomy 34:10).

Rather than spoiling our *simḥat yom tov,* the reading of the death of Moses gives content to the real meaning of *simḥat yom tov.*

In laying out for us the essence of *simḥat yom tov,* Maimonides notes that there is an individualistic element, to ensure that everyone will maximally enjoy the festival. We should be sure to eat meat and drink wine, and to give our wives colorful garments, and children candies. But if *simḥat yom tov* stops here, it is only *simḥat kriso* (lit., "gladdening his belly"). It must include gladdening the hearts of the unfortunates.[3]

Well, this is exactly the purpose of Hashem's eulogy of Moses. We focus on the highlights of his career. First, we are told that he was a miracle man, "as evidenced by all the signs and wonders that Hashem sent him to perform in the land of Egypt" (Deuteronomy 34:11). He was an *ish ha-Elokim.* Then, that he was a great friend of the Jewish people. First, "*ha-yad ha-ḥazakah,*" "the strong hand" (Deuteronomy 34:12). This refers to his refusal to believe that the Children of Israel sinned in the incident of the Golden Calf. He refused to let go of the Tablets.[4] The lesson is that one must not lose faith in a friend, no matter how suspicious and incriminating the circumstances look, until you are absolutely sure.

Then came "the awesome power that Moses performed before the eyes of all Israel" (Deuteronomy 34:12). This refers to the breaking of the Tablets, the pure self-denial to give to *Klal Yisrael.*[5]

Klal Yisrael deified him. They thought that he had inherent *kedushah.* That was the mistake. To correct it, he took the Tablets, which were described as "*ma'aseh Elokim,*" "God's handiwork," and etched with "the

3. Ibid.
4. Exodus Rabbah 46:1.
5. *Rashi* to Deuteronomy 34:12, s.v. "*le-einei kol Yisrael.*"

script of God" (Exodus 32:16), a double splendor that no mortal could have produced, and shocked them by showing them that they are only a vessel. So, too, I am only a vessel.[6] *Shekhinah medabberet mi-tokh geroni*, "the Divine Presence speaks through my throat."[7]

I would ask, when did this ever happen in history when a mortal is deified by the people that the leader should deny this totally! An unforgettable friend.

6. See R. Meir Simhah ha-Kohen of Dvinsk (*Meshekh Ḥokhmah*, Latvia, 1843–1926), *Meshekh Ḥokhmah*, Exodus 32:19.
7. R. Moses Sofer (*Ḥatam Sofer*, Hungary, 1762–1839), *Torat Mosheh*, *Shemot*, s.v. "*mah omar aleihem*"; *Terumah*, s.v. "*ve-asu aron*"; *Perush Maharzu* to Exodus Rabbah 3:15, s.v. "*moreh ani devarai ke-ḥetz*." See also Zohar, *Pinḥas*, *Ra'aya Meheimena* 3:232a.

The Prayer for Rain

October 16, 1995

From Passover until now, the second blessing of *Shemoneh Esreh* was, in a manner of speaking, lonely. The theme of the blessing, *gevurot,* had only one theme of *teḥiyyat ha-metim*. Now the short phrase *mashiv ha-ruaḥ u-morid ha-geshem* (lit., "Who makes the wind blow and the rain descend") adds the theme that Hashem causes the rain to descend. By adding this phrase, we are not merely coupling a theme. Belief in the resurrection of the dead is the most demanding article of faith in our religion. Hashem, in His great mercy, gives us help in furthering the belief through the phrase that is common to both themes, *matzmiaḥ yeshuah,* "sprouts forth salvation."

Rain is the agent that causes the seed in the ground to decompose and disintegrate, and then produce vegetation. Analogously, death is not the end. Before a person dies, Hashem reveals Himself to that person. The soul separates from the body. The soul goes to the world of the souls and the body is literally planted in the ground. It decays, it decomposes, and at the right moment, Hashem will reunite the soul and the body for an eternal union.[1]

---

1. See Nahmanides (*Ramban,* Spain, 1194–1270), *Torat ha-Adam, Sha'ar ha-Gemul,* last paragraph. Cf. Maimonides, *Ma'amar Teḥiyyat ha-Metim, sha'ar* 6 (expressing the

The union of rain with *teḥiyyat ha-metim* is accomplished amidst the spectacle of *Tefillat Geshem,* the Prayer for Rain. During the entire Festival, we fret about the rain lest the mitzvah of sukkah be spoiled.[2] Even though it is the rainy season, we should recite *Tefillat Geshem* in the evening, during *Maariv*. Why was the prayer placed in the morning services, during *Musaf*? In the thinking of the Belzer Rav, it is to connect the prayer to the first prayer for rain, which was said by Adam during the seventh hour of the day, corresponding to the time of *Musaf*.[3]

"Now all the trees of the field were not yet on the earth and all the herb of the field had not yet sprouted, for Hashem God had not sent rain upon the earth and there was no man to work the soil" (Genesis 2:5). After man was created and he realized the need for rain, he prayed for rain.[4] We need to appreciate the intrinsic value of rain and then we can use it as a model to understand that *teḥiyyat ha-metim* is a plausible concept.

There is another meaning in *matzmiaḥ yeshuah*. In the *Gra*'s thinking,[5] children can cause parents who are deceased to achieve a higher level of existence by means of *bera mizakkei abba* (lit., "a son can earn merit for a father").[6] This is the *peshat* of *Magen Avraham* and why the closing blessing does not refer to all the Patriarchs or to Jacob,[7] the *beḥir ha-Avot*, "the choicest of the Patriarchs."[8] It is because *bera mizakkei abba*.[9] This is a kind of *teḥiyyat ha-metim*.

---

view that the resurrection of the body will be for a temporary period, followed by the return of only the souls of the righteous for the World to Come).

2. *Ta'anit* 2a; *Rashi* ad loc.; *Sukkah* 28b.
3. R. Issachar Dov Rokeah (Belz, 1854–1926), cited in R. Yissachar Dov Rubin, *Talelei Orot: Mivkhar Be'urim Ḥiddushim u-Pheninim al Mo'adei ha-Shanah*, vol. 2 (Benei Berak, 1993), 613–614.
4. *Rashi* to Genesis 2:5.
5. R. Elijah b. Solomon Zalman (Vilna Gaon or *Gra*, Vilna, 1720–1797), *Be'ur ha-Gra: Mishlei*, ed. R. Meir Yehoshua Katzenellenbogen (Jerusalem: Mossad HaRav Kook, 2006), Proverbs 17:6, s.v. "*ateret zekenim benei vanim*," 190n25.
6. *Sanhedrin* 104a.
7. *Pesaḥim* 117b.
8. Genesis Rabbah 76:1.
9. R. Jacob b. Joseph Reischer (Prague, ca. 1670–1733), *Iyyun Yaakov*, *Pesaḥim* 117b. See also R. Shelomoh Friedman (Chortkov, 1894–1959), *Divrei Shelomoh: Mo'adim*, ed. R. David Mosheh Spiegel (Jerusalem, 1961), 53.

Kindness within Kindness

(Undated)

Each *yom tov* has a dual character. At once, it is a celebration of a unique gift that Hashem conferred upon us, His chosen people, and also demands of us by means of the performance of mitzvot unique to the holiday a demonstration that we appreciate these gifts.

Sukkot is the festival on which we commemorate the loving-kindness that Hashem showed to us, His people. Besides commemorating that we were enveloped by the Clouds of Glory, it was also the gift of *rishon le-ḥeshbon avonot,* "the beginning of the accounting period for sins."[1] This is at first glance peculiar, as Rosh Ha-Shanah should mark the new accounting period for sins. But as R. Levi Yitzhak of Berdichev explains, it is a matter of *ḥesed Elyon* that Hashem juxtaposes Sukkot to the Days of Awe.[2]

1. *Midrash Tanḥuma, Emor* 22.
2. R. Levi Yitzhak of Berdichev (*Berdichever Rav,* Ukraine, 1740–1809), *Kedushat Levi, Ha'azinu.*

Every Jew is to some extent caught up in the awesomeness of the Days of Awe, and his repentance accomplishes something. But if we repent out of fear, the repentance has limited accomplishment. What happens is only that the *zedonot,* "intentional sins," become *shegagot,* "unintentional sins."[3]

But Hashem, in His mercy, does not want any sentiment of piety to dissipate, God forbid. Hashem wants us to build the sentiment of piety into something even more noble and sublime. He does this by allowing us to blend the feeling of piety into our natural feeling of joy on the *Ḥag ha-Asif,* the "Festival of the Ingathering." By means of the performance of the mitzvot of the Four Species and sukkah, we can purify fear of God into love of God and convert the sins into merits. Hence, Sukkot is *rishon le-ḥeshbon avonot.*[4]

Now, if Sukkot represents the proverbial second chance, then Shemini Atzeret is a third chance. Hashem beckons us to stay another day, another day to purify and transform the fear into love. But this time, we are not given the obligation of mitzvot, but rather "*ve-hayyita akh same'aḥ,*" "you shall be completely joyous" (Deuteronomy 16:15). Just the mitzvah of rejoicing serves as the vehicle of our elevation.

If Shemini Atzeret is the *ḥesed she-be-ḥesed,* "kindness within kindness," then the Torah reading of the day tests us to see whether we have this innate quality in our relationships *bein adam le-ḥavero.* First we are confronted with the challenge of *ma'aser sheni.* Someone can be a *ba'al ḥesed,* but he may have the attitude that at certain times, he is not available. He simply retreats to a family festivity. "You shall rejoice on your festival" (Deuteronomy 16:14). And we are told, "The Levite who is in your cities, do not forsake him, for he does not have a portion or an inheritance with you" (Deuteronomy 14:27).

And then we encounter the man who is willing to do a *ḥesed,* but not the *ḥesed* of *Shemittah,* the release of an obligation.[5]

3. *Yoma* 86b.
4. *Kedushat Levi,* loc. cit.
5. Deuteronomy 15:2.

Then we encounter the challenge of *tzedakah*. "*Naton titten lo*," "you shall surely give him" (Deuteronomy 15:10), even one hundred times.[6] Our heart should not feel deprived.

Finally, we have the challenge of the Israelite bondsman. The obligations to the Israelite bondsman are spelled out in *Parashat Mishpatim*.[7] Then we hear of the obligation of *ha'anakah*, the gratuity that we are required to give him upon setting him free.[8] While he is a servant, we must treat him decently, with equality. We cannot eat rye bread and give him pumpernickel.[9] We think that this relationship is *ḥesed*. Well, alas, we are given the shock that *ḥesed* first begins after we free him. We must put him on his feet to start his life again.

How well have we done in *ḥesed she-be-ḥesed*?

6. *Rashi* to Deuteronomy 15:10.
7. Exodus 21:1–6.
8. Deuteronomy 15:14 ("Extend, you shall extend to him from your flocks, from your threshing floor, and from your wine cellar; as Hashem, your God, has blessed you, so shall you give him.").
9. See *Kiddushin* 20a.

Ḥanukkah

Self-Restraint, Self-Sacrifice, and Self-Denial

December 3, 1983

The ancient Greeks dazzled mankind with the beauty of their art form and architectural design, the genius of their mathematical science, and most of all, with the apparent omnipotence of their military might. Alexander the Great practically conquered the world. Accompanying this dazzle of achievement was an equally spectacular conceptualization of their self-worth. This conceptualization amounted to nothing less than self-deification.

The spectacular never fails to impress, to excite, and secretly to evoke a desire of emulation. And hence, according to Tradition, long before the ancient Greeks embarked upon their nefarious plan to spiritually annihilate the Jewish people, the fervor of the religious striving of our people had already dampened, and observance of the commandments amounted to a mere mechanical exercise.[1]

---

1. See R. Joel Sirkes (*Baḥ*, Poland, 1561–1640), *Baḥ* to R. Jacob b. Asher (*Tur*, Spain, 1270–1343), *Tur, Oraḥ Ḥayyim* 670, n. 4, s.v. "*ve-hayah omer Maharam*"; *Shem*

The spectacular can be counterbalanced only by the spectacular. The display of apparent omnipotent power can be counterbalanced only by a grand act of self-restraint. Self-deification can be counterbalanced only by self-denial.

The Greeks concentrated their program on what they thought threatened them most, three Jewish institutions that had the potential of producing the grand acts of self-restraint, self-sacrifice, and self-denial: *milah*, the Sabbath, and Rosh Ḥodesh.[2]

The Greeks prohibited circumcision, the laws that inspire restraint in the most primitive aspect of our lives. This restraint is the basis of our salvation. Abraham stands at the door of Gehinnom and fights that a *shomer ha-brit* should not go there.[3] In a broader sense, the basis of the highest human love, the love between a husband and a wife, is the grand act of sacrifice. When true human love is produced, there is a spark of divinity, which counteracts the moral climate of the arrogance of self-love. The purity of the inner feeling goes beyond its boundary and softens the arrogance of self-love.

The Sabbath represents restraint from material striving. When the Jewish people restrain themselves from material striving and turn their energies toward spiritual attainments, true Torah wisdom and wisdom that can approach the primordial source of wisdom itself are created, as indicated by the blessing *she-ḥalak me-ḥokhmato li-re'av*, "Who has given of His knowledge to those who fear Him."[4]

And Rosh Ḥodesh represents self-denial. If *beit din* would not pronounce the New Moon, the Festivals would not take place.[5] With the Festivals, three times during the year, the entire Jewish nation crowded

---

mi-Shemuel, vol. 1, *Miketz* (5671/December 1910), p. 131.

2. *Megillat Antioḥus; Midrash Ḥanukkah*, reprinted in Adolph Jellinek (Vienna, 1821–1893), *Beit ha-Midrash* 1:139.
3. Genesis Rabbah 48:8.
4. This blessing is recited upon seeing an outstanding Torah scholar. *Berakhot* 58a; *Rif* ad loc.; R. Asher b. Jehiel (*Rosh*, Germany, ca. 1250–1327), *Rosh, Berakhot* 9:8; *Tur, Oraḥ Ḥayyim* 224; R. Joseph Caro (Safed, 1488–1575), *Shulḥan Arukh, Oraḥ Ḥayyim* 224:6. Cf. Maimonides (*Rambam*, Egypt, 1135–1204), *Mishneh Torah, Berakhot* 10:11 ("*she-natan me-ḥokhmato li-re'av*").
5. See Leviticus 23:4; *Rosh Ha-Shanah* 25a.

into the *Azarah* and were *omdim tzefufim u-mishtaḥavim revaḥim,* they stood pressed but prostrated themselves with plenty of room.[6] The power of the multitude translates into a mass action of self-denial and submission to the demands of the Al-Mighty. A spark of divinity is precious when the power of the nation is inwardly drawn toward obedience to Hashem.

It is not coincidental that the personality of Joseph always unfolds during the Festival of Ḥanukkah, for Joseph was the exemplar of *milah,* the Sabbath, and Rosh Ḥodesh, the man capable of the grand act of restraint.[7]

"*Va-yema'en,*" "he adamantly refused" (Genesis 39:8), corresponds to *milah.* If Joseph would not have passed this test of restraint, he would have disappeared into oblivion.

And then Joseph chose not to reveal himself to his brothers when he first recognized them. "Joseph saw his brothers and he recognized them, but he acted like a stranger toward them" (Genesis 42:7). This grand act of restraint was done to promote the highest love. He did not want to reveal himself as a despot, with the brothers as servile servants. Rather, he wanted to be readmitted into the family circle. He wanted a profound reconciliation, not a superficial one. He taunted his brothers and made up false charges to show them that their suspicions about him were wrong.

His wisdom was always accompanied by a self-denial. When Pharaoh asked Joseph to interpret his dream, Joseph responded, "That is beyond me; it is God Who will respond with Pharaoh's welfare" (Genesis 41:16). And he never used his wisdom to exploit people. He always showed restraint. Joseph acquired all the land of Egypt for Pharaoh during the famine, but "the land of the priests he did not buy, since the priests had a stipend from Pharaoh" (Genesis 47:22). When the Egyptians asked that Joseph acquire them as slaves, he acquired only their land

6. Mishnah, *Avot* 5:5.
7. R. Zevi Elimelech Dynow (*Benei Yissaskhar,* Poland, ca. 1785–1841), *Benei Yissaskhar, Ma'amerei Ḥodeshei Kislev ve-Tevet,* no. 13. See also Genesis Rabbah 92:4 and Numbers Rabbah 14:2 (stating that Joseph observed the Sabbath before the Torah was given to the Children of Israel).

but made them *arisim*, "tenant farmers," not all-purpose slaves.[8] Their tax was only 20 percent, not the customary 80 percent that the landowner would take.[9] Moreover, Joseph transacted with the entire world – "Jacob perceived that there were provisions in Egypt" (Genesis 42:1) – contrary to the typical practice of imposing protective tariffs.

The celebration of Ḥanukkah concentrates on the flask of oil that was found, not the military conquest. The *Al ha-Nissim* comes to a crescendo with "thereafter, Your children came to the Holy of Holies... and kindled lights in the Courtyards of Your Sanctuary." As the *Ne'ot ha-Deshe* says, the burning of the oil represents complete self-denial of the intellect to the will of Hashem.[10] This is the basis of the brightness that follows in ever-increasing amounts.

8. Nahmanides (*Ramban*, Spain, 1194–1270), to Genesis 47:19.
9. Ibid.
10. R. Avraham Bornsztain (*Avnei Nezer*, Poland, 1838–1910), *Ne'ot ha-Deshe*, vol. 1, *Miketz ve-Shabbat Ḥanukkah* ¶ 12, vol. 2, *Nes Ḥanukkah*.

Mehadrin min ha-Mehadrin

December 27, 1986

Unique is the mitzvah of *ner Ḥanukkah*. It is only in connection with this mitzvah that the Sages established three different categories of fulfillment: (1) the minimal requirement, *ner ish u-beito*, "one candle for each household"; (2) *mehadrin*, "those who wish to enhance the mitzvah," *ner le-khol eḥad ve-eḥad*, "one candle for each member of the household"; and (3) *mehadrin min ha-mehadrin*, "enhancement of enhancement," *kol eḥad mosif ve-holekh*, "each member of the household lights an additional candle each night," in accordance with *Beit Hillel*.[1] Elsewhere, only two categories are set, i.e., the minimum requirement and the general dictum of *hiddur mitzvah ad shelish*, "enhancement of the mitzvah up to one-third."[2]

It is not too difficult to see why three categories are not set for *kashrut*. This would involve kosher, glatt kosher, and glatt glatt kosher.

1. *Shabbat* 21b.
2. *Bava Kamma* 9b.

But the addition of the third category would undoubtedly result in a new wave of devout vegetarians! And having two categories of *kashrut* is not so far-fetched. According to Tradition, the *Ribbono shel Olam* will arrange a lavish feast for the righteous *le-atid lavo*.[3] The Leviathan and the *Shor ha-Bar* (wild ox) will be served. But this is puzzling. If meat is available, why would anyone want fish? The answer must be that some people don't trust the *sheḥitah*!

I would submit that the Sages would not establish three separate categories of a mitzvah unless each one represented a qualitatively different level of performance of the mitzvah.

The mitzvah of *ner Ḥanukkah,* as we all know, commemorates the finding of the canister of pure oil by the Hasmoneans and its lasting eight days. Now, the design of the ancient Greeks was not to spill out the oil, but rather only to contaminate it. The darkness of Greece descended upon the Jewish people when the Greeks translated the Torah into Greek.[4] This marked the beginning of their insidious campaign to undermine the uniqueness of the Torah. They began by signaling that the Torah should be incorporated in the general scheme of knowledge.

The divine will and wisdom reveal themselves, as R. Hutner points out, in two different media, the medium of the *Asarah Ma'amarot,* "the Ten Utterances,"[5] and the medium of the *Aseret ha-Dibberot,* "the Ten Commandments." The former represents the laws of nature. Our recognition of the Divine is acquired by means of observation, deduction, logic, and the scientific method. The second, however, is represented in the form of the Ten Commandments, meaning articles of faith. We accept by our own free will the will of Hashem. Faith is our underlying acceptance of even the commandments that we feel we understand on a logical basis.[6]

3. *Bava Batra* 75a.
4. *Megillat Ta'anit, perek ha-aḥaron*; R. Aaron b. Jacob ha-Kohen of Lunel (Provence, end of 13th and first half of 14th cent.), *Orḥot Ḥayyim, Hilkhot Ta'anit* 24; *Kol Bo,* no. 63; *Tur, Oraḥ Ḥayyim* 580; *Shulḥan Arukh, Oraḥ Ḥayyim* 580:2.
5. The "Ten Utterances" are the ten statements that Hashem made in creating the world, which are recorded at Genesis 1:3, 1:6, 1:9, 1:11, 1:14, 1:20, 1:24, 1:26, 1:29, and 2:18. Mishnah, *Avot* 5:1.
6. R. Yitzhak Hutner (Brooklyn, 1907–1980), *Paḥad Yitzḥak: Kuntrus ve-Zot Ḥanukkah* (Brooklyn, NY: Mossad Gur Aryeh, 1984), *ma'amar* 4, pp. 39–41.

Now, the Greeks wanted to blur the distinction between the Ten Utterances and the Ten Commandments. In their view, the Torah must be incorporated into the extant body of knowledge. It must be subject to the laws of logic, scientific method, and deduction. Some parts could survive, other could not. The ultimate test of usefulness was whether it was aesthetically pleasing.

Not with the crude bestiality of Canaan, but with the culture of Japheth, the Greeks blurred the distinction between the fleeting pleasure that comes from scientific discovery or the beauty of architecture, poetry, and art, and the permanent beauty of the transformation of one's personality that comes from the sweetness of Torah study and the meticulous observance of the commandments.

How do we react to protect ourselves against the inroads of Hellenism? Well, there are three reactions, symbolized by the three levels of observance of the mitzvah of *ner Ḥanukkah*. There is the basic fulfillment of the mitzvah, *ner ish u-beito*. The Jewish home is a microcosm of the Jewish nation. This represents the minimalist's response. Each Jew must do his part. It is a nation of specialists, with a division of labor where each does his part. The light will glow from the totality and collective of the Jewish people. It is not necessary for any Jew to think about uniqueness and singularity. This quality is something that glows only from the Jewish people as a whole.

But there is a higher response, *ner le-khol eḥad ve-eḥad*. Each person feels an individual responsibility to embrace the Torah and make it central in his life! Each Jew feels a sense of responsibility to produce a light all by himself. And he does this by enhancing all the mitzvot.

But there is an even higher response, *mehadrin min ha-mehadrin*. That is a need to do something very dramatic and shocking. How is this done? One way is to become R. Shimon b. Yohai and leap for nothing else than the Crown of Torah, the total immersion in Torah, rejecting worldly pursuits unless there is no bread in the house.[7] With this response, we can accomplish *mosif ve-holekh*, enlarging the Torah.

7. See *Shabbat* 33b. R. Shimon b. Yohai and his son R. Eleazar hid in a cave for twelve years to escape a decree of death by the Romans. During that time, R. Shimon and his son immersed themselves in Torah study. They were miraculously sustained through

But there is another *mehadrin min ha-mehadrin* response that is also *mosif ve-holekh*. This is to realize that Hellenism was a perversion of the true role of Japheth. The response is to restore Japheth to his rightful place: "May God extend Japheth, but he will dwell in the tents of Shem" (Genesis 9:27).

So what is the role of Japheth? Beauty will not be an end in itself but rather the wisdom of the Ten Utterances will be used to rationalize and embellish the Torah to add to our understanding. Also, the Torah will give direction and infuse science with meaning and purpose.

The reaction of R. Shimon b. Yohai is much easier. Why? Anyone can assume this role and take it as far as he can go. But in order to put Japheth in his right place, one cannot act alone. No. We need the assistance of those who have deepened the understanding of Torah. We need the close cooperation and guidance of R. Shimon b. Yohai and his colleagues.

Extremism usually repels society at large. But when two polar opposites cooperate and become integrated, the entire society is lifted up to the level of *mehadrin min ha-mehadrin*. This gives new meaning to the dictum of "he who habitually practices the lighting of the lamp will have sons who are *talmidei ḥakhamim*."[8]

If one understands the *mehadrin min ha-mehadrin* response to Greek Hellenism, then an ideological merger between two different types of *talmidei ḥakhamim* will be taking place. And this will represent the impact of *talmidei ḥakhamim* in their finest moments, *talmidei ḥakhamim marbim shalom ba-olam*, "the disciples of the Sages increase peace in the world."[9]

---

a carob tree and a well of water that appeared at the mouth of the cave. When they emerged from the cave and saw a man ploughing and sowing, they exclaimed, "They forsake eternal life and engage in temporal life." R. Shimon and his son had attained such an exalted state as a result of their Torah study, that when they cast their eyes upon anything, it would immediately be consumed by fire.

8. *Shabbat* 23b.

9. *Berakhot* 64a; *Yevamot* 122b; *Nazir* 66b; *Tamid* 32b; *Keritot* 28b.

One Light for Each Household

December 15, 1990

One aspect of the uniqueness of Ḥanukkah is that our Sages instituted three levels of observance of the mitzvah of *ner Ḥanukkah*. Basic fulfillment of the mitzvah is achieved by *ner ish u-beito,* each household lights one candle for each day of Ḥanukkah. Those who want to enhance the mitzvah fulfill it with each member of the household lighting one candle corresponding to each day of Ḥanukkah. *Mehadrin min ha-mehadrin* is effected when each member of the household lights candles in increasing number, corresponding to each day of Ḥanukkah.[1]

The establishment of three categories of fulfillment of *ner Ḥanukkah* is a mystery. In connection with all mitzvot of the Torah, there are only two categories, i.e., the basic mitzvah and the *hiddur mitzvah,* with the general rule that *hiddur mitzvah* is *ad shelish,* up to one-third.[2]

1. *Shabbat* 21b.
2. Ibid.; *Bava Kamma* 9b.

Moreover, *hiddur mitzvah* should only enhance the basic mitzvah, not overwhelm it or put it to shame. Enhancement of the mitzvah cannot take on a life of its own and qualitatively change the basic mitzvah. By adding the dimension of *mehadrin min ha-mehadrin,* it appears as if *mosif ve-holekh* qualitatively changes the mitzvah of *ner Ḥanukkah* and the basic mitzvah is put to shame!

Permit me to suggest that the question is itself the answer. Only a mitzvah that in its basic form is a family mitzvah has the inherent power and beauty to generate *mehadrin min ha-mehadrin.* The Greeks' campaign was *le-hashkiḥam Toratekha,* "to make the Jews forget the Torah."[3] Then it is the family unit that must provide the remedy. The light of Torah of the father and mother in the form of transmitting the content of Sinai and its experience is what will counteract the objective of the Greeks.[4] If the Greeks aimed at *le-ha'aviram me-ḥukkei retzonekha,* to compel the Jews to stray from the *ḥukkim,*[5] then parental love and devotion for a child blurs the distinction between *ḥok* and *mishpat.* There is no human relationship that is more one-sided than the parent-child relationship. It goes beyond all boundaries of logic and reason. Parents never give up on children.

Joseph's personality unfolds on Ḥanukkah. It was his exemplary *kibbud av* that stood him in a crisis, enabling him to overcome the wiles of Lady Potiphar.[6] It was the feeling that submission to Lady Potiphar would amount to betraying his father. It personalized his moral dilemma and hence saved him.

The brighter that the light of each home sparkles, the further society will leap in the direction of *mehadrin min ha-mehadrin.* This is the potential for good of *ner ish u-beito.*

The converse is also true. Even a subtle failure in the Jewish home can spell disaster for the entire Jewish nation. When the Greeks were at

3. *Al ha-Nissim* Prayer.
4. In the thinking of R. Ahron Soloveichik (Chicago, 1917–2001), the father's mission is to transmit the content of Sinai, but the mother's role is to transmit the experience of Sinai. See R. Ahron Soloveichik, *Logic of the Heart, Logic of the Mind: Wisdom and Reflections on Topics of Our Times* (Jerusalem: Genesis Jerusalem Press, 1991), 16–19.
5. Ibid.
6. *Sotah* 36b.

the height of their power, when they entered the Sanctuary, Miriam b. Bilggah entered and desecrated the Altar, stomped on it, and proclaimed, "*Lukos, lukos* [wolf, wolf]. How long will you consume the money of Israel, and you do not stand by them in a time of pressing need!" She represented the epitome of success for the Greeks,[7] to make the Jews forget the Torah and to stray from the statutes.

When the Hasmoneans drove the Greeks out of the Temple, the members of the Bilggah family, who were Priests, were punished together with the entire *mishmar*. *Oy le-rasha, oy le-shekheno*, "woe to the wicked one, woe to his neighbor."[8]

Permit me to suggest that the punishment, which fell short of banishment, but instead was public humiliation of the Bilggah clan, was instituted *middah ke-neged middah*. Miriam's father, Bilggah, was not an apostate. If he were, he would have been disqualified from performing the service in the Temple.[9] The Sages understood the insidious process of moral decay. A subtle failure in the family could spell disaster for the Jewish nation.

Perhaps the entire failure was a matter of not exuding the highest enthusiasm for the *avodah*, making it central and a delight in his life. *Middah ke-neged middah*, Bilggah was relegated to the south corner. He could no longer occupy the north corner, a place of honor and distinction.[10] Lack of enthusiasm would be a short step away from regarding the *avodah* as a burden. Bilggah projected the sentiment that he preferred to be elsewhere, so *middah ke-neged middah*, his clan was made to borrow someone else's ring.[11] They were made to feel that they did not belong.

---

7. *Sukkah* 56b.
8. Ibid.
9. See II Kings 23:9; *Rashi* ad loc.; Mishnah, *Menaḥot* 13:10; *Menaḥot* 109a–b; *Zevaḥim* 22b; *Tur, Oraḥ Ḥayyim* 128.
10. Each Priestly family served in the Temple for one week at a time. At the end of the week, the incoming and outgoing families would divide the Showbread between themselves. The incoming family would divide it in the north of the Courtyard, while the outgoing family would divide it in the south. The Bilggah clan was thus treated as if it were always the outgoing family. *Sukkah* 56a–b.
11. Twenty-four rings were affixed to the stone floor of the Courtyard in the Temple, corresponding to the twenty-four Priestly families that would serve in the Temple on a rotating basis one week at a time. The rings were used to facilitate the ritual

And finally, once we reach this stage, we are not too far from conveying an impression that we do not really believe in the *avodah*. So, *middah ke-neged middah*, Bilggah was made to borrow the other Priests' knives and his storage alcove was blocked, as if to say, since you had no interest, we do not trust you; we do not trust your *sheḥitah*.

May we merit the blessing of our Sages, "He who habitually practices the lighting of the lamp will possess scholarly sons."[12] He who is accustomed with *nerot* – with *ner Shabbat*, purity, domestic tranquility, and strengthening the role of the family as moral educators – will be producing a new generation of *mosif ve-holekh*.

---

slaughter of the animals that were brought as offerings in the Temple. Each ring was in the shape of a circle with an open section. When an animal was to be slaughtered, the ring was rotated so that the open section faced upward. The animal's neck was placed in the open section. The ring was then rotated until the open section was located in a groove beneath the Courtyard floor. Bilggah's ring was permanently fixed to the floor so that it could not be rotated and opened. Bilggah was thus forced to use a ring of one of the other groups. *Sukkah* 56a–b.

12. *Shabbat* 23b (statement of R. Huna).

A Critique of the Modern Treatise on *Azut*

December 7, 1991

In the teaching of the hasidic master the *Shem mi-Shemuel,* the kindling of the menorah on Ḥanukkah not only commemorates the miracle of the flask of oil that was found, but also evokes the imagery of the military victory of the Hasmoneans.[1]

When oil is squeezed out of an olive, the extract, the oil, takes on a character that is the diametric opposite of that of the fruit itself. The olive is bitter, but the oil is sweet.[2] And eating the olive promotes forgetfulness,[3] but olive oil signifies the wisdom of the Torah.[4]

1. R. Shmuel Bornsztain (*Shem mi-Shemuel,* Poland, 1855–1926), *Shem mi-Shemuel,* vol. 1, *Ḥanukkah* (5677/December 1916), *leil* 8, p. 224; *Ḥanukkah* (5680/December 1919), *leil* 8, p. 250; *Ḥanukkah* (5683/December 1922), p. 261.
2. See Deuteronomy Rabbah 7:3.
3. *Horiyot* 13b.
4. *Berakhot* 57a.

So, too, the Hasmoneans leaped out of their natural roles. As a band of Priests, their life's work was "*yoru mishpatekha le-Yaakov*," "they shall teach Your ordinances to Jacob" (Deuteronomy 33:10), and to be *ohavei shalom*, "peace-loving people." But these people assumed a military role, becoming brutal and devious, doing whatever it took to win militarily. This is *azut*, "brazenness."

Any time that we practice *azut*, we run the danger of going too far and becoming an *azut panim*. "*Az panim le-Gehinnom*," "the brazen go to Gehinnom."[5] So the menorah reminds us that *azut she-be-kedushah*, "brazenness that is in holiness," requires *shemirah* so that it does not go out of bounds. This is symbolized in the oil realizing its fullness and mission of illumination by self-denial.

Well, if the menorah evokes *azut she-be-kedushah*, then *Al ha-Nissim* is an elaboration of the *azut she-be-kedushah*. The *azut she-be-kedushah* was five-dimensional: (1) the strong in the hands of the weak; (2) the many in the hands of the few; (3) the impure in the hands of the pure; (4) the wicked in the hands of the righteous; and (5) the willful sinners in the hands of the diligent students of Your Torah.

Permit me to suggest that *Al ha-Nissim* is a critical review of the modern treatise on *azut*, called *Chutzpah*, by Alan M. Dershowitz.[6]

The *Al ha-Nissim* review of Dershowitz, I think, would begin with lavish praise and admiration for his fulfillment of the mitzvah "love your fellow as yourself" (Leviticus 19:18). True, his love is so deep that he can claim an *azut* of *kedushah*, the strong in the hands of the weak. He never perceived himself as weak or handicapped when he went up against an entire superpower, the USSR, to secure the release of Natan Sharansky, even when Israel would not help because it refused to declare Sharansky a Prisoner of Zion until way into his nine-year sentence in the Gulag.[7]

And his *azut* for Israel took the form of "the many in the hands of the few." Can we imagine being more alone than when he took on the defense of Jonathan Pollard? All the major Jewish organizations were

5. Mishnah, *Avot* 5:20.
6. Alan M. Dershowitz, *Chutzpah* (Boston: Little Brown, 1991).
7. Ibid., 250–260.

silent and distanced themselves so as not to be accused of a double standard of loyalty.[8]

But then there is the stridently critical review as well. We must take exception to his views as a civil libertarian in the free market of ideas. As he sees it, all ideas, no matter how offensive, how heretical, how erotic, must be permitted to be expressed.[9] And if we are concerned about the polluted element that will result, don't worry; Dershowitz and others can be relied upon to knock down any offensive idea, and a world of beauty and nobility will then emerge. But we cannot allow Dershowitz's love affair with the First Amendment to repeal the law of the Torah regarding the prohibition against inciting the Evil Inclination, or the prohibitions against *lashon ha-ra* and *motzi shem ra*.

Azut must have as its ultimate objective: "the impure in the hands of the pure." And we are not content to say *tumah huttrah be-tzibbur*.[10] We must take exception to his statement that just as Reagan will not define his Americanism, it will be decided instead by the interaction of 230 million Americans, by American values, so, too, Halakhah will not define his Jewishness.[11] We must object to his agreement with Mordecai Kaplan's attitude toward Halakhah, who quipped, "Jews are not in the antiques business. Just because something is old, does not make it 'authentic.'"[12] We cannot accept that because the objective of *azut* is ultimately "the evil in the hands of the righteous."

And finally, he gives us a glimpse into his motives. Here again, we must object. He relates a story about the first dinner party of Dean Griswold that he attended when he was a professor at Harvard Law School. At the party, the Dean's wife served roast beef and vegetables.

---

8. Ibid., 289–292.
9. Ibid., 205–206.
10. See R. Jacob Joshua b. Tzvi Hirsch Falk (Poland, 1680–1756), *Penei Yehoshua, Shabbat* 21b, s.v. "*sham mai Ḥanukkah*." The expression "*tumah huttrah be-tzibbur*" refers to the halakhah that if a majority of the congregation is in a state of ritual impurity, a public offering may be offered. See *Yoma* 6b; *Pesaḥim* 77a. This principle applies also to the kindling of the Menorah in the Temple. See *Torat Kohanim, Emor* 13:12; Maimonides, *Mishneh Torah, Temidim* 3:10.
11. Dershowitz, *Chutzpah*, 195.
12. Ibid., 197.

Dershowitz ate the vegetables but not the meat. The next day, the Dean asked him why he had not eaten the meat. When he explained that the meat was not kosher, the Dean asked him whether he did not think that it was time for "your people" to adapt the old rules to modern times. Recalling the incident, Dershowitz said, "I think that the dean's well-intentioned remark kept me kosher for another year."[13]

The ultimate goal of *azut* is the delivery of the willful sinners into the hands of "*oskei Toratekha,*" the diligent students of Torah, not "*lomdei Toratekha,*" those who learn Torah. It is the triumph of a much broader ideal, when the whole society revolves around Torah, when those who learn, those who observe, and those who support Torah want to find guidance and inspiration from the Torah in everything they do.

If *azut* is to play a role in everyday life, we must remember: "It is a nation that will dwell in solitude and not be reckoned among the nations" (Numbers 23:9). Therefore *azut* must be the source for our internal motivation. We must put a tiger in our own talk – "be bold as a leopard, light as an eagle, swift as a deer, and strong as a lion to carry out the will of your Father in Heaven."[14]

---

13. Ibid., 64.

14. Mishnah, *Avot* 5:20.

Sevarah and the Celebration of Ḥanukkah

December 11, 1993

What cannot be conquered with military might may rather be won by attrition. This seems to be the case for the Greeks, who fought against *Ḥodesh*. What did they object to? They saw a paradox in the Jewish people. On the one hand, they are submissive to all the *ḥukkim*; they are mindless. But Hashem gave them the authority of "*ha-ḥodesh ha-zeh lakhem*," "this month shall be for you the beginning of the months" (Exodus 12:2). The months are yours. You make your calculations and the Festivals will be set. The greatest power in the area of creativity is the legislative authority of rabbis. And with the triumph, the Sages created a new holiday.

But it would seem that now the Greeks have accomplished their goal to eradicate our *Ḥodesh* because rabbinical authority today, in the post-Sanhedrin age, is totally by voluntary compliance.[1]

But I would say the opposite. We commemorate Ḥanukkah with the reading of the offerings of the Princes because on Ḥanukkah, we celebrate the rededication of the Temple. The offering of each Prince was identical, although each Prince put a different sentiment into his offering.[2] But on *Zot Ḥanukkah,* we read "*be-ha'alot'kha et ha-nerot,*" "when you kindle the lamps" (Numbers 8:2).[3] We place Aaron into prominence. The Divine Presence spoke through the throat of Moses,[4] but "Aaron your brother will be your spokesman" (Exodus 7:1). Aaron represented the attribute of *hod,* splendor, the very limits of the role of human action.[5]

The first time *sevarah,* "reasoning," is found in the Torah is when Aaron answers Moses regarding the he-goat offering of Rosh Ḥodesh. "Moses inquired insistently regarding the he-goat of the sin offering" (Leviticus 10:16).[6] And Aaron, who was a bereaved father, comes up with sharp *sevarah* of a distinction between *kadshei sha'ah* and *kadshei dorot.*[7]

---

1. See R. A. Yehudah (Ronnie) Warburg, *Rabbinic Authority: The Vision and the Reality; Beit Din Decisions in English* (Jerusalem: Urim, 2013), 17–32; Eli Turkel, "The Nature and Limitations of Rabbinic Authority," *Tradition: A Journal of Orthodox Jewish Thought* 27, no. 4 (Summer 1993): 83–84.
2. Numbers Rabbah 13:14; Nahmanides to Numbers 7:2.
3. *Shulḥan Arukh, Oraḥ Ḥayyim* 684:1.
4. R. Moses Sofer (*Ḥatam Sofer,* Hungary, 1762–1839), *Torat Mosheh, Shemot,* s.v. "*mah omar aleihem*"; *Terumah,* s.v. "*ve-asu aron*"; R. Zev Wolf Einhorn (*Maharzu,* Vilna, d. 1862), *Perush Maharzu* to Exodus Rabbah 3:15, s.v. "*moreh ani devarai ke-ḥetz.*" See also Zohar, *Pinḥas, Ra'aya Meheimena* 3:232a.
5. Zohar, *Bereshit* 1:21b.
6. R. Gedalia Schorr (Brooklyn, 1910–1979), *Or Gedalyahu: Mo'adim ve-Likkutim* (Jerusalem, 2001), 48–49.
7. R. Solomon b. Isaac (*Rashi,* France, 1040–1105), *Rashi* to Leviticus 10:19. Aaron was an *onen* after the death of his sons Nadab and Abihu. As a result, he was generally prohibited from partaking of the he-goat of Rosh Ḥodesh. Moses told Aaron that he should eat the offering because the law of *anninut* was waived in this case. Aaron and his sons Eleazar and Ithamar burned the he-goat of Rosh Ḥodesh. Moses became upset. Aaron explained that Hashem made an exception from *anninut* only for *kadshei*

As R. Zadok ha-Kohen says, anything that is first is the prototype of an attitude.[8] So on Ḥanukkah, we try to replicate the *hod* of Aaron. And how? By *ner le-eḥad, ner le-me'ah* (lit., "a light for one, a light for one hundred"),[9] with one hundred answers to the *Beit Yosef*'s question of why we celebrate Ḥanukkah for eight days instead of seven days if the oil that was found was enough to last one day.[10]

The blessing of *she-asah nissim* can be recited only if one sees the Ḥanukkah lights.[11] Why? The *Ḥiddushei ha-Rim* says that Ḥanukkah is not like the Three Festivals, which today are automatically sanctified. Rather, we must be spiritually aroused by observing the Ḥanukkah lights and then we can say the blessing of *she-asah nissim.*[12]

But to what should we be aroused? Permit me to say that we are expected to make the association of *ner Ḥanukkah* to the lights of the Menorah in the Temple. There were two appurtenances in the Temple that represented Torah: the Ark and the Menorah. The Ark represents the Written Law, and the Menorah represents the Oral Law, and specifically the role of *sevarah.*[13] This is the source of *ḥiyyut* for the Jewish people. It is our light. Every time Jews sit together and pour over a page of the Talmud, we are reenacting the battle of the Hasmoneans and we are reliving their triumph.

---

sha'ah (lit., "sacrifices for the current time"), i.e., the *milu'im* and the first offering of the Princes, which are brought only once in history, but did not make an exception for *kadshei dorot* (lit., "sacrifices for the generations"), the he-goat of Rosh Ḥodesh, which is brought every month. Moses acknowledged that Aaron was correct.

8. R. Zadok ha-Kohen Rabinowitz (Lublin, 1823–1900), *Tzidkat ha-Tzaddik, ot* 1.
9. The phrase is used in the talmudic discussion at *Shabbat* 122a regarding whether a Jew may benefit on the Sabbath from a lamp that was lit by a gentile on the Sabbath. The Mishnah states that if a gentile lit a lamp for himself, a Jew may use its light on the Sabbath. Mishnah, *Shabbat* 16:8. The Talmud notes that because a lamp that is lit for one person also illuminates for many people, the gentile is not considered to have performed an extra action for a Jew on the Sabbath from which the Jew would be prohibited to derive benefit.
10. R. Yerahmiel Zelcer, *Ner le-Me'ah: Al Inyanei Ḥanukkah* (Brooklyn, NY, 1975).
11. See *Shabbat* 23a; *Sukkah* 46a; *Tur, Oraḥ Ḥayyim* 676; *Shulḥan Arukh, Oraḥ Ḥayyim* 676:3.
12. See *Sefat Emet, Ḥanukkah* (5631/December 1870), *leil* 1 (quoting *Ḥiddushei ha-Rim*).
13. R. Naphtali Tzvi Yehudah Berlin (*Netziv*, Russia, 1816–1893), *Ha'amek Davar*, Exodus 27:20.

To Make Them Forget Your Torah

December 3, 1994

The phrase in *Al ha-Nissim* "*le-hashkiḥam Toratekha*," "to make them forget Your Torah," encapsulates the objective of our ancient Greek-Syrian oppressors.

Permit me to suggest that the campaign to effect this design did not begin with the specific prohibition against religious practice on the pain of death consisting of the Sabbath, Rosh Ḥodesh, and *milah*. It began in a much more subtle and indirect way with the translation of the Torah into Greek, which Ptolemy II Philadephus ordered the seventy-two Sages to do.[1] This apparently innocent event is regarded by our Sages as a tragedy.[2]

And why? Because when a lover of knowledge who denies the divine origin of the Torah wants to translate the Torah, he desires to bring

1. *Megillah* 9a.
2. *Masekhet Soferim* 1:7.

it into the corpus of knowledge on an equal footing. He has knocked the Torah from its pedestal. This is the first blow to making the Torah central in our lives and viewing it in its unique character. In Hellenistic thought, the Torah must be subjected to the same test of practicality and scientific method as secular knowledge; some parts may survive, but others might be rejected or regarded as irrelevant.

The lesson that an indirect, subtle attack can strike a bigger blow than a frontal attack is particularly brought home on the eighth day of Ḥanukkah. Each day of Ḥanukkah corresponds to a *korban* offered by a Prince in connection with the dedication of the Tabernacle.[3] The eighth day corresponds to *Menasheh*.[4]

In today's *sidrah*, we are told that Joseph called his firstborn *Menasheh, "Ki nashani Elokim et kol amali ve-et kol beit avi,"* "For God has made me forget all my hardship and my father's household" (Genesis 41:51). *Ha-Ketav ve-ha-Kabbalah* asks, what type of person would not be ashamed to openly thank God that his present situation is so satisfying that he forgets family and heritage?[5]

Without asking the question, the *Malbim* says that Joseph thanked Hashem because he felt pain for forgetting his father's home.[6] Joseph was the Horatio Alger of the ancient world, experiencing a spectacular rise from lowly felon to Viceroy of Egypt. "The daughters climbed heights to gaze [at Joseph]" (Genesis 49:22). He certainly made the cover of *Time* and *Newsweek* in the same week!

For a lesser person, all the honor, wealth, and adulation would have drowned out any longing for his father and heritage, with absolutely no pain. But Joseph felt pain for forgetting his father. He named his firstborn *Menasheh* so that every time he would pick up and embrace his child or

---

3. Mishnah, *Megillah* 3:6; *Megillah* 31a. The biblical account of the offerings of the Princes at Numbers 7:1–8:4 is read on Ḥanukkah because the dedication of the Tabernacle was completed on the twenty-fifth day of Kislev, the first day of Ḥanukkah. *Tur, Oraḥ Ḥayyim* 684 (citing *Pesikta Rabbati* 6).
4. See Numbers 7:54.
5. R. Yaakov Tzvi Mecklenburg (Germany, 1785–1865), *Ha-Ketav ve-ha-Kabbalah*, Genesis 41:51, s.v. *"ve-et kol beit avi."*
6. R. Meir Loeb b. Jehiel Michel Weisser (*Malbim*, Poland, Romania, and Russia, 1809–1879), *Malbim* to Genesis 41:52.

call him by his name, he would be reminded of his responsibility to preserve the heritage of his father, review the lessons that his father imparted, and implement the Jewish ideal of *ḥesed* in the policies of the government.

Our Sages well understood the insidious process of *le-hashkiḥam Toratekha*. It is no better illustrated than with the tragic story of Miriam b. Bilggah. She was an apostate who married a Syrian-Greek military officer. When the Greeks broke into the Sanctuary, she came to the Altar, which was a severe prohibition. She then took off her sandal and beat the Altar, proclaiming, "Wolf! Wolf! How long will you consume the money of Israel, and you do not stand by them in a time of pressing need!" When the Hasmoneans prevailed and restored order, the Sages prohibited not only Bilggah from being a Priest, but his entire clan. This was not overkill. Instead, it reflected the Sages' insight into how the process of *le-hashkiḥam Toratekha* worked.[7]

Three prohibitions were instituted. First, they permanently affixed the ring of the Bilggah family to the floor of the Courtyard, to tell them that they were not in charge; they were not the boss.[8]

Second, the members of the Bilggah family were required to divide their share of the *leḥem ha-panim* on the southern side of the Courtyard, even when they were the incoming family. This was contrary to the usual procedure. Each priestly family served in the Temple for a week. At the end of the week, the incoming and out going families would divide the *leḥem ha-panim* between themselves. The incoming family would divide it in the north of the Courtyard, while the outgoing family would divide it in the south. The Bilggah clan was thus treated as if it were always the outgoing family.

---

7. *Sukkah* 56b.
8. The rings were used to facilitate ritual slaughter. Twenty-four rings were affixed to the stone floor of the Courtyard in the Temple, corresponding to the twenty-four priestly families that would serve in the Temple on a rotating basis one week at a time. Each ring was in the shape of a circle with an open section. When an animal was to be slaughtered, the ring was rotated so that the open section faced upward. The animal's neck was placed in the open section. The ring was then rotated until the open section was located in a groove beneath the Courtyard floor. Bilggah's ring was permanently fixed to the floor so that it could not be rotated and opened. Bilggah was thus forced to use a ring of one of the other groups. *Sukkah* 56a–b.

Third, the alcove where the Bilggah family stored its knives for ritual use was closed because the Sages did not trust their *sheḥitah*. The members of the Bilggah family conducted themselves in their private lives without exuding the requisite *yir'at Shamayim* and trust – or *bittaḥon* – in Hashem. This was *middah ke-negged middah,* to demonstrate that the Sages did not trust them.

On the eighth day of Ḥanukkah, the religious rituals of Ḥanukkah, reach a crescendo. We have eight candles, the longest reading of the Torah of all the days of Ḥanukkah, *Zot Ḥanukkah,*[9] and the *ḥasimah* of Yom Kippur (i.e., the closure of judgment).[10] But the final impression that we are left with is the last verse of *mizmor shir* at Psalms 30. We say, "Hashem, my God, forever will I thank You" (Psalms 30:13). If this is not to be a sham, we must be equipped to nip in the bud the subtle and indirect forces that make mitzvot mechanical. This means that the end of the verse must be connected to the beginning, "So that my soul may sing to You and not be stilled" (Psalms 30:13). We must eternally be in the *shirah* mode. If we do not have enthusiasm, we must generate it so that we do not chill the burning candles.

9. The Torah reading for the eighth day of Ḥanukkah is Numbers 7:54–8:4. The phrase "*zot ḥanukkat ha-mizbe'aḥ,*" "this was the dedication of the Altar," is at Numbers 7:84.
10. R. Yehudah Leib of Zaklików (Poland, d. 1826), *Likkutei Maharil, Miketz, Derush le-Ḥanukkah.*

The Military Victory of the Hasmoneans

(Undated)

We are all familiar with the question of why Ḥanukkah is celebrated for eight days. If the flask of pure oil that was found would have in any case naturally lasted one night, the miracle of the oil was only a seven-day miracle.[1] One answer to this question given by the *Maharal* of Prague is that the extra day is to commemorate the miracle of the military victory.[2]

Now, the Sages of that generation were genuinely impressed with the military triumph, but they were not sure what to make of it. Did it reflect merely superior military strategy and the intense motivation of the Hasmoneans, or did it represent divine intervention, a real miracle? They were groping for divine guidance. This guidance came with the

1. R. Joseph Caro (Safed, 1488–1575), *Beit Yosef* to *Tur, Oraḥ Ḥayyim* 670, s.v. "*ve-ikha.*"
2. See R. Judah Loew b. Bezalel (*Maharal*, Prague, ca. 1525–1609), *Shabbat* 21b; *Ner Mitzvah.*

unmistakable miracle of the oil lasting eight days. With this miracle, everyone became sure that the military victory was a miracle as well.

I think that we can extend this thought a bit further by combining it with a thought of the *Shem mi-Shemuel.*[3] In Daniel's vision, the Greek nation is represented by a leopard.[4] Now, the leopard is not the strongest of animals. The lion is. But the leopard is a very bold and audacious creature. *Hevei az ka-namer,* "be bold as a leopard."[5] This was the essence of the ancient Greeks; they were brazenly arrogant. They felt superior to the entire human race and believed that anything that they could not understand with their reasoning should be rejected.[6] It is for this reason that, most of all, they could not tolerate the *ḥukkim*. As we say in *Al ha-Nissim,* they attempted "to compel them to stray from the statutes of Your will." Their culture was superior, and anyone who refused to embrace it would be put to death.

The miracle of the military triumph was that the Hasmoneans embraced the personality trait of *azut,* "brazenness." The Hasmoneans were Priests, gentle people of peace. They acted completely out of character by becoming warriors, having the chutzpah to stand up to the organized military power of the day. This is *azut*. To make the Hasmoneans focus on the obvious, that the military victory was a miracle, the miracle of the flask of oil occurred. The Hasmoneans resembled the oil. Just as the olive is transformed into oil, which is a substance of an entirely different character than the olive, so, too, the Hasmoneans were transformed. The olive, our Sages tell us, is *kasheh le-shikheḥah,* "it promotes forgetfulness."[7] And it is bitter, while the oil is sweet and signifies the wisdom of the Torah.[8]

At the same time, the Hasmoneans were given a powerful message of their vulnerability. *Azut* is prone to be directed toward destruction, so it needs *shemirah* and Torah. This vulnerability was to be understood from the miracle of the flask of oil. Just as the oil achieves its mission when it destroys itself, i.e., through self-denial, so, too, the *azut* could

3. *Shem mi-Shemuel,* vol. 1, *Ḥanukkah* (5673/December 1912), *leil* 6, p. 196.
4. Daniel 7:6; *Rashi* ad loc.
5. Mishnah, *Avot* 5:20.
6. See Nahmanides to Leviticus 16:8.
7. *Horiyot* 13b.
8. Deuteronomy Rabbah 7:3; *Berakhot* 57a.

retain its characteristic of *kedushah* only if it could be combined with the trait of submissiveness to the will of Hashem.

Indeed, the tragic flaw of the Hasmoneans, as Nahmanides points out, was that they violated the legacy of Jacob: "The scepter shall not depart from Judah nor a scholar from among his descendants" (Genesis 49:10).[9] The Hasmoneans should have turned over the reins of government to Judah, its rightful heir, and resumed their mission of the Priesthood, elevating the moral climate of society by fulfilling their role of being preoccupied with learning Torah and being lovers of peace.

The miracle of military triumph is recited in *Al ha-Nissim*. First we say "the many in the hands of the few," and then "the evil in the hands of the righteous." We may very well ask, but of course, could it be any other way? Should the wicked triumph over the righteous? The answer is that this is the miracle, the miracle of character transformation. The meek became valiant soldiers, even though the righteous recoil from physical confrontation and the pure recoil from violence.

In the contemporary, post-Holocaust era, we are reliving the miracle of Ḥanukkah in a special way. If our Sages regard the ancient Greeks as symbolized by the leopard, then *kal ve-ḥomer*, this is how we should regard the Nazis. While the Greeks felt that they were superior and, on the pain of death, wanted everyone to join them, the Nazis felt the same way but had such a disdain for the chosen people of Hashem, that they would be satisfied with nothing less than to reduce us to ashes. They marshalled the most advanced technology to efficiently reduce us to ash, to blot out our memory from the face of the earth as quickly as possible.

The miracle of the post-Holocaust era is that we have embraced the personality trait of the persecutor, the trait of *azut*. We, the people who were made into ashes, dared to rise out of the ashes, excel, and exert a tremendous influence on the world in every area of human endeavor. Yes, we dared to establish a State amidst twenty million hostile enemies.[10]

9. Nahmanides to Genesis 49:10.

10. Within hours of Israel's declaration of independence on May 14, 1948, Egypt, Syria, Transjordan, Iraq, and Lebanon invaded Israel. Reginald Seigel, "Arab Nations Attack Israel," *UPI NewsTrack*, May 15, 1948. The combined population of those countries then was at least twenty million. See Department of Economic Affairs, Statistical Office of the United Nations, *Demographic Yearbook, 1949–1950* (New York, 1950),

Jewish survival is predicated on our ability to adopt the characteristic of *azut*. But the challenge for us is to give the proper shape to the *azut* so that it is should remain an *azut* of *kedushah*. It is for us to combine the *azut* with the oil of the menorah and fulfill *mosif ve-holekh* according to *Beit Hillel*.[11]

71, 77 (estimating the population of Egypt, Syria, Jordan, and Lebanon in 1948 to be approximately 19.5 million, 3.1 million, 0.4 million, and 1.2 million, respectively; estimating the population of Iraq in 1947 to be 4.8 million).

11. *Shabbat* 21b.

Tu bi-Shevat

The Four Types of Rosh Ha-Shanah

February 14, 1987

On this resplendent Sabbath, we have both *Shabbat Shirah* and Tu bi-Shevat. But we also have an element of solemnity, for Tu bi-Shevat is one of the four days that our Sages designate as Rosh Ha-Shanah in the Jewish calendar.[1] Rosh Ha-Shanah is a serious time. It is a time for soul-searching. It is a time when we face challenges and demands head-on.

The human personality, in the oft-quoted talmudic dictum, manifests itself in four ways: *be-koso*, "by his cup"; *be-kiso*, "by his purse"; *be-ka'aso*, "by his anger"; and some say also *be-saḥako*, "by his laughter."[2] Perhaps each dimension of the human personality requires a separate Rosh Ha-Shanah.

Let us first take *be-koso*. This seems to be the light aspect of the talmudic dictum. But I would propose that it is the most serious

1. Mishnah, *Rosh Ha-Shanah* 1:1 (opinion of *Beit Hillel*).
2. *Eruvin* 65b.

because *nikhnas yayin, yatza sod,* "the wine goes in and the secret comes out."[3] The cup hence represents the inner world of man, his ambitions, his longings, his striving, and his vision. Where do they lie? This is the most profound type of *ḥeshbon ha-nefesh*. And it is capsulated in the Rosh Ha-Shanah of the first day of Tishrei in *Hashem menat ḥelki ve-kosi,* "Hashem is my allotted portion and my cup [i.e., my share]" (Psalms 16:5).

Then there is *be-kiso*. How a man spends his money reveals much about himself. It tells us of his priorities in life and his sense of responsibility or lack of it. This corresponds to the Rosh Ha-Shanah of the first day of Elul. This is the Rosh Ha-Shanah of *ma'aser behemah,* the tithing of the firstborn animal.[4] It is a significant test of integrity and responsibility in the financial realm. In order for *ma'aser behemah* to be operative, all ten animals must be born in the same fiscal year, which begins with the first day of Elul.[5] This law leaves plenty of room for manipulation – I don't think the county clerk keeps records of the birth of animals!

Then there is *be-saḥako,* what the individual finds entertaining. This corresponds to the first day of the month of Nisan. All the Festivals are set for us according to the first day of Nisan.[6]

The challenge here is: How do we view the Festivals? Are they just an opportunity for self-gratification? Or do we look upon them as occasions to reach out to the disadvantaged and the forlorn, and bring them into our joy as well?

Then there is Tu bi-Shevat, which is celebrated today. What is the practical significance of Tu bi-Shevat? Tu bi-Shevat is the Rosh Ha-Shanah for the trees.[7] All the tithes of fruits in the *Shemittah* cycle are set in reference to this date.[8]

---

3. *Sanhedrin* 38a.
4. Mishnah, *Rosh Ha-Shanah* 1:1.
5. Mishnah, *Bekhorot* 9:6; *Bekhorot* 58a.
6. Exodus 12:2; Mishnah, *Rosh Ha-Shanah* 1:1.
7. Mishnah, *Rosh Ha-Shanah* 1:1 (opinion of *Beit Hillel*).
8. *Rosh Ha-Shanah* 15b; Maimonides (*Rambam,* Egypt, 1135–1204), *Mishneh Torah, Ma'aser Sheni* 1:2.

Now, we know that in the third and sixth year, *ma'aser ani* substitutes for *ma'aser sheni.*[9] The difference in obligation is very substantial. Whereas in four of the six years of the *Shemittah* cycle, we get to take one-tenth of our produce and go with our family for a holiday in Jerusalem, consuming the fruits there, in the case of *ma'aser ani,* we give one-tenth of our produce to the poor.

Herein lies the test of anger, *be-ka'aso*! The man who is observant, who discharges all his tithing obligations, may very well harbor some resentment, some hidden anger, for, after all, he is already making considerable sacrifices. Now he is asked to do more. Here is the test. Will he harbor resentment, or will he assume the additional responsibility with aplomb, grace, and alacrity?

9. Deuteronomy 14:28–29, 26:12.

Rosh Ha-Shanah for the Trees

February 10, 1990

The practical significance of the Festival of Tu bi-Shevat is that it sets an accounting period and a cutoff point for *ma'aserot* of fruits. Fruit that blossomed before Tu bi-Shevat is in a different accounting period for *ma'aserot* compared with fruit that blossomed after Tu bi-Shevat.[1]

Without this accounting period, as R. Moshe Feinstein points out, we would be able to postpone giving tithes indefinitely into the future.[2] We would be able to combine the crops of this year with those of next year, give 10 percent of the combined crop, and then decide to make good on this obligation in the third year, and so on.

1. *Rosh Ha-Shanah* 15b; Maimonides, *Mishneh Torah, Ma'aser Sheni* 1:2.
2. R. Moshe Feinstein (New York, 1895–1986), *Derash Mosheh: Ḥiddushei Aggadah al ha-Torah* (Benei Berak, 1988), *Be-Shallaḥ*, p. 52.

Reinforcing this is the fact that the obligation is directed to the Tribe;[3] no individual member of the Tribe of Levi has a right to put in a claim for *ma'aser*. Instead, the *ba'al ha-bayit* has *tovat hana'ah*, the right to give the *ma'aser* to the person of his choice.[4] The accounting period is hence a *simḥah* because it makes the remainder of the field really the property of the *ba'al ha-bayit* without a hint of theft.

This can be generalized to the obligation to adopt the shortest accounting period for all our mitzvah obligations. The shorter the accounting period that we adopt, the greater the urgency we feel to fulfill our mitzvot.

If we are to adopt a short accounting period for accounts payable, we are to adopt a long accounting period for accounts receivable. This is seen in the story of Honi ha-Me'aggel, who learned that one must plant for posterity because our ancestors planted for us.[5] When it comes to dividends from mitzvot, we must show the utmost forbearance and patience! In addition, we must develop a taste for what is a dividend and what is an asset that is unthinkable to acquire. The Torah imposes discipline upon us. The discipline sweetens life and does not make it bitter. "Hashem showed him a tree. He threw it into the water and the water became sweet" (Exodus 15:25).[6]

---

3. Numbers 18:21 ("To the sons of Levi, behold! I have given every tithe in Israel as a heritage in exchange for the service that they perform, the service of the Tent of Meeting.").
4. *Bekhorot* 27a.
5. *Ta'anit* 23a. The Talmud records that the righteous man, Honi ha-Me'aggel, was troubled by the meaning of the verse "A song of ascents, When Hashem returned the captivity of Zion, we were like dreamers" (Psalms 126:1). He wondered whether it was possible for a man to dream continuously for seventy years. One day when he was traveling on the road, he saw a man planting a carob tree. Honi ha-Me'aggel asked him, "How long does it take for this tree to bear fruit?" "Seventy years," the man replied. Honi ha-Me'aggel then asked, "Are you certain that you will live another seventy years?" The man replied, "I found carob trees in the world; as my forefathers planted those for me, so, too, I plant these for my children." Honi ha-Me'aggel sat down to have a meal and fell into a slumber that lasted seventy years. When he awoke, he saw a man gathering the fruit of the carob tree and asked him, "Are you the man who planted the tree?" "I am his grandson," the man replied. Thereupon, Honi ha-Me'aggel exclaimed, "It is clear that I slept for seventy years."
6. See *Mekhilta* to Exodus 15:5 (interpreting the "tree" as a reference to the Torah).

Shabbat Shekalim

The Struggle between the Three *Haftarot*

February 28, 1987

On this resplendent Sabbath, a colossal and desperate struggle is taking place between three *haftarot*: *Parashat Mishpatim, maḥar ḥodesh,* and *Parashat Shekalim*. Each is insisting on its right to be read today. The dispute is apparently resolved by conferring complete victory on *Parashat Shekalim*. Not even a remembrance of the other two *haftarot* remains.

Bludgeoning rivals into total defeat appears a bit unseemly on this Sabbath, when we have the theme of unity ushering in Rosh Ḥodesh Adar.

Rather than understanding the reading of the *haftarah* of *Parashat Shekalim* as pushing aside the other *haftarot,* I would propose that the *haftarah* of *Parashat Shekalim* merely represents the other two, and is the pinnacle of a developmental process in achieving nobility of spirit.

In today's *haftarah,* we encounter a mysterious initiative of King Jehoash. It is 155 years since the construction of the Temple. There has been a succession of eight kings and no one undertook a project for beautifying and repairing the Temple. The initiative certainly carried with it a tremendous potential for inspiration and elevation. But the King's approach was misguided. He transforms the Priests and Levites into mendicant workers. He asks them to collect donations for the project from their acquaintances. They may keep the money, but they are obligated to see to it that the repairs are made. Hence, he relied on a combination of economic incentives and social pressure to effect the desired outcome.

But the plan met with passive resistance. "The Priests did not repair the deterioration of the Temple" (II Kings 12:7). And why? Because, as R. Samson Raphael Hirsch points out, the approach lacked the spontaneity that should mark one's attitude toward the Temple.[1]

Jehoiada approved a different scheme, that of setting up a chest near the Altar, and thus free-willed donations would be called for. And the plan was met with such enthusiasm and alacrity. "Whenever they saw that there was much money in the chest, the King's scribe and the High Priest would come up and they bagged and counted the money that was found in the Temple of Hashem" (II Kings 12:11).

Now, how could King Jehoash have been so misguided? The answer, I submit, lies in his preparation for royalty. We are told that Jehoash was seven years old when he became King.[2] The first six years of his life were spent in secret hiding in the Holy of Holies.[3] The nobility of Judah wanted to deify him, but as long as his mentor, Jehoiada, was still alive, he resisted.[4] When Jehoiada died, there was back-sliding with idolatry and even the brutal murder of Zechariah b. Jehoiada by the hand of Jehoash.[5] How could the son of the great benefactor have been murdered? Where was the *hakkarat ha-tov*? It seems that even this

1. R. Samson Raphael Hirsch (Germany, 1808–1888), *Haftarat Parashat Shekalim*, II Kings 12:6.
2. II Kings 12:1.
3. II Kings 11:2–3.
4. II Kings 12:3; R. Solomon b. Isaac (*Rashi*, France, 1040–1105), *Rashi* ad loc.; II Chronicles 24:17; R. Jehiel Hillel b. David Altschuler (Galicia, 18th cent.), *Metzudat David* ad loc.
5. II Chronicles 24:21–22.

was attributable to a warped development of the King, someone who had been isolated from society.

One can never leap to the level of spontaneity in *bein adam la-Makom* if he skips the developmental stage of *bein adam le-ḥavero*. And indeed, Jehoash skipped the two *haftarot* of *Parashat Mishpatim* and *maḥar ḥodesh*. In these two *haftarot,* we have to climb a ladder of increasing nobility in interpersonal relations.

In the *haftarah* of *Parashat Mishpatim,* we are transported to a period just before the destruction of the Temple. A brief respite is granted to the Jewish people before the terrible onslaught of Nebuchadnezzar. In gratitude to Hashem for the temporary withdrawal of the troops, Zedekiah proclaims with pomp and ceremony the emancipation of Jewish slaves.[6] This means that we are taking a bold stride in ending exploitation of the lowest echelon of society, the Israelite bondsman, who is either the homeless or the reformed criminal. We must turn our attention to the lowest element of society. We must treat the Israelite bondsman better, and develop a sensitivity to the needs of our fellow man.

Then we can proceed to the *haftarah* of *maḥar ḥodesh,* where we encounter Jonathan. Then we can climb the ladder of nobility and achieve the ebullient spirit of Jonathan, who felt the most profound spirit of friendship for a rival who would wrest the kingdom from him.[7] It is only then that we can develop this ebullience of spirit for a *davar she-be-kedushah* (holy matter), which was the plan of Jehoiada the Priest.[8]

6. Jeremiah 34:8.
7. See I Samuel 20:1–42.
8. R. Samson Raphael Hirsch, *Haftarat Parashat Shekalim.*

Counteraction

March 4, 2000

This Sabbath, the evil Haman bursts forth to the forefront of our consciousness and makes a pre-Megillah appearance. The *Ribbono shel Olam* tells us, "It is revealed to Me that Haman will plot to annihilate My people and offer Ahasuerus a bribe of ten thousand talents of silver to implement his plan. So, to counteract Haman's *shekalim,* I am giving you the mitzvah of *maḥatzit ha-shekel* for the Tabernacle."[1]

How does this counteraction work? Haman slandered the Jewish people, telling Ahasuerus, "Their laws are different from every other people's and they do not observe the King's laws" (Esther 3:8). The Jews are not loyal citizens. You must annihilate them, and you need not fear reprisals because they are *mefuzar u-meforad,* "scattered and separate" (Esther 3:8).[2]

1. *Megillah* 13b.
2. See R. Jonathan Eybeschuetz (Prague, 1690–1764), *Ya'arot Devash,* vol. 2 (Jerusalem: Mekhon Or ha-Sefer, 1988), 36.

Our situation would depend upon our ability to put Haman's word to a lie. We would have to show that we are a unified people of deep bonds. The first plan was for the Jews to unify and rally around Esther. The time had come for her to reveal her Jewish identity. Jews would rally around their friend in high places, the Queen herself. The plan catapulted Esther to an indispensable asset for the Jewish people. Everything must revolve around making Esther's intervention a success.

Esther says that we cannot be impetuous because "I have not been summoned to come to the king for these past thirty days" (Esther 4:11). So we must wait for the opportune time. Even if some Persians are trigger-happy and jump the gun, or some Jews go wayward because of despair and there is collateral damage, Esther must be preserved at all costs.

But to this plan Mordecai objects in the most strident manner. He responds with no element of kindness or gentleness. He does not say that it is a good plan but it must be finessed. Instead, he responds with a ferocity and harshness. He says essentially that the plan is fundamentally flawed. The salvation is not to make Esther an indispensable asset. No! "For if you persist in keeping silent at a time like this, relief and deliverance will come to the Jews from another place, while you and your father's house will perish" (Esther 4:14).

To defeat Haman, Esther must bond with her people and make the most profound bond possible. This is what the second plan is all about. Esther proposes a three-day fast. The third day falls out on Passover. But Esther says that if there is no Jewish nation, there is no need for Passover. So it is permissible for the Jewish people to fast.[3]

And it is a three-day fast. That way, she connected with the Jew who she does not want to be, the one we never want to know about. This is the *evyon*, "pauper," who is so desperate that a morsel of bread and a drop of water are the most precious sight possible.

Even after all this, Hashem makes it clear to Esther that she would succeed not because she was the friend in high places. In Psalm 22, "*la-minatze'aḥ al ayyelet ha-shaḥar,*" we are given a glimpse of what

3. Esther Rabbah 8:7; R. Issachar Berman b. Naphtali ha-Kohen (Poland, ca. 1520–1590), *Mattenot Kehunnah* ad loc., s.v. "*lammah hu Pesaḥ.*"

happens to Esther as she makes her way to the throne room.[4] Coming to the palace without being summoned was a capital offense. You would imagine that as she made her appearance and nervously approached the throne room, the courtiers would be rooting her on, hoping for her success. No! "They divide my garments among themselves, and cast lots for my clothing" (Psalms 22:19).

And Ahasuerus himself is initially unwelcoming. Esther hears him snarling that he yearns now for Vashti. He thinks, Vashti had dignity; Esther is aggressive and forward.[5] When Esther feels that "she won his favor" (Esther 5:2), she knows the truth, that it was a gift from Hashem.

Each year, we try to recapture some of the counteraction in the mitzvah of *maḥatzit ha-shekel.* In the time of the building of the Tabernacle, each Jew gave a half-shekel – "the wealthy shall not increase and the destitute shall not decrease" (Exodus 30:15) – so that no one could think that unity involves an indispensable personality around whom everyone rallies. No, each Jew by himself is a non-entity, only a half. And you do not become whole by connecting only with your neighbor because it is still only a shekel, a drop in the bucket for the entire project.

To become something, you must connect with the entire Jewish people. And for each successive generation, we have the mitzvah of *maḥatzit ha-shekel. "Ve-asu li mikdash ve-shakhanti be-sokham,"* "they shall make a Sanctuary for Me, and I will dwell among them" (Exodus 25:8), *be-sokh kol eḥad ve-eḥad,* "in each and every one of them."[6] This is possible only when each Jew views himself as a half and embraces the entire Jewish people.

---

4. See *Megillah* 15b.
5. *Midrash Shoḥer Tov,* Psalms 22, s.v. "*ki atah goḥi mi-baten.*"
6. See R. Moses Alshekh (*Alshekh,* Safed, 1508–1593), *Torat Mosheh,* Exodus 25:8, s.v. "*ve-od yitakhen derekh sheni*"; R. Isaiah ha-Levi Horowitz (*Shelah ha-Kadosh,* Prague, ca. 1565–1630), *Shenei Luḥot ha-Berit, Sha'ar ha-Otiot, ot ha-lamed lev tov; Masekhet Ta'anit, Inyan ha-Avodah*; R. Elijah de Vidas (Palestine, 1518–1592), *Reshit Ḥokhmah, sha'ar ha-ahavah,* ch. 6, s.v. "*u-shenei pesukim.*" The commentators explain that the use of the plural term "*be-sokham,*" "in them," instead of the word "*be-sokho,*" "in it," i.e., the Tabernacle, signifies that each person should sanctify himself so that Hashem will rest His Divine Presence in him.

Shabbat Zakhor

The Anti-Climax of the Megillah

March 22, 1986

The intensity of a drama is often diluted and even spoiled by the appearance of an unwelcome anti-climax. And so it seems the case with the Megillah. For all intents and purposes, the climax of our deliverance is reached with the reading of the verse "they hanged Haman on the gallows that he had prepared for Mordecai" (Esther 7:10).

Instead of leaving the various other details surrounding our salvation to the Oral Law, the authors of the Megillah chose to chronicle them in three chapters, which follow the climax of deliverance.

Far from constituting an anti-climax, the last three chapters of the Megillah represent, I would suggest, an all-out attempt to impress upon us that our salvation from certain annihilation was not the result of the confluence of natural events, but instead was a spectacular miracle of the most wondrous kind.

Yes, it was Ahasuerus' love for his Queen, Esther, that was the proximate cause of his revoking the decree of genocide. But Esther's intercession met with success only because of her profound love for her people and the fasting, repentance, and prayer of her people that stood behind her. How do we know this? It was the element of mystery in the Megillah, the mystery of Esther's nationality, that could have provided Haman with a credible defense.

Esther exposes Haman's plot. She takes great pains to make a dramatic buildup. Ahasuerus is expecting a request of no less than half of his kingdom. And what does she ask for? First and foremost, her own life. "Let my life be granted to me as my request" (Esther 7:3). She makes it look as though Haman engineered the decree only to destroy her. It was aimed at her, but to cover his tracks, to camouflage his design, he included all the Jewish people. How then could we understand Ahasuerus' shocking surprise, "Who is this? Where is this one who dared to do so?" (Esther 7:5). Now, was he a child? A fool? An idiot? How many decrees of annihilation of a whole people were then outstanding?

What Ahasuerus could not believe was that someone was so filled with hatred that he would go to such extraordinary lengths to include a whole nation in his nefarious plot, all to get one person. The King was incensed, not because of the annihilation decree, but only because Haman wanted to destroy his Queen.

So Haman had a credible defense. He could have said, "I did not know that Esther was Jewish." The whole kingdom was mystified by the enigma of Esther's nationality. "Esther had not told of her people or her kindred" (Esther 2:10). This was the reason that the King had announced a tax amnesty for the provinces to celebrate his marriage to Esther, so people should say, "See how generous he is. Imagine the generosity that he will show to the Queen's family." All this to induce Esther's relatives to come forward. And this was the purpose of the second beauty pageant, "*be-hikkavetz besulot shenit*" (Esther 2:19), to pry out of her the secret of her origin.[1] But all to no avail.

---

1. *Megillah* 13a. Ahasuerus took counsel of Mordecai regarding how to induce Esther to reveal her origin. Mordecai advised Ahasuerus to organize a second pageant so that Esther would fear being replaced as Queen and then would divulge her secret.

Why did Haman not think of the simple defense of ignorance of Esther's origin? He meant no harm to the Queen. This was a miracle. It was the righteousness of Esther that caused Haman to forget.

But perhaps the skeptic will insist that Ahasuerus had an elemental sense of decency and justice, so that once Esther exposed her slander, Haman's fate was doomed. But this is not so. Ahasuerus had absolutely no personal regard for the Jewish people. To him, they were nothing but a collection of marbles. And how do we know this? This is the purpose of the last three chapters of the Megillah.

Esther waits two months before she entreats the King to annul the evil decree.[2] What is the basis of her plea? Does she appeal to his sense of decency and justice, to spare the lives of perhaps millions of innocent people? No. Does she even elaborate on her own claim "had we been sold as slaves and maidservants, I would have kept quiet, for the adversary is not worthy of the King's damage" (Esther 7:4)? No. She makes no mention of the loyalty of the Jewish people, as evidenced by the first citizen, patriot Mordecai, or the productivity of the Jewish people, with the resultant loss of revenue. No. She simply builds on her intimate relationship with the King, saying that she will pine away witnessing the destruction of her people. "For how can I bear to witness the disaster that will befall my people" (Esther 8:6).

This appeals to the King. He understands that theoretically, he should save the Jewish people, but as a practical matter, how is it to be done? "An edict that is written in the King's name and sealed with the King's signet may not be revoked" (Esther 8:8); the authority of the King will be undermined by revoking a decree.

Is this not mind-boggling? Think for one moment of a parallel situation. Our President orders a nuclear attack on our enemy. Before

---

2. According to the *Ralbag*, Haman was killed on the seventeenth day of Nisan, but Esther waited until the twenty-third day of Sivan to request that the decree be retracted. One reason for the delay was that Esther wanted to wait until Ahasuerus' anger regarding Haman had subsided. Another possible reason for the delay was that Esther was waiting until the King called her so that she would not be required to jeopardize her life by approaching him without being called. R. Levi b. Gershom (*Ralbag*, France, 1288–1344), *Ralbag* to Esther 8:9–10. See also *Yalkut Me-Am Lo'ez*, Esther 8:3, 8:9.

the missile hits the target, the President learns that the perceived threat was a computer error. Would it not be unthinkable to say that we cannot recall the missile because we will lose our credibility? There is no justice, no decency, no compassion of any sort. All the genius of Mordecai had to be put to work to devise a scheme so that a new decree would be issued that would save the Jews but not contradict the old decree.

The original decree proclaimed that on the thirteenth day of Adar, all citizens should gather in the center of town, when the Jew-hater would be given permission to kill the Jews.[3] The new missive declared that the Jews would have the right to defend themselves.[4] This presents no contradiction with the first decree. And it might create confusion or doubt as to where the sympathies of the government lie. When there is no justice and no decency, the tide can easily turn in the other direction.

It is only in this context that we can understand that every small victory was of vast importance to rescue the Jews from the danger that they faced. It was enormously important that Ahasuerus give Haman's estate to Esther.[5] It was enormously important that a special day of fighting be granted to the Jews of Shushan, and that the ten sons of Haman be hanged.[6] Each victory gave a signal to the populace where the sympathies of the government lay.

Now we have a *kal ve-ḥomer* of the highest order. If after Esther revealed her origin, such fantastic efforts were necessary to secure the salvation of her people – who were the clear victims of slander, who could count among them the most loyal citizen of the Kingdom, Mordecai – then how vulnerable are we today in the Diaspora? Can we even imagine a replication of the circumstances that worked in favor of the Jews in the time of Mordecai and Esther?

If we are so vulnerable, then Mordecai's challenge to Esther, which marks the triumphant point of the Megillah – "and who knows whether it was just for such a time as this that you attained the royal position!" (Esther 4:14) – hits us with crushing poignancy. We must all regard

3. Esther 3:13.
4. Esther 8:10–12.
5. Esther 8:1.
6. Esther 8:11, 9:1–10.

ourselves as placed in a circumstance to respond immediately without hesitancy. Not responding is an opportunity forgone. Mordecai said to Esther that it was for this very reason she was made Queen, to intervene to help her people. Tomorrow, she may no longer be Queen and will not be able to do anything.

We are all Esthers, placed by Hashem in the world to accomplish a unique task in His *malkhut Shamayim*. We must respond with zeal, commitment, and alacrity, and never allow an opportunity to go by unanswered.

Days of Feasting and Joy

March 14, 1987

The miracle of Purim is celebrated for all time by means of "days of feasting and joy" (Esther 9:22). And how fitting this is. For it was the conduct of the Jewish people at the feast of Ahasuerus that is described at the very beginning of the Megillah that precipitated a crisis of existence for them, and it was the two feasts that Queen Esther arranged at the end of the Megillah that sealed the doom of our archenemy Haman.

The decree of genocide was laid upon the Persian Jews more than 2,300 years ago, our Sages tell us, because they participated in the party of Ahasuerus.[1] But what a harsh assessment. There were extenuating circumstances. The Jews, after all, were coerced to attend. According to one view, they brought along their own kosher food.[2] And some say

1. *Megillah* 12a.
2. R. Jacob Culi (Constantinople, ca. 1685–1732), *Me-Am Lo'ez*, Esther 1:5, trans. R. Shemuel Yerushalmi, *Yalkut Me-Am Lo'ez: Esther* (Jerusalem: Wagshal, 1974), 23. See also *Pirkei de-Rabbi Eliezer* 49; R. Samuel Eliezer b. Judah ha-Levi Edels (*Maharsha*, Poland, 1555–1631), *Ḥiddushei Halakhot ve-Aggadot*, *Megillah* 12a, s.v. "*la'asot ke-retzon ish va-ish.*"

that the motivation was to better appreciate the Feast of the Leviathan by comparison.[3]

Now, from the standpoint of an individual response, we may see extenuation. But from a nationalistic standpoint, it was nothing less than devastation. Ahasuerus made the party in the third year of his reign.[4] It marked the end of the seventy years since the prophecy of Jeremiah that the Temple would be rebuilt.[5] The party hence imparted a mocking statement to the Jewish people that God had abandoned them, that this promise was false. To rub in the statement, Ahasuerus donned the vestments of the *Kohen Gadol* and blatantly used the holy vessels of the Temple.[6] Participating in such a feast of mockery of Jewish destiny amounted to nothing less than idolatry!

It took a man possessed with the most sublime sense of national pride to feel the pain and ignominy of the failure of the Jewish people at that time. Only such a man would be desperately searching for an opportunity to make amends for this dastardly act. Only a grand act of loyalty to Hashem would make up for the travesty of participation in Ahasuerus' party.

The opportunity was quick to come. When Haman was expecting everyone to bow down to him, all the other Sages avoided him. But Mordecai was defiant and sought confrontation with him.[7]

It took a man of intense Jewish pride such as Mordecai, called *ha-Yehudi*, "the Jew," to detect the personalized response to an objectively nationalistic overture. Esther's offer to intervene on behalf of the Jewish people when she would be called seemed very sound and reasonable. After all, the Jewish people were in no immediate danger. The decree had been issued, but it would not become operative until a full eleven months later. Intervening now ran the risk of total failure. She desired nothing less than a successful mission.

3. R. Jacob Culi, *Yalkut Me-Am Lo'ez*, loc. cit. According to Tradition, Hashem will arrange a lavish feast for the righteous in the World to Come. The Leviathan and the *Shor ha-Bar* (wild ox) will be served. *Bava Batra* 75a.
4. Esther 1:3.
5. *Megillah* 11b (referencing Jeremiah 29:10).
6. *Megillah* 12a.
7. Esther 3:2.

But this did not satisfy Mordecai. He decides that this approach will not be enough to deliver the Jews from the decree. A double failure on the part of the Jews, participating in the party of Ahasuerus and the failure to defy Haman, meant that the mockery of the feast was still hanging over their heads. It would take a grand embrace of the entire Jewish people to arouse the compassion of Hashem, that is, to be concerned with even the Jew who lives in a distant province. Revocation of the decree might not come in time to save these Jews. Moreover, it had to be an embrace of the Jewish communities for all eternity. The natural intervention of a queen for her people, where she put herself in no danger in making her request, would surely evoke admiration and gratitude of the highest order from that generation, but it would never inspire future generations. It would not uplift the faith of future generations.

Esther learned her lesson well! When her life is miraculously spared after approaching the King without being called, she resists making an immediate plea to save her people. She realizes that to save the Jewish people, she must go full circle. She must transform what is a national issue for the King into a personal issue. The extermination of the Jews was undertaken because it served the Persian national interest, to remove an "*am mefuzar u-meforad*," "a people scattered and dispersed" (Esther 3:8).

By transforming the Jewish question from a national issue to a personal level, the Jew is humanized in the eyes of Ahasuerus. The Jew is no longer a composite portrait, but a person with feelings.

Esther would cause Ahasuerus' love for her to lead to a jealousy of Haman. She invited Haman to the party only to arouse Ahasuerus' jealousy.[8] The first party was for Ahasuerus: "the banquet that I have prepared for him" (Esther 5:4). The next party, to draw out the drama and suspense, is described as "for them" (Esther 5:8). Now Haman becomes part of the eternal triangle, the man who stands between Ahasuerus and the Queen. Because Haman makes Esther miserable, he must go. Perhaps this is the origin of the *hamantash*, the three-cornered cookie.

8. *Rashi* to Esther 5:4, s.v. "*yavo ha-melekh ve-Haman.*"

Let us merit to rejoice as the Jews of Persia rejoiced, with a new appreciation of their collective identity. "*La-Yehudim hayetah orah ve-simḥah ve-sasson viykar*," "the Jews had light, and gladness, and joy, and honor" (Esther 8:16). This phrase captures many aspects of our collective identity. *Orah* is Torah, *simḥah* is *Yom Tov*, *sasson* is *milah*, and *yakar* is *tefillin*.[9]

9. *Megillah* 16b.

Mi Hu Zeh ve-Ei-Zeh Hu?

March 18, 1989

In delving into the personality of Ahasuerus, our Sages dispute whether he should be regarded as a wise king or a foolish king. The dispute revolves around the advisability of his throwing a party for his distant provinces before he gave a party for his local subjects.[1]

It is astonishing that our Sages did not focus on the reaction of Ahasuerus to Esther's shocking revelation that she asks for her own life as her wish and her people as her request.[2] To this Ahasuerus responds, "*Mi hu zeh ve-ei zeh hu*?" "Who is this? Where is this one who dared to do so?" (Esther 7:5). Now, was annihilation of a whole people an ordinary, routine item on Ahasuerus' agenda? Did he have such a short memory?

1. *Megillah* 12a. According to the view that Ahasuerus was a clever king, he was wise to entertain his distant subjects first because he could win over the inhabitants of his own city at any time. According to the view that he was a foolish king, he should have entertained the inhabitants of his own city first so that if others rebelled against him, his local subjects would defend him.
2. Esther 7:3.

Rather than reflecting a dense intellect or a short memory, Ahasuerus' statement reflected the depths of the depravity of the enemies of our people. Ahasuerus' response reflected the success of the master slanderer, Haman, to depersonalize and dehumanize the Jewish people, reducing them to an abstraction and caricature, which in turn made despoliation and annihilation acceptable, even applaudable.

Haman began, "There is a certain people scattered abroad and dispersed among the peoples in all the provinces of your realm." The Jews manifest their humanity only as individuals, not as a single people, united and concerned about each other. Then the second stage, "Their laws are different from every other people's." In their individuality, they are peculiar. They cannot be useful to the empire. They cannot be integrated. They have no economic value. Then the next stage, "and they do not observe the King's laws." They are a threat to the empire. And finally, the hint of extermination – "It is not befitting for the King to tolerate them" (Esther 3:8).

In the argument, Haman anticipated by almost 2,500 years the diabolical plan of the Nazi regime. From 1933 to 1939, almost four hundred laws were passed to deal with the status of the Jew, for the purpose of dehumanizing the Jew. Starting in 1935 with the law that banned Jews from military service, then proceeding to the infamous Nuremberg Laws, which made it a crime for a non-Jew to marry a Jew, these laws made Jews second-class citizens.[3] Additional laws barred Jews from the civil services and the universities, and set quotas for Jewish physicians and lawyers. These laws made Jews lesser beings, dehumanizing them. It was then a small matter to proceed to Kristallnacht in 1938, and a slew of new laws that further dehumanized the Jew, requiring him to wear a yellow badge, imposing a special income tax on the Jews, prohibiting friendly relationships with Jews, setting special hours for Jews to shop.[4] No indignity was too trivial to legislate, even the law that Jews could not buy or sell books, or use a non-Jewish hairdresser![5] This dehumanization

3. Meyer Weinberg, *Because They Were Jews: A History of Antisemitism* (New York: Greenwood, 1986), 106–107.
4. Ibid., 109.
5. Ibid.

made it easier for the German people to accept expulsion, persecution, and then annihilation and the Final Solution.

Well, Esther had her answer to the big lie of *am mefuzar u-meforad*. Yes, she rejects the cowardly path of continuing to hide her Jewishness out of fear that Ahasuerus' love for her would abruptly turn into hatred when he would learn of her ethnic origin. She also rejects the path of caution of "I have not been summoned to come to the King for these past thirty days" (Esther 4:11). Instead, she readily risks her life for her fellow Jews. No social barrier here. The Queen risks her life for the commoners in the most distant provinces, as this was the only recourse, to act with such dispatch. The decree would not go into effect until almost a year later. The intervention was necessary only to save the most distant Jews because it was feared that there would not be enough time for the missives reversing the original decree to reach them.

And yes, Esther delivers a much more impassioned plea for her people than she does for herself, the plea of "*nafshi be-she'elati*," "let my life be granted to me as my request" (Esther 7:3). It is the culmination of a carefully crafted plea. It is her answer to Ahasuerus' question, "What is your request, Queen Esther? It shall be granted to you. And what is your petition? Even if it is until half of the kingdom, it shall be fulfilled" (Esther 7:2). Her plea for her people, *ammi be-vakkashati*, "let my people's lives be granted to me as my petition" (Esther 7:3), is her initiative – "*va-toseph Esther*," "Esther spoke again" (Esther 8:3). And for them she marshals all her resourcefulness, the whole gamut of human sentiment and manner of persuasion. She speaks, *va-tidabber*, persuasively (Esther 8:3). Then comes the expression of desperation and the tears of high tension: "She fell at his feet, and wept, and implored him" (Esther 8:3). All this to save her people.

What she accomplishes is to be the opposite of Haman. Haman's hatred for one person, Mordecai, translated into a hatred for *am Mordekhai*, the entire nation of Mordecai. But Esther transformed Ahasuerus' love for her into a love for her people. "For how can I bear to witness the disaster that will befall my people?! How can I bear to witness the extermination of my kindred?!" (Esther 8:6).

She tells him that without her people, she will perish. Life for her is unthinkable without her people. She will be nothing but a demoralized vegetable without them. This is what humanizes the Jewish people for Ahasuerus and enables him to have sympathy for them. This point transforms the Jewish people from a caricature back to people of human qualities.

The coupling of the annihilation of Esther with the decree of Jewish annihilation is what throws Ahasuerus off. He would never associate the perishing of his object of love with the destruction of the people that he regarded as merely an abstraction and caricature.

Esther gave humanity even to the individual Jew in the distant provinces because it was for him that the urgency existed. Hence, she was the opposite of Haman who gave abstraction and caricature to even the Jew who was Ahasuerus' great benefactor, Mordecai.

Shabbat Parah

The Privilege Element of *Ḥok*

March 25, 1989

The concept of *ḥok* conjures up the image of the thickening of the Heavenly yoke, blind adherence to the commands of Hashem, even if their logic eludes us or is contrary to our basic intuition. This approach to *ḥok*, I submit, is only a half-truth and represents misplaced emphasis.

Today, in *Parashat Parah*, we focus on the *ḥok* of *parah adummah*.[1] But to shatter the erroneous concept that *ḥok* centers on responsibility and duty, the *haftarah* makes us aware of the privilege aspect of *ḥok*.

Ezekiel prophesizes that we will be driven from the Land of Israel and our exile will constitute a *ḥillul ha-Shem*. "They desecrated My holy Name when it was said of them, 'These are the people of Hashem, but

1. The *maftir* for *Parashat Parah* is at Numbers 19:1–22, which describes the laws of the *parah adummah*.

they departed His land'" (Ezekiel 36:20). The nations will jeer at us and say that the people who claim that they are special, that they are the Chosen People, have sinned egregiously and have been, in consequence, driven from their land. This constitutes a *ḥillul Hashem.*

But Ezekiel tells us that we will be restored even without merit. "I will sanctify My great Name that is desecrated among the nations" (Ezekiel 36:23). This is nothing less than a *ḥok.* It violates the normal rules that we are taught, that the punishment for *ḥillul Hashem* is death.[2] At the very least, this means diminished expectations for the future. But we will be restored.

Nahmanides explains that we are Hashem's link to mankind. Man was created only so that he should apprehend divinity.[3] But none of the nations acknowledge Hashem. Only we do. So any sin that we commit will not destroy our inner core of holiness. We will still be worthy of our mission of being a "light unto the nations."[4]

But the *ḥok* continues because not only will we be restored, but Hashem will spare us the disgrace of the nations, and the Land of Israel will be amazingly productive.

And the *ḥok* will continue because Ezekiel tells us that Hashem will remove our stone hearts. "I will give you a new heart and put a new spirit within you" (Ezekiel 36:26).

And the *ḥok* continues in that the Land of Israel will be rebuilt.

It behooves us to find the privilege element of *ḥok* on the personal level as well. We find this in connection with *teshuvah.* The Jerusalem Talmud tells us of an amazing dialogue with regard to what should become of the sinner.[5] *Ḥokhmah* (wisdom) says that it is hopeless. Man is a creature of habit. Once caught in the net of sin, there is no hope. Yes, *teshuvah* is there, but man will never avail himself of it.

Nevuah (prophecy) says that *teshuvah* is possible only by suffering death of some sort, such as diminished expectations for the future, and a diminished quality of life.

---

2. Maimonides (*Rambam,* Egypt, 1135–1204), *Mishnah Torah, Teshuvah* 1:4.
3. Nahmanides (*Ramban,* Spain, 1194–1270) to Deuteronomy 32:26, s.v. "*ashbisah me-enosh zikhram.*"
4. Isaiah 42:6, 49:6.
5. Jerusalem Talmud, *Makkot* 2:6.

And finally, the Torah says that the sinner is redeemable but only by bringing a guilt offering. *Teshuvah* entails the eradication of our past, which carries with it heavy guilt and the severing of even cherished relationships.[6]

But Hashem says that *teshuvah* redeems the sinner without a *korban* and without death because *teshuvah* can be out of love of Hashem, which, in the words of Resh Lakish, results in *ha-zedonot na'asot lo ke-zekhuyyot*, "the intentional sins become considered as merits."[7]

This is indeed a *ḥok* of unparalleled proportions, that the sinner is conferred a bonus! The explanation, according to R. Joseph B. Soloveitchik, is that every Jew longs to be closer to Hashem and do His will. This is the essence of the Jew. This is his inner core. Sinning squashes this longing for holiness. Repentance therefore acts as a dynamic force, energizing the individual with a zeal and zest to do Hashem's will, a zeal that he never had before, a vigor that he never had before.[8]

This notion is encapsulated in the mitzvah of *haramat ha-deshen*, the "lifting of the ashes," symbolic of the residue of the sins of those who repented.[9] The ashes are elevated and then deposited on the east side of the Altar, becoming part of the Altar itself, which means no reduced expectations for the future.

The privilege aspect of *ḥok* not only supplies us with our sense of destiny, with confidence and optimism for the future. It is also a powerful unifying force because the sinner of today is capable of being transformed – *ha-zedonot na'asot lo ke-zekhuyyot. Mah she-ya'aseh ha-zeman lo ya'aseh ha-sekhel*, "what time will do, the intellect would not do!"[10]

---

6. *Yalkut Shimoni*, Ezekiel 358.
7. *Yoma* 86b.
8. Pinchas H. Peli, *On Repentance: In the Thought and Oral Discourses of Rabbi Joseph B. Soloveitchik* (Jerusalem: Oroth, 1980), 275.
9. Leviticus 6:3; R. Menahem b. Moses Bavli (Safed, 16th cent.), *Ta'amei Mitzvot, mitzvat aseh* no. 59.
10. For examples of use of the exact phrase, see R. Natan Friedland (Lithuania, 1808–1883), *Kos Yeshuah ve-Neḥamah, Kos Tar'elah* 1:4; R. Mosheh Meir Yashar, *He-Ḥafetz Ḥayyim be-Netivot ha-Tefillah* (Jerusalem: Mekhon Ḥatam Sofer, 1974), 77. An earlier formulation is "*mah she-ya'aseh ha-zeman ya'aseh ha-sekhel.*" See R. Isaac b. Joseph Caro (Spain, 1458–1535), *Toledot Yitzḥak, Va-Yeshev*, s.v. "*va-yima'en le-hitneḥam*"; R. Jair Hayyim

The *ḥok* is truly the *netzaḥ she-be-netzaḥ*, the twenty-fifth *sidrah* of the Torah, the eternity of the eternity of the Jewish people![11]

b. Moses Samson Bacharach (*Ḥavvot Yair*, Germany, 1638–1702), *She'elot u-Teshuvot Ḥut ha-Shani* (Frankfurt am Main, 1679), no. 97, p. 112b.

11. The mitzvah of *haramat ha-deshen* is found in *Parashat Tzav*, at Leviticus 6:3. *Parashat Tzav* is the twenty-fifth *parashah* in the Torah. *Netzaḥ she-be-netzaḥ* is the twenty-fifth level of the *Sefirot*.

Shabbat ha-Ḥodesh

Elevating and Exalting the Beginning

March 28, 1987

The month of Nisan is governed by a divine providence. Even if our enemies hatch a plan against us, not only will it not succeed, but it will be the basis of a blessing. And why? Because in this month at the time of the Exodus, the entire natural order was turned aside. We experienced redemption after hopelessness.

We can always effect renewal of the entire Jewish nation just by emulating what Hashem did for us in this month, simply by emulating *ka-zeh re'eh ve-kaddesh,*" "see it like this and sanctify it."[1] We must sanctify the forsaken man whom nobody thinks of.

1. The Midrash explains that when Hashem informed Moses regarding the requirement to sanctify the New Moon, Moses was uncertain of the precise size that the moon must appear in the sky for it to be fit to be sanctified. Hashem therefore showed Moses the moon with His finger, so to speak, and said, "See it like this and sanctify it." *Mekhilta de-Rav Shimon bar Yoḥai* to Exodus 12:2; R. Solomon b. Isaac (*Rashi*, France, 1040–1105), *Rashi* to Exodus 12:2, s.v. "*ha-zeh.*"

We are reminded of this in *barkhi nafshi* (Psalms 104). We are told, "*ḥasidah beroshim beitah*," "among the cypresses is the home of the stork" (Psalms 104:17). *Radak* explains that this psalm illustrates that even the lowest level of creation serves a purpose for higher levels of creation. The stork, a *ḥai*, rests on a tree, a *tzome'aḥ*, which is on a lower level in the hierarchy of creation.[2] Increasing the bonds of friendship or strengthening family ties does not rejuvenate society. But reaching out to the forsaken man will uplift the whole society and all relationships will become close.

Also, we must sanctify the beginning of knowledge. Society must give priority to Jewish education. We should not be fascinated only with the Nobel Prize. We should make the necessary sacrifices so that elementary education is a high priority item in our spending. If the typical *rebbe* must take on two jobs or even a third, what effect will this have on his productivity? If we would esteem primary education, then our aspiration for higher education would expand.

We are told that three things were made difficult for Moses to understand until Hashem showed him the prototype of the object: the size of the New Moon at the first moment when it may be sanctified; the forbidden species of *sheratzim*;[3] and the design of the Menorah.[4] It would seem that after they were shown to Moses, he understood some aspect of their inter-relationship.

In today's world, we can easily confuse the *sheratzim* for the Menorah. It is only when we recognize good in its incipient stage, symbolized by the New Moon, that we can learn to make distinctions and really separate the *sheratzim* from the Menorah.

---

2. R. David Kimhi (*Radak*, Provence, ca. 1160–ca. 1235), *Radak* to Psalms 104:17.
3. *Sheratzim* are animals that slither along the ground or appear to do so because they have short legs and their movement is not readily noticeable. See *Rashi* to Genesis 1:24 and Leviticus 11:41.
4. *Menaḥot* 29a; Numbers Rabbah 15:4.

Preparation for the Permanent Renewal

March 19, 1988

The further in time we are removed from a momentous event, the more difficult it is to recapture its aura. We stand now more than twenty years from the electrifying triumph of the Six-Day War. World Jewry basked then in a glamour, religious nationalism, and sense of destiny.

Today, more than twenty years later, we are experiencing a profound anguish in the aftermath of the armed struggle in the Arab uprisings, the riots, and the seeming impasse that we have reached with the reaction of the governmental authorities. The official policy of beatings and deportation has prompted some of our brethren to distance themselves from the policy, claiming that this constitutes moral courage.[1]

If we are now groping to find the key to recapture the spirit of '67, perhaps we should refer to today's *haftarah*. Here, we find that we should

1. Alan Cowell, "Prominent U.S. Jews, Visiting Israel, Voice Unease," *New York Times*, March 2, 1988, 3.

prepare for the Third Temple, the *beit olamim* that will be a restoration after which we will never revert to exile or defeat. It will therefore be a renewal that will never be lost.

Now, all *ḥanukkot* (inaugurations) are celebrated with the offering of sacrifices. The types of animals offered for sacrifice, as well as their number, carry, according to R. Samson Raphael Hirsch, a symbolic meaning.[2] Generally, for the Festivals, the Torah prescribes sacrifices from three types of animals: the *ayal* (ram), the *par* (bullock), and the *keves* (lamb). The ram is the mature and strong animal, the one that goes to the head of the herd, displaying the personality of leadership. The bullock is the work animal, symbolizing toil in the service of Hashem. And the lamb represents passive acceptance of guidance and direction from Hashem.

The number of each animal prescribed for the offerings, R. Hirsch tells us, will be one, two, or seven. One symbolizes the nation as a collective, a perfect unity. Two represents the multiplicity of the nations, signifying the individuality of each nation. And finally, seven is really six plus one. Six represents the first six days of the week, the realm of the material and the physical, but linked to Hashem.[3]

Now, if we relate R. Hirsch's theory to the image of the Third Temple described in Ezekiel, we are shocked to find a major departure from the order of sacrifices as the *ḥanukkah* stretches from the eve of Passover to the end of Sukkot.[4] And we surprisingly find a recurrence of the number six.

First we encounter the significant fact that the *korban pesaḥ* is not to be brought from a lamb but rather from a bullock.[5] Perhaps the significance is that unlike the Exodus from Egypt – which involved *mesirut nefesh* by the Children of Israel in their submission to Hashem, but was orchestrated by Moses, and they received clear-cut instructions – the preparation for the Third Temple will, at least in the initial stage, not

2. R. Samson Raphael Hirsch (Germany, 1808–1888), Numbers 29:13; *Haftarat Parashat ha-Ḥodesh.*
3. Ibid., Numbers 29:13.
4. Ezekiel 45:21–25.
5. Ibid., v. 22; R. Hirsch, *Haftarat Parashat ha-Ḥodesh.*

be orchestrated. There will not even be a single leader to whom we will all look. Instead, all we will be able to do is devote our energies to persevere and work for the service of Hashem.

When we come to the Sabbath, which symbolizes a routinized mode, we find the *korbanot* to include six lambs,[6] because we will face the mesmerizing attraction of the status quo. It will be comfortable to be suspended between the past and the promise of peace in the future. We can defer the important decisions. But it is precisely in this state of calm, the conditions of status quo, that we must elicit the leadership quality, to move forward with a positive progress. Hence, the addition of a *korban* from one *par*.

Then we find the *korbanot* of Rosh Ḥodesh. Here we are dealing with a breakthrough, a sign of renewal. Again, we are confronted with six lambs.[7] Everyone is willing to latch on to an imaginary momentum that will somehow carry us forward to the next step. But this is why we cannot be *mesiaḥ da'at*. No! We must build upon every achievement. The *par* aspect of the national character must advance and build on the past successes with action and follow-up. Hence, again, we have a *korban* from one *par*.

But now we reach the framework for negotiations with our enemies! This is discerned by looking at the set of offerings prescribed for Sukkot. Normally, there are thirteen bullocks, two rams, and fourteen lambs.[8] This set is, as R. Hirsch points out, in reality two sets – seven, one, and seven; and six, one, and seven, setting up a contrast between us and the nations of the world.[9] The contrast, however, diminishes as we move through the Festival of Sukkot, as the bullocks are progressively decreased. What we are saying is that we are projecting our enemies into the Messianic era, when they will be transformed and become redeemable. Israel will have its mission, the Sinaitic covenant, and the nations of the world, the Noahide covenant.

---

6. Ezekiel 46:4.
7. Ezekiel 46:6.
8. Numbers 29:13.
9. R. Hirsch, Numbers 29:13.

This optimistic, visionary view of our enemies does not take place in the Sukkot of the *ḥanukkah* of the Third Temple.[10] Nay! The number of bullocks never changes. In this era, in preparing for the inauguration of the Third Temple, we must adopt a realistic view of our enemy, never to underestimate it.

There are those who would ask nothing more than to be relieved of the anguish of the moment and capitulate with some form of unilateral concessions. But that cannot be. We must have minimum conditions for beginning negotiations. We must have a true, sincere negotiation partner, one who gives us first a *quid pro quo,* a party that will offer peace in return for what we give up. It must be a party that is not a cover or a conduit for a group that is bent upon our destruction. And finally, it must be someone who will guarantee the peace that follows.

We have no choice other than to devote the *par* and the *ayal* character of the Jewish nation toward producing and finding the sincere partner. When that happens, the *par* and *ayal* will be transformed into a *keves,* and we will feel intensely a renewed sense of destiny.

---

10. See Ezekiel 45:25.

Shabbat ha-Gadol

Bridging the Generation Gap

April 14, 1984

According to Tradition, Elijah visits the Jewish home on two occasions: one, at every *brit milah*,[1] and also during the Seder.[2] It is Elijah who will bridge the generation gap. "He will turn back [to God] the hearts of fathers with their sons and the hearts of sons with their fathers" (Malachi 3:24).

Now, Elijah seems like an unlikely intimate guest, as he is a zealot.[3] Would not Aaron, who is a lover and pursuer of peace,[4] be a much

1. *Pirkei de-Rabbi Eliezer* 29; Zohar, *Lekh Lekha* 1:93a.
2. It is customary to place a cup of wine on the Seder table for Elijah the Prophet. See R. Jacob b. Joseph Reischer (Prague, ca. 1670–1733), *Ḥok Yaakov*, end of *siman* 480; R. Hayyim b. Israel Benveniste (*Ba'al Knesset ha-Gedolah*, Smyrna, 1603–1673), *Pesaḥ Me'uvin*, ¶ 182; R. Moses Hagiz (*Maharam Ḥagiz*, 1672–ca. 1751), *She'elot u-Teshuvot Shetei ha-Leḥem*; R. Hayyim Palaggi (Smyrna, 1788–1869), *Mo'ed le-Khol Ḥai* 4:30.
3. I Kings 19:10.
4. Mishnah, *Avot* 1:12.

more appropriate guest? Moreover, it appears that Elijah to some extent failed in his mission. The high point of his career occurred on Mount Carmel. There, he offered a contrast between himself on the one hand and the 450 prophets of the Baal on the other hand. Twin bulls were selected. The prophets of the Baal could not manage to cause a fire to descend to consume their bull. "There was neither sound nor response" (I Kings 18:26). Elijah ordered that a trench be built on his altar, filled with water. Then he prayed, "Answer me, Hashem, answer me" (I Kings 18:37). It was at this point that Elijah reached the zenith of his career, when all the people pronounced, "Hashem, He is the God! Hashem, He is the God!" (I Kings 18:39).

Now, was this a permanent victory? Did it provoke mass conversions? No! Immediately after this, Jezebel tells Elijah that she will kill him as she did the 450 prophets of the Baal.[5] Elijah flees and barely escapes with his life. He finally gets to the cave in Mount Carmel, and then Hashem asks him, "Why are you here, Elijah?" (I Kings 19:9). Was he not shocked at this question? He answers, "I have acted with great zeal for Hashem, God of Legions, for the Children of Israel have forsaken Your covenant" (I Kings 19:10). At this point, Elijah is assigned to appear at every *brit milah* and report on the merit of the Jewish people.[6]

To summarize Elijah's approach, he was very sensitive to evil and disillusioned with sinners. To counteract this, he wanted to do nothing less than recreate the Exodus from Egypt and the Splitting of the Sea of Reeds, that is, completely change the natural order, and create an aura of certitude. The way to deal with evil is with open confrontation.

Elijah needs to be re-educated regarding all these points. With respect to the disillusionment, the *brit milah* testifies to the Jewish people's commitment to Hashem.

With respect to our certitude, we have the Wise Son's question, "What are the testimonies, and the decrees, and the ordinances that Hashem, our God, commanded you [*etkhem*]?" (Deuteronomy 6:20). This is a general question, asking for the categorization of mitzvot. But the author of the Haggadah applies it to the *korban pesaḥ*. The Wise Son

5. I Kings 19:2.
6. *Pirkei de-Rabbi Eliezer* 29; Zohar, *Lekh Lekha* 1:93a.

is a tough guy who seeks a profound understanding of the mitzvot. First he wants to understand how the mitzvah is a testimony regarding the bond between Hashem and the Jewish people. The Wise Son is therefore interested in not just the mechanical performance of the mitzvot but also their symbolic meaning. Then he is interested in finding out what he does not know. The *korban pesaḥ* is called a *ḥok*, but certainly it is understood. The Children of Israel aimed to nullify the *avodah zarah* of the Egyptians.[7]

But the Wise Son wants to find an element that he does not understand in the *pesaḥ*. He wants to find *mishpat* in the *pesaḥ* as well. This is how a *mitzvah bein adam la-Makom* relates to *bein adam le-ḥavero*. The Wise Son understands that the Torah is interpreted as a whole.

These are very tough demands on the teacher. In fact, if the teacher himself is an *eino yode'a lish'ol*, that is, he is incapable of asking the right questions, he might regard the Wise Son as the Wicked Son. After all, he could easily seize upon the word "*etkhem*," "you" (Deuteronomy 6:20), that the Wise Son uses, which makes him akin to the Wicked Son who uses the phrase "*lakhem*," "to you" (Exodus 12:26).

But the teacher must understand that the question springs from the Wise Son's passion for learning the mitzvot. Accordingly, the approach to him must be like the laws of the *pesaḥ* – *ein maftirin aḥar ha-pesaḥ afikoman*,[8] that one may not eat anything after the *pesaḥ*.[9] This is intended to show the *ḥavivut ha-mitzvah*. This is how the teacher should understand the probing of the Wise Son. The Wise Son wants to remain with a taste of the *pesaḥ* in his mouth, something that he can always savor.

To illustrate the inherent danger of certitude, we look at the Wicked Son. The Wicked Son takes what appears as logical, the *korban pesaḥ*, and is sure that he understands it totally, and complains, "What is this service to you?" (Exodus 12:26). The *Beit ha-Levi* says that the Wicked Son is very sophisticated. He does not want to nullify the mitzvot.[10] No. He wants only to introduce something irrelevant.

---

7. *Pesikta de-Rav Kahana, Parashat ha-Ḥodesh* 23, s.v. "*dabru*"; *Yalkut Shimoni, Bo* 191.
8. *Haggadah, Maggid*; *Mekhilta, Bo* 18, s.v. "*ve-hayah ki yish'alekha*."
9. Mishnah, *Pesaḥim* 10:8; *Pesaḥim* 119b.
10. R. Yosef Dov Soloveitchik (*Beit ha-Levi*, Belarus, 1820–1892), *Beit ha-Levi al Derush u-Milei de-Aggadata* (Jerusalem, 1985), *Bo*, s.v. "*ve-higgadeta le-vinkha*."

The Wicked Son does not get an answer. We blunt his teeth by teaching the Son Who Does Not Know How to Ask. Both the Wicked Son and the Son Who Does Not Know How to Ask get the same answer.[11] By upgrading society's moral climate, the Wicked Son will disappear.

The Simple Son asks, "*Mah zot*?," "What is this?" (Exodus 13:14). During the Seder, as the *Keli Yakar* points out, the Simple Son is being fed exotic foods and delicacies, so he asks nothing.[12] But the next day, *maḥar*, when he is asked to redeem his firstborn, he asks, "*Mah zot*?" He does not want to part with the five coins. This goes beyond *derekh ha-melitzah* (satire) because what best arouses someone's curiosity is not being a passive spectator, but real involvement on a personal and financial basis.

Two of the questions, those of the Wise Son and the Simple Son, are asked *maḥar* to show that the Four Sons are really cyclical.[13] The same child who is today the Wicked Son can someday be the Wise Son. There might *ḥas ve-shalom* be a retrogression. If the Wise Son is rebuffed, he might turn into the Wicked Son. The Wicked Son might then lose interest, and turn into the Simple Son. The Simple Son could then be lost completely, becoming the Son Who Does Not Know How to Ask.

But indeed the reverse is also possible. The Son Who Does Not Know How to Ask could become the Wicked Son, which is a slight reversion, but eventually could become the Wise Son.

Yesh maḥar she-hu aḥar zeman, "there is a tomorrow that is after a long period of time."[14] So patience is needed in bridging the generation gap.

---

11. In the Haggadah, the answer to the Wicked Son and the Son Who Does Not Know How to Ask is: "It is because of this that Hashem acted on my behalf when I left Egypt" (Exodus 13:8). The answer provided to the Wicked Son in the Torah, by contrast, is: "It is a *pesaḥ* feast offering to Hashem Who passed over the houses of the Children of Israel in Egypt when He smote the Egyptians, but He saved our households" (Exodus 12:27). See R. Ephraim Solomon b. Aaron of Luntshits (*Keli Yakar*, Łęczyca, 1550–1619), *Keli Yakar* to Exodus 12:26.
12. *Keli Yakar* to Exodus 13:14.
13. R. Isaac Nissenbaum (Poland, 1868–1942), *Hagut Lev* (Vilna: L. Apel, 1910), 142–144; R. Mosheh Yaakov Weingarten, *Ha-Seder ha-Arukh* (Jerusalem: Otzer ha-Mo'adim, 2011), 143.
14. R. Solomon b. Isaac (*Rashi*, France, 1040–1105), *Rashi* to Deuteronomy 6:20.

Passover – First Days

The Blood Shall Be a Sign for You

April 17, 1984

The climactic moment of *ge'ullah*, the midnight event of the slaying of the Egyptian firstborn, is described by the Torah and the author of the Haggadah as singular, as something set apart from the *ge'ullah* process up to this point. No intermediary of any kind was involved here. "Not through an angel, not through a seraph, and not through a messenger, but the Holy One, Blessed is He, He alone, in His Glory."[1]

Now, given the uniqueness and singularity of the event of the Plague of the Firstborn, the preparations that the Children of Israel were instructed to make in anticipation of the event are quite perplexing. The Children of Israel were instructed to slaughter a lamb for the *korban pesaḥ*, dip a bundle of hyssop in the blood, and smear the blood

1. *Haggadah, Maggid.*

on the two doorposts and the lintel.[2] For what purpose? "I will see the blood and I shall pass over you" (Exodus 12:13).

But did the Holy One, Blessed is He, need any signs to identify the Jewish home? *Rashi* provides us with the answer to this question. We were told, "The blood shall be a sign for you" (Exodus 12:13). *Rashi* explains, "for you it shall be a sign, but not for others a sign."[3] The sign was not for the public. Instead, it was intended as a sign for each Jew. The blood, as *Rashi* explains, had to be smeared not in the public domain, but rather on the inner doorpost and the inner lintel.

But what was the nature of the inner sign? We were asked to make the symbolism of the *pesaḥ* touch the private, inner recesses of our heart.

The *pesaḥ* was a paradoxical symbol. On the one hand, it represented the deity of the Egyptians.[4] And on the other hand, as the *Maharal* points out, it represented the perfect harmony and unity of *Knesset Yisrael*.[5] Every aspect of the service of the *pesaḥ* indicates this. The *pesaḥ* had to be slaughtered in a *ḥaburah* (group).[6] It had to be eaten in a *ḥaburah*.[7] It had to be a lamb,[8] which is an extremely sensitive animal. If one limb is injured, the entire lamb feels the pain acutely.[9] The *pesaḥ* had to be eaten only *tzeli esh*, "roasted," which would preserve its wholeness, rather than cooked in water, which would cause it to disintegrate.[10] And even a bone could not be broken,[11] as breaking bones symbolizes discord.[12]

2. Exodus 12:7, 12:22.
3. R. Solomon b. Isaac (*Rashi*, France, 1040–1105), *Rashi* to Exodus 12:13.
4. Exodus 8:22; *Rashi* ad loc., s.v. "*to'avat Mitzrayim*"; Exodus Rabbah 16:3.
5. R. Judah Loew b. Bezalel (*Maharal*, Prague, ca. 1525–1609), *Gevurot Hashem*, ch. 60.
6. Mishnah, *Pesaḥim* 8:7 (opinion of R. Judah); *Pesaḥim* 64a–b, 91a; *Rashi* to Exodus 12:6, s.v. "*kehal adat Yisrael*"; Maimonides (*Rambam*, Egypt, 1135–1204), *Mishnah Torah, Korban Pesaḥ* 1:9–11, 2:2; R. Joseph Caro (Safed, 1488–1575), *Kesef Mishneh* to *Mishnah Torah, Korban Pesaḥ* 2:2.
7. Exodus 12:46; *Rashi* ad loc., s.v. "*be-vayit eḥad ye'akhel*"; *Pesaḥim* 86a; *Mishneh Torah, Korban Pesaḥ* 9:1.
8. Exodus 12:3.
9. Leviticus Rabbah 4:6.
10. Exodus 12:8.
11. Exodus 12:46.
12. *Maharal, Gevurot Hashem*, ch. 60.

And the *pesaḥ* symbolizes the perfect unity of the *Ribbono shel Olam*. The *pesaḥ* must be eaten with matzah and *maror*.[13] It is the same God Who brings the servitude (*maror*) Who brings the *ge'ullah* (matzah). *Hu ha-Moḥetz, Hu ha-Rofeh*, "He is the inflictor, He is the healer."[14]

Taking all these factors together, the *pesaḥ* appears to symbolize that the false belief in idolatry can be defeated only by *Knesset Yisrael* in unison. When the false belief dissipates, we will realize the Oneness of the Al-Mighty and His inseparable bond with us.

The bringing of the *korban pesaḥ* marked the formation of *Knesset Yisrael*. As the *Or Same'aḥ* points out, the *korban pesaḥ* was in fact a *korban gerut*, the offering of a convert.[15] The formation of *Knesset Yisrael* at that historic moment was, however, a spontaneous event. The command of Hashem through Moses and Aaron to bring the offering was given to the entire people.[16] Though it demanded nothing less than risking their very lives to demonstrate their devotion, the spectacular Plagues that preceded the command of the *korban pesaḥ* certainly emboldened the Jewish people to carry out the command, and in the process, bring into being *Knesset Yisrael* for the first time.

The blood of the *pesaḥ* had to be spread on the inner doorpost and the inner lintel because the Jew needed a strong symbol that he could not rely upon spontaneity in the formation of the community in the future. Indeed, the magnificent achievement of space exploration by the United States in the 1960s and the British recapture of the Falkland

13. Exodus 12:8; Numbers 9:11.

14. Cf. Deuteronomy 32:39; Job 5:18; R. Moses Isserles (*Rema*, Poland, 1525 or 1530–1572), *She'elot u-Teshuvot ha-Rema*, no. 20.

15. R. Meir Simhah ha-Kohen of Dvinsk (*Or Same'aḥ* or *Meshekh Ḥokhmah*, Latvia, 1843–1926), *Meshekh Ḥokhmah* to Numbers 9:7, s.v. "*ve-yitakhen*" (referencing *Or Same'aḥ* on Maimonides, *Mishneh Torah, Meḥusrei Kapparah* 1:2). In general, in the time of the Temple, a convert to Judaism was prohibited from eating *kodashim*, "portions of sacrificial offerings," until he brought a *korban gerut*, even if he had undergone circumcision and performed ritual immersion. *Keritot* 8b. If he was circumcised on the eve of Passover, however, he was permitted to partake of the paschal offering without bringing a *korban gerut*. See *Pesaḥim* 92a. The *Meshekh Ḥokhmah* finds support for this exception in that the Children of Israel partook of the paschal offering without first bringing a *korban gerut*.

16. Exodus 12:3.

Islands after its invasion by Argentina created a surge of nationalism and jingoism in those countries.[17] Similarly, an external threat of war unites a people and makes them aware that they are not merely a collection of individuals, but a nation.

The Jew must be different. He cannot rely on spontaneity to form his awareness of *Knesset Yisrael.* He must always be ready to take the initiative to form the *tzibbur* himself. To drive home this concept, the Jew was bidden to sprinkle the blood in the inner, secret, hidden part of his home, reminding him that it is the individual's responsibility to form the *klal.*

According to our Sages, the two doorposts symbolize Isaac and Jacob, while the lintel symbolizes Abraham.[18] Following on this theme, the Jew must imagine himself as Isaac although he feels adversity and envy. He must take the initiative in forming the *tzibbur*. He must imagine himself as Jacob, who in his lifetime had many setbacks, but was never fazed. Though he did not experience a steady progression, he thrusted onward.

But the Jew's obligation in forming the *tzibbur* goes even to "*ve-higga'tten el ha-mashkof*" (Exodus 12:22), reaching the lintel, which is symbolic of our Forefather Abraham. Now, we know that Jacob is usually regarded as the *beḥir ha-Avot*, "the choicest of the Patriarchs."[19] Why, then, is Abraham symbolized by the lintel? The answer must be that the Jew's obligation in forming the *tzibbur*, in taking the initiative in this regard, extends even to imagining himself to be Abraham, who stood *be-ever eḥad*, "on one side," and the world on another side.[20] He stood

17. See Andrew Chaikin, "Live from the Moon: The Societal Impact of Apollo," in *Societal Impact of Spaceflight*, eds. Steven J. Dick and Roger D. Launius (Washington, DC: Government Printing Office, 2007), 54; Jean Houbert, "The Falklands: A Hiccup of Decolonisation," *Current Research on Peace and Violence* 5, no. 1 (1982): 15; Carlos Escudé, "Argentine Territorial Nationalism," *Journal of Latin American Studies* 20, no. 1 (May 1988): 139. In April 1982, Argentina seized the Falkland Islands from the United Kingdom. British administration was restored two months later at the end of the Falklands War.
18. Exodus Rabbah 1:36.
19. Genesis Rabbah 76:1.
20. Abraham is referred to in the Torah as the "*Ivri*" (עברי). Genesis 14:13. The Midrash interprets this term to signify that Abraham stood on one side (עבר אחד) and the world on another side. Genesis Rabbah 42:8 (opinion of R. Judah).

alone. Because he stood alone, he could not rely on anyone; the onus was entirely upon him. To such an extent is the individual's responsibility to establish the *tzibbur.*

The ritual of spreading the blood on the lintel and the two doorposts was done only in connection with the *korban pesaḥ* in Egypt. All subsequent paschal offerings dispense with this requirement.[21] But there is always a reminder of the *ever eḥad* aspect of communal responsibility. We were saved from Egypt in the merit of the blood of the *pesaḥ* and in the merit of the blood of circumcision.[22] At every *brit milah,* we give the *rakh ha-nimmul* (lit., "the tender circumcised one") the blessing "May God make you like Ephraim and Manasseh" (Genesis 48:20).[23]

Now, since the aspiration of the Jew is always for *ge'ullah,* what kind of blessing is this? Do we wish that the child be brought up among gentiles, in the forty-nine levels of impurity?

The answer is that we are speaking to the responsibility of the parents. We are telling the father: Do not imagine that someone else will assume responsibility to educate your child in Torah values. Do not abrogate your responsibility, no matter that there are *yeshivot* and a good moral climate. Imagine that you are Joseph bringing up his sons Ephraim and Manasseh in Egypt, who could not rely on anyone else.

---

21. Mishnah, *Pesaḥim* 9:5; Abraham b. Meir ibn Ezra (Ibn Ezra, Spain, 1089–1164), Ibn Ezra to Exodus 12:24.

22. *Pirkei de-Rabbi Eliezer* 29 (interpreting the repetition of the phrase "in your blood you shall live" at Ezekiel 16:6 as a reference to the blood of circumcision and the blood of the *pesaḥ*); *Mekhilta, Bo* 5; Exodus Rabbah 17:3, 19:5; *Targum Yonatan,* Exodus 12:13; *Rashi* to Exodus 12:6, s.v. "*ve-hayah lakhem le-mishmeret.*"

23. *Targum Yonatan,* Genesis 48:20; R. Shalom Perlow (Belarus, 1850–1925), *Mishmeret Shalom* 18:10. See also R. Menahem b. Solomon (*Meiri,* Perpignan, 1249–1316), *Midrash Sekhel Tov,* Genesis 48:20 (stating that the blessing "May God make you like Ephraim and Manasseh" is implicit in the statement "*zeh ha-katan gadol yihiyeh,*" "this little one, great may he become," recited as the *brit milah*); R. Dovid Kviat (Brooklyn, 1920–2009), *Sukkat David* (Jerusalem, 2008), *Brit Milah,* p. 47, ¶ 6 (explaining that the blessing is implicit in the statement "just as he has entered into the covenant, so may he enter into the study of Torah, the marriage canopy, and the performance of good deeds").

Emet ve-Yatziv and *Emet ve-Emunah*

April 18, 1984

Recounting the Exodus, which takes the form of a special mitzvah on the night of the Seder, is not a separate mitzvah the entire year, but rather part of the mitzvah of the recitation of *Shema*. It takes the form of reciting the third paragraph of *va-yomer*, in which the Exodus is mentioned.[1]

In regard to the recitation of *Shema*, our Sages tell us that he who does not recite *emet ve-yatziv*, "true and fair," in the morning, and *emet ve-emunah*, "true and faithful," in the evening, does not fulfill his obligations.[2] Analysis of these two texts reveals a fundamental difference between them. The morning text of *emet ve-yatziv* speaks in the past tense

1. Numbers 15:37–41. The Exodus is mentioned at Numbers 15:41 ("I am Hashem, your God, Who has removed you from the land of Egypt to be a God unto you; I am Hashem your God.").
2. *Berakhot* 12a.

and recounts the miracles that Hashem wrought for us, beginning with "from Egypt You redeemed us, Hashem, our God, and from the house of slavery You liberated us. All their firstborn You slew, but Your firstborn You redeemed; You split the Sea of Reeds."[3] In contrast, the *emet ve-emunah* text is written in the form of continuous action. We express the hope that these miracles, which were the substance of *emet ve-yatziv*, will continue in the future, that we will continue to be the beneficiaries of this special divine providence. "He is the One Who redeems us from the power of kings, our King Who delivers us from the hand of all the cruel tyrants."[4]

We often have a tendency to compartmentalize these two texts, believing that the era of *emet ve-yatziv* is over and we now find ourselves in the inferior era of *emet ve-emunah*. A little reflection, however, reveals that the two texts must be integrated. Unless we connect *emet ve-emunah* to *emet ve-yatziv*, what hope does our future hold for us? It is only because we believe that our destiny is redemption that we have faith in the future.

But I would submit that the integration works the other way as well. What imparts real meaning to the open miracles that we experienced in the era of *emet ve-yatziv*? It is only the *emunah* that preceded them. The Splitting of the Sea of Reeds provides a proof of this contention. The miracle, as the *Maharal* points out, was qualitatively different from the Ten Plagues.[5] The Ten Plagues represented a change in the natural order to punish the Egyptians, but the natural order remained intact for the Children of Israel. The Splitting of the Sea was the opposite. For the Children of Israel, the natural order was changed – "the Children of Israel walked on dry land amid the sea" (Exodus 15:19) – but for the Egyptians, the natural order remained intact. The Sea of Reeds was a sea as they all drowned upon entering it.

If the Splitting of the Sea was such a great miracle, how is it possible that just three days later, a rebellion took place when there was no water? Had the Children of Israel quickly forgotten the lesson of the Sea of Reeds?

3. Morning Prayer, *Shema*.
4. Evening Prayer, *Shema*.
5. *Maharal, Gevurot Hashem*, ch. 40.

The answer, I submit, is that because the miracle was overwhelming and so magnificent, qualitatively different from the past, the Children of Israel quickly lost focus on the *emunah* that preceded it. When they left Egypt, they were commanded to borrow gold and silver vessels.[6] That was to be their spoils, which they would never return. The command to borrow, in the context of the Plagues, must have been very perplexing to the Children of Israel. If Hashem was All Powerful, why display such weakness? Their rightful spoils – "and afterward they will leave with great wealth" (Genesis 15:14) – should have been taken forcefully. The lingering doubt was clarified only at the Sea of Reeds. The Children of Israel left under circumstances that would deceive the Egyptians into thinking that they had a chance to vanquish them because of the weakness of the request of "we will go on a three-day journey" (Exodus 8:23).

If the weakness was done deliberately to lull the Egyptians into a false sense of confidence, at the Sea of Reeds, the doubt was resoundingly resolved. The Egyptians were merely a vehicle to reveal the Divine Glory. "*Sus ve-rokhevo ramah va-yam*," "having hurled horse and its rider into the sea" (Exodus 15:1). Both the horse and the rider, glued together, were cast into the sea.[7] Both were only instruments to reveal the Divine Glory.

Now, if the Children of Israel had retained their focus on the *emunah* preceding the magnificent miracle at the Sea of Reeds, there would have been no rebellion three days later. Instead, the *emunah* was forgotten, and the entire focus was on the miracle itself. When we focus only on a miracle itself, without the *emunah* that preceded it, when another crisis arises, we expect another miracle to occur for us. When it does not, we are left with a feeling of abandonment and disillusionment. This makes us ripe for rebellion. It is therefore *emunah* that actually imparts meaning to miracles.

Not only are *emet ve-yatziv* and *emet ve-emunah* integrated, but *emunah* is regarded by our Sages as stronger than open miracles in aspiring to perfect faith. Moses described Hashem in his prayer as "the great, powerful, and awesome God" (Deuteronomy 10:17). Jeremiah, by contrast, omitted the description "awesome" because he saw gentiles

6. Exodus 11:2.
7. *Mekhilta, Be-Shallaḥ* 2 to Exodus 15:1; *Midrash Tanḥuma, Be-Shallaḥ* 13; *Rashi* to Exodus 15:1, s.v. "*sus ve-rokhevo*."

reveling in the holy places.[8] Daniel omitted the description "powerful" when he saw the gentiles enslaving the Jewish nation.[9] Ezra, however, reinstated Moses' formulation, describing Hashem as "the great, powerful, and awesome God" (Nehemiah 9:32). He reasoned that, on the contrary, those events were a magnificent display of Hashem's strength in that Hashem restrains His will by showing a long-suffering countenance to the wicked. And these are great displays of the awesomeness of Hashem because if it were not for the awe of the nations for the Holy One, Blessed is He, how could one solitary nation survive among the nations of the world?[10]

R. Moses Hayyim Luzzatto, in *Da'at Tevunot,* points out that nothing brings us to the realization of "*ein od mi-levaddo,*" "there is none beside Him" (Deuteronomy 4:35), more than when we make a stupendous effort to accomplish something and it comes to naught.[11] When we witnesses a divine manifestation of wisdom or strength, our minds can always play tricks on us, causing us to imagine that somehow there could be greater acts of wisdom or prowess from another source. But when we do not succeed despite our concerted best efforts, and naturally we should have succeeded, this proves *ein od mi-levaddo*.

The modern era gives us so much opportunity to observe the phenomenon that progress of all different varieties carries with it an undertone of powerlessness and vulnerability. The development of the atom meant the enormous increase in the standard of living of the world, but at the same time brought the specter of nuclear holocaust. Our prodigious ability to produce is not an unqualified good because it makes us vulnerable to greater fluctuation of the business cycle due to the inability of demand to meet supply. The integration of the world economy because of tremendous advances in communications and transportation has made the international monetary systems more delicate.

---

8. See Jeremiah 32:18 ("the great and powerful God, His name is Hashem, Master of Legions").
9. See Daniel 9:4 ("I beg of You, O Lord, the great and awesome God").
10. *Yoma* 69b.
11. See R. Moses Hayyim Luzzatto (*Ramḥal,* Italy, 1707–1746), *Da'at Tevunot* (Jerusalem: Goldblatt, 2001), 62–63.

Powerful forces now exist to demonstrate our powerlessness amidst prodigious achievement, and what emerges is *ein od mi-levaddo*.

But the element of powerlessness goes one step further. The Exodus is the model for all future salvations of the Jewish people. Just as the savior of the Jewish people, Moses, was born despite the most stupendous effort to destroy him, so, too, despite all the efforts of our enemies to thwart our progress, we will not only overcome them, but they, in an unknowing manner, will themselves contribute to our progress. The opposite of their evil intention will come to pass!

The Four Cups

April 6, 1985

The mitzvah of the Four Cups is different from all the other mitzvot of the night of Passover. It is only in connection with this mitzvah that our Sages prescribe that even a pauper must sell his chattel, if necessary, in order to fulfill the mitzvah.[1] Also, even if he does not enjoy the wine, he must drink it at the Seder.[2]

Along with this distinctiveness comes, as we would expect, the most lofty and noble symbolism. The Four Cups correspond to the four expressions of *ge'ullah*;[3] the proverbial four cups of retribution that Hashem will

1. *Mishnah, Pesaḥim* 10:1; R. Samuel b. Meir (*Rashbam*, France, ca. 1080–1174), *Rashbam* to *Pesaḥim* 99b, s.v. "*ve-afillu*"; Maimonides, *Mishneh Torah, Ḥametz u-Matzah* 7:7; *Tur, Oraḥ Ḥayyim* 472; R. Joseph Caro (Safed, 1488–1575), *Shulḥan Arukh, Oraḥ Ḥayyim* 472:13.
2. R. Solomon b. Abraham Adret (*Rashba*, Spain, 1235–1310), *She'elot u-Teshuvot ha-Rashba* 1:238; *Shulḥan Arukh, Oraḥ Ḥayyim* 472:10.
3. Genesis Rabbah 88:5 (statement of R. Huna in the name of R. Benayah); Jerusalem Talmud, *Pesaḥim* 10:1 (statement of R. Yohanan in the name of R. Benayah).

make our enemies drink;[4] the Four Matriarchs;[5] the Four Patriarchs;[6] the four redeemers;[7] the four elements in the hierarchy of creation;[8] the four banners that accompanied the Children of Israel in the Wilderness;[9] and the four rows of precious gems in the breastplate of the High Priest.[10] It is therefore with almost a sense of disappointment that we read the Jerusalem Talmud's reason that the Four Cups correspond to the four times that the cups of Pharaoh are mentioned in the dream of the *Sar ha-Mashkim* and in the interpretation of the dream.[11]

Now, if an evil man had a dream about four cups, is that a reason for us to drink four cups at the Seder?

I would submit that the Jerusalem Talmud's reason is the most relevant one for the twentieth-century Jew. The twentieth-century Jew is steeped in a history and a sense of our destiny as a people. Our

---

4. Genesis Rabbah 88:5 (statement of R. Joshua b. Levi); Jerusalem Talmud, *Pesaḥim* loc. cit.
5. *Maharal, Gevurot Hashem*, ch. 60; R. Isaiah ha-Levi Horowitz (*Shelah ha-Kadosh*, Prague, ca. 1565–1630), *Shenei Luḥot ha-Berit, Masekhet Pesaḥim, Matzah Ashirah, derush* no. 1.
6. The "Four Patriarchs" are Abraham, Isaac, Jacob, and Joseph. Although generally only Abraham, Isaac, and Jacob are referred to as the Patriarchs, Joseph is included in this context based on the verse "with Your powerful arm You redeemed Your nation, the sons of Jacob and Joseph, Selah" (Psalms 77:16). R. Menahem Mendel Kasher (Israel, 1895–1983), *Torah Shelemah, ḥelek* 9 (Jerusalem: Beit Torah Shelemah, 1992), Exodus 6:6, *milu'im* to n. 38; R. Kasher, *Haggadah Shelemah*, 3rd ed. (Jerusalem: Mekhon Torah Shelemah, 1967), 92. In discussing the mitzvah of the Four Species on Sukkot, *Mishnat Rebbe Eliezer* provides twenty explanations for the religious significance of the number four, one of which is the Four Patriarchs. *Mishnat Rebbe Eliezer*, ch. 5. R. Kasher states that those reasons may be applied to the Four Cups as well.
7. *Midrash ha-Gadol*, Exodus 6:7. The Four Redeemers are Elijah the Prophet, the Messiah b. David, the Messiah b. Joseph, and the High Priest. The High Priest is identified as Shem, the son of Noah. *Rashi* to *Sukkah* 52b, s.v. "*ve-Kohen Tzedek*."
8. R. Moses Isserles (*Rema*, Poland, 1525 or 1530–1572), *Torat ha-Olah, ḥelek* 3, ch. 51.
9. *Maharal, Gevurot Hashem*, ch. 60.
10. R. Menahem Mendel Kasher, *Torah Shelemah, ḥelek* 9, Exodus 6:6, *milu'im* to n. 38; R. Kasher, *Haggadah Shelemah*, 3rd ed. (Jerusalem: Mekhon Torah Shelemah, 1967), 92. In discussing the mitzvah of the Four Species on Sukkot, *Mishnat Rebbe Eliezer* provides twenty explanations for the religious significance of the number four, one of which is the four rows of precious stones in the breastplate of the High Priest. *Mishnat Rebbe Eliezer*, ch. 5. R. Kasher states that those reasons may be applied to the Four Cups as well.
11. Jerusalem Talmud, *Pesaḥim* 10:1 (statement of R. Joshua b. Levi).

model of redemption is not the wretched slave, burdened by misery, whose only wish is to be released from his suffering. Such a man has no higher goal or purpose and is not aware of the *ge'ullah* as it is unfolding. Only when he reaches the climax of *ge'ullah* can he trace it backward and understand how the whole process fits together. In retrospect, he understands the *ge'ullah.*

Rather, our model is a prospective one. We identify with the *Sar ha-Mashkim,* as Joseph did. The *Sar ha-Mashkim* is one who tasted and experienced the delight of being part of the royal entourage but is now despised and yearns for reinstatement. Such a man will seize upon any event and read redemption and restoration into it, and feel that his restoration is imminent. Once he feels that the process is under way, he can project himself into the future and imagine that he is already there. He is always thinking ahead and imagining that events are moving in his favor much more quickly than they actually are.

And so it is with the *Sar ha-Mashkim.* He sees a cup of Pharaoh. It is significant to him, only because he remembers his former position. The goblet is the tool of his trade. He seizes upon it as an indication that he will be restored to power and experience his former delight.

But then he sees himself pressing the grapes into the cup. Now, is this any way to serve a king? The wine must be delicately manufactured and properly aged. But the *Sar ha-Mashkim* feels that this is *ge'ullah* too because he is, after all, in a dungeon, and this is the best that he can do. The King would therefore be very pleased with his work.

Each cup is looked upon as coming closer to being reconstituted. The *Sar ha-Mashkim* does not interpret any of the cups in the sequence as a regression, but rather as a rising crescendo. He is part of a process, fully confident in what the end result will be. Each stage serves as a spur for the next. And the *Sar ha-Mashkim* will not be satisfied until he reaches his former position, "*ka-mishpat ha-rishon*" (Genesis 40:13).

Joseph regards the *Sar ha-Mashkim* as his model and identifies with him. He is convinced that he, too, will return to his former position. It is only in this light, as it seems to us, that we can understand Joseph's subsequent conduct. He chooses to reveal that he is a Jew.[12]

12. Genesis 40:15.

This is astounding. Such a revelation would not serve him well, as the Egyptians held the Jews in abomination.[13]

But Joseph views himself in the future. There, he is no longer living in a decadent society that does not recognize the Jew, but rather in a world where the Jew occupies the center. And in this very same vein, we can understand Joseph's plea to the *Sar ha-Mashkim.*

The *Malbim* interprets the plea as consisting of three elements. First, it is a matter of justice for the *Sar ha-Mashkim* to put in a good word for Joseph. Then, it is a matter of *ḥesed.* And even if it not regarded as *ḥesed,* it is really nothing.[14]

Well, is it nothing? Did the incident not topple the Egyptian aristocracy, Lady Potiphar?

The same answer must be given. Joseph imagines that he is living in a different era and a different society that has a much more refined concept of justice, a much grander concept of mercy, and a much more noble concept of what is an inconvenience.

When the redemption process is looked upon as a prospective one rather than as a retrospective one, even the pauper does not feel as if he is a pauper. He feels as in the proverbial story that he made a loan to someone and it is due immediately.[15] And similarly for the tender child. He is viewed as if he is already mature and can enjoy the wine.[16]

This is one main aspect of the Four Cups, as *Tosafot* point out, that it is not enough to listen to the blessings over the Four Cups, but one must drink the cups.[17] We cannot be a passive participant, but must be actively aware that the *ge'ullah* is in motion.

---

13. See Genesis 43:32.
14. R. Meir Loeb b. Jehiel Michel Weisser (*Malbim,* Poland, Romania, and Russia, 1809–1879), *Malbim* to Genesis 40:14.
15. See R. Jacob b. Wolf Kranz (*Dubner Maggid,* Poland, 1741–1804), *Emet le-Yaakov, Haggadah shel Pesaḥ,* s.v. "*kol dikhvin,*" reprinted in R. Avraham Berush Flahm (Ukraine, 1804–1873), *Berit Avot al Haggadah le-Leil Shimurim.*
16. See *Pesaḥim* 108b; *Shulḥan Arukh, Oraḥ Ḥayyim* 472:15 (stating that children who have reached the age of *ḥinnukh* should be given the Four Cups at the Seder). Cf. R. Jacob b. Joseph Reischer, *Ḥok Yaakov, Oraḥ Ḥayyim* 472:27 (ruling that even children who have not attained the age of *ḥinnukh* should be given the Four Cups).
17. *Tosafot* to *Pesaḥim* 99b. See also Maimonides, *Mishneh Torah, Ḥametz u-Matzah* 7:7, 7:9.

The Disorder of the Seder: The Upstaging of *Maror*

April 15, 1987

For the past two evenings, we have subjected ourselves to the discipline of a Seder. If *seder* implies an orderly, systematic arrangement, our sense of order is almost immediately assaulted as we encounter what appears to be a reversal of order in *karpas* and *yaḥatz*. We arrive at the meaning of *karpas* by reading it backward, *samakh perakh*, i.e., sixty myriads of Jews subjected to crushing labor.[1] Hence, *karpas* denotes the most wretched part of our servitude.

1. R. David b. Joseph Abudirham (Spain, 14th cent.), *Sefer Abudraham, Seder ha-Haggadah u-Peirusheha*; R. Jacob b. Moses Moellin (*Maharil*, ca. 1360–1427), *Sefer Maharil: Minhagim*, ed. Shlomo Y. Spitzer (Jerusalem: Mekhon Yerushalayim, 1989), 96, ¶ 14; *She'elot u-Teshuvot Maharil*, no. 58:1; R. Joseph Caro (Safed, 1488–1575), *Beit Yosef* to R. Jacob b. Asher (*Tur*, Spain, 1270–1343), *Tur, Oraḥ Ḥayyim* 473, n. 3, s.v. "*tamkha*" (citing *Maharil*); R. Abraham Abele Gombiner (*Magen Avraham*, Poland, ca. 1635–1682), *Magen Avraham* to *Shulḥan Arukh, Oraḥ Ḥayyim* 473:4 (citing *Maharil*).

We then proceed to *yaḥatz*. The breaking of the middle matzah and the placing of the smaller half in between the other two matzot signifies *leḥem oni*, "bread of affliction," which symbolizes the Servitude in general.[2]

What we have here is a reversal of order. We first project the crushing labor with *karpas* and then we project the Servitude with *yaḥatz*. But historically, the reverse took place. It was *be-peh rakh* (i.e., soft words). First we were inveigled to work.[3] This then degenerated into slavery, and finally into crushing labor. Moreover, does the *karpas-yaḥatz* sequence not upstage the official commemoration of *maror* that is made later in the Seder with the blessing of *al akhilat maror*? Then we commemorate the crushing labor with the *maror* by dipping the *maror* in *ḥaroset*.

Perhaps the second question answers the first. Our most heartfelt desire is to eradicate the element of *maror* in Jewish life, both the physical and spiritual varieties, and with it, to eradicate *maror* of the human race. The *karpas-yaḥatz* sequence demonstrates how this can be done. Hashem always sends the *refuah* (cure) before the *makkah* (plague).[4] It is only by focusing on the most ghastly aspect of our persecution and the most virulent form of assimilation that we arouse our spirit and sensitivities to *maror* of any kind, even to what we might think is the most mellow kind. The moment we are willing to blot out the most ghastly aspects of the Holocaust, we begin to give credence to the Bitburg mentality that human forgiveness demands that after fifty years, we must blot out the episode of the Holocaust entirely.[5]

---

2. *Berakhot* 39b; *Rashi* ad loc., s.v. "*leḥem oni kesiv*"; Maimonides, *Mishneh Torah, Ḥametz u-Matzah* 8:6.
3. *Midrash Tanḥuma, Be-Ha'alot'kha* 13.
4. *Megillah* 13b. The Talmud applies this principle to the sequence of events in the Book of Esther. Before Ahasuerus promoted Haman (Esther 3:1), Esther had already become Queen.
5. On May 4, 1985, President Ronald Reagan placed a wreath at the Bitburg military cemetery in West Germany as part of the observance of the fortieth anniversary of V-E Day. The cemetery included graves of forty-nine members of the Nazi SS. The visit was widely criticized outside Germany. See Robert D. McFadden, "Americans Voice Anger on Bitburg," *New York Times*, May 6, 1985, A8; "Tears, Anger as Reagan Visits Belsen and Bitburg," *Jerusalem Post*, May 6, 1985, 1.

Karpas was inserted into the Haggadah ritual for the purpose of arousing the curiosity of the children so that they should not fall asleep.[6] Now, why arouse their curiosity with this aspect of the Seder, the crushing labor? Why not pick something else for special emphasis, such as one of the symbols of freedom?

The choice of *karpas* for this purpose demonstrates that it is an obligation to make our children aware of the most ghastly aspects of the Servitude. As painful as it is, we may not anesthetize them, shield them, protect them, from the unpleasantries. And this is equally valid with respect to spiritual *maror*. If we admire the completely assimilated Jew for his stellar achievements in politics, finance, or statesmanship, and tend to overlook his ultimate blasphemy of intermarriage, then a sensitivity toward Tradition has already begun to erode!

We must be on guard. To ensure that our sensitivities are attuned to all kinds of *maror*, we must always keep in our consciousness its extreme forms!

If *maror* is upstaged by the *karpas-yaḥatz* sequence, then it is assaulted a second time in Rabban Gamliel's statement "whoever does not explain the following three things at the Passover festival has not fulfilled his duty: *pesaḥ*, matzah, and *maror*." Here again, Rabban Gamliel does not follow the correct order. Historically, we first experienced *maror*. Then, the *pesaḥ* came, and finally the matzah.

Now, Rabban Gamliel is perhaps also giving us a subtle hint of how to eradicate the *maror* in our lives by suggesting what we must emphasize in our lives. First, we must emphasize the element of compassion of the *pesaḥ*. "It is a *pesaḥ* feast offering to Hashem, Who passed over the houses of the Children of Israel in Egypt when He smote the Egyptians, but He saved our households" (Exodus 12:27). We must spare no effort to arouse compassion in interpersonal relations.

Then, we must proceed to matzah. The emphasis here is the awareness of the divine intervention in human affairs. For later generations,

6. *Pesaḥim* 116a; *Rashbam* ad loc., s.v. "*ḥiyyuva le-darddekei*"; *Tur, Oraḥ Ḥayyim* 473; R. Shneur Zalman of Liadi (Russia, 1745–1812), *Shulḥan Arukh ha-Rav, Oraḥ Ḥayyim* 473:14; R. Israel Meir ha-Kohen Kagan (*Ḥafetz Ḥayyim*, Radin, 1838–1933), *Mishnah Berurah* 473:21.

it is indeed very tempting to theorize that an oppressed people simply rebelled against their tormentors, without any divine intervention, as happens so often in history. To dispel this notion, we emphasize that "their dough did not have time to become leavened."[7] If we indeed rebelled, we would have surely prepared adequate provisions for our departure. The fact that we did not, and the actual redemption took place with such suddenness, proves that there was divine intervention.[8]

Matzah therefore represents the need to cultivate within ourselves an awareness of a divine presence in our lives. *Pesaḥ* and matzah prevent *maror*!

Finally, we can perhaps understand that *karpas* is indeed a double symbol. Yes, it represents crushing labor, but it is also a symbol of freedom. Some *posekim* take the view that it requires *hesebah*.[9] This tells us that it is within our hands to transform *perakh* into *ḥerut* for our great benefit and for *ḥerut olam*!

7. *Haggadah, Maggid.*
8. R. Samson Raphael Hirsch, Exodus 12:39.
9. R. David b. Joseph Abudirham, *Sefer Abudraham, Seder ha-Haggadah u-Peirusheha*, s.v. "*ve-aḥar ha-Kiddush notel yado*"; R. Solomon Ganzfried (Hungary, 1804–1886), *Kitzur Shulḥan Arukh* 119:3. But see R. Zedekiah b. Abraham Anav (Rome, ca. 1210–1280), *Shibbolei ha-Leket, Seder Pesaḥ* 218; R. Isaac Tyrnau (Austria, 14th cent.), *Sefer ha-Minhagim, Minhag shel Pesaḥ*; R. Moses b. Abraham Mat (Poland, ca. 1551–ca. 1606), *Matteh Mosheh* 625.

Everlasting Freedom

April 2, 1988

In the everyday prayer of *emet ve-emunah,* we affirm that the special designation of Passover as *zeman ḥerutenu,* "the season of our freedom," is meant to impart a permanent freedom – "He removed His people Israel from their midst to everlasting freedom."[1] Now, in light of the return to *galut* that we experienced after the Exodus from Egypt, we can only take it to mean that the Exodus transformed the spirit of the Jew in a fundamental way. This transformation was permanent and irreversible. And therefore, despite the return of a physical servitude, we celebrate a permanent freedom.

We express the thought quite plainly in the *Dayyenu* song. Here, we list fifteen levels, beginning with "if He had brought us out of Egypt but had not executed judgments upon the Egyptians, it would have sufficed for us!"

Now, each level, of course, was a building block in the further development of our spiritual personality, but each was sufficient in

1. Evening Prayer, *Shema.*

and of itself to warrant giving Hashem everlasting praise. Each represents a gift of either the Exodus process itself or of its aftermath. These divine gifts permanently changed our personality and were not taken away from us.

The central theme of the Haggadah is expressed immediately after *Dayyenu* in the words of Rabban Gamliel: "Whoever does not explain the following three things at the Passover festival has not fulfilled his duty: *pesaḥ*, matzah, and *maror*."

Perhaps Rabban Gamliel picks up on the *Dayyenu* theme and concerns himself with the concept of *ḥerut olam*, "everlasting freedom." He wants to show that with an order of *pesaḥ*, matzah, and *maror*, we can redefine *maror*. Whatever the Jewish nation will experience in the form of *maror* or *galut* after the Exodus from Egypt would be seen in the proper perspective by first delving into the *pesaḥ* and matzah, in that order. We do not approach *maror* of the generations without first being armed with *pesaḥ* and matzah.

First, *pesaḥ* tells us that we should not God forbid equate adversity with *maror*. *Pesaḥ* represents the repudiation of alien beliefs to the extent of *mesirut nefesh* because the lamb was the deity of the Egyptians. The *mesirut nefesh* extended even to taking the struggle to the period of repose by tying the paschal lamb to the bedpost.[2] We must be willing to take on challenges even though it means meeting adversity.

Then we must be armed with matzah. Historians will also try to diminish the significance of the Exodus. They will tell us it represents the old story of an armed rebellion. The Ten Plagues and the Splitting of the Sea of Reeds are reduced to natural phenomena. But all the facts point to the divine intervention, that the *ge'ullah* took place suddenly, without preparation. If it were really an armed rebellion, the Children of Israel would have prepared provisions. The fact that they were not prepared for the *ge'ullah* shows that it was entirely the Hand of Hashem.[3]

2. *Pesikta de-Rav Kahana, Parashat ha-Ḥodesh* 23, s.v. "*dabru*"; *Yalkut Shimoni, Bo* 191.
3. R. Samson Raphael Hirsch, Exodus 12:39.

Now, we all know that the *ge'ullah* had to take place when it did. If we would have been in Egypt any longer, we would have sunk to the fiftieth level of impurity and would have been irredeemable.[4]

What does it mean to be in the fiftieth level of impurity? R. Moshe Feinstein[5] relates it to R. Eleazar ha-Kappar's statement, "Jealousy, lust, and glory remove a person from the world."[6] We were influenced by a society where these three elements were rampant with such intensity that we would have completely lost our elemental sense of community. But we were redeemed, as a *mattenat Elokim* (divine gift). And therefore it represents a gift from Hashem that no matter how much division there would be among Jews, the jealousy, lust, and desire for glory would never cause us to lose our elemental sense of community. The harmony and unity of the Jewish people would always be possible.

This is all symbolized in matzah, which represents our freedom from Egypt. The ingredients of matzah – flour and water – are the same as those of *ḥametz*. The only difference is *se'or*, "yeast," which in itself has no taste and no nourishment, but blows up the dough. The difference between *ḥametz* and matzah is very little. The letters are the same and only a small stroke marks the differences between the *ḥet* and the *heh*. Numerically, the difference is three, i.e., *ḥametz* is 138 and matzah is 135, representing the jealousy, lust, and desire for glory that remove a person from this world.[7]

As we approach the future, we must always be equipped first with a willingness to submit to turmoil and challenge for the purpose of destroying and denying false beliefs, and also with a belief that Hashem intervenes in the history of man. Then we will have a different perspective on *maror*.

---

4. R. Isaac b. Solomon Luria (*Arizal* or *Ha-Ari*, Safed, 1534–1572), *Siddur ha-Ari, Seder Haggadah*, s.v. "*matzah zu*"; R. Moses Alshekh (*Alshekh*, Safed, 1508–1593), *Torat Mosheh*, Exodus 12:41; R. Isaiah ha-Levi Horowitz, *Shenei Luḥot ha-Berit, Masekhet Pesaḥim, Matzah Shemurah*, ¶ 158, s.v. "*ve-illu lo hotzi ha-Kadosh Barukh Hu*"; R. Hayyim b. Moses ibn Attar (*Or ha-Ḥayyim*, Morocco, 1696–1743), *Or ha-Ḥayyim* to Exodus 3:7, s.v. "*va-yomer Hashem.*"
5. See R. Moshe Feinstein (New York, 1895–1986), *Derash Mosheh, derush* 8, p. 251.
6. Mishnah, *Avot* 4:21.
7. R. Moses Sofer (*Ḥatam Sofer*, Hungary, 1762–1839), *Pesaḥim* 30a; *Torat Mosheh, Bo*, s.v. "*shivat yamim matzot tokhelu.*"

The Fifth Cup

April 10, 1990

One of the most prominent features of the Seder is the drinking of the Four Cups. Since the Four Cups correspond to the four expressions of *ge'ullah*, i.e., *ve-hotzeti, ve-hitzalti, ve-ga'alti, ve-lakaḥti*, which heralded the Exodus experience,[1] the question naturally arises: Why did our Sages not institute a fifth cup to correspond to "*ve-heveti*," "I shall bring you [into the Land of Israel]" (Exodus 6:8), the fifth expression of *ge'ullah* mentioned in conjunction with the other four expressions of *ge'ullah*?

Perhaps the answer lies in the proposition that our Sages assessed that the limit for most people in their tolerance of liquor is four cups of

1. Genesis Rabbah 88:5; Exodus Rabbah 6:4; Jerusalem Talmud, *Pesaḥim* 10:1. The First Cup corresponds to "I shall take you out [*ve-hotzeti*] from under the burdens of Egypt" (Exodus 6:6), the Second Cup corresponds to "I shall rescue you [*ve-hitzalti*] from their service" (ibid.), and the Third Cup corresponds to "I shall redeem you [*ve-ga'alti*] with an outstretched arm" (ibid.), each denoting freedom from physical oppression. The Fourth Cup corresponds to "I shall take you [*ve-lakaḥti*] as a people" (Exodus 6:7), denoting spiritual redemption.

wine. If we would drink a fifth cup, we would become giddy and drunk. Giddiness would only slight *ve-heveti*. When we focus on *Eretz Yisrael,* we want to be in an exalted state, full of pride, but we want to be sober!

R. Mosheh Shternbukh posits that whereas liberation from tyranny and oppression is a prerequisite for us to accept *ol malkhut Shamayim,* we celebrate each stage in the process of liberation from oppression. But once *ve-lakaḥti* has taken place, the whole function of *ve-heveti* is to implement the divine plan of *ve-lakaḥti* in a Jewish State. *Ve-heveti* is hence not a blessing without the integration of *ve-lakaḥti.*[2]

We are now witnessing in *Eretz Yisrael* a monumental struggle of the religious parties to be once again the kingmakers in the Israeli government. For some, these times represent a golden opportunity for the achievement of a new integration of *ve-lakaḥti* and *ve-heveti*. Other quarters would like to take away the influence of all the little parties by means of parliamentary reform.[3]

As we observe the struggle for the higher integration of *ve-lakaḥti* with *ve-heveti,* we note that historically a much greater leap of the sort was attempted in 1538, the renewal of the Sanhedrin.[4]

I do not propose that as a practical matter, but only for its shock value. Who would be the person whom all the Sages of Israel would ordain?

I submit that the greater the integration of *ve-lakaḥti* with *ve-heveti* that we can achieve within the framework of a theoretical Sanhedrin, the greater the integration we can achieve of *ve-lakaḥti* with *ve-heveti* within the framework of the *Medinah*.

---

2. R. Mosheh Shternbukh (Jerusalem, contemp.), *Ta'am va-Da'at: Peshatim, Be'urim ve-Divrei Ḥizzuk she-Ne'emru be-Siḥot al Parashat ha-Shavua be-Yohanesburg,* vol. 2, Exodus 6:8, s.v. "*ve-heveti el ha-aretz.*"
3. Asher Wallfish, "Reforming the System," *Jerusalem Post,* April 4, 1990, 5.
4. In 1538, R. Jacob Berab (*Mahari Berav,* Safed, 1474–1546) assembled twenty-five of the leading rabbis in Safed and re-instituted *semikhah.* The rabbis appointed R. Berab as the Chief Rabbi. R. Bareb then ordained R. Joseph Caro. R. Yehudah Leib ha-Kohen Maimon (Israel, 1875–1962), *Ḥiddush ha-Sanhedrin be-Medinatenu ha-Meḥudeshet* (Jerusalem: Mossad HaRav Kook, 1951), 106–108.

The Power of Symbolism

March 30, 1991

Symbolism is a powerful educational device. In the hands of the creative mind, symbolism can develop a theme beyond its superficial level and bring nuances and subtleties to the fore. But there is the danger that we might get carried away with the symbolism and lose sight of the basics. And so it is with the theme of *maror* on the night of Passover.

To make us feel that we are not merely descendants of those who experienced the Servitude, but actually experienced it ourselves, our Sages instituted various rituals for the night of Passover. One ritual is *yaḥatz*. We take the *leḥem oni* and develop the theme further. By breaking the middle matzah, we conjure up the lifestyle of the pauper. The pauper always partakes of only a *perusah*, "portion," and then puts away the lion's share of his sustenance for the next day.[1] As R. Hai Gaon explains,

1. *Pesaḥim* 115b.

because the pauper has no confidence in his earning capacity, he always feels a sense of insecurity and uncertainty for the future.[2]

Then there is *karpas*, the symbol of the crushing labor of the Children of Israel in Egypt. We arrive at this symbolism by reading the word "*karpas*" backward: *samakh perakh*.[3] But we might not realize that *karpas* represents *maror* at all. So to ensure that we do make the symbolic association, we must dip the *karpas* in salt water, representing bitterness and Jewish tears.[4]

The Sages also developed the theme of *maror* with *maror* itself. If we take *maror* in the form of *tamkha*, "horseradish,"[5] the bitterness of the herb reminds of us the bitterness of the Exile. But the preferred species is *ḥazeret*, which is pure Romaine lettuce or Iceberg lettuce. We are reminded that *teḥilato matok, ve-sofo mar*, "its beginning is sweet but its end is bitter."[6] Lest we lose sight that lettuce represents the Servitude, we recite a blessing on it of *al akhilat maror*.

But then there is one more symbol of the Servitude, and that is *ḥaroset*. We follow the opinion that *ḥaroset* was instituted not just to counteract the bitterness of the *maror*, but as an independent mitzvah,[7]

---

2. *Ḥiddushei ha-Ran*, *Pesaḥim* 115b, in the name of R. Hai Gaon (Pumbedita, 939–1038).
3. R. David b. Joseph Abudirham, *Sefer Abudraham*, *Seder ha-Haggadah u-Peirusheha*; R. Jacob b. Moses Moellin, *Sefer Maharil: Minhagim*, ed. Shlomo Spitzer (Jerusalem: Mekhon Yerushalayim, 1989), 96, ¶ 14; *She'elot u-Teshuvot Maharil*, no. 58:1; R. Joseph Caro (Safed, 1488–1575), *Beit Yosef* to *Tur*, *Oraḥ Ḥayyim* 473, n. 3, s.v. "*tamkha*" (citing *Maharil*); R. Abraham Abele Gombiner (*Magen Avraham*, Poland, ca. 1635–1682), *Magen Avraham* to *Shulḥan Arukh*, *Oraḥ Ḥayyim* 473:4 (citing *Maharil*).
4. R. Shaul Yedidyah Elazar Taub (Poland, 1886–1947), quoted in *Haggadah shel Pesaḥ: Ashei Yisrael*, 2nd ed. (Brooklyn, NY: Moriah, 1988), *Yisa Berakhah*, *be-Inyan Mei Melaḥ*, 16.
5. *Tamkha* is one of the types of bitter herbs that may be used as *maror*. Mishnah, *Pesaḥim* 2:6; *Pesaḥim* 39a. *Tamkha* is commonly defined as horseradish. See R. Israel Meir ha-Kohen Kagan, *Mishnah Berurah* 473:36.
6. Jerusalem Talmud, *Pesaḥim* 2:5. Initially, the Egyptians allowed the Children of Israel to live in the best part of the land of Egypt (Genesis 47:6), but eventually enslaved them and made their lives bitter (Exodus 1:13–14).
7. R. Eliezer b. Tzadok, Mishnah, *Pesaḥim* 10:3; *Pesaḥim* 114a; Maimonides, *Mishneh Torah*, *Ḥametz u-Matzah* 7:11; R. Vidal Yom Tov of Tolosa (*Maggid Mishneh*, Spain, ca. 1300–1370), *Maggid Mishneh* to *Mishneh Torah* ad loc. Cf. Maimonides, *Perush ha-Mishnayot*, *Pesaḥim* 10:3.

and its purpose is to remind us that "they embittered their lives with hard work, with mortar, and with bricks" (Exodus 1:14).[8]

Now, is this not a paradox? The taste of *ḥaroset* is sweet, but it is supposed to remind us of perhaps the most heart-wrenching aspect of the Servitude – the building that we did just for the sake of building, Pitom and Ramses, and the Jewish blood that was put into those bricks.[9] It would seem that the Sages should have decreed the adding of an ingredient that would at the very least neutralize the sweet taste.

Perhaps the hint of the answer lies in the halakhah that we must shake off the *ḥaroset,*[10] as if to say that the sweetness is not for us, but for the onlookers. At times, Jewish suffering might evoke sympathy and even outcry. But when Jewish suffering occurs in relation to the bricks-and-mortar activities of the nations, or if it occurs in obstruction to their bricks and mortar, our suffering will be regarded as sweet to the onlooker. The *maror* of *yaḥatz* may evoke sympathy; the world can identify with the scrounging pauper who pulls himself up by his bootstraps. The *maror* associated with exploitation, the maror of *karpas,* can be commiserated with by the nations of the world, and certainly the *maror* of genocide, i.e., the *maror* of *tamkha.* But when the gentiles will be involved in building, and Jewish blood will be spilled in consequence, no sympathy will be found. Then, *ḥaroset* redefines the other *marors.* It shakes us out of our delusion that we can relax our guard when it comes to the threats of the various *maror*s because there will always be a bricks-and-mortar element.

Sure, the world can cheer on the Horatio Alger who leaps from rags to riches. But just let Horatio come into conflict with the production activities of the least educated and trained individual. Then there will be a fierce jealousy, and the success of the pauper will be begrudged with all intensity. The *maror* of insidious exploitation will evoke a sigh, but society will do nothing about it because it is a necessary evil that accompanies the sweep of economic progress. And even *tamkha* has its

8. *Pesaḥim* 116a (opinion of R. Yohanan); *Mishneh Torah, Ḥametz u-Matzah* loc. cit.; R. Vidal Yom Tov of Tolosa, *Maggid Mishneh* to *Mishneh Torah* ad loc.
9. Jerusalem Talmud, *Pesaḥim* 10:3.
10. *Shulḥan Arukh, Ḥoshen Mishpat* 475:1.

limits because in building for the future, society will say, "We cannot be weighed down by guilt; we must forget the evils of the past and move forward." So empathy, and comfort, and outcry are all in the abstract and hypothetical. We observe it now in the vehement opposition to the deportation policy and the settlement of the Russians in the liberated territories.[11]

Ḥaroset is the most powerful educational form of *maror*. It is the last ritual of *maror* because *korakh* is in remembrance of the time of the Temple and *afikoman* is in remembrance of the *korban pesaḥ* and hence is not *leḥem oni*. *Ḥaroset* redefines the other forms of *maror* and shatters our delusions that we can relax our guard in respect of the threat of Jewish suffering.

Let us merit that *karpas*, the representation of the worst form of the Servitude, be transformed into *ḥerut*, as is the opinion of some that *karpas* is an appetizer and requires *hesebah* because it is one of the symbols of freedom.[12]

---

11. Howard Rosenberg, "U.S. Urges Israel Not to Deport Palestinians," *American Israelite*, March 28, 1991, A6; Jonathan Schachter, "UN Adjourns Discussion on Expulsions by Israel," *Jerusalem Post*, January 13, 1991, 2.
12. R. David b. Joseph Abudirham, *Sefer Abudraham, Seder ha-Haggadah u-Peirusheha*, s.v. "*ve-aḥar ha-Kiddush notel yado*"; R. Solomon Ganzfried, *Kitzur Shulḥan Arukh* 119:3. But see R. Zedekiah b. Abraham Anav, *Shibbolei ha-Leket, Seder Pesaḥ* 218; R. Isaac Tyrnau, *Sefer ha-Minhagim, Minhag shel Pesaḥ*; R. Moses b. Abraham Mat, *Matteh Mosheh* 625.

As though He Himself Had Gone Out of Egypt

April 18, 1992

One of the unique mitzvot of the night of Passover is spelled out in the Haggadah as "in every generation, one is obligated to regard himself as though he himself had gone out of Egypt."[1] But this appears impossible. No matter how vivid and expansive our imagination, nor how much we have refined the art of vicarious living, we still have not invented the time machine, which would allow us to travel back in time thousands of years.

But if the Torah prescribes an obligation, it cannot be impossible to fulfill. Its prescription is derived from the verse *ve-higgadeta le-vinkha,* "You shall tell your son on that day saying, 'It is because of this that Hashem acted on my behalf when I left Egypt'" (Exodus 13:8). So within the context of dialogue of the father with his son, it is possible to create the feeling that "Hashem acted on my behalf." And yes, the

1. *Haggadah, Maggid.*

father who is prepared to meet the challenge of the Wise Son has the patience and resourcefulness to build on the curiosity of the Simple Son. He has the creativity to get the uninterested interested, and all the tact and diplomacy to prevent the Wicked Son from boycotting the Seder. Such a person has demonstrated a commitment to Jewish survival and identity. Such a person feels the power of the decree "Every son who will be born, into the River shall you throw him" (Exodus 1:22), and the vapidity of the *mem-tet sha'arei tumah*, "forty-nine levels of impurity."

If the obligation to regard oneself as if he himself left Egypt is accomplished by telling over the story of the Exodus to his son, the deeper the reaching out to the next generation, the more authentic will be the feeling that the father himself went out of Egypt. How is the deepest bond accomplished? It is by meeting the challenge of the three questions of the Wise Son: "What are the *edot* (testimonies), *ḥukkim* (decrees), and *mishpatim* (ordinances) that Hashem, our God, commanded you?" (Deuteronomy 6:20).

Now, *edot* are mitzvot that testify regarding a historical event.[2] Most basically, if the parent has done his homework, he will be able to explain the symbolism inherent in each item in the Seder and relate it to the historical events.

But to be most effective in *ve-higgadeta le-vinkha* and reach a vicarious experience of the Exodus, the challenge must work the other way as well. The historical experience of the Generation of the Exodus from Egypt must form our Weltanschauung and lifestyle today. And hence, do we display the selfsame *mesirut nefesh* that our ancestors showed in bringing the *korban pesaḥ*, and slaughtering the deity of the Egyptians, in our commitment to Torah and mitzvot? And when the climactic moment of the Exodus came, and we were busy making bread and suddenly left Egypt, do we realize that it was not due to our efforts but only the work of Hashem? And does the *maror* of the Exodus form our attitude toward anti-Semitism and heighten our sensitivity toward incipient threats to

2. R. David Kimhi (*Radak*, Provence, ca. 1160–ca. 1235), *Radak* to Psalms 119:1; R. Levi b. Gershom (*Ralbag*, France, 1288–1344), *Ralbag* to II Kings 17:15, s.v. "*ve-et edvotav asher he'id bam*"; R. Obadiah b. Jacob Sforno (*Sforno*, Italy, ca. 1470–1550), *Sforno* to Deuteronomy 4:45.

the State of Israel? When historical experiences form the basis of our Weltanschauung and lifestyle, there is no break with the past. We are then connecting to the Generation of the Exodus from Egypt.

The implication of the linking between *ve-higgadeta le-vinkha* and the connection with the past is at once frightening and exhilarating. Why? Because the Four Sons are not different people but different phases of the same personality.[3]

The *mishpatim* refer to mitzvot *bein adam le-ḥavero*.[4] The Wise Son wants to know the relevance of interpersonal conduct that can be derived from the *korban pesaḥ*. Now, if we did our homework, we can show how every aspect of the *korban pesaḥ* denotes unity of the Jewish people. It is sacrificed in a group,[5] and eaten in a group.[6] But we have a much greater expectation. If the father's personal life belies this integration between *bein adam le-ḥavero* and *bein adam la-Makom*, the father will be looked upon as a hypocrite. Then he will not reach even his child, to say nothing of reaching the Generation of the Exodus from Egypt.

To the extent that we are successful in *edot* and *mishpatim*, *ḥukkim* will also become a means of actually reaching the Generation of the Exodus from Egypt. Reaching that generation requires a teacher who engages in an exhaustive search for the truth, extending himself beyond all reason for the student. It is the teacher who admits when he identifies matters beyond his ken who will evoke respect. The student will say, if the teacher does not fudge, then he is intellectually honest and a humble person, admitting ignorance. This approaches the humility that we had at Sinai, saying "*na'aseh ve-nishma*," "we will do and we will listen"

3. See *Sefat Emet, Pesaḥ* (5634/April 1874); R. Yehudah Leib Chasman (Lithuania and Hebron, 1869–1935), *Or Yahel: Iyyunim be-Musar ve-Yir'at Hashem*, 3rd ed., vol. 1 (Jerusalem, 1969), 257; R. Hayyim Shmulevitz, cited in R. Mosheh Yaakov Weingarten, *ha-Seder ha-Arukh: Haggadah shel Pesaḥ* (Jerusalem: Otzer ha-Mo'adim, 2011), 144.
4. *Radak* to Psalms 119:1; *Malbim* to *Sifra*, Leviticus 133.
5. Mishnah, *Pesaḥim* 8:7 (opinion of R. Judah); *Pesaḥim* 64a–b, 91a; *Rashi* to Exodus 12:6, s.v. "*kehal adat Yisrael*"; Maimonides, *Mishnah Torah, Korban Pesaḥ* 1:9–11, 2:2; *Kesef Mishneh* to *Mishnah Torah, Korban Pesaḥ* 2:2.
6. Exodus 12:46; *Rashi* ad loc., s.v. "*be-vayit aḥat ye'akhel*"; *Pesaḥim* 86a; *Mishneh Torah, Korban Pesaḥ* 9:1.

(Exodus 24:7). And then even *ḥukkim* connect to the Generation of the Exodus and the crescendo of the *ge'ullah – ve-lakaḥti.*

But if we fail in both *edot* and *mishpatim,* we are left with only *ḥukkim,* which will turn off the inquisitive child. The obedient one will become only the Simple Son. He will be polite and ask in general terms, "What is this?" (Exodus 13:14). He knows that he will not get an intellectually or emotionally acceptable answer from the father for his detailed and pointed questions. The failure at the *edot* and *mishpatim* level could even cause a total lack of interest, converting the Wise Son into the Son Who Does Not Know How to Ask. With time, he may even become the Wicked Son. Finally, the Wicked Son disappears and does not even show up at the Seder.

But the cyclical nature of the Four Sons also denotes an exhilarating aspect. Through self-education and moral striving of the parent generation, *edot* and *mishpatim* can come alive. This will bring back the lost generation! "He will turn back the hearts of fathers with their sons and the hearts of sons with their fathers" (Malachi 3:24).

The Four Matriarchs

April 6, 1993

A story is told of a family sitting at the Seder table on the first night of Passover reading the portion of the Haggadah that describes the Ten Plagues. As each Plague is mentioned, everyone removes a drop of wine from their cup. The woman of the household was sitting at the table, bleary eyed, drained, and utterly exhausted after a long day of preparation. After the Ten Plagues were counted, she removed an eleventh drop from her cup. "Mama," asked one of her children, "why eleven?" "For me," she answered, "the day before Passover is also a plague."[1]

I am sure that the poor woman would take some consolation from the insight of the *Shelah*, who finds a correspondence between the Four Cups and the Four Matriarchs.[2] In the Kiddush that we recite over the First Cup, the lifework of Sarah leaps forward – "Who has

1. R. Jacob J. Schachter, "A Little at a Time," in R. David Stavsky, ed., *Sermons for Passover: Presented by Members of the Rabbinical Council of America* (5753/1993), 1.
2. *Maharal, Gevurot Hashem*, ch. 60; R. Isaiah ha-Levi Horowitz, *Shenei Luḥot ha-Berit, Masekhet Pesaḥim, Matzah Ashirah, derush* no. 1.

chosen us from every people, exalted us above every tongue."[3] This is Sarah, who converted the women, bringing them "under the wings of the Divine Presence."[4] *Maggid* is recited over the Second Cup. A poignant passage is "*Arami oved Avi*," "an Aramean tried to destroy my Forefather" (Deuteronomy 26:5). Here, Rebecca, who was raised in the house of Laban, is a counteracting force. The *Birkat ha-Mazon* is recited over the Third Cup. This cup is therefore associated with Rachel, whose son Joseph sustained the entire world.[5] And then the Fourth Cup, over which Hallel is recited, is associated with Leah, who said, "This time let me gratefully praise Hashem" (Genesis 29:35).

Permit me to expand on this. The ideal that the Torah sets for women is *tzeniut* – "*Kol kevudah bat melekh penimah*" (lit., "every honorable princess dwelling within") (Psalms 45:14).[6] But *tzeniut* goes beyond modesty in dress and speech. It also includes purity of purpose, and authenticity in thought, motive, and sentiment.

The first cup is a celebration of the spiritual power of the Jewish people. In the Kiddush, the phrase "*Mekaddesh Yisrael*," "He who sanctifies Israel," appears before "*ve-ha-zemanim*," "and the festive seasons," because it is an act of sanctification that generates the *kedushah* of the Festivals.[7] But spiritual power can at times manifest itself in an aggressive, crude, and barbaric way, through zealotry. It needs refinement and

3. Kiddush for Passover.
4. Genesis Rabbah 39:14, 84:4; *Rashi* to Genesis 12:5.
5. See Genesis 50:20.
6. Jerusalem Talmud, *Horiyot* 3:2; *Rashi* to *Yoma* 47a, s.v. "*lo ra'u korot beiti*." This verse is applied to Kimhit, who merited having seven sons serve as the High Priest. She attributed that merit to her modesty in never uncovering her hair even inside her home.
7. See *Berakhot* 49a; *Rashi* ad loc., s.v. "*mekaddesh ha-Shabbat ve-Yisrael ve-ha-zemanim*." The Kiddush concludes with the blessing "Blessed are You, Hashem, Who sanctifies Israel [*mekaddesh Yisrael*] and the festive seasons [*ha-zemanim*]." According to a *baraita*, we do not conclude one blessing with two subjects. The Kiddush appears to be a blessing on two matters, the sanctification of Israel and the sanctification of the Festivals. The Talmud explains, however, that the blessing should be understood to mean that Hashem sanctifies the Jewish people, who in turn sanctify the Festivals through the declaration of the New Moon by *beit din*. Under that interpretation, the concluding blessing of Kiddush is recited over only one matter, the sanctification of Israel.

moderation. This is the role of women, as demonstrated by our Matriarch Sarah.

Rebecca's personality bursts forth at the point that we read *Arami oved Avi*. But when do we see Laban's intent? R. Avraham Mordekhai of Gur posits that it is when Laban says "the daughters are my daughters, the children are my children" (Genesis 31:43).[8] It is his embrace desiring to assimilate us.

Throughout the Diaspora, we have been subjected to so much torment, anguish, discrimination, and hatred that we grope for a kind word and certainly an embrace of love. It takes a very delicate sensitivity to discern that the love of the possessive father, Laban, is not unqualified, but covers up an insidious desire to ensnare us, to tear us away from our Father in Heaven, and ultimately from our Jewish brethren.

And when we are intoxicated with *ve-ga'alti*, reaching affluence reminiscent of the spoils of Egypt, we have to remove ourselves from selfishness and remind ourselves of Joseph, Rachel's son. He told his brothers, "Although you intended me harm, God intended it for good; in order to accomplish – it is as clear as this day – that a vast people be kept alive" (Genesis 50:20).

And finally, *ge'ullah* may make us arrogant, causing us to believe that we fully deserve everything and are entitled to everything. At this juncture, we need Leah's personality. When Judah was born, she said, "This time let me gratefully praise Hashem" (Genesis 29:35), that I took more than my portion.[9]

The heroines of the Exodus from Egypt do not appear openly in the Haggadah, but assuredly their personality pops up in the blend and the texture of the wine.

8. R. Avraham Mordekhai Alter of Gur (*Imrei Emet*, Poland, 1866–1948), *Imrei Emet*, vol. 3 (Israel, 1986), First Days of Passover, p. 100.
9. *Rashi* to Genesis 29:35. Judah was Leah's fourth son. The Matriarchs knew prophetically that Jacob was destined to have twelve sons. *Rashi* to Genesis 29:34, s.v. "*ha-pa'am yillaveh ishi*." Because Jacob had four wives, Hashem could have apportioned the sons equally among them, with each wife giving birth to three sons. When Leah gave birth to her fourth son, she considered it as if she had taken more than her portion.

Opening the Door for *Shefokh Ḥamat'kha*

April 23, 1997

One of the rituals of the Seder that is chock full of symbolism and shrouded in mystique is that immediately after *Birkat ha-Mazon*, we open the door of our home, stand outside, and recite *shefokh ḥamat'kha*.

In the thinking of R. Menahem Mendel of Rimanov, the opening of the door recounts a historical event, the blessing of Isaac.[1] It was on the fifteenth of Nisan that Jacob received the blessing of Isaac.[2] But recall that Jacob masqueraded as Esau and "it was when Jacob had scarcely left from the presence of Isaac, his father, that Esau his brother came back from his hunt" (Genesis 27:30). *Zeh yatza ve-zeh nikhnat*

1. R. Menahem Mendel of Rimanov (Poland, 1745–1815), *Menaḥem Tziyyon, Derushim le-Pesaḥ*.
2. *Pirkei de-Rabbi Eliezer* 32; *Yalkut Shimoni, Toledot* 114; *Rashi* to Genesis 27:9, s.v. "*shenei gedi'ei izzim*."

(lit., "this one departs, and this one enters").[3] They missed each other by a fraction of a second. Just as Jacob was ready to leave, Esau made his entry. Jacob, feeling the presence of Esau, hid behind the door. Just as the door opened, Jacob managed to escape unnoticed. The opening of the door hence commemorates Jacob's escape.

Another tradition is that the opening of the door is a welcome to Elijah the Prophet.[4] Some even say "*barukh ha-ba*" on this occasion.[5]

If we combine these two traditions, the opening of the door represents a meeting in the flesh between Elijah and Jacob. Each represents the attribute of Truth – "*titten emet le-Yaakov*," "grant truth to Jacob" (Micah 7:20), and "*shelaḥ or'kha ve-amit'kha*," "dispatch Your light and Your truth" (Psalms 43:3)[6] – but indeed manifest different concepts of truth. In Elijah's world, there is no room for extenuation for the Children of Israel. "The Children of Israel have forsaken Your covenant" (I Kings 19:10), with no qualifications. But Jacob's concept of truth is one against a backdrop of constraint. In disguising himself as Esau, Jacob acted upon the urging of Rebecca: "Your curse be upon me, my son" (Genesis 27:13).

And Elijah's world of *emet* is the truth of the moment. For Jacob, *emet* is what is understood with distance from the event when the facts can be viewed dispassionately and new data is allowed to elucidate and clarify original intentions and ambiguities.

Let's speculate for a moment. Suppose that the timing of Esau's arrival was a fraction of a second earlier. Then Jacob would have encountered Esau. Jacob's masquerade would have exploded in his face. Would Isaac still have said "*gam barukh yihiyeh*," "he shall remain blessed" (Genesis 27:33)? Esau never caught Jacob in the act. He only later learned of the deception and hence was removed from the emotional rage that he would have experienced had he arrived just a fraction of a second earlier and caught Jacob in the act. Even with only knowing what Jacob did to him instead of witnessing it himself, Esau said, "May the days of mourning for my father

3. *Midrash Tanḥuma, Toledot* 11. See also Genesis Rabbah 66:5; *Rashi* to Genesis 27:30.
4. R. Jehiel Michal Epstein (Belorus, 1829–1908), *Arukh ha-Shulḥan, Oraḥ Ḥayyim* 480:1.
5. Ibid.
6. *Rashi* to Psalms 43:3, s.v. "*shelaḥ or'kha ve-amit'kha*."

draw near, then I will kill my brother Jacob" (Genesis 27:41). You could imagine what he would have done had he discovered Jacob in the act!

Jacob's greatest fear in his life was "perhaps my father will feel me and I shall be as a mocker in his eyes" (Genesis 27:12). Now, imagine how Jacob would have felt if he had been caught red-handed. What would his self-image have become? Would his spiritual potential and path in life been different? Indeed, distance from an event sometimes radically changes one's perspective. Witness Esau's encounter with Jacob twenty-two years later. "Esau ran toward him, embraced him, fell upon his neck, and kissed him; then they wept" (Genesis 33:4).

Now, the Festival of Passover is a family *yom tov* par excellence. The Four Sons are at the Seder, including the Wicked Son. We commemorate the *korban pesaḥ,* which is the *korban* of our first sense of national unity. Elijah's job is "he will turn back [to God] the hearts of fathers with their sons and the hearts of sons with their fathers" (Malachi 3:24). He bridges the generation gap. And how? By rising to Jacob's level of *emet.*

Our Sages tell us that in five instances in the Torah, Elijah is written *ḥaser* (lit., "missing"), without a *vav,* and corresponding to this, Jacob is written five times *maleh* (lit., "full"), with a *vav.*[7] This signifies that Jacob took the *vav* from Elijah, representing *emet* and *yashrut,* as a pledge, and in the future, Elijah will come to Jacob to claim the pledge and announce the *ge'ullah.*

Well, on the night of the Seder, Elijah and Jacob symbolically meet when we open the door. We pray that this year, Elijah reclaimed his *vav* from Jacob and will proclaim the *ge'ullah* speedily in our days.

7. *Rashi* to Leviticus 26:42. Elijah is spelled without a *vav* (i.e., אליה instead of אליהו) at II Kings 1:3, 1:4, 1:8, and 1:12, and Malachi 3:23. Jacob is spelled with a *vav* (i.e., יעקוב instead of יעקב) at Leviticus 26:42 and Jeremiah 30:18, 33:26, 46:27, and 51:19.

The Loneliest Man at the Seder

April 2, 1999

The loneliest man at the Seder is the Wicked Son. For his impudence and mockery, "What is this service to you?" (Exodus 12:26), we do not dignify him with an answer. Instead, we set his teeth on edge and insult him. "Had he been there, he would not have been redeemed."[1]

Now, are we not too hard with the Wicked Son? Consider that the Torah gives an answer to him: "You shall say, 'It is a *pesaḥ* feast offering to Hashem'" (Exodus 12:27). Why does the author of the Haggadah not give the same answer to the Wicked Son?

Perhaps the Wicked Son in the Haggadah is not the same one as in the Torah. No, it is the same person, says the *Netziv*.[2] But the answer in the Torah is not for the Wicked Son. It is what we tell ourselves when

1. *Haggadah, Maggid.*
2. R. Naphtali Tzvi Yehudah Berlin (*Netziv*, Russia, 1816–1893), *Ha'amek Davar*, Exodus 12:27.

we are exposed to the mockery of the Wicked Son. The Wicked Son's mockery hurts us and demoralizes us. We need *ḥizzuk*. We must reach out to our very essence and strengthen our identity.

Now, the Torah could have placed the Wicked Son's question in the context of matzah or *maror*. Why did it choose *pesaḥ*? If the question is on *maror*, then we would decide that we need not get upset with the Wicked Son. After all, it is just part of a pattern of "in every generation, they rise up against us to destroy us,"[3] and the Wicked Son is the enemy from within.

The Wicked Son's question could have been put in the context of the matzah. But that would be strengthening ourselves with the statements "their dough did not have time to become leavened"[4] and "they had not made provisions for themselves" (Exodus 12:39). True, the fact that we did not make provisions is proof that Hashem effected the *ge'ullah* for us, because if it were attributable to our own efforts, we would have had preparation.[5] But we could also get a superiority complex from Hashem's praise of our faith – "your following Me into the Wilderness, into an unsown land" (Jeremiah 2:2).[6]

So we go to the *pesaḥ* to reinforce our personality with a dosage of *anavah* (humility) – "It is a *pesaḥ* feast offering to Hashem, Who passed over the houses of the Children of Israel in Egypt when He smote the Egyptians, but He saved our households" (Exodus 12:27). The essence of the Jewish people is *anavah*. Because of a deep *anavah*, we were saved.[7] This realization leads directly to a rarefied sense of responsibility. This is the key essence of a Jew. Judah said, "I will personally guarantee him [i.e., Benjamin]; of my own hand you can demand him" (Genesis 43:9). And when we feel a heightened sense of responsibility, we go back to

3. *Haggadah, Maggid, Ve-Hi she-Amedah.*
4. *Haggadah, Maggid, Matzah Zu.*
5. R. Samson Raphael Hirsch, Exodus 12:39.
6. See *Rashi* to Exodus 12:39, s.v. "*ve-gam tzedah la asu lahem.*"
7. Exodus Rabbah 1:36; R. Enoch Zundel b. Joseph (Białystock, d. 1867), *Etz Yosef* ad loc., s.v. "*she-hishppilu atzman.*" See also R. Ephraim Solomon b. Aaron of Luntshits (*Keli Yakar*, Łęczyca, 1550–1619), *Olelot Ephraim, ḥelek 2, ammud 7, ma'amar* 71; R. Solomon ha-Kohen Rabinowich (*Tiferet Shelomoh*, Radomsk, 1801–1866), *Tiferet Shelomoh, Be-Shallaḥ*, s.v. "*ve-hinneh zeh ha-inyan.*"

the Seder and ask ourselves, maybe we were too harsh with the Wicked Son. Did he really exclude himself from the *klal*?

Let us note that the *Keli Yakar* tells us that there is little difference between the Wicked Son and the Simple Son.[8] Why do we say that he removes himself from *klal* only with respect to the Wicked Son but not the Simple Son? The answer is that the Simple Son asks *maḥar*, "tomorrow."[9] First he observes the mitzvah and then, and only then, does he ask "What is this?" In the *Keli Yakar*'s opinion, the Simple Son is not asking out of curiosity but instead is also mocking. But first he does the mitzvah and then questions why. He is a *meḥutzaf* (brazen) and also obnoxious, but not one who removes himself from the *klal*.

When we react to "you shall say, 'It is a *pesaḥ* feast offering to Hashem'" (Exodus 12:27), then we get to the most inclusive concept of the *klal* possible.

---

8. *Keli Yakar* to Exodus 13:14.
9. Exodus 13:14.

The Prayer for Dew on the First Day of Passover

April 20, 2000

In a short while, we will be joining in *Tefillat Tal,* the Prayer for Dew. Its exalted poetry, mood, and melody, combined with the trapping that the *Shatz* will don a *kittel,* all evoke Yom Kippur. We may well ask, why do we have this prayer altogether?

Consider that Hashem made a covenant that dew will not be withheld.[1] Dew is an immutable law of nature. When Elijah prays "there will not be dew or rain during these years, except by my word" (I Kings 17:1), only the rain was withheld, but not the dew. We find a similar incident with Gideon. Gideon was desperately groping for a sign that the Children of Israel were worthy of victory against Midian. He proposed, "If there will be dew only on the fleece, and the entire ground will be dry, then I will know that You will help Israel through my hand" (Judges 6:37). When he arose the next morning and squeezed the fleece, it took

1. *Ta'anit* 3a; *Rashi* to Judges 6:38.

an entire bowl to draw out the dew from the fleece.[2] But the dew hit the ground because the dew is not withheld.

Moreover, there is no halakhic consequence for forgetting to recite *tal*. The Sephardim begin to say *morid ha-tal* with *Tefillat Tal,* but forgetting to say *morid ha-tal* does not require one to repeat *Shemoneh Esreh.*[3]

Perhaps the juxtaposition of *Tefillat Tal* right after the first Seder is the key to the answer. On the night of the Seder, we are bidden with a mitzvah that is well neigh impossible to fulfill, "In every generation, one is obligated to regard himself as though he himself had gone out of Egypt."[4] The crux of the mitzvah is not just to offer thanksgiving to Hashem for our status as descendants of the Generation of the Exodus from Egypt, but to feel vicariously that we ourselves are the ones who experienced the miracle. No matter how hard we try, honest self-evaluation will tell us that we fall short. So at night, we realize that the grand expression of *hakkarat ha-tov* that is demanded of us requires us to develop a more refined sensitivity to *hakkarat ha-tov,* that is, to increase our capacity to express *hakkarat ha-tov*. We discover this point in the process of fulfilling "whoever tells the story of the Exodus from Egypt at length is praiseworthy."[5]

We come across the midrash that explains why Aaron inaugurated the first three Plagues. We are told that Moses owed a debt of gratitude to the Nile for protecting him as an infant. "She placed it [i.e., the basket] among the reeds at the bank of the River" (Exodus 2:3). He could therefore not smite the Nile and transform it into blood.[6] Similarly, he could not smite the Nile and make it produce frogs.[7] Likewise, he could not smite the earth to produce lice because the earth covered up his crime of killing the Egyptian and allowed him to escape.[8]

---

2. Judges 6:38.
3. *Shulḥan Arukh, Oraḥ Ḥayyim* 114:3.
4. *Haggadah, Maggid.*
5. Ibid. (paragraph beginning with "We were slaves to Pharaoh in Egypt").
6. Exodus Rabbah 9:10; *Rashi* to Exodus 7:19.
7. Exodus Rabbah 10:4; *Rashi* to Exodus 7:19.
8. Exodus Rabbah 10:7; *Rashi* to Exodus 8:12.

But what are we being told here, that Moses owed a debt of gratitude to inanimate objects, the Nile and the Egyptian soil? In the thinking of R. Hayyim Shmulevitz, the lesson here is that we should not regard our benefactors as an inanimate object.[9] It is often tempting to deny our obligation to the benefactor by deciding that the benefactor is doing the favor for ulterior motives – He is giving only to get back something greater, or the benefit is entirely an unintended side effect. There are so many ways that we can render the benefactor an inanimate object.

Well, because we realize that we need to cultivate a greater sensitivity to *hakkarat ha-tov*, we have *Tefillat Tal*. Yes, dew is an immutable law of nature, but we should not take it for granted. We must imagine a world with periodic cessations of dew. It would be a world with a new element of instability, lowering the quality of life. We realize that we owe a tremendous debt to Hashem that He arranged the world with dew as an immutable law of nature.

The more we cultivate the attribute of *hakkarat ha-tov*, the greater the expression of *hakkarat ha-tov* we become capable of.

9. See R. Hayyim Leib Shmulevitz (Poland and Jerusalem, 1902–1979), *Siḥot Musar: Sha'arei Ḥayyim*, 5731–5732 (Jerusalem, 2013), *ma'amar* 73.

Moses and the Haggadah

April 7, 2004

The mandate of the author of the Haggadah to us is "whoever tells the story of the Exodus from Egypt at length is praiseworthy."[1] The author of the Haggadah apparently violates his own dictum with respect to the treatment of Moses. Moses was the human hero of the Exodus experience. We expect that he should be given his due. The entire Haggadah should be chock full of recognition and praise for him.

Yet, we are terribly disappointed. In the entire Haggadah, we find only one explicit reference to Moses, and it is incidental to the thrust of the text. R. Yose ha-Gelili wants to prove that the Egyptians were smitten five-fold at the Sea of Reeds compared to the Plagues in Egypt. He demonstrates this by pointing out that the "finger of God" is used to describe the Plagues in Egypt,[2] while the "great hand" is the phrase used

1. *Haggadah, Maggid* (paragraph beginning with "We were slaves to Pharaoh in Egypt").
2. Exodus 8:15.

at the Sea of Reeds.[3] Hence hand is equal to five times finger. Then the author of the Haggadah adds the next verse, "Israel saw the great hand that Hashem inflicted upon Egypt; and the people revered Hashem; they had faith in Hashem and Moses, His servant" (Exodus 14:31). The last verse is unnecessary for the proof that the Egyptians were smitten five-fold at the Sea of Reeds.

The other reference to Moses is a veiled reference. The veiled reference is "*ha-otot,*" "the signs" (Deuteronomy 26:8). This refers to the Staff, as it says "and this Staff you shall take in your hand, with which you shall perform the signs" (Exodus 4:17).[4]

Rather than slighting the honor of Moses, I would propose that the author of the Haggadah heaps lavish praise on him. The key here is that the veiled reference to Moses is connected to the Staff. Moses' mission was to be a faithful servant of Hashem and carry out His charge. The Staff represented Moses' opportunity to deflect some of the Divine Glory on himself and project himself as a human being possessing supernatural powers rather than as the mouthpiece of the Master of the Universe.

The story of the Staff began when Moses plucks out the Staff, which was a sapphire rod, from the garden of Yitro.[5] No one before was able to pluck out the Staff. Yitro was amazed and told Moses, "Since you plucked it out, you must be the redeemer." On the Staff was emblazoned *d'tzakh adash b'aḥav*.[6] The Plagues were inaugurated with the Staff, three by Aaron and three by Moses. Moses had the opportunity to project himself as a magician. The lesson that the Staff had no inherent power was not likely to be learned when Moses transferred the Staff to Aaron for the first three Plagues. It was the same Staff in the hands of Moses that performed miracles before the Elders and the nation, and in the hands of Aaron, miracles are performed again.

---

3. Exodus 14:31.
4. *Haggadah, Maggid.*
5. *Pirkei de-Rabbi Eliezer* 40; *Yalkut Shimoni, Shemot* 168.
6. Exodus Rabbah 8:3; *Pirkei de-Rabbi Eliezer* 40. *D'tzakh adash b'aḥav* is an acronym for the Ten Plagues. "*D'tzakh*" stands for *dam, tzefardde'a,* and *kinnim* (i.e., blood, frogs, and lice); "*adash*" stands for *arov, dever,* and *sheḥin* (i.e., wild beasts, pestilence, and boils); and "*b'aḥav*" stands for *barad, arbeh, ḥoshekh,* and *bekhorot* (i.e., hail, locusts, darkness, and the slaying of the firstborn).

The question is why do the sorcerers say "it is a finger of God"? (Exodus 8:15). Logically, they should have said to Moses, "We concede your superiority over us; your sorcery is in a qualitatively different league than ours." In a Godless society, how do the sorcerers come to say "it is a finger of God"? If Moses had projected himself in even a small way as having independent power, the sorcerers would never have said "it is a finger of God." The fact that they said this is eloquent testimony that Moses executed his mission of being a servant of Hashem, that he was merely an instrument to promote the Divine Glory. It is precisely because Moses comported himself in an entirely veiled and incidental way that he succeeded in his mission with perfection.

Yes, the author of the Haggadah gives Moses his due. The mention of Moses in the verse "they had faith in Hashem and Moses, His servant" gives Moses credit for why the sorcerers said "it is a finger of God." It is only because Moses was the servant of the Holy One, Blessed is He, and resisted all attempt to deflect the Divine Glory on himself. So R. Yose ha-Gelili informs us that the exposition that the Egyptians were smitten five-fold at the Sea of Reeds is known to us only because Moses motivated the Egyptians to say "it is a finger of God." If there is no "finger," there is no *derashah* that can be made from the "great hand."

It is with the same purity and integrity that Moses transmitted the lesson of the second and third phases of the Plagues – "so that you will know that I am Hashem in the midst of the land" (Exodus 8:18) and "so that you shall know that there is none like Me in all the world" (Exodus 9:14).

The author of the Haggadah speaks to us and asks us to emulate Moses' character of giving total recognition to Hashem. It is the forty-eighth attribute that is necessary to acquire the Torah, repeating a saying in the name of the one who said it.[7] "Whoever repeats a thing in the name of the one who said it brings redemption to the world, as it is said, 'Esther informed the King [regarding the plot to kill him] in the name of Mordecai'" (Esther 2:22).[8]

7. Mishnah, *Avot* 6:6.
8. Ibid.

Yes, we bring *ge'ullah* to the world when we recognize our fellow's virtue, something redeeming and something good. It is when we can elevate our fellow that we achieve the highest level of unity and bring *ge'ullah* – may it come speedily in our days.

Hallel

(Undated)

One of the unique features of the Festival of Passover is that it is only on this Festival that we recite Hallel at night. We usher in the Festival with a double recitation of Hallel, once during the Evening Prayer and again at the Seder. Yet, our ancestors who lived through the *ge'ullah* process did not recite Hallel at the Exodus. Instead, they waited until the Splitting of the Sea of Reeds.

Why did they wait? R. Hayyim Soloveichik suggests that the man of profound faith believes that his salvation is imminent.[1] "But as for me, I trust in Your kindness; my heart will exult in Your salvation. I will sing to Hashem, for He has dealt kindly with me" (Psalms 13:6). But he does not break out in spontaneous *shirah* until he actually experiences the *ge'ullah*. It was not until the Children of Israel felt the decisiveness of *ge'ullah* – "and

1. See R. Isaac Zev ha-Levi Soloveitchik (*Brisker Rav*, Jerusalem, 1886–1959), *Ḥiddushei Rabbenu ha-Griz Soloveitchik mi-Pi ha-Shemu'ah al ha-Torah*, no. 127 (recording the statement of R. Hayyim Soloveitchik [*Rav Ḥayyim Brisker*, Brest-Litovsk, 1853–1918]).

Israel saw the Egyptians dead on the seashore" (Exodus 14:30) – that they broke out in *shirah.*

I would like to suggest another approach, which I think has much relevance for the contemporary scene. The Splitting of the Sea of Reeds marked a fundamental change in the conduct of Hashem toward the Children of Israel. In Egypt, the miracles, the Ten Plagues, were a necessary show of force to make the Egyptians do the will of Hashem. But now that Pharaoh sent the Children of Israel out and he himself escorted them, and the divine promise of "and afterward they will leave with great wealth" (Genesis 15:14) was also fulfilled, what else was needed? The Children of Israel could have been led over a direct route to the Land of Israel "by way of the land of the Philistines" (Exodus 13:17).

After three days, the Children of Israel began to turn back, encamping in front of Baal-zefon.[2] This was all to lure the Egyptians into a trap. The miracle of the Sea of Reeds was not necessary to punish the Egyptians. It was done just to demonstrate to the Children of Israel that they are special.[3] It was a miracle for the sake of miracle. This evokes *shirah.*

It is from the *parashah* of *shirah* that we derive *zeh Keli ve-anvehu,* "this is my God and I will glorify Him" (Exodus 15:2). Abba Saul understands the word "*anvehu*" as a contraction of two words, *ani ve-hu,* "I and Him," meaning that "I will be like Him; just as He is merciful and gracious, so too will I be merciful and gracious."[4] At the Sea of Reeds, Hashem showed the Children of Israel three dimensions of specialness, which we should imitate in the performance of mitzvot.

First, Hashem wrought the miracle of the Splitting of the Sea of Reeds not to punish the Egyptians, but rather to convey to the Children of Israel that they are special. One should never perform a religious act as a means of showing someone else that we are superior to them, or that some leaders have failed and we know better.

---

2. Exodus 14:2.
3. R. Shmuel Bornsztain (*Shem mi-Shemuel,* Poland, 1855–1926), *Shem mi-Shemuel: Al Seder Parshiyyot ha-Torah u-Mo'adei Kodesh,* 9th ed., vol. 2 (Jerusalem, 1992), *Be-Shallaḥ* (5671/February 1911), p. 171.
4. *Shabbat* 133b; *Rashi* ad loc., s.v. "*hevei domeh lo.*"

Second, the specialness that Hashem showed us had meaning only after the redemption from Egypt took place. The Splitting of the Sea of Reeds was icing on the cake. Timing is everything. Before the basic *ge'ullah* was achieved, a demonstration of our specialness through the performance of miracles for the sake of miracles could evoke mockery. There is no icing without a cake first. So, too, in the performance of mitzvot, we cannot leap to the esoteric and the remote before we fulfill the basic mitzvot. Take the mitzvah of *tallit* as an example. It is an optional mitzvah, and for a woman, it is a doubly optional mitzvah, quite remote.[5] Leaping to the mitzvah before we fulfill the basic mitzvot is *yuhara* (false piety).[6] It is not a sign of extra piety. It is fake religious pride.

Third, at the Sea of Reeds, there were spoils.[7] And we ask, why was it necessary? There were already the spoils of Egypt.[8]

I would submit that perhaps a contrast was being set up with respect to how a divine promise would be fulfilled in a minimal way so as to be *yotzei* and how it would be fulfilled with maximum generosity and grace. In Egypt, the Children of Israel did not even want the spoils. Hashem told Moses, "Please speak [*dabber na*] in the ears of the people: Let each man request of his fellow and each woman from her fellow silver vessels and gold vessels" (Exodus 11:2). *Ein "na" ela lashon bakkashah*; the word "*na*" denotes a request.[9] And they had to resort to deceit and self-humiliation. They had to shame the Egyptians into giving it to them. But at the Sea of Reeds, Hashem demonstrated the most profound grace and generosity, to show them that it is not only the result, but how it comes about, that matters.

It is only when we have these elements that we can say that the specialness is demonstrated, and it is only then that we can experience the decisiveness and finality of the *ge'ullah*.

---

5. In general, women are not obligated in time-bound mitzvot, of which *tallit* is one. See *Shulḥan Arukh, Oraḥ Ḥayyim* 17:2; R. Moshe Feinstein, *Iggerot Mosheh, Oraḥ Ḥayyim* 4:49.
6. *Berakhot* 17b; *Pesaḥim* 55a; R. Moses Isserles (*Rema*, Poland, 1525 or 1530–1572), *Rema* to *Shulḥan Arukh* loc. cit.
7. *Mekhilta de-Rav Shimon bar Yoḥai* 12; *Rashi* to Exodus 15:22.
8. Exodus 12:35–36.
9. *Berakhot* 9a; *Rashi* to Exodus 11:2.

You Shall Tell Your Son

(Undated)

Each one of the Three Festivals sparkles in its own distinctive way. We would imagine that the special mitzvot of each Festival would not detract or slight any of the other Festivals. The mitzvah of matzah on Passover, for example, in no way slights the Festival of Sukkot, as the latter festival has its own distinctive mitzvot, i.e., sukkah and the Four Species.

But a disturbing question arises. Why is the Festival of Passover singled out by the Torah for *ve-higgadeta le-vinkha,* "you shall tell your son" (Exodus 13:8), to relate the essence of the message of this festival to our children, but no similar demand is made of us to transmit to our children the essence of the character of the other two of the Three Festivals? Is the eternal message of the other Festivals any less important than the message of Passover?

Perhaps the answer lies in the proposition that *haggadah* is not the optimal medium to transmit the essence of Sukkot or Shavuot. On Sukkot, the focus is on the frail roof of the *dirat arai* that we reside in during the seven days of Sukkot, and the overriding message is our total dependence upon Hashem and the futility of relying on human beings. This idea cannot be transmitted by means of preaching. Preaching and exhortations cannot directly inculcate *emunah* and *bittaḥon*. How is this best achieved? It is, as the *Ḥinnukh* points out, by the meticulous performance of mitzvot.[1] The mitzvot have a mystical quality about them. *Emunah* and *bittaḥon*, and love and fear of Hashem, are byproducts of the performance of mitzvot. *Haggadah* is hence not the optimal means of transmitting *bittaḥon*.

On Shavuot, we commemorate the *mysterium tremendum* of *ma'amad har Sinai*. But as we become increasingly removed historically from the event of Mount Sinai, the ability to transmit the actual experience of Sinai becomes diminished and eventually is lost entirely. How then is the experience preserved? It cannot be achieved through *haggadah*. Instead, it must be achieved when parents demonstrate to their children that the Torah is central to their life, by showing them their willingness to sacrifice for it and set priorities around it. This type of conduct recaptures the emotions of centrality that we had as a people thousands of years ago when all creation stood silent in awe as Hashem spoke to us, His people, and revealed to us His Torah.

But on Passover, we have a mitzvah of *haggadah* because it is through the medium of *haggadah* that we can fulfill our obligation of "in every generation, one is obligated to regard himself as though he himself had gone out of Egypt."[2] We are bidden to somehow leap the generations and touch the lives of our ancestors, to make the biblical figures come alive and vicariously feel their pain and triumph, to feel the birth pangs of a nation of Hashem.

---

1. *Sefer ha-Ḥinnukh* teaches *ha-adam nif'al aḥar pe'ulotav* (lit., "a person is made according to his deeds"). See R. Aaron b. Joseph ha-Levi, *Sefer ha-Ḥinnukh*, eds. R. Yitzhak Yeshayah Weiss, R. David Zicherman, and R. Yitzhak Weinstein (Jerusalem: Mekhon Yerushalayim, 1992), mitzvah no. 16 (prohibition against breaking a bone of the paschal offering). See also ibid., mitzvah no. 40 (prohibition against building an altar from hewn stone); mitzvah no. 99 (commandment that Priests wear the Priestly Vestments); mitzvah no. 264 (obligation for a Priest to become impure for a close relative); mitzvah no. 299 (commandment to bring a *Musaf* offering on each of the seven days of Passover); mitzvah no. 324 (commandment to take a *lulav* on Sukkot); mitzvah no. 401 (commandment to bring two lambs as a burnt offering daily).
2. *Haggadah, Maggid.*

This ability to make contact with previous generations, as R. Soloveitchik points out, was first demonstrated by Jacob.[3] It was he who not only communicated with his grandchildren, but pronounced that the closeness that he felt to them was the same as with his own sons. "And now, your two sons who were born to you in the land of Egypt… shall be mine; Ephraim and Manasseh shall be mine like Reuben and Simeon" (Genesis 48:5).

On Passover, we must reach the generation of the Exodus and be creative teachers, addressing ourselves to our children on whatever level they are on, to the inquisitive child, the searching child, and the bewildered child. We must even get the wicked child to participate in the Seder and conduct something of a dialogue with him, unlike the fifth son, who does not show up altogether. We are bidden to tap our resourcefulness to reach the children and make the Exodus and its personalities come alive.

Making contact with the previous generations is one of the endowments that a father gives his son. Beside the genetic code, the father gives his son *mispar dorot ha-rishonot*.[4] And this, in R. Akiva's words, is the secret of the *keytz* (lit., "end," i.e., Messianic times), because this is what provides us with the passion and intensity of our Jewish identity.[5]

---

3. R. Abraham R. Besdin, *Man of Faith in the Modern World* (Hoboken, NJ: Ktav, 1989), 18–19.
4. Mishnah, *Ediyot* 2:9.
5. Ibid.; see R. Besdin, *Man of Faith in the Modern World*, 20.

Passover – Shabbat
Ḥol ha-Mo'ed

Song of Songs – Holy of Holies

(1990s)

All the songs recorded in the Torah are holy, teaches R. Akiva, but the Song of Songs is holy of holies.[1] In all the other songs, either God praises Israel or Israel praises God. The Song of Songs is the song of reciprocal praise.

In the Song of Songs, we shed our usual appellation as servants or children. Instead, we are described as Hashem's bride, and Hashem as the bridegroom.[2] What is intended is to depict a relationship of equality. The *Ribbono shel Olam* calls *Knesset Yisrael* "*tammati*" (lit., "my perfection") (Song of Songs 5:2). As R. Yannai expounds, this could be understood as *te'omati*, "my twin," as if the *Ribbono shel Olam* is not greater than you and you are not greater than Him.[3] Within this framework of equality,

1. Mishnah, *Yadayim* 3:5; *Midrash Tanḥuma, Titzavveh* 5.
2. Song of Songs 4:8–12.
3. Song of Songs Rabbah 5:3; *Tashlikh* Prayer, *Kel Maleh Raḥamim*.

both the *Ribbono shel Olam* and *Knesset Yisrael* recognize each other's singularity.

In this vein, the *Ribbono shel Olam* praises the Jewish people as not only superior to the other nations, but that relative to *Knesset Yisrael,* the other nations have no value at all. "As a rose among thorns, so is My beloved among the daughters" (Song of Songs 2:2).[4] Notice that it is a rose among thorns, not a rose among roses.[5]

Knesset Yisrael returns the compliment. "Like an apple among the barren trees of the forest, so is my Beloved among the sons" (Song of Songs 2:3).[6] God is a beautiful, fragrant, and fruitful apple tree among barren, useless trees. This is a recognition of *ein od mi-levaddo,* "there is none beside Him" (Deuteronomy 4:35).

When each party in a relationship recognizes the other party's singularity, the deepest communication of souls is achieved. Eloquent and elegant speech become superfluous. *Ve-diglo alai ahavah* (lit., "His banner upon me is love") (Song of Songs 2:4) is understood by our Sages to mean that even the babbling and mistakes of *Knesset Yisrael* are dear to Hashem.[7] If an ignorant and sincere man says *ve-oyavta,* "you shall estrange," instead of *ve-ahavta,* "you shall love," his prayer is accepted and the egregious mistake is overlooked![8] With such a profound love existing between Hashem and *Knesset Yisrael,* there can never be a severance of relationship or clean break.

Different expressions are employed in the Song of Songs to describe the singularity of both Hashem and *Knesset Yisrael,* but there are two words that are used to describe both Hashem and *Knesset Yisrael.* They are *tzvi,* "gazelle," and *ayal,* "hart."[9] A characteristic of the

---

4. "Daughters" refer to the other nations that try to influence the Jewish people to worship their gods. *Rashi* to Song of Songs 2:2.
5. Cf. R. Shelomoh Harkavi (Grodno, 1890–1941), *Me-Imrei Shelomoh,* vol. 2 (Jerusalem, 1994), 29–30.
6. "Sons" refer to the gods worshipped by other nations. *Rashi* to Song of Songs 2:3.
7. Song of Songs Rabbah 2:13. The Midrash associates the word "*diglo*" with the word "*digul,*" omission or mistake.
8. Ibid.
9. Song of Songs 2:9, 2:17, 8:14.

gazelle is that when it runs away, it is always turning his head.[10] And a characteristic of the young hart is that it never sleeps with both eyes shut, only with one eye shut.[11] The gazelle and hart thus symbolize that even in the worst alienation, there is always a longing for reconciliation and a readiness for it at any time by both Hashem and *Knesset Yisrael.*[12]

There is, however, one final aspect of a *Shir ha-Shirim* relationship, that every profound love must be accompanied by profound jealousy. Indeed, Solomon tells us, "For strong till the death is my love; though their zeal for vengeance is hard as the grave" (Song of Songs 8:6).

The entire Song of Songs is written in delicate, soft, and tender terms, but in three places, an abrupt outburst of jealous emotion appears, two on the part of *Knesset Yisrael,* and one on the part of Hashem. In connection with *Knesset Yisrael,* the phrase "*hishbati etkhem benot Yerushalayim… im tit'oreru et ha-ahavah,*" "I adjure you, O nations destined to ascend to Jerusalem… if you dare to disturb His love for me," appears twice.[13] In both instances, it comes after *Knesset Yisrael* reflects upon the singular gifts of endearment that Hashem bestowed upon them, gifts that were not given to anyone else.

First, in chapter two, elaborate mention is made of the gift of Torah, including "He brought me to the *beit ha-yayin*" (lit., "the house of wine") (Song of Songs 2:4).[14] In addition, "*semolo taḥat roshi, vi-yimino teḥabbekeni,*" "His left hand supports my head and His right hand embraces me" (Song of Songs 2:6). By connecting *semolo,* "His left hand," to *simlah,* "dress," our Sages take "His left hand supports my head" to allude to *tzitzit.*[15] Noting that the right hand embraces the left when we put on *tefillin,* our Sages connect "His right hand embraces me" to *tefillin.*[16]

---

10. *Targum Yonatan* to Song of Songs 8:14; *Malbim* to Song of Songs 2:9.
11. *Targum Yonatan* to Songs of Songs 8:14.
12. See *Malbim* to Song of Songs 2:9.
13. Song of Songs 2:7, 8:4.
14. Song of Songs Rabbah 2:13 (stating that the "house of wine" refers to Mount Sinai, where the Torah was given); *Rashi* to Song of Songs 2:4, s.v. "*el beit ha-yayin*" (associating the "house of wine" with the Tent of Meeting, where Moses expounded the Torah).
15. Song of Songs Rabbah 2:17.
16. Ibid.

Now, the Oral Law is our exclusive gift – *yeinah shel Torah* (lit., "the wine of Torah"), the secrets of the Torah, which the nations of the world cannot comprehend.[17] It is not their domain at all. Also, as an endearment, Hashem gives us *tefillin* and *tzitzit*, with which we can display our Jewish identity in an open manner.

In chapter three, just before the outburst of this emotion of jealousy, *Knesset Yisrael*'s frantic journey through time is described. The nation waited impatiently for forty years in the Wilderness, and finally, in the time of Joshua, after he vanquished the thirty-one Kings, there is an ecstatic outburst after getting the Land of Israel. *Knesset Yisrael* says, "I grasped Him, determined that my deeds would never again cause me to lose hold of Him, until I brought Him to my mother's house and to the chamber of the one who conceived me" (Song of Songs 3:4). *Knesset Yisrael* fully seizes the *shekhinah* and wants to bring Hashem into the Tabernacle of Shiloh.

Knesset Yisrael forewarns the nations that they will be defenseless if they dare disrupt or interfere with the love that these gifts evoke for them. Interference with these singular gifts evokes a feeling of nothing less than an invasion with the singular relationship that the Al-Mighty bestowed upon us, His chosen people.

Now, if we feel the singularity of our relationship with Hashem, then emotions of jealousy are quite proper in relation to three issues. First, we must be proud that we are Jews. We must want to be Jews, not only secretly, but to display our Jewishness in an open manner. Any reticence on our part to display our Jewishness openly bespeaks a lack of recognition of our singular relationship with Hashem. Any intrusion on our right to display our Jewishness openly must be reacted to with intense emotion. Jealous guarding of our Jewishness is a proper expression of our relationship with Hashem.

Second, we must be aware that it is only the Jewish people who were brought to the *beit ha-yayin*. When we discuss social issues, there is only one standpoint, the Jewish one.

---

17. See *Midrash ha-Ne'elam, Va-Yetze*, ch. 18, *ma'amar "ve-hinnei sullam mutzav artzah"*; R. Samuel Eliezer b. Judah ha-Levi Edels (*Maharsha*, Poland, 1555–1631), *Ḥiddushei Halakhot ve-Aggadot, Berakhot* 34b.

Finally, any threat to the existence of the Land of Israel, or even to the suggestion that it is not our exclusive domain, must be reacted to with jealousy. The talk now of the sectionalization of Jerusalem, or that the Jewish State should not have its capital in Jerusalem, must be rejected out of hand.[18]

When *Knesset Yisrael* responds in its proper form with the emotion of jealousy, we can expect the *Ribbono shel Olam* to respond accordingly. And what does this involve? It involves the declaration on the part of the Al-Mighty "the vineyard is Mine!" And the nations of the world reply, "The thousand silver pieces are Yours, You to Whom peace belongs, and two hundred more to those who guarded the fruit" (Song of Songs 8:12). *Knesset Yisrael* is treated as *hekdesh,* "consecrated property." Any expropriation by the nations of the world will be treated as *me'ilah ba-kodesh* (i.e., trespass with respect to a holy matter), with the consequence that everything that was extracted will be returned, with a penalty of a fifth as well.[19]

18. James D. Besser, "Rabin: Jerusalem Is Ours: Prime Minister at AIPAC Conference Emotionally Describes His Lifelong Commitment to the Israeli Capital," *New York Jewish Week* (Manhattan ed.), March 24, 1994, 35.
19. *Rashi* to Song of Songs 8:12, s.v. "*le-notrim et piryo.*"

It Is I and No Other

April 22, 2000

The Song of Songs is linked to the Festival of Passover. Permit me to suggest that one rationale for the pairing is to sensitize us to one aspect of the Exodus from Egypt that would otherwise probably not receive sufficient attention and focus.

We know that the overriding theme of the Song of Songs is the Jewish people's yearning for a direct, personal, and intimate relationship with Hashem. *Yishakeni mi-neshikot pihu* (lit., "May He kiss me with the kisses of His mouth") (Song of Songs 1:2). This refers to *Mattan Torah*, and specifically to the first two Commandments that we heard directly from Hashem.[1]

By reading the Song of Songs, we hence draw attention to the finale of *ge'ullah*, the Plague of the Firstborn, which is described by the Torah and the author of the Haggadah, and is a Song-of-Songs-type of phenomenon. "I shall go through the land of Egypt on this night … I am Hashem" (Exodus 12:12).

1. Song of Songs Rabbah 1:13; R. Elijah b. Solomon Zalman (Vilna Gaon or *Gra*, Vilna, 1720–1797), *Be'ur ha-Gra*, Song of Songs 1:2.

"Not through an angel, not through a seraph, and not through a messenger, but the Holy One, Blessed is He, He alone, in His Glory."[2]

Now, all the Plagues violate the natural order, so what was so special about the Plague of the Firstborn? Should we understand the Torah's words of "I shall go through the land of Egypt" that it is just an article of faith that an angel cannot distinguish between *tippah shel bekhor ve-tippah she-einah shel bekhor*?[3]

Permit me to theorize that during the Plague of the Firstborn, the Jewish people felt a qualitative difference between this experience and witnessing and being saved from the previous Plagues. The Jewish people really felt that the *ge'ullah* was now being brought about by the Holy One, Blessed is He, by Himself. And why? Because there are a number of fundamental differences between the salvation that Hashem effects through an angel and the salvation that Hashem effects directly.

An angel, within the framework of effecting salvation, can disappoint and even demoralize the one he saves. Recall that the angel said to Lot, "Flee for your life" (Genesis 19:17). This implied, as the *Mizraḥi* points out, that Lot was expecting more.[4] He was expecting that his property would also be saved. He thought that his home along with his fine furniture would miraculously be transported to safety. No. He thought that perhaps his stock portfolio would be saved. No. The record of it was erased in a computer file. And what about my gold and silver bullion? It was looted by fellow Sodomites. And what about my secret bank account in a Swiss bank? The only scrap of paper that is evidence of your ownership of the account was lost! You only get to have your life saved and no more. What a disappointment!

---

2. *Haggadah, Maggid.*

3. Hashem distinguished between a drop that brought forth a firstborn and a drop that did not bring forth a firstborn. *Bava Metzia* 61b; *Pesikta Rabbati* 17; *Yalkut Shimoni, Shemini* 546; *Rashi* to Leviticus 12:38, s.v. "*asher hotzeti etkhem.*" In the Plague of the Firstborn, an Egyptian who was born first to either his mother or his father was killed. The Egyptian women committed adultery and would bear several children, each of whom was a firstborn to a different father. Hashem Himself discerned who was a firstborn and killed him in the Plague. *Rashi* to *Bava Metzia* 61b, s.v. "*she-hivḥanti be-Mitzrayim.*"

4. R. Elijah Mizrahi (*Re'em*, Constantinople, ca. 1450–1526), *Sefer ha-Mizraḥi*, Genesis 19:16.

And the angel also says, "*Al tabbit aḥarekha*," "Do not dare look behind you" (Genesis 19:17). You have taken part in the sin of Sodom. You do not really deserve to be saved. You are being saved only in the merit of Abraham.[5]

Whereas an angel can disappoint and demoralize, Hashem effected our *ge'ullah* not just by saving us, but also by suffusing us with a feeling of self-worth and merit, a feeling that we deserved to be redeemed. And how? By coupling the Plague of the Firstborn with the paschal offering. On the tenth day of the month of Nisan, we were bidden to take a *pesaḥ*.[6] This required an act of courage because the lamb was the *avodah zarah* of the Egyptians.[7] But it was a measured act of courage for Hashem knew that the Egyptians would not question us or harass us for taking possession of their deity for an unspecified purpose.

But *isarusa de-la-Ela* was already working. We got past the test of measured courage and proceeded to the next one – *Shabbat ha-Gadol* – of tying the deity of the Egyptians to our bedposts. Again, Hashem intervened with *isarusa de-la-Ela*. Hashem paralyzed the Egyptians. They could do nothing even though they knew that the Children of Israel were preparing to slaughter their deity.[8]

Momentum was building, and the path was already paved for the final act of courage, to slaughter the deity of the Egyptians. We were already emboldened to take the courageous act without fear. *Isarusa de-la-Ela* was working well to propel us to great heights. In the end, we dipped the hyssop in the blood of the *pesaḥ* and spread the blood on the doorposts and the lintel.[9] This is how Hashem would know to skip over our homes.[10] All this was designed to make us feel that we had done something courageous that demonstrated our faith in Hashem, and hence we deserved to be redeemed.

One angel cannot go on two missions, and certainly cannot do two things at the same time.[11] But at the same time that Hashem suffused

---

5. See Genesis 19:29.
6. Exodus 12:3.
7. Exodus 8:22; *Rashi* ad loc., s.v. "*to'avat Mitzrayim*"; Exodus Rabbah 16:3.
8. *Mekhilta de-Rav Shimon bar Yoḥai*, Exodus 12:6; *Tur, Oraḥ Ḥayyim* 430.
9. Exodus 12:22.
10. Exodus 12:23.
11. Genesis Rabbah 50:2; *Rashi* to Genesis 18:2.

us with a feeling of self-worth, He demoralized the Egyptians by "against all the gods of Egypt I shall mete out punishment" (Exodus 12:12).

Another difference is that an angel is concerned only with doing its mission. If executing the mission generates changed expectations for us, that is entirely incidental. But in the Plague of the Firstborn, Hashem changed our expectations for the future. He gave the Angel of Death a vacation. "He will not permit the destroyer to enter your homes to smite" (Exodus 12:23). Without this factor, we would, of course, have felt catapulted to great heights in the Plague of the Firstborn. But at the same time, we might have felt a backdrop of natural order and expected the natural order to return. By sending the Angel of Death on vacation, Hashem created an excitement that the natural order was permanently changed and that we should expect a very bright future.

The ideal for us is derived from the Thirteen Attributes of Mercy, which are mentioned in today's Torah reading.[12] "Just as He is 'merciful and gracious,' so must you be merciful and gracious."[13] Well, there are all kinds of kindness. There is human kindness and there is kindness that imitates the kindness of Hashem.

Now, if a problem or demand makes its way to an individual or the community and the supplicant feels disappointed with the response, then the response is the kindness of an angel, not an imitation of the kindness of Hashem. It is shades of "flee for your life; do not look behind you" (Genesis 19:17).

If our response is that we are over-extended and too busy, then again, this is the response of an angel, not the response of divine kindness. And if the feeling is that we are concerned only with stop-gap measures and not extended or long-term solutions, then again, this at best is an angel's response and not a response that imitates divine kindness.

Let it be our lot to imitate our ancestors at the Sea of Reeds who shouted "*Zeh Keli ve-anvehu,*" "this is my God and I will glorify Him" (Exodus 15:2). They felt *ani ve-Hu,* "I and Him," and were driven to imitate Hashem's kindness.[14]

---

12. The Torah reading is at Exodus 33:12–34:26. The Thirteen Attributes of Mercy are at Exodus 34:6–7.
13. *Shabbat* 133b; *Rashi* ad loc., s.v. "*hevei domeh lo.*"
14. Abba Saul understands the word "*anvehu*" as a contraction of two words, *ani ve-hu,* "I and Him," meaning that "I will be like Him; just as He is merciful and gracious, so too will I be merciful and gracious."

Make Your Way Known to Me

April 19, 2003

We are all comfortable with the notion that the Torah portion that the Sages instituted for a holy day relates to the theme of the day.[1] Well, today, the beginning of the Torah reading is Moses' request to Hashem "make Your way known to me" (Exodus 33:13). This is arguably the most abstruse passage in the Torah. It takes place historically after the Sin of the Golden Calf and appears to have no relevancy for the theme of the Festival of Passover.

Permit me to suggest that "make Your way known to me" relates critically to the essential reason for Passover, the reason of freedom.

In the thinking of the *Sforno,* the essence of freedom is control or mastery over time.[2] "This month shall be for you the beginning of

1. See Mishnah, *Megillah* 3:5–6; *Megillah* 30b–32a.
2. *Sforno* to Exodus 12:2.

the months" (Exodus 12:2). Hashem tells the Jewish people, "You will now be master over time."

In the thinking of R. Joseph B. Soloveitchik, the free man enjoys life by exuberating in the three dimensions of time. Because he is free, he can participate in and create experiences that will form a cherished memory. This is retrospection. He can reminisce. Only one's imagination limits the joys one can anticipate. Because retrospection and anticipation are very bright, appreciation of the present moment is intensified.[3]

In sharp contrast, a slave has no retrospection, no cherished moments to recollect, because his existence is a continuous state of misery. And because the slave is brutalized and intimidated, his horizons are effectively lowered. His bleak condition even destroys his imagination and hope for something better. For the slave, there can therefore be no appreciation of the moment.[4]

When the Children of Israel left Egypt, the Exodus is described as "the Children of Israel went forth with an upraised hand" (Numbers 33:3), triumphantly.

I would ask you, does this mean that freedom for the Jewish people began with the *ḥerut* of anticipation and as appreciation, but the worst part was simply blotted out? No. This is the lesson of "make Your way known to me." Commentators understand Moses' request as seeking an understanding of divine justice – *tzaddik ve-ra lo ve-rasha ve-tov lo,* "why do the righteous suffer and the wicked prosper?"[5] Hashem's answer is: "You will see My back, but My face may not be seen" (Exodus 33:23). You will understand divine justice only retrospectively, but while events are unfolding, you will not understand anything.[6] You will have many troubling questions. "You will see My back" makes the very essence of a Jew a questioning individual, searching for understanding Hashem by means of retrospection. If retrospection is how a Jew quests for Hashem,

---

3. R. Abraham R. Besdin, *Reflections of the Rav: Lessons in Jewish Thought* (Jerusalem: World Zionist Organization, 1979), 200–202.
4. Ibid.
5. *Berakhot* 7a.
6. *Ḥatam Sofer, Torat Mosheh,* Exodus 33:23.

retrospection must also have been a part of the *ḥerut* personality that the Jews acquired in the Exodus from Egypt.

We cannot blot out the past. No. If we look back enough, the Servitude was not continuous misery. There were cherished moments to remember.

Permit me to suggest that the event for retrospection was "He performed the signs in the sight of the people. And the people believed, and they heard that Hashem had remembered the Children of Israel" (Exodus 4:30–31). This was a major moment, a cherished memory. Why? Moses mesmerized the Jewish people in that not only did he have the code words of redemption, "*pakod pakadeti,*" "I have surely remembered" (Exodus 3:16),[7] but he was the living embodiment of that code and therefore testimony that Hashem had already visited the Jewish people in the Servitude.

Consider that when Pharaoh heard his astrologers say that the savior of Israel had been born, Pharaoh set out to destroy every male child.[8] The resources of the nation were mobilized toward this end. He pursued the goal monomaniacally. Every woman had to go to a hospital to give birth.[9] He had detectives encircle homes where pregnant women were known to hide.[10] With all these stupendous efforts to stillborn the savior of Israel, Pharaoh ends up bringing him up in his own palace![11] Moses' survival is the spectacular miracle of Jewish survival. This is a cherished moment of retrospection. *Ḥerut* of retrospection fuels the *ḥerut* of anticipation in a way that cannot be done if there is no retrospection.

The second part of *ḥerut* is the *ḥerut* of anticipation. "It shall be that when your children say to you, 'What is this service to you?'

---

7. Exodus Rabbah 5:13. The code was transmitted from Jacob to Joseph, from Joseph to his brothers, and from Asher b. Jacob to his daughter Serah. Serah was still alive when Moses said the code words in Egypt and verified the code for the Children of Israel.
8. Exodus 1:22; *Rashi* ad loc.; Exodus Rabbah 1:18; *Midrash Tanḥuma, Va-Yak'hel* 4.
9. R. Hezekiah b. Manoah (*Ḥizkuni,* France, 13th cent.), *Ḥizkuni* to Exodus 1:21, s.v. "*va-ya'as lahem.*"
10. See R. Jacob Culi (Constantinople, ca. 1685–1732), *Me-Am Lo'ez,* Exodus 1:21, trans. R. Shemuel Yerushalmi, *Yalkut Me-Am Lo'ez: Sefer Shemot* (Jerusalem: Mossad Yad Ezra, 1968), 14.
11. Exodus Rabbah 1:26.

you shall say, 'It is a *pesaḥ* feast offering to Hashem'... and the people bowed their heads and prostrated themselves" (Exodus 12:26–27). Now, the prostration was for the tidings of the sons that they would have.[12] R. Moshe Feinstein asks, this is the question of the Wicked Son, so why was there jubilation?[13] The answer is that once we recognize the miracle of survival, we have a certainty that the condition of the Wicked Son is but a transitory phenomenon. Why? Because if Hashem performed for us a spectacular miracle for our survival, then it will not be survival for the sake of survival, or survival for the sake of mediocrity, but rather survival for the sake of greatness!

In our time, Hashem has given us the gift of a Jewish State. The entire fifty-five-year history of the State of Israel is the survival of "one lamb among seventy wolves."[14] Just before Operation Iraqi Freedom, analysts were giving dire predictions that once hostilities would begin, Saddam would launch chemical warheads to Israel, and sleeper terrorist cells would be activated in Israel and the United States.[15] "In every generation, they rise us against us to destroy us; and the Holy One, Blessed is He, rescues us from their hands."[16]

Because the miracle of survival is also reaffirmed and reinforced by the survival from every generation's dangers, we are living currently the *ḥerut* of retrospection. Let the *ḥerut* of retrospection fuel the *ḥerut* of anticipation. Let's think big. The *ḥerut* of anticipation is *Meshiaḥ Tzidkenu*; may he come speedily in our days.

---

12. *Rashi* to Exodus 12:27. The news that they would have sons is implied at Exodus 12:26, "When your children say to you." R. Simeon b. Isaac ha-Levi Aschenberg (Germany, d. 1598), *Devek Tov*, Exodus 12:27, s.v. "*va-yikkod ha-am.*"
13. R. Moshe Feinstein (New York, 1895–1986), *Derash Mosheh*, Exodus 12:27, s.v. "*va-yikkod ha-am va-yishtaḥavu.*"
14. *Pesikta Rabbati* 9 (on Psalms 35:10 [*matzil ani me-ḥazak*]).
15. Herb Keinon, "Israel Readies for Dirty Bombs, Missiles," *Jerusalem Post*, February 7, 2003, A5; John Solomon, "FBI, Police Prepare for Attacks in the US," *Jerusalem Post*, February 17, 2003, 5.
16. *Haggadah, Maggid, Ve-Hi she-Amedah.*

The Dry Bones

April 10, 2004

King Solomon describes the redemption from Egypt with the imagery of *medalleg al he-harim*, "leaping over the mountains" (Song of Songs 2:8). We were destined to wallow in servitude for 400 years, but Hashem lopped off 190 years.[1] The Future Redemption will also be accelerated. It is described in the next phrase, *mekappetz al ha-geva'ot*, "skipping over the hills" (Song of Songs 2:8).

What is the difference between leaping and skipping? The *Sefat Emet* tells us that leaping is with one foot, while skipping is with two feet.[2] Thus, skipping is even more accelerated than leaping.

In what manner will skipping manifest itself? Permit me to suggest that it is laid out in today's *haftarah*. Ezekiel describes a vision of

1. Song of Songs Rabbah 2:19.
2. R. Yehudah Aryeh Leib Alter (*Sefat Emet*, Poland, 1847–1905), *Sefat Emet, Pesaḥ* (5642/1882).

teḥiyyat ha-metim in the valley of the dry bones.[3] His vision departs from our traditional notion of how *teḥiyyat ha-metim* will take place.

It is our tradition, as the *Malbim* points out, that *teḥiyyat ha-metim* will take place similarly to the development of the embryo. First comes the seed of life. Then a membrane forms, upon which flesh grows and sinews develop. Finally, the limbs attach themselves to the sinews and bones. So it will be with *teḥiyyat ha-metim*. First the body totally disintegrates, with only the *luz* bone remaining. The *luz* bone is the life force, the *ruaḥ*, to begin *teḥiyyat ha-metim*.[4]

What Ezekiel describes is different. The bones are "*atzamot yeveshot*," "completely dry" (Ezekiel 37:2). There is no *luz* bone, no *ruaḥ ḥayyim*, "spirit of life," at all. So the first thing is that Hashem blows a spirit into the bones. "Behold, I bring a spirit into you, and you will come to life" (Ezekiel 37:5). The spirit makes the bones functional, and the process of reconstituting the human body begins, but without a spiritual life force. The spiritual force comes when the body is fully reconstituted. And it is the real thing because it says about the spirit "then you will know that I am Hashem" (Ezekiel 37:6). So sinews develop on the bones, then flesh develops on the sinews, and skin develops on the flesh. Only then does the spiritual life force enter.

Ezekiel speaks to us in our own period of exile. It is a message of hope because the dry bones in life were people who did not have the *laḥluḥit* (lit., "moisture," i.e., freshness) of mitzvot.

But, I think that Ezekiel speaks most poignantly to the portion of the Exile in the post-Holocaust period. There was never a time in Jewish history when a stronger judgment prevailed that the Jewish people are a heap of dry bones with no hope for a future. But Hashem reconstituted the body of the Jewish people in a spectacular manner that allows us full expression as we never had it before. In all previous exiles, the potential for the Jew in the material, intellectual, cultural, and political spheres was very limited. The mundane world for the Jew was totally barren and primitive. The gentiles set so many barriers and limitations around us.

---

3. Ezekiel 37:1–14.
4. *Malbim* to Ezekiel 37:4.

But now, in the post-Holocaust period, we are living in a wealthier and more open society. The material, intellectual, and cultural potential for the Jew is unlimited. And, indeed, Hashem has reconstituted the Jewish body in full. In every field of endeavor, excellence is achieved by Jews in a far disproportionate rate to their number. When we look at stellar achievement rather than just prominence, the percentage rises even higher. There are twelve million Jews, which is only 0.2 percent of the total population. Only two out of every 1,000 people are Jews, yet one out of five of all Nobel Prizes were earned by Jews.[5] The fullness that Hashem gave us rises even to the level of a national existence, achieving the status of a nation among the nations of the world. So it is the gift of Hashem of reconstituting us with a full body and a spirit, but not the gift of "you will know that I am Hashem."

In the reconstitution of the body, there is a noise, a rattling of the bones as they come together and form the body.[6] What is the noise? It is the jealousy of the nations of the world. Only recently, the President of Malaysia, using the medium of the Arab League Convention, but speaking on the world stage to billions of people, said that the Jews control the world.[7] He said that with hatred and jealousy, but he is right.

Hashem reconstituted the body for us. It is the first stage of *teḥiyyat ha-metim*. The final stage, the second *ruaḥ*, which is the spirit of "you will know that I am Hashem," can come in either of two times – *be-ittah*, "in its time," Hashem will blow the second *ruaḥ* in us, or *aḥishennah* (lit., "I will hasten it"), if we arrive at a knowledge of Hashem on our own.[8]

So there are enormous opportunities for *kiddush Shem Shamayim* in every sphere of life, in the sphere of family, community, business, politics, public policy, and international relations. It is in the period of *mekappetz al ha-geva'ot* that we have an abundance of opportunities to make a *kiddush Hashem*.

---

5. Baruch Aba Shalev, *100 Years of Nobel Prizes* (New Delhi: Atlantic Publishers, 2003), 57.
6. Ezekiel 37:7.
7. "Malaysian Leader: Palestinian Fight Has Been Futile; Jews Rule the World, He Tells Muslim Body," *Detroit Free Press*, October 17, 2003, A4; "Malaysian Attacks Jews," *New York Times*, October 17, 2003, A8.
8. See Isaiah 60:22; *Rashi* ad loc.

Passover – Seventh Day

Hallel on Yom ha-Atzma'ut

April 26, 1989

We are all familiar with the principle that the Festival of Passover predicts the day of the week on which each of the Jewish holidays falls. This is arrived at by means of the "*at bash*" system wherein the first letter of the Hebrew alphabet is interchanged with the last, the second with the next to last, and so forth.[1] Hence, the day of the week on which the first day of Passover falls is the same day of the week on which the *ta'anit*, Tishah be-Av, falls, and the day of the week on which the second day of Passover falls is the same day of the week on which Shavuot falls.[2]

Throughout the millennia, each day of Passover had its pairing, except for the seventh day of Passover. But with the establishment of Yom ha-Atzma'ut on the fifth day of Iyar, this ended. The fifth day of Iyar always falls on the same day of the week as the seventh day of Passover.[3]

---

1. *Sabbath* 104a.
2. *Shulḥan Arukh, Oraḥ Ḥayyim* 428:3.
3. Dr. Yom Tov Levinsky, *Sefer ha-Mo'adim: Parashat Mo'adei Yisrael*, vol. 8 (Tel Aviv: Devir, 1956), 467.

The link between Yom ha-Atzma'ut and the seventh day of Passover goes further.

In rabbinic circles, there is an ongoing controversy regarding whether one should recite Hallel, at least without a blessing, to mark this momentous event.[4] The debate revolves around applying a *kal ve-ḥomer* that is mentioned in the Talmud. We are told that the Jewish nation was blessed with forty-eight Prophets and seven Prophetesses. None of them ever added to, or subtracted from, what was written in the Torah. How then, questions the Talmud, did the Sages institute the reading of the Megillah?

To this the Talmud answers, now, if the Jews, who were delivered from slavery in Egypt said *shirah,* then certainly we should commemorate our deliverance from death at the hands of Ahasuerus and Haman with a public reading of the Megillah. Then, continues the Talmud, we should recite Hallel on Purim on the basis of the *kal ve-ḥomer*. The Talmud answers that we do not recite Hallel for a miracle that occurred outside the Land of Israel; alternatively, the reading of the Megillah is equivalent to the recitation of Hallel; and lastly, we were still servants of Ahasuerus.[5]

Since these three technical objections to Hallel do not apply to Yom ha-Atzma'ut, the *kal ve-ḥomer* apparently should legitimize the recitation of Hallel on Yom ha-Atzma'ut.

But the detractors of the *kal ve-ḥomer* make two major points. First, we cannot recite *Hallel* solely on the basis of witnessing a miracle. It is legitimate to recite *Hallel* only if the miracle is followed by a revival and renewed commitment to Torah and mitzvot. Second, the event itself, the establishment of the State, falls far short of the demands of the Torah.

Most relevant to the discussion, I would submit, is a study of a great figure in Jewish history, King Hezekiah. He, too, apparently rejected the *kal ve-ḥomer*. He along with his generals witnessed the decimation of Sennacherib, who besieged Jerusalem. Sennacherib was defeated not by

4. See R. Nahum Rakover, *Hilkhot Yom ha-Atzma'ut ve-Yom Yerushalayim: Berurei Halakhah* (Jerusalem: Misrad ha-Datot, 1973), 125–236.

5. *Megillah* 14a.

any human battle, but rather by an angel sent by Hashem, which killed the soldiers in the Assyrian camp.[6] Yet, Hezekiah chose not to recite Hallel!

Hezekiah is described in II Kings as "he trusted in Hashem" (II Kings 18:5), unsurpassed in the attribute of *bittaḥon*! He was ever alert to any threat that would diminish the pristine environment of *emunah*. Out of fear that people would reduce their reliance on Hashem, he found it necessary to hide the Book of Cures that King Solomon had authored.[7] Out of concern that people naturally regard their monarch as a role model, he took the bold step of publicly humiliating his father, who was an idolater, by dragging his remains in public.[8]

But a policy that is praiseworthy for a generation that finds itself at the zenith of *emunah* is not always appropriate for a generation of a lesser degree of *emunah*, and perhaps for a *dor yatom*. A case in point is the *neḥash ha-neḥoshet*, the "Copper Serpent." Hezekiah destroyed it because people were deifying it.[9] Hezekiah was praised for destroying it, but his righteous predecessors, Asa and Yehoshafat, who were renowned for eradicating idolatry in their time, were not criticized for keeping the Copper Serpent.[10]

Well, was it an idol or not? The choices required to be made by Jewish leaders are often not between good and evil, but rather the selection of a lesser evil.

The Copper Serpent had its good points. Let's look at the events leading up to its creation and its original purpose. An ungrateful people murmured against the manna and complained why Hashem had taken the Children of Israel out of Egypt. To poignantly demonstrate the ingratitude, Hashem sent the Copper Serpent.[11] The phrase used is in the *pi'el* – *va-yishlakh Hashem*, "Hashem sent" – not the in the *kal*, *ve-shalakh*.[12] As Nechama Leibowitz points out, all Hashem did was

6. II Kings 19:35.
7. *Berakhot* 10b.
8. *Makkot* 24a.
9. II Kings 18:4.
10. See *Ḥullin* 6b.
11. Numbers 21:6.
12. In Hebrew grammar, *kal* is the simple active form of a verb whereas *pi'el* is the intensive active form of the verb. For example, a *kal* form of the root *shin-bet-resh* (ש-ב-ר) is *shavar* (שָׁבַר, "broke"), whereas a *pi'el* form of that root is *shibber* (שִׁבֵּר, "shattered").

simply remove the restraints that He had imposed on the serpents in the Wilderness.[13] The natural state was for the serpents to attack. The miracle was that they did not attack. Now, the contribution of the Copper Serpent was to serve as a reminder of the constant danger that the Children of Israel were exposed to in the Wilderness, so anyone who looked at it got *ḥiyyut*, "life."[14] As our Sages put it, people became submissive to Hashem by looking at the Copper Serpent and absorbing its poignant message.[15]

For a generation that found itself at the pinnacle of *emunah*, the main concern was that people were deifying the Copper Serpent. Notwithstanding that the destruction of the serpent would remove a force to bring people closer to Hashem, this had to be sacrificed. Other hooks to *emunah* could easily be found. But Asa and Yehoshafat were concerned with producing *emunah*. For them, primacy was given to the need to preserve any force that would bring people closer to Hashem. In that context, they were willing to tolerate the untoward consequence that some people would deify the Copper Serpent.

What a striking parallel. Is not the Jewish State also a Copper Serpent in our times? Yes, the secular Zionists were ensnared by the State. They deify the State. This is a terrible tragedy. But for many others, the State is like the Copper Serpent in Moses' time, the reminder that we as a people are in constant mortal danger. It is indeed a reminder of "plan a conspiracy and it shall be annulled; speak your peace and it shall not stand, for God is with us!" (Isaiah 8:10). Yes, for many, its establishment is not merely a miracle that we witnessed, but indeed something that constantly rededicates our faith.

And we have a *kal ve-ḥomer*. Hezekiah was criticized for not saying *shirah*. If he would have said *shirah*, our Sages tell us, he would have been made the Messiah, and Sennacherib would have been Gog and Magog.[16]

---

13. Nechama Leibowitz (Israel, 1905–1997), *Gilyonot*, Numbers 21:4–9 (1968) (citing R. Isaac b. Moses Arama [*Akedat Yitzḥak*, Spain, ca. 1420–1494]).
14. Numbers 21:8–9.
15. See *Targum Yonatan* to Numbers 21:9; Nahmanides (*Ramban*, Spain, 1194–1270) to Numbers 21:9; *Or ha-Ḥayyim* to Numbers 21:9.
16. *Sanhedrin* 94a; Song of Songs Rabbah 4:19.

Now, we can well understand why Hezekiah did not say *shirah*. The man of faith does not presume to understand the scope and depth of the salvation that Hashem wrought for him. He is overwhelmed with a tremendous sense of humility. The kindness of Hashem extends beyond his wildest imagination and comprehension. How dare he say *shirah*, praising Hashem for what He did, when he does not even begin to understand it? The man of extraordinary faith celebrates the event by achieving an even higher level of submissiveness and humility and recognition of Hashem.

But our Sages tell us that for such a generation, this was not the correct approach. *Kal ve-ḥomer* for a *dor yatom*, which is groping for ways to produce *emunah* and *bittaḥon*. As the *Ḥinnukh* asks, why do so many mitzvot commemorate the Exodus from Egypt? The answer is that we want to produce *emunah*, and we do this by performing mitzvot. It is mitzvot and *ma'asim tovim* that shape character and produce *emunah*.[17]

Today, we must strive for new opportunities to intensify our fulfillment of mitzvot and find new settings for *ma'asim tovim*. For our generation, hiding the Book of Cures perhaps would not be correct, as the book would allow an opportunity to find *tzelem Elokim* in *ḥokhmah* and in the deductions of the medical profession. We could accept the side effect of self-deification of man. So, too, the State represents the medium of bringing new life to the mitzvah of settling the Land of Israel. The Israeli flag, as R. Joseph B. Soloveitchik said, is holy because it is drenched with the blood of the IDF who defended the Land of Israel with their lives.[18]

It is striking that the Copper Serpent was put on a banner.[19] So, too, the symbol of the State in the flag will be hoisted on a pole on Yom ha-Atzma'ut.

---

17. R. Aaron b. Joseph ha-Levi (*Ra'ah*, Spain, ca. 1235–1300), *Sefer ha-Ḥinnukh*, eds. R. Yitzhak Yeshayah Weiss, R. David Zicherman, and R. Yitzhak Weinstein (Jerusalem: Mekhon Yerushalayim, 1992), mitzvah no. 16 (prohibition against breaking a bone of the *pesaḥ* offering).
18. R. Joseph B. Soloveitchik (New York, 1903–1993), *Ḥamesh Derashot* (Jerusalem: Mahon Tal Orot, 1974), 89–90.
19. Numbers 21:8–9.

The State, too, reflects a new setting for *ma'asim tovim* in the form of sanctifying the political and legislative processes.

Let us merit *az nashir shir ḥadash* (lit., "then we will sing a new song").[20]

20. See Isaiah 42:10; Psalms 96:1, 98:1, 149:1; Song of Songs Rabbah 1:35; *Haggadah*, Blessing of "*Asher Ge'alanu*" ("Then we shall thank You with a new song for our redemption and for the deliverance of our souls."); R. Jacob b. Joseph Reischer (Prague, ca. 1670–1733), *Iyyun Yaakov, Berakhot* 13a, s.v. "*hinneni oseh ḥadashah.*"

Passover – Last Day

Juxtaposing *Go'el* to *Ga'al*

April 21, 1987

Intensive probing and extensive analysis of a topic runs the risk of causing one to lose sight of its central theme. So, too, in respect of our obligation to recount the Exodus from Egypt. Its unique feature of "whoever tells the story of the Exodus from Egypt at length is praiseworthy"[1] runs the risk of losing focus on the main point. We would therefore expect that the last official reading of the Festival, the *haftarah* of the day, would set us straight in this regard. But to our surprise, the *haftarah* deals with two themes that are peripheral to the Haggadah: the defeat of Sennacherib and a description of the personality of the Messiah.[2]

Upon reflection, we can well understand why we dwell on the personality of the Messiah. Since the Haggadah focuses on the anguish that the Egyptians caused us and the divine visitation of punishment that was meted out to them, we may very well be left with a vindictive

1. *Haggadah, Maggid* (paragraph beginning with "We were slaves to Pharaoh in Egypt").
2. Isaiah 10:32–12:6.

aftertaste, which might build into visions of a reconstituted society with the oppressed taking the place of those who are exploiting us.

No, we do not even want to entertain such horrendous thoughts. We want it to be clear that what we want is nothing less than a just society. The type of society that we desire is the Messianic era, described for us in today's *haftarah*, an age of stellar achievement in Torah, a refined sense of justice, and universal peace, even in the animal kingdom.[3]

But why is the defeat of Sennacherib inserted in the *haftarah*? The answer perhaps is that we want to follow *ga'al Yisrael*, "He redeemed Israel," with *Go'el Yisrael*, the "Redeemer of Israel," Hashem.[4] "In every generation, they rise up against us to destroy us."[5] We want to emphasize that Hashem is the Redeemer, continuously intervening in human society to extricate us from all kinds of dangers.

The defeat of Sennacherib is the prototype of the type of danger that we face and the miraculous intervention that Hashem executes for us in each generation. Sennacherib descended upon Jerusalem with his hosts. He ignores the advice of his stargazers to attack Jerusalem. Instead, he haughtily proclaims that it is but a simple matter to conquer Jerusalem, and there is no need to attack immediately. Tomorrow will do.[6]

Well, that night, an angel descended and wrought havoc in the camp of the Assyrians. The enemy was defeated without the waging of any sort of battle![7]

Now, this is the sort of danger we face, a crisis of existence on a daily basis. The Jewish State is surrounded by hostile forces bent on its destruction. But Hashem is always sending angels to save us. He sent the angel of diplomacy to neutralize Egypt and eliminate the threat of a

---

3. Isaiah 11:6–9.
4. See *Pesaḥim* 117b. After the completion of first portion of Hallel in the Haggadah, we recite the blessing "Blessed are You, Hashem, Who has redeemed Israel [*ga'al Yisrael*]." The blessing regarding redemption in the *Shemoneh Esreh*, by contrast, concludes with "Who redeems Israel" [*Go'el Yisrael*]. That blessing in *Shemenoh Esreh* looks to the future because the blessing is a request for divine mercy.
5. *Haggadah, Maggid, ve-Hi she-Amedah.*
6. *Sanhedrin* 95a.
7. II Kings 19:35.

two-front war against Israel.[8] He then sent the angel of irrationality and a seven-year war is waging between two sworn enemies of Israel.[9] Hashem even sent the angel of greed in the form of the profit motive to convert an energy crunch into an energy glut.[10] What a collection of angels!

A grave criticism was hurled against the generation of Hezekiah – Why did they not say *shirah* when Sennacherib was decimated? We are told that Hashem wanted to make Hezekiah the Messiah and Sennacherib Gog and Magog, but because the generation of Hezekiah failed to recite *shirah*, this was not to be![11]

Now, just missing this cue to say *shirah* could not possibly evoke such a consequence. But I would suggest that the meaning of the failure to say *shirah* is spelled out in today's *haftarah*. Hezekiah's generation was challenged with the verse that links the Sennacherib episode with the description of the great personality of the Messiah – "A staff will emerge from the stump of Jesse and a shoot will sprout from his roots" (Isaiah 11:1). The challenge was whether they wanted to be a staff or only a sprout. The subsequent growth of the tree is not perceptively connected with the roots. But if the stump remains, the connection between the full growth and the stump is evident.

Hezekiah, do you want to be the Messiah himself, or part of the ancestors of the Messiah? If the miraculous defeat of Sennacherib made an impression, there can be nothing less than a religious renaissance. The generation would soar to the greatest heights in emulating the character of the Messiah. The generation of Hezekiah prided itself on its Torah

8. On March 26, 1979, following the 1978 Camp David Accords, Prime Minister Menachem Begin and President Anwar El Sadat signed a peace treaty between Israel and Egypt. Bernard Gwertzman, "Egypt and Israel Sign Formal Treaty, Ending a State of War after 30 Years: Sadat and Begin Praise Carter's Role; Ceremony Is Festive," *New York Times*, March 27, 1979, A1.
9. From September 1980 to August 1988, the Islamic Republic of Iran and the Ba'athist Republic of Iraq were engaged in war. The war is known as the "Iran-Iraq War" and the "First Persian Gulf War." See generally Efraim Karsh, *The Iran–Iraq War, 1980–1988* (Oxford: Osprey, 2002).
10. See Elizabeth Eder, "OPEC: Demise of a Cartel?" *Harvard International Review* 6, no. 1 (September/October 1983): 33–34; David Toufic Mizrahi, "If Oil Isn't Important, Who in the Middle East Is?" *Washington Post*, November 3, 1985, C1.
11. *Sanhedrin* 94a; Song of Songs Rabbah 4:19.

scholarship. "They searched from Dan until Beer Sheba, and no ignoramus was found."[12] That generation should have risen to new heights of Torah and then proceeded from there to develop a finer sensitivity to justice and strides toward universal peace.

We are faced with the same challenge. Do we want to be a "staff" or only a "sprout"?

On this day, we are challenged to connect the First Redeemer to the Final Redeemer with a magnanimous expression of *tzedek*.

12. *Sanhedrin* 94b.

The-Song-of-Songs Demand

April 9, 1988

One who identifies with the Song-of-Songs relationship between Hashem and *Knesset Yisrael* is emboldened to make strident, aggressive, and even outrageous demands.

For the millennia, an ongoing dispute rages between Hashem and *Knesset Yisrael.* Hashem says that *Knesset Yisrael* must make the first move – "return to Me and I will return to you" (Malachi 3:7). But *Klal Yisrael* says that Hashem should make the first move – "bring us back to You and we shall return" (Lamentations 5:21).

Now, in the Song of Songs, *Klal Yisrael* makes the same point by saying "*mashkheni aḥarekha narutzah,*" "draw us near, Hashem, then we will run after You with alacrity!" (Song of Songs 1:4).

The Song-of-Songs personality knows that by virtue of the closeness of his relationship, there is no need for pretenses, and masquerades are useless. But "*sheḥorah ani ve-navah*" (lit., "I am black, yet comely")

(Song of Songs 1:5). Since I confess my sins, my sins should not be a barrier impeding my advance or my progress.

Then comes the outrageous demand of recalling the Sin of the Golden Calf – "While the King was yet at his table, my nard gave forth its scent" (Song of Songs 1:12).[1]

The Song-of-Songs personality does not navigate in the world of logic and natural law. "The voice of my Beloved! Behold it came suddenly, leaping over mountains, skipping over hills" (Song of Songs 2:8).

But what gives one license to make these demands? It is only because one can unabashedly proclaim "*azah ka-mavet ahavah*," "strong till the death is my love" (Song of Songs 8:6). And if anyone could offer to barter that love for all his possessions, that person would be ridiculed – "*boz yavuzu lo*," "they would scorn him to the extreme" (Song of Songs 8:7).

But how do we prove the love? What is "strong till the death"? Only by the answer that we give the nations when they ask us in chapter five of Song of Songs why we still cling to Hashem after He abandoned us. Our answer is to depict Hashem in anthropomorphic terms and say that we are drawn to His Torah; we are absolutely infatuated with it. *Kevutzotzav taltallim* (lit., "His locks are wavy") (Song of Songs 5:11),[2] and "*ḥikko mamtakkim ve-khullo maḥmaddim*" (lit., "His palate is most sweet, and all of Him is a delight") (Song of Songs 5:16)![3]

We can demonstrate our loyalty and infatuation with the Torah by pointing to the pride of *Knesset Yisrael* when it says, "Let us rise early for the vineyards. Let us see if the vine has budded, if the blossom has opened, if the pomegranates are in bloom" (Song of Songs 7:13).

The vine "gladdens God and men" (Judges 9:13). The "blossom" is the *talmid ḥakham* who is not quite finished his studies but benefits

1. See *Shabbat* 88b; *Rashi* to Song of Songs 1:12, s.v. "*nirddi natan reiḥo*"; *Targum Yonatan* to Song of Songs 1:12.
2. This verse is interpreted to mean that from every one of the crowns of the letters of the Torah, many mounds of *halakhot* are derived. See *Targum Yonatan* to Song of Songs 5:11.
3. These expressions refer to the sweetness of the words of the Torah and the ability to transform willful misdeeds into merits through repentance. *Rashi* to Song of Songs 5:16, s.v. "*ḥikko mamtakkim*."

society.[4] And the "pomegranates" are those who go to the hinterlands and educate the masses in the basic fundamentals of the mitzvot.[5]

And we can point to what the nations say about us, "*sugah ba-shoshannim*," "hedge of roses" (Song of Songs 7:3). The rose is not an imposing barrier. It is only the aesthetic person who will not trample over the roses.[6]

4. *Rashi* to Song of Songs 7:13, s.v. "*pitaḥ ha-semadar*"; *Eruvin* 21b.
5. See *Rashi* to Song of Songs 7:13, s.v. "*henetzu ha-rimmonim*."
6. R. Mordechai Gifter (Ohio, 1915–2001), as heard from *Gedolei Telz*, cited in R. Meir Zlotowitz and R. Nosson Scherman, *Shir haShirim* (Brooklyn, NY: Artscroll, 2010), 179, Song of Songs 7:3.

Gebrukts on Passover

May 1, 2005

Throughout *Klal Yisrael*, a leniency in the strictures of Passover has set in for the last day of Passover. In some quarters, people are very meticulous that matzah should not come into contact with water. It is a remote concern, perhaps even a wild or irrational one, that fermentation might begin. These people refrain from eating *gebrukts* during Passover.[1] Also, these same people politely decline invitations the entire Passover because the standards of their neighbors might not be up to theirs. Come

1. *Gebrukts* means "broken" in Yiddish. The Hebrew term for *gebrukts* is *matzah sheruyah* (lit., "soaked matzah"). For a discussion of the custom of not eating *gebrukts*, see generally R. Aaron Wertheim, *Halakhot ve-Halikhot be-Ḥasidut* (Jerusalem: Mossad HaRav Kook, 2003), 173–174; R. Daniel Sperber, *Minhagei Yisrael: Mekorot ve-Toledot*, vol. 2 (Jerusalem: Mossad HaRav Kook, 1991), 144–146; R. Gedaliah Oberlander, "*Ḥumrat Iy Akhilat Matzah Sheruyah be-Pesaḥ*," in *Or Yisrael: Kovetz le-Inyanei Halakhah u-Minhag* 15 (Nisan 5759/1999): 134–148. For a discussion of this topic in English, see R. Aaron Wertheim, *Law and Custom in Hasidism*, trans. R. Shmuel Himelstein (Hoboken, NJ: Ktav, 1992), 261–262; R. Daniel Sperber, *Why Jews Do What They Do: The History of Jewish Customs throughout the Cycle of the Jewish Year*, trans. Dr. Yaakov Elman (Hoboken, NJ: Ktav, 1999), 60–64.

the last day of Passover, the same people both dip their matzah in soup with *kneidlach* and take up invitations. Does the leniency not constitute a *zilzul* (denigration) of the last day of Passover?

Many answers are given.[2] One is that we are saying, "*Ḥakhamim*, you have done so well with your safeguards. You have sealed the boundaries so well with your *ḥumrot* so that there is certainly no breach of Torah law. So today, we cut ourselves some slack. We even retreat a bit."[3] This is a big complement to our Sages, but it is also a big complement to our women who do all the *avodat perakh* preparing for Passover and enforce the *ḥumrot* of our Sages. Today is therefore a Mother's Day of sorts.

There are other answers. Permit to combine a number of them and add my own twist here. *Ḥametz* has the stringency of *mashehu*; it is prohibited even in a minute amount.[4] How do we define *mashehu*? Is it something visible to the naked eye? At what distance? Perhaps even something microscopic? The answer is that *mashehu* depends on who you are, what your level of religiosity is, and the sensitivity that you have for the prohibition of *ḥametz*.

Because our Sages do not quantify *mashehu*, it makes it possible for everyone to define it differently. The result is fragmentation and segmentation. So we need to break down these barriers. This is the rationale for the custom of eating *gebrukts* on the last day of Passover. It is an exercise in *aḥdut*.[5]

What promotes *aḥdut*? It is the medium of the matzah. During the entire Passover, it had a defined border that it would never breach. The whole Passover, it would not think of touching water. But on the last day of Passover, it breaches the boundary.

So the dual symbolism of matzah can reach new places. It is the symbol of *avdut*, the unleavened bread, the bread of slavery that we had for 210 years. We took it with us out of Egypt. It tells us, as R. Samson

2. See R. Gedaliah Oberlander, "*Ḥumrat Iy Akhilat Matzah*," 145–146.
3. See R. Zevi Elimelech Dynow (*Benei Yissaskhar*, Poland, ca. 1785–1841), *Derekh Pikudekha, mitzvat lo ta'aseh* 12, *ḥelek ha-dibbur*, 4.
4. Exodus 12:20; *Pesaḥim* 30a; Maimonides, *Mishneh Torah, Ma'akhalot Asurot* 15:9; *Tur, Oraḥ Ḥayyim* 447; *Shulḥan Arukh, Oraḥ Ḥayyim* 447:1.
5. See R. Naphtali Tzvi Horowitz of Ropshitz (Poland, 1760–1827), *Zera Kodesh*, vol. 2 (Jerusalem, 1954), 30b.

Raphael Hirsch says, that we did not seize our freedom.[6] No, Hashem gave it to us as a gift.

Matzah is also the symbol of freedom because we eat it with the *korban pesaḥ*. "With matzot and bitter herbs shall they eat it" (Numbers 9:11). So matzah is *ḥerut*. And how? The numerical difference between matzah and *ḥametz* is three.[7] So the difference between the tasteless wafer and the bread that has height and taste is in the three manifestations of the Evil Inclination: "Jealousy, lust, and glory remove a person from the world."[8] On the last day of Passover, the matzah breaches its boundaries a bit further and becomes an integrative force in *Klal Yisrael* for the entire year.

---

6. R. Samson Raphael Hirsch (Germany, 1808–1888), Exodus 12:39.
7. *Ḥatam Sofer, Pesaḥim* 30a; *Torat Mosheh, Bo*, s.v. "*shivat yamim matzot tokhelu.*" The numerical equivalence of *ḥametz* is 138, and the numerical equivalence of matzah is 135.
8. Mishnah, *Avot* 3:28; *Ḥatam Sofer, Pesaḥim* 30a.

Shavuot

Orpah Kissed Her Mother-in-Law but Ruth Clung to Her

May 27, 1985

At the crossroads of eternity stood two widowed, tearful sisters-in-law, Orpah and Ruth, together with their bereaved mother-in-law Naomi. Orpah chose to part with her mother-in-law and return to her homeland. Orpah kissed her mother-in-law.[1] Her kiss was sincere and was recorded as one of the pristine moments in human history. Because she triumphed for a moment, she merited to have a descendant, Goliath, who would also have his moment of glory, and through his defeat, would be instrumental in sanctifying the name of Hashem.[2] But the irony is that a *neshikah*, a kiss, has the same root

1. Ruth 1:14.
2. Orpah shed four tears over her departure from her mother-in-law. In that merit, she had four sons who were mighty warriors: Saf, Madon, Goliath, and Yishbi be-Nov.

as *neshek*, a weapon.[3] The kiss can be transformed into a weapon on account of the emotion of the moment.

But of Ruth, it is said, "Ruth clung to her" (Ruth 1:14). When Ruth embraced Naomi, her embrace not only encompassed the tangible and discernable, but touched the Jewish past and future in a singular way. And hence, her embrace caught hold of a piece of eternity. Ruth, the mother of the Messiah, embodied the characteristics of the Messiah in at least their incipient form. This was the scope of her embrace.

We are told that the Messiah has four names.[4] One name is Shiloh. The *Sforno* identifies this word with the root *shul* (ש-ו-ל), the bottom hem of a garment, as well as with *shalom*, which means peace.[5] Taken together, the Messiah will end the era of war and subjugation, and will usher in the era of eternal peace.

For someone to have the gift to reconcile profound differences, he must be able to correct all the errors of the past. This was one of the traits of Ruth. Mahlon's sin was that he deserted the Land of Israel; he showed disloyalty.[6] Well, Ruth went to the other extreme. She demonstrated the highest attachment to her mother-in-law Naomi – "your people are my people, and your God is my God" (Ruth 1:16) – as people testified to Naomi, "She is better to you than seven sons" (Ruth 4:15).

Ruth Rabbah 2:20; *Sotah* 42b. David sanctified Hashem's name in killing Goliath. See I Samuel 17:45 ("David said to the Philistine… 'I come to you with the Name of Hashem, Master of Legions, the God of the battalions of Israel that you have ridiculed.'").

3. See R. Jonah ibn Janah (Spain, first half 11th cent.), *Sefer ha-Sharashim*, and R. David Kimhi (*Radak*, Provence, ca. 1160–ca. 1235), *Sefer ha-Sharashim*, s.v. "*neshek*." Verses in which the root word *neshek* means to kiss include Genesis 31:28; Genesis 45:15; I Samuel 20:41; I Kings 19:20; Proverbs 7:13; Proverbs 24:26; and Song of Songs 1:2. Verses in which *neshek* means a weapon include Ezekiel 39:9–10; Psalms 78:9; and Psalms 140:8.
4. *Sanhedrin* 98b. The first letter of the four names, Menahem, Shiloh, Yinnon, and Haninah, form the word "*Mashiaḥ*" (משיח). R. Issac b. Judah Abrabanel (Portugal, 1437–1508), *Yeshu'ot Meshiḥo, iyyun* 2, ch. 3.
5. R. Obadiah b. Jacob Sforno (*Sforno*, Italy, ca. 1470–1550), *Sforno* to Genesis 49:10, s.v. "*ad ki yavo Shiloh*."
6. *Bava Batra* 91a.

Another name of the Messiah is Yinnon. This word means progeny. The hope that the Messiah brings is that of everlasting progeny. "May his name endure forever; may his name connote mastery [*yinnon shemo*] as long as the sun endures" (Psalms 72:17). His progeny should be everlasting as the sun. Ruth so treasured her heritage that she did not want it to end with her. She wanted it to be forever, throughout posterity.

It is only in this light that we can understand her audacious and bold plan to fall at the feet of Boaz on that fateful night and propose to him. She knew that the legitimacy of her right to enter *Klal Yisrael* would be a matter of dispute. The exposition of *Moavi ve-lo Moaviyah,* that only a male Moabite convert may not marry into the Jewish nation, was not widely known or accepted in her time and, for that matter, not even in King David's time.[7] People questioned his right to royalty! She knew that the only way that she could save her progeny from oblivion and prevent alienation was to maneuver to have the stamp of legitimacy placed on her marriage and entering into the Jewish nation. This could best be achieved by Boaz, who was the *gadol ha-dor*. Some take Toviah's refusal to marry Ruth as proceeding from pure motive.[8] He felt that only if the *gadol ha-dor* would marry her, people would not question the marriage. Ruth cared about her progeny, her unborn future generations. Only one who cherishes his or her heritage thinks along these lines.

Perhaps the most difficult mission of the Messiah is the one that is encompassed in the name Menahem, comforter. Jeremiah laments, "*Ein lah menaḥem mi-kol ohaveha,*" "She has no comforter among all her lovers" (Lamentations 1:2). We know this so poignantly today. We can have allies and friends, even loved ones, but not comforters. A comforter is someone who can suffuse suffering with meaning, with an understanding of the value of the suffering. Really, only Hashem can be the true comforter. "I, only I, am He Who comforts you" (Isaiah 51:12). But

7. *Yevamot* 76b. The Torah states: "An Ammonite or Moabite shall not enter the congregation of Hashem... because they did not meet you with bread and water on the road when you were leaving Egypt" (Deuteronomy 23:4–5). The Sages understand these verses as prohibiting only a male Ammonite and Moabite convert from marrying into the Jewish nation because it was customary only for men, and not women, to go to the desert to meet travelers.
8. R. Joel Sirkes (*Baḥ*, Poland, 1561–1640), *Meshiv Nefesh*, Ruth 4:6.

we must do our part. Our part consists of always connecting ourselves to the past, contrary to the concept of the gentiles that reconciliation consists of forgetting and blotting out history.

Ruth did her part to connect to the past. Her inspiration to become a convert came from Mahlon.[9] So now she rejected the option of marrying outside the Levirate marriage, which, as Boaz says, would have allowed her, a woman of beauty and charm, to marry anyone of her choice.[10] But instead she chose to perpetuate the name of her deceased husband Mahlon through the Levirate marriage. Through the Levirate marriage, the mission of the deceased on this earth can continue through the children of the marriage.[11]

If Mahlon was her original inspiration, she would not just use him as a vehicle, but would build his name and infuse meaning into his wretched life. She would not sever her ties with the past. This is the Menahem.

For someone with these qualities, there is the life of Haninah, the last name of the Messiah, which means grace and charm. One with grace and charm is liked by all. This will give us the hope of becoming the beacon to the world, leading the world in the Messianic age.

9. *Meshiv Nefesh*, Ruth 1:4.

10. See Ruth 3:10; Abraham b. Meir ibn Ezra (Ibn Ezra, Spain, 1089–1164), Ibn Ezra to Ruth 3:10, s.v. "*im dal ve-im ashir*"; R. Meir Loeb b. Jehiel Michel Weisser (*Malbim*, Poland, Romania, and Russia, 1809–1879), *Malbim* to Ruth 3:10.

11. R. Aaron b. Joseph ha-Levi (*Ra'ah*, Spain, ca. 1235–1300), *Sefer ha-Ḥinnukh*, eds. R. Yitzhak Yeshayah Weiss, R. David Zicherman, and R. Yitzhak Weinstein (Jerusalem: Mekhon Yerushalayim, 1992), mitzvah no. 598.

The Balanced Personality

June 10, 1989

If the reading of the Book of Ruth on Shavuot is designed to reinforce the theme and message of the day, we may well ask, would not the reading of the Song of Songs provide a more natural pairing for Shavuot? *Zeman mattan Toratenu,* "the giving of the Torah," in the imagery of our Sages, is depicted as the wedding of *Klal Yisrael* to the *Ribbono shel Olam.*[1] Relatedly, would not the reading of the Book of Ruth blend naturally with Passover? This would pair the story of the lowly beginnings of the Jewish people with the lowly beginnings of Jewish royalty.

But the objective of the Torah is to produce a balanced personality. On Shavuot, we leap in the category of *bein adam la-Makom. Hevi'ani el beit ha-yayin* (lit., "He has brought me into the house of wine"), *ve-diglo alai ahavah* (lit., "His banner upon me is love") (Song of Songs 2:4).[2]

---

1. Mishnah, *Ta'anit* 4:8; R. Solomon b. Isaac (*Rashi,* France, 1040–1105), *Rashi* to Song of Songs 3:11, s.v. "*be-yom ḥatunnato*"; Song of Songs Rabbah 3:21.
2. The Midrash interprets "the house of wine" as an allusion to Sinai, and "His banner upon me is love" to the loving acceptance of the Torah and mitzvot by the Jewish

We recognize that Hashem is prominent because of His profound Torah teachings. It is then that we become vulnerable to neglect *bein adam le-ḥavero*. So we must make a great leap in the direction of *bein adam le-ḥavero* and reach out to the most alienated and distant Jew. We do that by identifying with Ruth.

Layer upon layer of hostility and distrust surrounded Ruth upon her arrival in the Land of Israel.[3] It would be hard to imagine a Jew against whom we would harbor more bias and scorn. Here is a woman who was a Moabite, a member of a despised nation, one that is the antithesis of *ḥesed* – "because of the matter that they did not greet you with bread and water on the road when you were leaving Egypt" (Deuteronomy 23:5). And she was part of a family that abandoned the Jewish people in a time of distress, taking up residence in Moab during a famine.[4]

But we must penetrate the thick layers of bias that surround her and look at her as an individual, as a person. And what we see is a beautiful *neshamah*, an individual of noble spirit. Her *neshamah* is so pure and magnificent that she is the progenitor of the Messiah![5]

On Passover, we very much get involved in the theme of the day. We vicariously feel that we went out of Egypt and therefore we relate to the wretched existence of a slave; we have no self-value. Our self-image desperately needs to be built up. We do this by pairing Passover with the Song of Songs to remind us that we, as Jews, have a singular relationship with Hashem.

On Passover, when we celebrate our freedom, there is a danger that the emphasis on freedom may turn into license. So we set out to destroy the *se'or*, "yeast"; we are obsessed with destroying every manifestation of the Evil Inclination.[6] *Ḥametz* is prohibited *be-mashehu*, even in a minute amount.[7]

---

people. Song of Songs Rabbah 2:13.

3. See *Meshiv Nefesh*, Ruth 2:6.
4. Ruth 1:1.
5. See Ruth 4:17.
6. *Berakhot* 17a; *Rashi* ad loc., s.v. "*se'or she-ba-issah*."
7. Exodus 12:20; *Pesaḥim* 30a; Maimonides (*Rambam*, Egypt, 1135–1204), *Mishneh Torah, Ma'akhalot Asurot* 15:9; R. Jacob b. Asher (*Tur*, Spain, 1270–1343), *Tur, Oraḥ Ḥayyim* 447; R. Joseph Caro (Safed, 1488–1575), *Shulḥan Arukh, Oraḥ Ḥayyim* 447:1.

But on Shavuot, instead of destroying the Evil Inclination, we take it in the form of the Two Loaves to the holiest place of the Jewish people, to the Temple, as a communal sacrifice.[8] Why? Because on Shavuot, we leap to the noble spirit. It is the culmination of the inspirational leap from the forty-ninth level of impurity to the forty-ninth level of purity. It is here that we become vulnerable to viewing the Torah as an abstract doctrine. But "*lo ha-midrash ha-ikkar, ela ha-ma'aseh*," "not study, but practice, is the primary thing."[9] So we must emphasize on Shavuot the theme of the sanctification of the mundane and the material.[10] This is done with the offering of the Two Loaves, which is eaten by the Priests, not consumed on the fire of the Altar.[11]

On Shavuot, when we make a leap of faith, "*na'aseh ve-nishma*," "we will do and we will listen" (Exodus 24:7), we express blind loyalty to Hashem by declaring a willingness to fulfill the mitzvot even before we hear what is involved. But when we leap in faith, we are prone to put a premium on promises, vision, and aspiration. We become oriented toward the future, blotting out the past, and developing a blind spot for appreciating the gifts that we already have. To ensure that our *hakkarat ha-tov* to Hashem for the past is not blunted, we must put an emphasis on this on Shavuot.

Indeed, *hakkarat ha-tov* is catapulted to an importance on Shavuot that surpasses that of the other festivals because the distinctiveness of Shavuot manifests itself not as on the other festivals in the form of a special ritual *bein adam la-Makom*, but rather in an increased emphasis on *seudat yom tov*. "All authorities concede that in the case of *Atzeret*, we require an assembly 'for you.' What is the reason? It is the day on which the Torah was given."[12] And the *leḥem mishneh* corresponds not only to the manna, which is the symbol of *bittaḥon*, but also to the Two Loaves,

---

8. Leviticus 23:17.
9. Mishnah, *Avot* 1:17.
10. See *Maharal, Tiferet Yisrael*, ch. 25.
11. Leviticus 23:20.
12. *Pesaḥim* 68b; R. Samuel Eliezer b. Judah ha-Levi Edels (*Maharsha*, Poland, 1555–1631), *Ḥiddushei Halakhot ve-Aggadot, Pesaḥim* 68b (noting that *Atzeret* refers to *Shavuot*).

which made it permissible to eat *ḥadash* in the time of the Temple[13] and hence injects an element of thanksgiving to Hashem.[14]

Having the *todah* in the *Birkat ha-Mazon* carries a special significance on Shavuot because everyone is drawn into the *seudah*. If we do not say *malkhut beit David* in the *Birkat ha-Mazon*, we do not fulfill our obligation.[15] This takes on a double meaning. Not only do we not fulfill our obligation to say *Birkat ha-Mazon*, but we also will not have absorbed the theme of the Book of Ruth and the message of *Atzeret*.

A focus on "he has brought me into the house of wine" may very well expose us to the sin of arrogance, so it is our duty to relate to Boaz who was the intellectual and spiritual elite of Israel, the head of the Sanhedrin. If anyone was to feel the scorn against Moab and against traitors, it should have been him – "the heart of the King reflects the heart of all of Israel."[16] But he was a man of humility, and one of humility can overcome all biases and penetrate to the core of the matter. In a series of steps, he was to see the inner purity of Ruth, marry her, and hence become the progenitor of the Messiah.

13. Mishnah, *Menaḥot* 10:6; *Menaḥot* 68b.

14. *Sforno* to Leviticus 23:17.

15. *Berakhot* 48b; Maimonides, *Mishnah Torah, Berakhot* 2:4; *Shulḥan Arukh, Oraḥ Ḥayyim* 187:4.

16. Maimonides, *Mishnah Torah, Melakhim* 3:6.

The Roots of Royalty on Shavuot

May 21, 1999

The Book of Ruth presents the roots of Jewish sovereignty. The fascinating story would blend well and enhance any festival in the Jewish calendar. If our Sages prescribed the reading of the Book of Ruth on Shavuot, it must be that Ruth does more for Shavuot than for any other holiday. Why?

In the teaching of the *Shem mi-Shemuel*, the Jewish people were inherently incapable of establishing *malkhut*.[1] We had to import the institution from Moab, and specifically from Ruth.

This is indeed a shocking statement for, after all, Moab is the very quintessence of immodesty. The Prophet Isaiah describes Moab as a

1. R. Shmuel Bornsztain (*Shem mi-Shemuel*, Poland, 1855–1926), *Shem mi-Shemuel: Al Seder Parshiyyot ha-Torah u-Mo'adei Kodesh*, 9th ed., vol. 4 (Jerusalem, 1992), *Shavuot* (5670/June 1910), p. 44 (citing his grandfather, R. Zev Nahum Bornsztain, a disciple of the *Kotzker Rebbe*).

haughty, arrogant people.[2] The birth of Moab was from incest. Moab was the offspring of Lot and his eldest daughter.[3] And when Moab was born, the eldest daughter broadcast to the world that he was fathered by her father.[4]

Now, on that fateful night when Ruth visited Boaz in the granary, she threw herself at his feet and proposed marriage.[5] This was an incredibly immodest act. Boaz's worst nightmare was that people would know that Ruth came to the threshing floor that night: "Let it not be known that the woman came to the threshing floor" (Ruth 3:14).

In what way was this immodest act different from the act of Lot's eldest daughter? After all, a Noahite is permitted to marry his daughter,[6] and Lot's daughters thought the world had been destroyed.[7] But what drove them? Was it a desire to repopulate Hashem's world? Were they doing a *ḥesed* for yet unborn generations? Or were they motivated primarily by self-interest, because they were terrified at the thought of a lonely death. The test is what the older daughter called her child. She called him Moab. She broadcast the immoral act. This shows that she was motivated by self-interest.

But as far as Ruth is concerned, her immodest act was done for a pure and noble reason. And she receives praise from Boaz, "You are blessed of Hashem, my daughter; you have made your latest act of kindness greater than the first" (Ruth 3:10). Boaz says that this *ḥesed* outdoes her previous *ḥesed* of taking care of her mother-in-law.[8] And why? Because Boaz knows the harsh realities of life. Ruth was a young, beautiful, vibrant woman, and she could have her pick. That is why Boaz said "in that you have not gone after the younger men, be they poor or rich" (Ruth 3:10).[9]

2. Isaiah 16:6 ("We have heard of Moab's pride – exceedingly proud – his haughtiness and pride and scorn are untrue deceptions.").
3. Genesis 19:30–37.
4. Genesis Rabbah 51:11; *Rashi* to *Bava Kamma* 38b, s.v. "*de-ke-amrah 'Moav'*"; *Rashi* to Genesis 19:37. The name Moab derives from *me-av hu,* "he is from a father."
5. Ruth 3:6–9; *Rashi* to Ruth 3:9, s.v. "*u-pharasta khenafekha.*"
6. *Sanhedrin* 58b. See also Nahmanides (*Ramban,* Spain, 1194–1270) to Genesis 19:32.
7. Genesis 19:31.
8. *Rashi* to Ruth 3:10; R. Levi b. Gershom (*Ralbag,* France, 1288–1344), Ruth 3:10.
9. Abraham b. Meir ibn Ezra, Ibn Ezra to Ruth 3:10, s.v. "*im dal ve-im ashir*"; R. Meir Loeb b. Jehiel Michel Weisser, *Malbim* to Ruth 3:10.

But Boaz is eighty years old.[10] Why did Ruth want to marry him? It was to give legitimacy to her children, to give legitimacy to the exposition of *Moavi ve-lo Moaviyah*, that the law that a Moabite convert may not marry into the Jewish nation applies only to a male Moabite.[11] Because she sought to have this done by the *gadol ha-dor*. She was driven to do a *ḥesed* for her yet unborn children. So the immodest act was committed for the purest and most selfless purpose.

This is the character of Jewish royalty. The King is the first citizen of the Torah. He carries with him a portable *sefer Torah* to remind him of all that is in it.[12] But to acquire Torah, one must be meek. It is the job of the King as part of his mission to be the first citizen of the Torah, to inspire and hence make the Torah central to the life of everyone, and to introduce an aspect of immodesty for a pure and noble purpose.

Part of the job of the King is to be the cheerleader to propose an ambitious plan for Torah study and observance, to boast of accomplishment of the people in Torah.

David does this. "One thing I asked of Hashem" (Psalms 27:4). He does not make his public agenda economics, tax ideologies, or international relations. No. "*Malkhut sha'al*," "he asked for royalty."[13] His public agenda is "one thing," to set the people straight. David fulfills the role, bringing an *azut* for Torah into Jewish royalty. "*David met ba-Atzeret*," "David passed away on Atzeret."[14] So, on Atzeret, we relive the drama. David defies death by being attached to the Torah.[15]

---

10. Ruth Rabbah 6:2.

11. *Yevamot* 76b. The Torah states: "An Ammonite or Moabite shall not enter the congregation of Hashem ... because they did not meet you with bread and water on the road when you were leaving Egypt" (Deuteronomy 23:4–5). The Sages understand these verses as prohibiting only a male Ammonite and Moabite convert from marrying into the Jewish nation because it was customary only for men, and not women, to go to the desert to meet travelers.

12. Deuteronomy 17:18–20.

13. *Midrash Shoḥer Tov*, Psalms 27.

14. Jerusalem Talmud, *Beitzah* 2:4, *Ḥagigah* 2:3. See also *Shabbat* 30a (stating that David passed away on the Sabbath); *Yalkut Shimoni*, Psalms 735 (stating that David passed away on Shavuot that fell on the Sabbath).

15. *Shabbat* 30a. David asked Hashem to reveal to him the day he would die. Hashem revealed to him only that he would die on a Sabbath. From then on, David would

When the humble man is ambitious, it often evokes mockery. It is the King who must set the highest ambition for Torah and the most lofty vision for the nation, the vision that the humble and the meek follow. This is the role of the King.

---

study Torah the entire day of Sabbath. When the day arrived upon which David's soul was destined to come to rest, the Angel of Death stood before him but was unable to overcome him because David's mouth did not cease from the study of Torah. To distract David from his studies, the Angel of Death shook the branches of a tree outside David's house. David went out to see the cause of the noise. As he ascended the stairs, a stair caved in under him. For a moment he was silent, and at that moment he passed away.

Human Perception and Potential

(Undated)

If there is any realm of human conduct that is above reproach, we would imagine that it would be deeds that display strength of character recorded in the Torah. Yet, in reference to three such deeds, our Sages put them under the scrutiny of the microscope and decided that they failed to live up to potential.

First, Reuben's deed is dissected. When he gets wind of the fact that his brothers convened a court and condemned Joseph to death, he protests and says, "We will not strike him mortally" (Genesis 37:21). The Midrash states that had he only known that the Torah would write of his action – "Reuben heard, and he rescued him from their hand" (37:21) – he would have carried Joseph home on his shoulders.[1]

What the Midrash is telling us is that within the framework of Reuben concurring with the decree of his brothers to execute Joseph,

1. Ruth Rabbah 5:6; *Yalkut Shimoni, Va-Yeshev* 141.

what he did, saving his life, was very admirable and sincere. Reuben thought that he was doing *ḥesed*, but in reality, Reuben and his brothers had a perverted perception of Joseph. Joseph was pure and innocent and did not deserve to die or to be punished in any way. It was a matter of justice, not mercy, that Joseph should be freed. Had Reuben only had a correct sense of justice, he would have protested the verdict with much more vigor. He would have carried the lad home on his shoulders.

The strength of character of Aaron is then dissected by the Midrash. When Hashem approached Moses to be the Redeemer of Israel, Moses initially showed much resistance, fearing that somehow his acceptance would encroach upon the honor of Aaron, who was the established prophet for eighty years.[2] Hashem tells him that his fears are unfounded. "When he sees you, he will rejoice in his heart" (Exodus 4:14). But had Aaron only known that the Torah would write this of him, he would have approached Moses with timbrels and dances.[3] His vision and imagination were limited. If he would have seen the redemption process in advance, he would have known that Moses was selected instead of him not because Moses had more wisdom, but because of Moses' *anavah*. There was no one who could reflect the Divine Glory more and not deflect an iota of the Divine Glory to himself.

And finally of Boaz. Had he known that the Torah would write of him "he handed her parched grain" (Ruth 2:14), he would have given Ruth fattened calves.[4] He thought that he knew her, but did not realize what a spiritual giant she was. As he himself says to her later on the fateful night when "she came stealthily" and proposes marriage, "You have made your latest act of kindness greater than the first, in that you have not gone after the younger men, be they poor or rich" (Ruth 3:10).

What can be accomplished through sincere action is indeed limited by our perception of reality and the breadth and depth of our vision. If only our perception were more accurate and our imagination and vision grand, the sincere person would do much more, beyond what he thinks are the limits of his capabilities.

---

2. Exodus Rabbah 3:16; *Rashi* to Exodus 4:10.
3. Ruth Rabbah 5:6; *Yalkut Shimoni, Va-Yeshev* 141.
4. Ruth Rabbah 5:6; *Yalkut Shimoni, Va-Yeshev* 141.

Shabbat Ḥazon

Kara Alai Mo'ed: Jewish Destiny

August 4, 1984

The day of our greatest tragedy and calamity, the ninth day of Av, was called by Jeremiah a *mo'ed*, a festival.[1] On this account, we do not say *Taḥanun* on Tishah be-Av[2] or on the eve of Tishah be-Av.[3]

Now, what affinity did the day of our deepest sorrow have with the days of deepest joy? The double meaning of *mo'ed* perhaps explains this kinship between Tishah be-Av and the Festivals. *Mo'ed*, as R. Samson Raphael Hirsch tells us, means both "festival" and "assembly."[4] On the occasion of the Festivals, the Jew, especially in the time of the Temple,

1. Lamentations 1:15.
2. R. Jacob b. Asher (*Tur*, Spain, 1270–1343), *Tur, Oraḥ Ḥayyim* 559; *Shulḥan Arukh, Oraḥ Ḥayyim* 559:4.
3. R. Meir b. Barukh of Rothenburg (*Maharam me-Rotenburg*, Germany, ca. 1215–1293), *Haggahot Maimuniyyot, Minhagei Tish'ah be-Av*, to *Mishneh Torah, Ta'aniyot*; R. Joseph Caro (Safed, 1488–1575), *Shulḥan Arukh, Oraḥ Ḥayyim* 552:12.
4. R. Samson Raphael Hirsch (Germany, 1808–1888), Exodus 12:2.

felt a special closeness to Hashem. Ten miracles were performed for our forefathers in the Temple.[5] One of these miracles that we all experienced together was "*omdim tzefufim u-meshtaḥavim revaḥim*," we stood crowded together yet we prostrated ourselves in ample space. This same poignant feeling of closeness to Hashem that we felt amidst joy was unfortunately felt amidst tragedy on Tishah be-Av.

The distribution in this world of pain and suffering on the one hand and reward on the other has never been a source to reinforce our faith. Quite to the contrary, it has been a source of testing our faith and giving rise to the age-old question of "*tzaddik ve-ra lo, rasha ve-tov lo*," "why do the righteous suffer and the wicked prosper?"[6] But on the fateful day of Tishah be-Av, we as a nation were made to feel so acutely that our anguish and suffering reflected divine retribution.

What forms the center stage of the destruction of the Temple? It is the discovery by Nebuchadnezzar's general, Nebuzaradan, of Zechariah's blood seething in the Courtyard of the Temple, and the resultant killing of 940,000 of the flower of Israel. For some peculiar reason, Nebuzaradan was obsessed with finding out the secret of the seething blood. The Priests thereupon brushed him off by telling him that it was the blood of an animal that was sacrificed. Nebuzaradan did not believe this. He tested the blood by comparing it with the blood of animals that were slaughtered at his command, and behold, the blood sample did not match.[7]

Now he grew irate and threatened a merciless death for those who would not reveal the secret to him. When they told him that it was Zechariah's blood, he took it upon himself to avenge it. First, he killed Torah scholars, then *tinnokot shel beit rabban*, and then Priests, totaling 940,000. Only then he asked, "Zechariah, is this enough? I have killed the flower of them." Zechariah said that it was enough.

We must have felt at that time, more than ever, that a grand public trial had been set. The enemy was a mere instrument of divine punishment, thrusting in our face that which we much preferred to keep concealed and buried. How different the episode was from the ordinary war

---

5. Mishnah, *Avot* 5:5.
6. *Berakhot* 7a.
7. *Gittin* 57b.

of conquest, when the powerful overwhelm the weak or want to impose their values or demonstrate the superiority of their culture or religion. When was it that the enemy wanted to show us that we were unfaithful to our own religion and wanted to focus only on this and serve as an instrument of divine punishment?

Indeed, Nebuchadnezzar ordered Zedekiah, the Head of State, to witness the execution of his ten sons. He then blinded Zedekiah and sent him off as a captive to Babylon.[8] But with respect to Jeremiah, the "Prophet of Doom," he ordered that he not be harmed in the slightest.[9] On that fateful day, there was an acute awareness of a meeting with Hashem, the *mo'ed* experience.

Now, there was more to the *mo'ed* experience on Tishah be-Av. Nations, in their sedate and rational moments, may make international accords regarding codes of conduct in war. But once a war breaks out, these rules are meaningless. War is chaos. There are no rules of civility or restraint.

Yet, the *ḥurban* was different. Nebuzaradan commanded that no married woman should be ravished because "the God of this people hates lewdness."[10] Amidst the untrammeled exercise of power, there was an element of restraint. The element of restraint amidst chaos and destruction was another manifestation of the perception of the Divine amidst the anguish of torment, for it is this that creates amazement and wonder in us. How can there be restraint amidst chaos? It must be the reflection of the Divine.

Another element of *mo'ed* was that Nebuchadnezzar commanded that we be driven mercilessly and not be permitted to rest until we were driven out of the Land of Israel. "By the rivers of Babylon, there we sat and also wept when we remembered Zion" (Psalms 137:1). He was afraid that the reflective Jew would weep and instantly, a decisive defeat would turn into a victory by the Children of Israel.[11]

Well, from our standpoint, we felt acutely that we were already defeated, a hopeless people, made homeless and desolate. How did

8. Jeremiah 39:6–7.
9. Jeremiah 39:11–12.
10. Lamentations Rabbah 5:11.
11. *Pesikta Rabbati* 29:2; *Midrash Shoḥer Tov*, Psalms 137.

the inhumanity of our tormentors serve their purpose? Was not their continuation of torture purely senseless? But it is precisely when logic completely evades us that we perceive the Divine, by making us reflect. Here, again, it was the *mo'ed* experience.

Our Sages tell us that in the time of the Messiah, the three-week period of *Bein ha-Metzarim* will be transformed into a *yom tov,* with the Seventeenth of Tamuz and Tishah be-Av becoming full festivals.[12] We are now in the Redemption period and we must perceive the *mo'ed* element of Redemption, just as we perceived the *mo'ed* element of servitude on Tishah be-Av. Just as Nebuzaradan gave us that feeling of the grand public trial, we must be aware that the Jew today is a public figure. We may be scattered physically all over the world, but the Jew today is performing on the center stage of the world.

No other event in the modern era thrusts the Jew into a public role, into a position of being constantly analyzed, scrutinized, and even subject to a double standard of morality, than the creation of the State of Israel. There are some in our own circles who fail to comprehend the religious significance of the establishment of the State of Israel. They fail to understand the *mo'ed* element of Jewish redemption.

Just as it was the self-restraint of inflicting power that brought a sense of *mo'ed,* it is the restraint that we impose on our own untrammeled power that gives us the *mo'ed* experience of redemption. We may marvel at how far we have come from the self-contained isolationism of the ghetto mentality to the free access to every avenue of creative human endeavor. We have also achieved dizzying accomplishment in so many areas. But it is not the sense of power that we feel when we observe this that represents for us a divine spark. Instead, it is the self-imposed

12. See Zechariah 8:19 ("Thus said Hashem, Master of Legions: 'The fast of the fourth [month], the fast of the fifth, the fast of the seventh, and the fast of the tenth will be to the House of Judah for joy and for gladness and for happy festivals. [Only] love truth and peace'"). The Sages explain that the fast of the fourth month refers to the seventeenth day of Tammuz, the fast of the fifth month refers to Tish'ah be-Av, the fast of the seventh month refers to the Fast of Gedaliah, and the fast of the tenth month refers to the Fast of the Tenth Day of Tevet. R. Solomon b. Isaac (*Rashi,* France, 1040–1105), R. David Kimhi (*Radak,* Provence, ca. 1160–ca. 1235), and R. Jehiel Hillel b. David Altschuler (Galicia, 18th cent.), *Metzudat David* ad loc.

restraint we set on the terms on which we choose to enter the secular society and the areas that we choose to enter at all.

Just as it was the sense of defeat after defeat that represented the *mo'ed* experience of servitude, so, too, it is not in the basking in the glory of past laurels and spiritual accomplishments of *ḥesed* that we perceive the Divine. Instead, it is in the restless drive of the perfectionist that we perceive the *mo'ed* experience of the Redemption.

It is our challenge today to perceive the *mo'ed* element of the Redemption. This is the key to transforming the three weeks of *Bein ha-Metzarim* into the three weeks of festivals that we are awaiting with such anticipation with the coming of the Messiah.

Naḥem and the Contemporary State of Israel

July 27, 1985

Several years ago, a serious-thinking rabbi, writing in the *Jewish Week*, openly confessed his ambivalence with respect to the fast of Tishah be-Av.[1] As a Jew deeply rooted in our Tradition, he would, of course, not do away with the fast. But why, he asks in doleful terms, do we still concentrate on the negatives? Should we not celebrate the miracle of Jewish Statehood? And does the reality not belie the description of Jerusalem in our prayers as a city in a state of ruins and as a city that is desolate?[2]

To you, Rabbi, I say, you are very easily consoled. Indeed, when it comes to a personal slight, injury, or harm, our Sages praised very

1. "Mixed Feelings on the 9th Day of Av," *Jewish Week*, July 15, 1983, 23.
2. *Naḥem* Prayer for Tish'ah be-Av. In Ashkenazic communities, the *Naḥem* Prayer is recited on Tish'ah be-Av only during *Minḥah* in the *Shemoneh Esreh* Prayer.

much the attribute of *no'aḥ le-retzot,* "easily appeased,"[3] but when it comes to our national tragedies, *no'aḥ le-retzot* effectively denies the singular nature of our mission and reduces our destiny and heritage to mediocrity.

Our Sages had a profound sensitivity to know exactly which elements of our national tragedy require consolation. They composed a special blessing with the word "*naḥem*" in the beginning and the word "*menaḥem*" at the end.[4] But we immediately encounter a disturbing repetition. We implore Hashem that he should console the mourners of Zion and the mourners of Jerusalem, and then also the City, which is described as *ha-avelah,* "mournful"; *ha-ḥarevah,* "ruined"; *ha-bezuyah,* "scorned"; and *ha-shomemah,* "desolate."

Now, the latter three expressions do not appear at the beginning, but the mourners of Zion and the mourners of Jerusalem do. Why? Well, there are two reasons to mourn for our tragedy. One is the void that we feel because of the lost splendor of the past. The second is our feeling of what is still missing now in our personal and national lives because of the *ḥurban.* One who is not chained to the past, who regards the events of two thousand years ago as something that we should by now completely blot out of our memory, will certainly be puzzled and mystified by the description of Jerusalem today as *ha-avelah mibeli vaneha,* "the mournful city without her children." Why? Israel is populated with many loyal children who defend the honor of the Land and will lay down their lives for it.

But one who mourns the glory of our past, the historical Jew, deeply connected to the past, has the highest concept of children, the spirit of R. Yeshevav of whom the heavens pronounced that he did not leave any detail from the Torah of Moses without observing it,[5] and

3. Mishnah, *Avot* 5:11.
4. The prayer begins "*Naḥem* [console], O Hashem, our God, the mourners of Zion and the mourners of Jerusalem, and the City that is mournful, ruined, scorned, and desolate," and ends with "Blessed are You, Hashem, *menaḥem* [Who consoles] Zion and rebuilds Jerusalem."
5. R. Meir b. Jehiel (Germany, 13th cent.), "*Arzei ha-Levanon*" (*kinah* recited on Tish'ah be-Av), reprinted in Alter Welner, *Aseret Harugei Malkhut ba-Midrash u-ve-Piyyut* (Jerusalem: Mossad HaRav Kook, 2005), 347.

the fervor of R. Hutzpit, of whom it is said that the passing bird was singed by his fiery breath of Torah.[6] When children argue and fight with each other, it tears their parents' hearts out. And he embodies the ideal of "hear my child, the discipline of your father, and do not forsake the teaching of your mother" (Proverbs 1:8), the child who is eager to hear *musar* and is so fearful to depart in any slight way from tradition, *Torat immekha*.

One who is not steeped in the past is surprised by the next phrase, *ha-ḥarevah*, "in ruins." The city is a ruin? Could we possibly describe Jerusalem as a city in ruins today, with its teeming population and laughing children, with the great promise of the future? No. But the historical Jew remembers the holiness of R. Judah b. Bava, the fervor of holiness of R. Hutzpit. He asks, "How can we contemplate allowing Brigham Young University to construct a center in Jerusalem, the Holy City?" He rejects the suggestion that as a democracy, Israel must allow it, that Israel should behave as all other democratic nations that subscribe to freedom of expression.[7]

The Jew not steeped in the past will also be very surprised by the next description, which is *ha-bezuyah*, "despised." Is Israel despised today? It is a sister nation, an ally of the United States, no longer a vassal to be manipulated. It is a mini superpower in military might. Despised? But the Jew steeped in history will remember "*al elleh ani bokhiyyah*," "for these do I weep" (Lamentations 1:16). He will remember the genius of Torah of R. Akiva, *oker harim ve-toḥanan zu ba-zu be-sevara*, "who would uproot mountains of halakhic problems and grind them one against the other by thorough analysis," and the charisma of Torah of R. Hanina b. Tradeyon, who assembled crowds to study Torah.[8]

---

6. R. Meir b. Jehiel, "*Arzei ha-Levanon*," op. cit.; R. Isaac b. Moses of Vienna (*Or Zaru'a*, Vienna, ca. 1180–1250), *Or Zaru'a, Hilkhot Bekhorot, siman* 510. R. Hutzpit was considered equivalent to Jonathan b. Uzziel, whose fiery breadth of Torah would singe a passing bird. *Sukkah* 28a; *Bava Batra* 134a.
7. Brigham Young University's planned construction of a center on Mount Scopus in 1985 sparked controversy in Israel over concern that the center would be used to convert Jews. See Max Arthur, "New Mormon Center in Jerusalem Incites Debate," *Sun-Sentinel*, July 12, 1985, 6D.
8. *Arzei ha-Levanon*, op. cit., 346.

And we ask ourselves, what would the giants of the spirit say about the state of *kevod ha-Torah* today? When the burning social issues of the day are discussed, from euthanasia to ERA to abortion to comparable worth, in whichever forum, whether it is judicial, legislative, or mass media, does anyone ask what the Jewish perspective is on the issue? Do Jewish professionals who live in the secular world want to know?

And finally, *ha-shomemah* is puzzling. Israel is not desolate. It is teeming with people. But *al elleh ani bokhiyyah*. We remember R. Shimon and Yishmael *Kohen Gadol*, the martyrs. Each could not bear to see the suffering of his friend and therefore begged to be killed first. The executioner found it amusing and cast lots.[9] When the High Priest, R. Yishmael, took sight of the decapitated head of R. Shimon b. Gamliel, "he placed his eyes upon his eyes and his mouth upon his mouth with absolute love [*ahavah gemurah*]."[10]

Yes, Israel may be populated with bright prospects, but if in the sea of humanity, *ahavah gemurah* does not prevail, each person is truly desolate. He is all alone with no connection to his fellow man.

Only a person who feels a tremendous need for consolation, who feels acutely the void in *kedushah* today, fully understands the end of the blessing, where we say "and with fire You will rebuild her in the future," that only Hashem can provide us with a *neḥamah*. And may the day come speedily in our time. Amen!

9. Ibid., 345.
10. Ibid.

How Has the Gold Dimmed?

August 9, 1986

Jeremiah gives prominence to the word "*eikhah*," "how," in expressing his profound grief over the destruction of the Temple. But he also uses this expression to convey his sorrow over the death of a single person. "*Eikhah yu'am zahav*," "How has the gold dimmed?" (Lamentations 4:1). This refers to Josiah,[1] the child King who assumed the monarchy at the age of eight, and who, up to his tragic death twenty-two years before the *ḥurban*, held out the hope for the Jewish people of reversing the decline and leading a national renaissance.[2]

How did Josiah do this? He had no delusions that a people steeped in idolatrous worship for many decades could suddenly leap to

1. *Rashi* to Lamentations 4:1. This is the lamentation referred to at II Chronicles 35:25.
2. II Kings 22:1–2, 23:1–25. After Josiah's death, Jehoahaz b. Josiah reigned three months, Jehoiakim b. Josiah reigned eleven years, Jehoiakhin b. Jehoiakim reigned three months, and Zedekiah b. Josiah reigned eleven years. II Kings 23:31, 23:36, 24:8, 24:18.

perfection. He started with a campaign to repair the deterioration of the Temple, which had not been done for over two hundred years.[3] That is, he started with externalities.

But in the midst of this project through which Josiah would reveal his unique genius of elevating his people, officers found a *sefer Torah* ominously opened to the verse "Hashem will lead you and your king who you will set up over yourself to a nation you never knew" (Deuteronomy 28:36). He took this to mean that the prophecies of doom would be imminently fulfilled and therefore actions had to be taken immediately to avoid desecration. He therefore had the flask of manna, the Ark, and the Tablets hidden in the subterraneous caves under the Temple.[4]

Today, we can well appreciate and relate to what Josiah did. Recently, we had the centennial celebration of the Statue of Liberty.[5] Can we imagine that amidst all the rhetoric and extolling of achievement of liberty, the President would shock us by dolefully proclaiming that we have perverted the meaning of liberty by becoming a drug culture? We do not deserve the symbol of liberty. He then presses a button and a huge white sheet descends and covers the entire statue. It will not be uncovered until major progress is made on the drug front, until we no longer equate liberty with license.

This is exactly what Josiah did. He simulated disaster and made us reflect for one moment on what life would be like for the Jewish people in exile. In exile, would we feel the singularity of the Oil of Anointment; the Staff of Aaron, the symbol of peace; or the flask of the manna, the deep faith in Hashem? And in *galut*, amidst abandonment, and exile, and humiliation, what would become of Torah observance and Torah learning. What would become of the Staves of the Ark, which symbolize the supporters of Torah?[6]

---

3. II Kings 22:4–7; R. David Kimhi (*Radak*, Provence, ca. 1160–ca. 1235), *Radak* to II Kings 22:5.
4. *Yoma* 52b.
5. Robert D. McFadden, "Nation Rekindles Statue of Liberty as Beacon of Hope: Light from Lasers," *New York Times*, July 4, 1986, A1.
6. R. Tobiah b. Eliezer (Mainz, 11th cent.), *Midrash Lekaḥ Tov* (*Pesikta Zutarta*), Exodus 25:13; R. Meir Simhah ha-Kohen of Dvinsk (*Or Same'aḥ* or *Meshekh Ḥokhmah*, Latvia, 1843–1926), *Meshekh Ḥokhmah*, Exodus 25:15.

When Josiah reached the climax of his campaign, the most dramatic moment when he buried the remains of Jeroboam b. Nevat, the symbol of rebellion, on his own idolatrous shrine in Beit El,[7] what did the ordinary Jew feel? Did he feel the shrill voice of condemnation? No. What he felt first and foremost was that the child King included himself in the rebuke. He felt a delicate voice similar to what Jeroboam heard from Hashem, "Repent, then I, you, and the son of Jesse will walk in the Garden of Eden."[8] He heard the voice of one whose deepest desire was to elevate society to new heights of magnificence and beauty.

How have we today implemented Josiah's formula of reproof? Well, usually when there is a *maḥloket* (controversy), we adopt one view. But when it comes to the mitzvah of "you shall reprove your fellow" (Leviticus 19:17), we have adopted the view to be *yotzei le-khol ha-de'ot,* "to fulfill our obligation according to all opinions," with three views: *ad kedei haka'ah,* "until the rebuker is struck by the sinner"; *ad kedei kelalah,* "until the rebuker is cursed by the sinner"; and *ad kedei nezifah,* "until the rebuker is scorned by the sinner."[9] Because of this stringency and little attempt, if any, to create the feeling of "I, you, and the son of Jesse will walk in the Garden of Eden," such actions invite the unthinkable on the part of the left.

Let us remember that Jeremiah refers to Josiah once more in *Eikhah* when he laments "*ruaḥ appeinu meshiaḥ Hashem,*" "the breath of our nostrils, the anointed of Hashem" (Lamentation 4:20).[10] If we would adopt the spirit of Josiah, we would be inexorably headed toward redemption and salvation.

---

7. II Kings 23:15–16.
8. *Sanhedrin* 102a.
9. *Arakhin* 16b (opinions of Rav, Samuel, and R. Yohanan, respectively).
10. *Ta'anit* 22b.

Ḥazon Yeshayahu

July 23, 1988

Today, on the eve of Tish'ah be-Av, we are made to read *Ḥazon Yeshayah*, "the vision of Isaiah." Of the ten expressions of prophecy, *Rashi* tells us, *ḥazon* denotes the most harsh and the most strident form of reproof.[1] Harsh, not because Isaiah's message of reproof is explicit in contrast to Moses' discourse, which only intimates reproof.[2] Harsh, not because Isaiah engages in name-calling, calling us "*ketzinei Sedom*," "chiefs of Sodom" (Isaiah 1:10). Harsh, not because he rails against specific evils and is devastating and unsparing. No. For the man who prophesized 150 years before the *ḥurban*, he perhaps knew that fulminating against specific evils would not shake up the Jewish people, despite his

1. *Rashi* to Isaiah 1:1, s.v. "*asher ḥazah al Yehudah vi-Yerushalayim*" (citing Genesis Rabbah 44:6).
2. *Rashi* to Deuteronomy 1:1, s.v. "*elleh ha-devarim*"; *Sifrei*, Deuteronomy 1; *Targum Onkelos* to Deuteronomy 1:1. Moses' reproof was stated indirectly by mentioning the names of the places where the Children of Israel sinned in the Wilderness.

sting. After all, he is a professional, and evil is the fodder of the prophet. People expect him to be repulsed by evil!

But with respect to our survival, we really have nothing to fear. We have some good and redeeming qualities as well. In any case, we are not worse than the generation that preceded us. We cannot be destroyed!

What will shake up the people, bait them, make them take the Prophet seriously, and make them think is to rip apart the good. That is what Isaiah does. He tears into the good. First, *bein adam la-Makom*. Isaiah tells us that Hashem is sated with our *korbanot*.[3] He finds our assemblages on the Sabbath, Rosh Ḥodesh, and the Festivals a bother.[4] Speaking to the pilgrims, he says, "Who asked you to trample My courtyards?" (Isaiah 1:12).

This is harsh! For what if someone injured his friend, yea, seriously injured or hurt him. Is he to give up *tefillah*, *talmud Torah*, and all mitzvot *bein adam la-Makom* because he has not yet done *teshuvah* for his transgressions *bein adam le-ḥavero*? Is any observance of mitzvot *bein adam la-Makom* hypocritical? No, I would say. If you are moved by a pious spirit to fulfill mitzvot *bein adam la-Makom* while you still have not repented *bein adam le-ḥavero*, by all means, do so. Perhaps the mitzvot *bein adam la-Makom* will reform your *bein adam le-ḥavero* as well.

Yes, we get angry! But Isaiah makes us think because he provokes us with a gauge to measure the quality and authenticity of our goodness. As R. Samson Raphael Hirsch explains, Isaiah gives us three images of what the most precious thing in Jewish religious life, the Temple, could represent. We are presented with one image of the ideal and two images that fail the ideal.[5]

First, the ideal. Does the Temple evoke the image of a sukkah, a booth, that is guarding over a vineyard? The vineyard represents something that is most precious; it symbolizes the blissful life – "the vintage of the grapevine gladdens God and men" (Judges 9:13). The sukkah is a hut that is occupied by a watchman day and night. By day, he guards

3. Isaiah 1:11.
4. Isaiah 1:13–14.
5. R. Samson Raphael Hirsch (Germany, 1808–1888), *Haftarat Devarim*, Isaiah 1:8.

the vineyard against foraging birds, and by night, against thieves.[6] The watchman is on guard to prevent any foreign influence from destroying the beauty and perfection of what the vineyard represents.

Or perhaps we cannot honestly relate to this image of the Temple but only to a *melunah ve-mikshah,* the sleeping quarters of the watchman who guards not a vineyard, but a cucumber field.[7] The cucumber field is not as valuable as a vineyard. The vegetable is not palatable to the birds. There is no need to stand guard by day, only at night to ward off thieves.[8] Maybe we do not regard the life that the Temple protects as the blissful life represented by the vineyard, but as something that has some value, along with other things in life. And we do not want to stand guard with such determination, anxiety, and ferocity; we do not need to stand a constant guard to prevent infiltration.

But now the shocking third image appears. Perhaps we regard the Temple as an *ir netzurah,* a city under siege.[9] The imagery is that of a determined enemy. The city is besieged and lets nothing out. Translate this as an attitude toward *kedushah.* We do everything we can to confine the influence of *kedushah* in our lives. We do not want it to spread to newer and different spheres and dimensions of our lives.

Now, we can ask ourselves, when we summon up extraordinary energy to lavish upon the Altar abundant sacrifices and go all out in other mitzvot *bein adam la-Makom,* does this reflect the fervor and enthusiasm that we have for mitzvot? If this energy will flow to other areas and will lead us to reform our ways *bein adam le-ḥavero,* then Hashem will not despise our mitzvot *bein adam la-Makom.* But if the mitzvot *bein adam la-Makom* are merely in the image of an *ir netzurah,* then we have no intent of expanding performance to other dimensions of our life. Quite to the contrary, we want to get spent up, exhausted, so that we will have no energy to proceed further. That will relieve our guilt. But the Evil Inclination will laugh!

---

6. *Rashi* to Isaiah 1:8, s.v. "*ke-melunah ve-mikshah.*"
7. Isaiah 1:8.
8. *Rashi* to Isaiah 1:8, s.v. "*ke-melunah ve-mikshah.*"
9. Isaiah 1:8.

Then Isaiah proceeds to tear away at our mitzvot *bein adam le-ḥavero*. He addresses *mishpat* (justice) and says, "You think you are practicing *mishpat*. No." – "*Limdu heitev, dirshu mishpat*," "learn to do good and seek justice" (Isaiah 1:17).

The past week, at the Democratic National Convention, we were exposed to various ideas of *mishpat*. One version was justice as envisioned by Jesse Jackson. He told us of a guilt concept of justice. Comparing America to a quilt of many patches, he said that the claim of labor for a fair wage is just a patch, but not big enough to be heard. So, too, the claim of women for comparable worth. It is just a patch, but it is not big enough.[10]

I think Isaiah was speaking to Jesse Jackson, too, when he said *limdu heitev, dirshu mishpat*. Jesse Jackson's concept of justice is a persecution one. It is no more than a rehashing of the political theory of logrolling. A claim is legitimate only if it forms the proper alliances – support me and I will support you. Not only does this conceptualization of justice allow for the possibility that totally outlandish claims will be realized, such as his pitch for self-determination for the Palestinians, but it even discredits truly legitimate claims by telling people that the only way they will be heard is if they appeal to naked self-interest – I'll support you if you support me.

Of such people, Isaiah said, "lovers of bribery and pursuers of payments; they do not render justice to the orphan; the grievance of the widow does not come to them" (Isaiah 1:23). Such people will never take up the cause of the helpless, the powerless, and the disenfranchised. And most importantly, "the grievance of the widow does not come to them." The widow will see how the case of the orphan was disposed of and she will turn away in discouragement.[11]

10. Rev. Jesse Jackson, Speech to the Democratic National Convention ("Common Ground and Common Sense"), July 19, 1988, reprinted in "Stresses 'Common Ground': Jackson Talks of Hope, Dreams as He Weaves 'Quilt of Unity,'" *Congressional Quarterly Weekly Report* 46 (July 23, 1988): 2057-2060. For excerpts of the speech, see "The Democrats in Atlanta: Excerpts from Jackson's Speech; Pushing Party to Find Common Ground," *New York Times*, July 20, 1988, A18.
11. *Rashi* to Isaiah 1:23, s.v. "*ve-riv almanah lo yavo aleihem*."

If we want to gauge society's sensitivity to justice, we merely have to ask, to what extent does society take up the cause of the powerless, the concern of those who cannot even articulate their claims, let alone form close alliances with others? Is their plight an item on our agenda? Justice, Jesse, is not a claim on society. It is best conceptualized as a duty that we all have. I'm afraid your quilt would be found to contain not only patches of silk, gabardine, and crockersack,[12] but wool and linen. It is a blend of *kil'ayim* and we cannot warm ourselves with your blanket!

Finally, *ḥazon* is reproof in the most noble tradition of our people because it pushes away only with the left hand, but draws close with the right hand,[13] as *ḥazon* stands for *ḥatzi za'am ve-ḥatzi neḥamah*, "half rage and half solace."[14] But where is the solace in Isaiah's words? It is there because Isaiah turns to even the most decadent elements of society and tells them that in but a moment's time, he sees them as redeemable. "If your sins are like scarlet, they will become white as snow; if they have become red as crimson, they will become [white] as wool" (Isaiah 1:18).

The crimson dye is in contrast to the crimson fabric. For one, the crimson dye is intrinsically crimson, which signifies the Jew whose very essence is sin. He is rebellious. And the crimson dye, unlike the crimson fabric, can make other substances crimson, hence denoting the Jew who causes others to sin.[15]

Isaiah says that despite this, you are not irredeemable. The doors of *teshuvah* are still open to you. "They will become [white] as wool." This point adds the final touch to Isaiah's message of "Zion will be redeemed through justice and those who return to her through righteousness" (Isaiah 1:27).

---

12. Rev. Jesse Jackson, Speech to the Democratic National Convention, *Congressional Quarterly Weekly Report*, 2058.
13. See *Sotah* 47a.
14. R. Jonathan Eybeschuetz (Prague, 1690–1764), *Ahavat Yehonatan, Haftarat Devarim*; R. Elazar b. Samuel Rokeah (Amsterdam, ca. 1665–1742), *Ma'aseh Roke'aḥ al ha-Mishnayot, Gittin*. R. Jacob Culi (Constantinople, ca. 1685–1732), *Me-Am Lo'ez*, I Kings 18:3, trans. R. Shemuel Yerushalmi, *Yalkut Me-Am Lo'ez* (Jerusalem: Wagshal, 1968), 271.
15. R. Meir Loeb b. Jehiel Michel Weisser (*Malbim*, Poland, Romania, and Russia, 1809–1879), *Malbim* to Isaiah 1:18. See also *Alshekh, Marot ha-Tzove'ot*, Isaiah 1:18.

Sinat Ḥinnam

August 8, 1992

We are all familiar with the dictum of our Sages that whereas the first Temple was destroyed because of the sins of immorality, bloodshed, and idolatry, the second was destroyed because of *sinat ḥinnam*, "unwarranted hatred," and this teaches us that *sinat ḥinnam* is equivalent to the three cardinal sins.[1]

This equation requires explanation. The three cardinal sins are something concrete, something objectively measurable. But *sinat ḥinnam* is entirely a subjective judgment. To be sure, in the mind and heart of the victim of hatred, the hatred is baseless. But the one who practices *sinat ḥinnam* will regard it as justified. And a third party, if equipped with all the facts, would often reserve judgment on whether the hatred was justified.

Perhaps the key here is the story of Kamtza and Bar Kamtza, which the commentators relate to the sin of *sinat ḥinnam*.[2] A wealthy

1. *Yoma* 9b.
2. *Gittin* 55b–56a; Lamentations Rabbah 4:3.

man made a party and asked his attendant to invite his friend Kamtza. The attendant erred and brought Bar Kamtza instead. Upon discovering Bar Kamtza, the host told him, "You are my enemy. What are you doing here?" Bar Kamtza replied, "I am here already. Let me stay." "No!" said the host. "I'll pay for my portion," pleaded Bar Kamtza. "No!" replied the host. "I'll pay for half the party," begged Bar Kamtza. "No!" repeated the host. "I'll pay for the entire party." "No!" Thereupon, the host escorted Bar Kamtza by the hand and evicted him.

Prominent rabbis were there and said nothing. The *Ḥatam Sofer* posits that the rabbis acted correctly,[3] because just as there is *sinat ḥinnam,* there is a permissible variety of hatred. This occurs when one observes someone doing a sin, such as murder, and there is no second corroborating witness. The witness may not report the sin to *beit din,* but must keep his own counsel. Informing on the sinner in that case is *lashon ha-ra.*[4]

Forty years before the destruction of the Temple, the Sanhedrin moved out of the *Lishkat ha-Gazit,* taking away the power of *beit din* of twenty-three to deal with capital cases.[5] Why? Because violence and lawlessness were rampant and people bought protection from the Roman government. With instances of rising crimes, with no capacity to do anything about them, the only thing one could do was to harbor hatred. So the Sages could do nothing at the party. A mere attempt to intervene would prove tempting for the host to spill the beans and speak the *lashon ha-ra* against Bar Kamtza.

Now, so embittered was Bar Kamtza that the Sages did not intervene that he decides to fabricate a story that the Jewish people were rebelling against the Roman government. He implants an invisible defect in a *korban.*

The case comes before R. Zechariah's court. He could decide that Bar Kamtza's vicious act was good confirmation that the Sages were justified in refusing to intervene. If so, the course of action is clear-cut:

3. R. Moses Sofer (*Ḥatam Sofer,* Hungary, 1762–1839), *Gittin* 55b.
4. See *Pesaḥim* 113b; *Rashbam* ad loc., s.v. "*shem ra hu*"; R. Israel Meir ha-Kohen Kagan (*Ḥafetz Ḥayyim,* Radin, 1838–1933), *Sefer Ḥafetz Ḥayyim, Hilkhot Lashon ha-Ra* 4:4.
5. *Sanhedrin* 41a; *Rashi* ad loc. See also *Shabbat* 15a; *Avodah Zarah* 8b.

Kill Bar Kamtza so that he will not be able to inform the Emperor and offer the sacrifice for the sake of *shelom malkhut*. But suppose, just suppose, that the Sages were mistaken, that Bar Kamtza was a victim of *sinat ḥinnam*. His outrageous act is not confirmation of his wickedness, but to the contrary, a manifestation of how far a victim of *sinat ḥinnam* could be driven by bitterness. An *anav*, someone who is always very hard on himself but always recognizes the good in others, would find it difficult to side with the host against the pleading of the guest and would find it unimaginable that Bar Kamtza would actually inform on the Jews to the Emperor.

Yes, to be realistic, there is a choice of two threats: the external threat of an invasion by Rome, but also the threat of the rabbis being totally discredited. People would say, "They care about *shelom malkhut*, but not about avoiding the embarrassment of an individual. That is too trivial to be concerned with." And if they would kill Bar Kamtza, then people would say, "The Sages would do anything to cover up the mistake, even snuff out a life." An *anav* decides that the internal threat is much more serious than the external one. Cut your losses and refuse to offer the sacrifice. Restore the integrity of the Sages as much as possible. Acknowledge the mistake, and to make amends, show that you are willing to put the Jewish people in danger.

R. Yohanan says that the *anavah* of R. Zechariah caused the Temple to be destroyed and for us to be put in exile. What is R. Yohanan saying? Is he ignoring all the terrible sins that existed at the time and finding a scapegoat in R. Zechariah? No!

What R. Yohanan is saying is, see the destructive, disintegrative power of *sinat ḥinnam*. It creates an environment that renders a hero of the Jewish people a villain and transforms his wisdom into conventional logic. It is only the background of *sinat ḥinnam* that makes him think this way. It is only the *anav* who would be particularly sensitized to it. *Sinat ḥinnam* disarms and also converts the wise and pure into villains. Hence, *sinat ḥinnam* is in a real sense equal to murder. Without an authoritative, restraining influence, there is *hefkerut*, "lawlessness." Then immorality and idolatry follow naturally.

The remedy for R. Yohanan can be found in his three requests to Vespasian. First, "*ten li Yavneh ve-ḥakhameha*," "give me Yavneh and her wise men."[6] We must teach the next generation moral values to create a better society without the sin of *sinat ḥinnam*. And Rabban Gamliel must be saved, because we must demonstrate to our enemies that we do indeed have common ground. The Biryonim had burnt provisions of twenty-one years to force the issue of Jewish sovereignty.[7] We, too, believe in Jewish sovereignty. And finally, restore R. Tzadok who fasted forty years to atone for the sins of the generation. *Ahavat ḥinnam* counteracts *sinat ḥinnam*.

May it be our lot to emulate R. Yohanan in our time.

---

6. *Gittin* 56b.
7. *Gittin* 56a. The Biryonim wanted the Jews to fight the Romans, but R. Yohanan disagreed because he thought that the Jews would lose. The Jews of Jerusalem had sufficient provisions to hold out for twenty-one years, but the Biryonim burned the storehouses of wheat, barley, and wood to force the Jews to fight.

Exaggeration

July 24, 2004

Probably, there is nothing more counterproductive for the objective of the one who gives reproof then to exaggerate the flaws of the object of his reproof. This will evoke nothing less than hostility and hatred, and will accomplish nothing.

Moses was apparently guilty of this conduct when he reported the sin of the Spies, stating that they said that the cities in the Land of Israel are "fortified to the very heavens" (Deuteronomy 1:28). But they never said this. They said only that the cities were "fortified" (Numbers 13:28). There is a qualitative difference between "fortified" and "fortified to the very heavens."

The *Ḥafetz Ḥayyim* says that exaggeration is a form of falsehood.[1] But our Sages tell us that what Moses did was an innocent form of exaggeration.[2] Why?

1. See R. Israel Meir ha-Kohen Kagan (*Ḥafetz Ḥayyim*, Radin, 1838–1933), *Sefer Ḥafetz Ḥayyim, Asin* 13; *Be'er Mayim Ḥayyim* ad loc.
2. See *Ḥullin* 90b; *Tamid* 29a.

Permit me to suggest that since the Spies said "we cannot ascend to that people because it is too strong for us" (Numbers 13:31), Moses took upon himself to summarize what the Spies said. The summary is not a distortion of the truth. It is only an innocent exaggeration, not a pernicious exaggeration.

The tragedy of exaggeration is what we face today. The International Court of Justice, by a vote of fourteen to one, ruled that Israel's security barrier is illegal. The Court denied a sovereign State the right to defend itself.[3]

How do we respond to the exaggerated form of hatred that absolutely defies all logic? It is with R. Akiva's approach, *metzaḥek*, "smiling."[4] The smile says that despite the tragedies that befall us, we as a people will prevail.

But it seems to me that R. Akiva was able to smile because he understood the profundity of the anguish that we should feel on Tish'ah be-Av. Only someone who feels the profundity of the tragedy is capable of imagining the profundity of the ecstasy that Hashem will bring with the *ge'ullah*. Only one who is an ultimate optimist can imagine that the *ge'ullah* is imminent.

The profundity of the anguish is expressed in *Naḥem* with the words *ha-avelah*, "mournful"; *ha-ḥarevah*, "ruined"; *ha-bezuyah*, "scorned"; and *ha-shomemah*, "desolate."[5] This is very accurate for the

---

3. International Court of Justice, "Legal Consequences of the Construction of a Wall in the Occupied Palestinian Territory," Advisory Opinion, July 9, 2004.
4. *Makkot* 24a–b. The Talmud records that after the destruction of the Temple, R. Gamliel, R. Eleazar b. Azariah, R. Joshua, and R. Akiva were traveling on the road and heard the sound of the Roman crowds from a distance. R. Gamliel, R. Eleazar b. Azariah, and R. Joshua began to weep, but R. Akiva was smiling. "Why are you smiling?" they asked R. Akiva. "Why are you crying?" he replied. They responded, "The heathens who worship idols live in security and in calm, but for us, the Temple is consumed in fire – should we not weep?" R. Akiva then explained that he is smiling because if such is the reward for those who transgress Hashem's will, those who do Hashem's will can expect a much greater reward.
5. *Naḥem* Prayer, *Shemoneh Esreh* for *Minḥah* on Tish'ah be-Av. The prayer begins "*Naḥem* [console], O Hashem, our God, the mourners of Zion and the mourners of Jerusalem, and the City that is mournful, ruined, scorned, and desolate," and ends with "Blessed are You, Hashem, *menaḥem* [Who consoles] Zion and rebuilds Jerusalem."

first fifty-two years of the destruction of the First Temple.[6] Jerusalem was literally a plowed field, desolate. But now, two thousand years later, the Land of Israel is not *shomemah*, not *ḥarevah*, and not *avelah*. The only thing that we can relate to is *bezuyah*, "scorned."

But if R. Akiva would come down now, he would say that the *ma'on* of the *Beit ha-Mikdash* is *ḥarevah*. The International Court of Justice is a travesty. We yearn for the justice of the Messiah – "He will be imbued with a spirit of fear of Hashem, and will not judge by what his eyes see nor decide by what his ears hear" (Isaiah 11:3). No superficial justice, relying on rumor and hearsay. Only one judge, an American, dissented. The Court did not discuss the repeated and deadly terrorist acts.[7]

R. Akiva would say that yes, there are inhabitants in the Land of Israel, but it is still *shomemah* if we have *sinat ḥinnam*. We can be surrounded by a sea of humanity, yet each and every one of us is alone and desolate if we exaggerate the faults of our friend.

R. Akiva was the *ohev Yisrael*. He understood that just a drop of *ahavat ḥinnam* in the form of exaggerating the virtues of our fellow is the key to move from the four expressions of desolation to the four expressions of jubilation, "the Jews had light, gladness, joy, and honor" (Esther 8:16).

We think that the present life is good, but in comparison to what we could have, it is now *avelut*. Only the man of faith who believes that the prophecies of *Eikhah* and Zechariah are linked can believe that one prophecy can follow the other in rapid succession.

The key is to move from *sinat ḥinnam* to *ahavat ḥinnam*, from exaggerating the faults of our fellow to exaggerating the virtues of our fellow. When this happens, we can hope that Hashem will bring forth on the outside *ḥomat esh saviv*, "a wall of fire around," and inside *u-le-khavod eheyeh ve-sokhah*, "and for glory will I be in its midst" (Zechariah 2:9).

---

6. *Shabbat* 145b.
7. The American judge Thomas Buergenthal said that the court should not have ruled until it had considered "all relevant facts bearing directly on issues of Israel's legitimate right of self-defense" and that the impact of "repeated deadly terror attacks" was something "never really seriously examined by the court." Gregory Couch and Greg Myre, "Major Portion of Israeli Fence Is Ruled Illegal," *New York Times*, July 10, 2004, A1.

Rosh Ḥodesh

He Made the Moon for Festivals

March 31, 1984

As would be expected, the first mitzvah that we were commanded to perform as a people went beyond prescribing a mere obligation. It did nothing less than capsulate our mission and secret of our continuous rejuvenation. The consecration of the New Moon was that mitzvah: "This month shall be for you the beginning of months" (Exodus 12:2).

Our Sages expound that the New Moon should be *le-dugmah*, as a model. Just as the moon is intrinsically not a luminous body, but merely reflects the light of the sun, we, too, in our personal lives must conduct ourselves so that we reflect glory upon our Creator.[1]

1. See Exodus Rabbah 15:27; R. Enoch Zundel b. Joseph (Białystock, d. 1867), *Etz Yosef* ad loc., s.v. "*hi shel or*"; R. Obadiah b. Jacob Sforno (*Sforno*, Italy, ca. 1470–1550), *Sforno* to Numbers 28:11; R. Jehiel Michal Epstein (Belorus, 1829–1908), *Arukh ha-Shulḥan, Oraḥ Ḥayyim* 426:2.

But from the vantage point of the observer, the moon does not appear to continuously reflect light. The moon has phases, ascending and descending. The period of its cycle of approximately thirty days corresponds, as our Sages tell us, to the thirty generations from Abraham to Zedekiah.[2] The ascendancy of Abraham, infusing light into a chaotic world, eventually wanes in the time of the bleakest darkness for the Jewish people.

Are we today in a prolonged *yoma arikhta* of this darkness? No, absolutely not. The moon is our model for rejuvenation and hope. Newtonian physics tells us that cosmic bodies have a tendency to unite. The gravitational pull between these bodies is a function of both their relative mass and the distance between them.[3] Were it not for the relative positions and course of the planets, they would all fuse into a single conglomerate. If the moon's orbit were closer to the earth, its gravitational pull might inundate the world.[4] If the moon were further away, the quality of life on earth as we know it today would not be possible.[5] What preserves the integrity of the moon and allows it to contribute to the well-being of the earth is its motion. The moon survives as an entity only because it is a part of a moving pattern. So, too, in our personal lives, we as the Chosen People are inexorably moving toward our ultimate destiny, salvation, and redemption.

But there are many different moving patterns of getting there, some more pleasant than others. To reinforce the notion that we are part of a moving pattern, we always invoke David in the prayer of consecrating the New Moon, "David, King of Israel, lives and endures."[6]

---

2. Exodus Rabbah 15:26.
3. The principle is known as "Newton's Law of Universal Gravitation." See Forest Ray Moulton, *An Introduction to Celestial Mechanics* (London: MacMillan, 1902), 77; Douglas W. MacDougal, *Newton's Gravity: An Introductory Guide to the Mechanics of the Universe* (New York: Springer, 2012), 8–10.
4. Peter Ward and Donald Brownlee, *Rare Earth: Why Complex Life Is Uncommon in the Universe* (New York: Copernicus Books, 2003), 223.
5. Ibid.
6. Prayer for Sanctification of the Moon. This verse was composed by R. Judah ha-Nasi and is based on Psalms 89:38 ("Like the moon, [David's throne] shall be established forever."). See *Rosh Ha-Shanah* 25a; R. Solomon b. Isaac (*Rashi*, France, 1040–1105), *Rashi* ad loc., s.v. "*David Melekh Yisrael.*"

David, as King, was well aware that everything he did in both a passive and active way would actually determine the course of history. His virtue would elevate society. His sin would bring it down. His repentance would again elevate society. Every action of his would generate a reaction and a definite course of history.

The realization that we are not isolated and that everything that happens to us puts us into a moving scenario is true not only for a king, but for each of us. "All Jews are sons of kings."[7]

Everyone's potential impact on society is enormous and can assume an important role in the overall scheme of events. To reinforce the centrality of man and particularly the Jew in the scheme, we always recite the *barkhi nafshi* prayer on Rosh Ḥodesh.[8] The overriding theme of this prayer is the hierarchy of creation. Creation is a series of ascending categories: the *domem*, the inanimate matter; the *tzome'aḥ*, the vegetative; the *ḥai*, the living creatures; and finally, the *medabber*, man, who is endowed with the gift of intelligent speech.[9]

Now, the lower order of creation exists only to serve the higher order. "He causes vegetation to sprout for the animals, and plants through man's labor, to bring forth bread from the earth" (Psalms 104:14). And we are told that even the most massive, impressive element of a lower form of life serves the lowest element of the higher order. The wild birds use the cedar trees as a nest, and the stork, a non-kosher bird, makes its home in a cedar.[10] This drives home the point that even the lowliest man stands at the crown of creation, with all forms of lower life serving him.

The sublime importance of man in the scheme of creation is further seen when it becomes evident that divine providence and special care extend to even the most remote and forsaken of Hashem's creatures.

---

7. Mishnah, *Shabbat* 14:4.
8. Psalms 104.
9. R. Bahya b. Asher (*Rabbenu Beḥaye*, Saragossa, 1255–1340), *Rabbenu Beḥaye al ha-Torah, Va-Yak'hel*, s.v. "*ekhol beni devash*"; R. Moses Alshekh (*Alshekh*, Safed, 1508–1593), *Torat Mosheh*, Deuteronomy 7:13; R. Isaac b. Solomon Luria (*Arizal* or *Ha-Ari*, Safed, 1534–1572), *Sefer ha-Likkutim, Bereshit, siman* 1, *Ekev, siman* 8 (Jerusalem: Lifshitz Brothers, 1913); R. Reuben Hoeshke b. Hoeshke Katz (Prague, d. 1673), *Yalkut Re'uveni, Va-Yikra*.
10. R. David Kimhi (*Radak*, Provence, ca. 1160–ca. 1235), *Radak* to Psalms 104:17.

The streams and rivers wade through the mountainous and underground channels and find their way to quench the thirst of the wild beasts.[11] The irregular terrain of the earth is designed to provide refuge to nature's threatened creatures, the high mountains for the goats, and the clefts for the gophers. If such meticulous concern is extended to these creatures, whose only purpose is to serve man, how much more so does the sublime importance of man follow. Even the most forsaken creatures are part of the divine scheme, and so even the lowliest man is esteemed by God.

The entire *barkhi nafshi* prayer is a description of natural phenomena, with two exceptions. We are told, "He made the moon for festivals; the sun knows its destination" (Psalms 104:19). The moon was made so that we could fix the seasons, i.e., the Festivals, by them. Indeed, it is by virtue of this verse that we recite *barkhi nafshi* on Rosh Ḥodesh.[12] The reference must be to the Festivals, not to the seasons, as the rotation of the sun rather than the moon makes the seasons. Now, this refers to the dictum of the Jerusalem Talmud that if *beit din* does not pronounce the New Moon, the Festivals do not occur.[13]

Similarly, our Sages propounded "*elleh mo'adei Hashem mikra'ei kodesh asher tikri'u otam be-mo'adam,*" "these are the appointed Festivals of Hashem, the holy convocations, that you shall designate in their appropriate time" (Leviticus 23:4). Do not read the word "*otam,*" "them," but rather "*atem,*" "you."[14] Even if you err inadvertently, even if you err deliberately, even if you are misled in designating the New Moon, these are the official Festivals.[15] If *beit din* erroneously pronounced the New Moon because of false witnesses, the pronouncement is valid and should not be reversed. The determination of our Festivals by *beit din* represents the highest creative potential of the Jew – "for it is your wisdom and discernment in the eyes of the people" (Deuteronomy 4:6).

11. Psalms 104:10–11.
12. *Tur, Oraḥ Ḥayyim* 423; R. Israel Meir ha-Kohen Kagan (*Ḥafetz Ḥayyim,* Radin, 1838–1933), *Mishnah Berurah* 423, n. 9 (citing *Tur*).
13. Jerusalem Talmud, *Rosh Ha-Shanah* 1:3.
14. *Rosh Ha-Shanah* 25a.
15. The phrase "*asher tikri'u otam*" appears at Leviticus 23:2, 23:4, and 23:37. Each time, the word "*otam*" (אתם) is spelled without a *vav.* The Sages therefore expound the word "*otam*" as *atem,* "you." *Rashi* to *Rosh Ha-Shanah* 25a, s.v. "*atem, atem, atem.*"

The Rosh Ḥodesh Jew

1986

Shabbat Malkheta is a very gracious and generous hostess. The Queen gives elaborate recognition to its guest, Rosh Ḥodesh. She relinquishes *maftir* and the *haftarah* to Rosh Ḥodesh,[1] and in a little while, will make another grand gesture in the *Musaf* Prayer.[2] If it were not for the fact that today is the Sabbath, the Festival of Rosh Ḥodesh would perhaps completely escape notice. The holiness of Rosh Ḥodesh is not outwardly evident. The prohibition against work does not apply,[3] and we are not bidden to honor Rosh Ḥodesh with festivities in the form of either *simḥah* or *oneg*.[4]

---

1. R. Joseph Caro (Safed, 1488–1575), *Shulḥan Arukh, Oraḥ Ḥayyim* 425:1. The *maftir* is at Numbers 28:9–15, and the *haftarah* is at Isaiah 66:1–24.
2. *Shulḥan Arukh, Oraḥ Ḥayyim* 425:3. When the Sabbath coincides with Rosh Ḥodesh, the fourth blessing of the *Musaf* Prayer of the Sabbath is substituted with a different blessing that includes aspects of the *Musaf* Prayer of the Three Festivals. In addition, the introduction of that blessing includes a unique prayer, *Atah Yatzarta*.
3. *Arakhin* 10b; *Shulḥan Arukh, Oraḥ Ḥayyim* 417:1.
4. *Rashi* to *Ta'anit* 15b, s.v. "*ve-im hit'ḥilu*"; R. Yehiel Avraham Zilber, *Berur Halakhah, Oraḥ Ḥayyim*, vol. 3, no. 418 (Benei Berak, 1976), 217.

What then does the Festival of Rosh Ḥodesh consist of? The clue is found in the unique phraseology that the Torah employs in connection with the *Musaf* offering on Rosh Ḥodesh, "*se'ir ḥatat la-Hashem*," "a male goat sin offering to Hashem" (Numbers 28:15). In connection with all the Festivals, there is a *se'ir ḥatat*.[5] But only in connection with Rosh Ḥodesh is the word *la-Hashem* used. This is taken to mean that the offering effects atonement for a sin that the sinner was not aware of either in the beginning or in the end, such as eating *kodesh* or entering the Sanctuary in a defiled state while not knowing of the sin.[6] Rosh Ḥodesh therefore represents the ability of the Jew to influence society without consciously exerting any effort toward this direction. How is this possible?

Perhaps best exemplifying the Rosh Ḥodesh personality is Joseph. Joseph was idolized by the Egyptian society. "The daughters climbed heights to gaze [at Joseph]" (Genesis 49:22), to catch a glimpse of the beauty and the symbol of absolute power. Pharaoh said to Joseph, "by your command shall all my people be sustained" (Genesis 41:40).

He was not idolized for his Jewishness. His spectacular achievement and physical beauty overshadowed his Jewishness. And when Joseph's brothers are caught in what they perceive to be an insidious plot against them, Joseph tells them that he will keep all the brothers except on the condition that they bring down Benjamin.[7] Then he locks them up for three days.[8] Then he changes his mind and says, "I fear God" (Genesis 42:18). I will lock up only one, Simeon. Only one is necessary and no more. Thereupon, the brothers say, "Indeed we are guilty concerning our brother" (Genesis 42:21).

The sequence here is very important. A stay of three days in jail does not bring the brothers to a realization of *teshuvah* for the sin. Why do they arrive at this realization when they have a lightening of the demand placed upon them? It is, I submit, because the brothers are shocked by hearing compassion from the seat of absolute power. This

5. Numbers 28:22 (Passover), 29:4 (Rosh Ha-Shanah), 29:11 (Yom Kippur), 29:16, 29:19, 29:22, 29:25, 29:28, 29:31, 29:34, 29:38 (Sukkot).
6. *Shevuot* 2a, 9a.
7. Genesis 42:14–16.
8. Genesis 42:17.

must have been the surprise of their lives! Compassion is contagious. The brothers now regret that they did not have compassion for their brother. Joseph's display of a spark of mercy in his role as a potentate generates a tremendous impact, a *hirhur teshuvah* (thought of repentance) in the brothers.

There are many Rosh Ḥodesh Jews around, the spectacular achievers in the business world and the professions, the Nobel Prize winners in the sciences. These people do not only achieve. They dazzle. They impress. They electrify! Once they are idolized, every aspect of their lives is scrutinized and people want to emulate them. If it is found that they wear *tefillin*, go to a *minyan* in the morning, or go to a *shiur*, people want to emulate them. Think, *ḥas ve-shalom*, if a Rosh Ḥodesh Jew is not faithful to even basic Torah values. For example, he marries outside our faith. Think of the damage that he causes to the moral climate for our people!

But there must be something more to the Rosh Ḥodesh Jew. The spectacular happens only rarely. Rosh Ḥodesh, by contrast, is every month. Yes, every Jew can be spectacular by being inconsistent! A Jew can be spectacular when it comes to *bein adam la-Makom*, but when it comes to *bein adam le-ḥavero*, he is just ordinary, business-like, mechanical, showing no special sensitivity.

Take Shraga Feivel, for example. He puts on two pairs of *tefillin*. *Tefillin* of *Rashi* is not enough; he must also put on *tefillin* of *Rabbenu Tam*.[9] And he is concerned with microscopic worms in his salad, and

---

9. See *Shulḥan Arukh, Oraḥ Ḥayyim* 34. *Tefillin* contain parchment on which four biblical passages are written. *Menaḥot* 34b. The four passages are: Exodus 13:1–10 ("*kaddesh li kol bekhor*"), Exodus 13:11–16 ("*ve-hayah ki yevi'akha*"), Deuteronomy 6:4–9 ("*Shema*"), and Deuteronomy 11:13–21 ("*ve-hayah im shamo'a*"). In the *tefillah* that is worn on the hand, the four passages are written on one piece of parchment and in the order in which they appear in the Bible. In the *tefillah* that is worn on the head, each passage is placed in a separate compartment. According to *Rashi*, the four passages are placed in the compartments from right to left in the order in which they appear in the Bible. *Rashi* to *Menaḥot* 34b, s.v. "*ve-ha-ko're ko're ke-sidran*." According to *Rashi*'s grandson, R. Jacob b. Meir (*Rabbenu Tam*, Ramerupt, ca. 1100–ca. 1171), the passage from Deuteronomy 11:13–21 precedes the passage from Deuteronomy 6:4–9 in their placement in the compartments from right to left. *Tosafot* to *Menaḥot* 34b, s.v. "*ve-ha-ko're ko're ke-sidran*."

that his barley is possibly *ḥadash*.[10] If, God forbid, Shraga Feivel would cheat someone in business, then what of his spectacular achievements *bein adam la-Makom*? They are no longer subject to admiration, but instead to ridicule.

What we need is "may You establish a new altar in Zion!"[11] And what is the new altar? The *Shem mi-Shemuel* says that it is the altar of the twelve stones of Elijah.[12] What he means is the integration of the Children of Israel to our Father in Heaven that comes when we achieve the spectacular both in *bein adam le-ḥavero* and *bein adam la-Makom*.[13]

---

10. The Torah prohibits eating from grain that has taken root after the sixteenth day of Nisan until the subsequent sixteenth day of Nisan. Leviticus 23:14. The prohibition applies to wheat, barley, rye, oats, and spelt. This prohibited grain is referred to as *ḥadash* (lit., "new"). In the time of the Temple, the consumption of *ḥadash* became permissible when the *korban omer* was brought on the sixteenth day of Nisan. After the destruction of the Temple, *ḥadash* becomes permissible on the seventeenth day of Nisan in the Land of Israel, and on the eighteenth day of Nisan outside the Land of Israel. *Shulḥan Arukh, Oraḥ Ḥayyim* 489:10.

    The issue of whether the prohibition of *ḥadash* applies to grain grown outside the Land of Israel is the subject of debate among the halakhic authorities. In accordance with the view of R. Eliezer recorded in the Mishnah, most *Rishonim* are of the opinion that the prohibition does apply in the Diaspora. See Mishnah, *Kiddushin* 1:9; R. Isaac b. Jacob Alfasi (*Rif*, Algeria, 1013–1103), *Rif* to *Kiddushin* 37a; R. Asher b. Jehiel (*Rosh*, Germany, ca. 1250–1327), *Rosh, Kiddushin* 1:62; Maimonides (*Rambam*, Egypt, 1135–1204), *Mishneh Torah, Ma'akhalot Asurot* 10:2; R. Jacob b. Asher (*Tur*, Spain, 1270–1343), *Oraḥ Ḥayyim* 489. The *Shulḥan Arukh* rules similarly. *Shulḥan Arukh, Oraḥ Ḥayyim* 489:10; *Yoreh De'ah* 293:2. For several centuries, however, the common practice of observant Jews outside the Land of Israel has been to follow various minority opinions with respect to *ḥadash*. See *Arukh ha-Shulḥan, Yoreh De'ah* 293:5–6 (citing minority opinions, including the opinion of R. Isaac b. Moses of Vienna (*Or Zaru'a*, Vienna, ca. 1180–1250), *Or Zaru'a, Hilkhot Ḥadash, siman* 328).
11. *Musaf* Prayer for Rosh Ḥodesh.
12. I Kings 18:31.
13. R. Shmuel Bornsztain (*Shem mi-Shemuel*, Poland, 1855–1926), *Shem mi-Shemuel: Al Seder Parshiyyot ha-Torah u-Mo'adei Kodesh*, 9th ed., vol. 1 (Jerusalem, 1992), *Noaḥ, Rosh Ḥodesh Ḥeshvan* (5673/October 1912), p. 53.

The Festival of Rosh Ḥodesh

January 7, 1989

Because there is neither a prohibition against work nor a novel ritual to mark the occasion, Rosh Ḥodesh remains essentially an invisible holiday. When Rosh Ḥodesh falls, however, on the Sabbath, the Festival of Rosh Ḥodesh spurts forward more than usual. This is mostly because the Sabbath is a very gracious host. In deference to its guest, the Sabbath gives the *maftir* and *haftarah* to Rosh Ḥodesh.[1] To ensure that we notice this, two *sifrei Torah* are removed from the ark on the Sabbath that coincides with Rosh Ḥodesh. In case we miss this too, the *gabbai* pounds on the *shulḥan* before *Musaf* and announces, "*Atah yatzarta*," which alerts us to the fact that *Musaf* will be dismembered and Rosh Ḥodesh will take over the Sabbath *Musaf*.[2]

---

1. *Shulḥan Arukh, Oraḥ Ḥayyim* 425:1. The *maftir* is at Numbers 28:9–15, and the *haftarah* is at Isaiah 66:1–24.
2. *Shulḥan Arukh, Oraḥ Ḥayyim* 425:3.

We are all familiar with the teaching of the *Tur* that the twelve New Moons correspond to the Twelve Tribes.[3] Each month corresponds to a different tribe. Rosh Ḥodesh hence celebrates the individual.

But what type of individual do we celebrate on Rosh Ḥodesh? Is it the man of stellar achievement? Do we celebrate man as the master of Torah and *ḥokhmah* and his creative genius and human endeavor, reflected in the diversity of the uniqueness of the Jewish people, as manifested in the Twelve Tribes? No. We can see this with an examination of the embellishments of Rosh Ḥodesh. In the *haftarah,* we are immediately struck by a contrast. We are confronted with the imagery of Hashem and His magnificent splendor: "The heaven is My throne and the earth is My footstool; what house could you build for Me, and what place could be My resting place?" (Isaiah 66:1).

But what kind of man does Hashem pay attention to? What kind of man is worthy of note? "It is to this that I look: to the poor and broken-spirited person who is zealous regarding My word" (Isaiah 66:2). It is the humble man, the man of crushed spirit who hastens to do Hashem's bidding. This theme is reinforced with the *barkhi nafshi* prayer. In that prayer, a major theme is the hierarchy of creation, as the *Radak* points out.[4]

What Rosh Ḥodesh celebrates is not man as a stellar achiever. No. It is the celebration of the humanity and dignity of man.

In a recent article in *Tradition,* R. Amital puts forward a positive theme.[5] His theme, I think, expands the reach of the type of man that Rosh Ḥodesh celebrates. Traditionally, we are taught that we must respond to the transgressor with all types of hatred,[6] the lowest-level transgressor and the highest-level transgressor.[7] But how do we develop a love for the transgressor? The answer lies in the embellishments that we say on Rosh Ḥodesh. We believe that it is not so important where

3. *Tur, Oraḥ Ḥayyim* 417.
4. *Radak* to Psalms 104:17.
5. R. Yehuda Amital (Israel, 1924–2010), "A Torah Perspective on the Status of Secular Jews Today," *Tradition: A Journal of Orthodox Jewish Thought* 23, no. 4 (Summer 1988): 1–13.
6. See *Pesaḥim* 113b; Maimonides, *Mishneh Torah, Rotze'aḥ* 4:10; 13:14.
7. For a distinction between these levels of transgressors, see R. Amital, "A Torah Perspective," 6.

we are, but where we are going. We believe that man is capable of being transformed quite speedily and suddenly – "before she even feels her labor pains, she will give birth" (Isaiah 66:7).

And we are already optimistic this can happen, as we omit two portions of Hallel, *Lo lanu*, "Not for our sake" (Psalms 115:1–11), which includes the verse "Why should the nations say, 'Where now is their God?'" (Psalms 115:2), and "*Ahavti*" (Psalms 116:1–11), which includes the verse "I said in my haste, 'All mankind is deceitful'" (Psalms 116:11). All this is perhaps capsulated in the purest line of *barkhi nafshi*, "sinners will cease from the earth" (Psalms 104:35).

Ḥaverim kol Yisrael ve-nomar amen! "All Israel shall be friends; let us answer 'amen'!"[8]

8. *Birkat ha-Ḥodesh* (blessing of the new month, recited on the Sabbath preceding the week in which Rosh Ḥodesh falls).

Hallel on Rosh Ḥodesh

(Undated)

Rosh Ḥodesh is practically an invisible *yom tov*. If it were not for Hallel, we perhaps would not be aware of its presence. And even when it comes to Hallel, we do not say it in its entirety,[1] as if to say Rosh Ḥodesh does not merit recitation of the full Hallel.

But it is precisely Hallel, and particularly what we choose to say and what we choose not to say, that contains the secret of how something invisible is transformed into something awe-inspiring, attaining universal recognition and admiration. What is emphasized is the component of human initiative in bringing about rejuvenation.

We leave out *Lo lanu*, "Not for our sake" (Psalms 115:1–11). Here, we plead desperately that Hashem should intervene in human affairs, not for our merit, but because Hashem's name is being desecrated and profaned among the nations. "Why should the nations say, 'Where now is their God?'" (Psalms 115:2).

1. *Ta'anit* 28b; *Shulḥan Arukh, Oraḥ Ḥayyim* 422:2.

We also leave out *Ahavti* (Psalms 116:1–11), where the famous verse "*shomer pesa'im Hashem,*" "Hashem protects the simple" (Psalms 116:6), appears.[2] Hashem is the guardian of the simpleton. We say, in effect, Hashem must intervene and rescue us because we are all simpletons. We lack the foresight and insight to help ourselves. The cumulation of the *tzarot* of the Exile has done this to us.

And the chapter ends on the most dismal note of all, "I said in my haste, 'All mankind is deceitful'" (Psalms 116:11). David says that he has lost all trust in humanity. When he was surrounded by Saul's hosts at the Stone of Divisiveness, the people of Zif betrayed his whereabouts and he was at his wits' end.[3] He proclaimed that the Prophet Samuel had been deceitful when he promised that David would become the King of Israel,[4] or, as the Abrabanel says, that we as a people feel that the prophecies for redemption are false, and we continue to suffer in the long tortuous exile.[5]

We omit these not out of despair. We say in effect that we are helpless to act. We cannot form any relationship of trust.

What do we say? We begin with the paragraph of the strange suffixes, *ha-magbbihi,* "enthroned on high";[6] *mekimi,* "raises";[7] *moshivi,* "transforms."[8] The suffix "*i*" denotes "me."[9] We are saying in effect that it is we who determine the design of Hashem's perceived involvement in human affairs. Do we want that Hashem should be merely enthroned on high, *ha-magbbihi la-shevet*? Or do we want Him to deign to interfere in human affairs, *ha-mashpili lir'ot*?

---

2. Maimonides, *Mishneh Torah, Ḥanukkah* 3:7–8; R. Israel Meir ha-Kohen Kagan, *Mishnah Berurah* 422:12.
3. I Samuel 23:19–28.
4. *Midrash Shoḥer Tov,* Psalms 18:2.
5. R. Issac b. Judah Abrabanel, *Zevaḥ Pesaḥ, Hallel,* Psalms 116:11.
6. Psalms 113:5.
7. Psalms 113:7.
8. Psalms 113:9.
9. R. Moses b. Jacob Albelda (*Maharam Alviladah,* Turkey, 16th cent.), *Derash Mosheh, Va-Era,* cited by R. Avrohom Chaim Feuer, *Tehillim: Psalms; A New Translation with a Commentary Anthologized from Talmudic, Midrashic and Rabbinic Sources* (Brooklyn, NY: Mesorah, 1996), 1367, Psalms 113:6. See also *Midrash Hallel,* s.v. "*mekimi me-afar dal*" (contrasting Psalm 113:7 with Hannah's prayer, "*mekim me-afar dal*" [I Samuel 2:8]).

And to what extent can our actions determine our transformation? It is "He raises the needy from the dust, from the trash heaps. He lifts the destitute, to seat them with nobles, with the nobles of His people. He transforms the barren wife into a glad mother of children" (Psalms 113:7–9).

How does this transformation come about? The element of human initiative is emphasized, as we read in the paragraph of "when Israel went out of Egypt" (Psalms 114:1). We focus on the grand act of faith of Judah. "Judah became His sanctuary" (Psalms 114:2).

We all know of the dispute that arose between the Tribes regarding who should have the privilege to plunge first into the Sea of Reeds. Judah wanted the honor, but Benjamin also wanted it.[10] I could never understand the dispute. The shoreline was certainly long enough to accommodate both Tribes.

The *Me-am Lo'ez* explains that Judah felt that if he would lead the way, a greater impact would be made on society. People would say that if the Tribe of the Princes is submissive to Hashem's will, then certainly ordinary people must be submissive.[11]

Benjamin, on the other hand, felt that the command was "*dabber el benei Yisrael va-yissa'u*," "speak to the Children of Israel and let them journey forth" (Exodus 14:15).[12] Only Benjamin was born after Jacob grappled with the Angel of Esau.[13] And so, only one who faces the decadent society, rather than being insular, can make a greater impact on society.

---

10. *Midrash Shoḥer Tov*, Psalms 114:2, s.v. "*hayesah Yehudah le-kad'sho*."
11. R. Jacob Culi (Constantinople, ca. 1685–1732), *Me-Am Lo'ez*, Exodus 14:21, trans. R. Shemuel Yerushalmi, *Yalkut Me-Am Lo'ez: Sefer Shemot* (Jerusalem: Mossad Yad Ezra, 1968), 319.
12. Ibid. The *Me-Am Lo'ez* explains that Benjamin interpreted Hashem's command to Moses "*va-yisa'u*" to mean that the Children of Israel should jump into the Sea first, and then Hashem would save them. The other Tribes, by contrast, thought that they were to wait until Hashem split the Sea.
13. Genesis 32:25–30 (struggle with the Angel of Esau); Genesis 35:16–18 (birth of Benjamin). After Jacob prevailed in his struggle with the Angel of Esau, he was granted the name "Israel." Genesis 32:29. Benjamin therefore interpreted the command "speak to the Children of Israel" as referring specifically to the Tribe of Benjamin. *Yalkut Me-Am Lo'ez* ad loc.

What follows from a grand act of faith is a new perception and a new outlook, a new sense of mission. "As for the heavens, the heavens are for Hashem; but the earth He has given to mankind" (Psalms 115:16). From the new sense of mission, we move to an approach to how we can effect our own rejuvenation in the sphere of everyday life. And it occurs in two ways. One is "my vows to Hashem I shall pay, in the presence, now, of His entire people" (Psalms 116:14). We make vows and fulfill them in public view. This is how we counteract the mistrust prevalent in society. We inject a dosage of integrity into an artificially contrived situation.

And how do we restore our fellowship in society? We find reason to express thanksgiving to Hashem. "To You I will sacrifice a thanksgiving offering [*todah*], and the Name of Hashem I will invoke" (Psalms 116:17). The *todah* had forty loaves[14] and had to be eaten in one day and one night.[15] Therefore, a *seudat hoda'ah* was held, where the bread was shared with others. Fellowship was promoted through the *seudah*.

When the climate of distrust is replaced with one of trust and fellowship, new inspiration is created. Reality is now perceived differently and much more optimistically. The Jew no longer perceives himself as a helpless creature. Quite the opposite, the tables are turned. The Jew views himself as the center of the world. He exhorts the nations to praise Hashem for His conduct toward us because "His kindness has overwhelmed us" (Psalms 117:2). The nations are told that they should praise Hashem.

We move from the notion of universal praise to the idea that "it is better to take refuge [*la-ḥasot*] in Hashem than to rely on nobles" (Psalms 118:9). *Ḥasyon* is the natural refuge of a boulder.[16] There is no need for assurances or promises. When we were weighed down by "I said in my haste, 'All mankind is deceitful'" (Psalms 116:11), we were able to say only "O, Israel, trust in Hashem; their help and their shield is He! House of Aaron, trust in Hashem; their help and their shield is He!" (Psalms 115:9–10). Now we become almost oblivious to any lurking dangers. We live in quite a smug world, and all the taunts and barbs of our enemies mean nothing to us. It is at this point that the element

14. *Menaḥot* 77b.

15. *Torat Kohanim, Tzav* 12; *Zevaḥim* 36a; *Rashi* to Leviticus 7:15.

16. *Rashi* to Psalms 118:9.

of *emunah* enters the realm of thanksgiving and we say, "Give thanks to Hashem, for He is good, for His kindness endures forever" (Psalms 107:1). We can say that Hashem's kindness is forever. We say that it transcends time. We believe that everything now, in the past and in the future, is a manifestation of Hashem's kindness.

Glossary

AFIKOMAN. Piece of matzah eaten at the end of the Seder.

AGUDDAH AḤAT. One unit.

AHAVAT ḤINNAM. Unwarranted love.

AḤDUT. Unity.

AKEDAH. The Binding of Isaac.

AL HA-NISSIM. Additional prayer recited in the *Shemoneh Esreh* and *Birkat ha-Mazon* on Ḥanukkah and Purim. The prayer consists of an introductory paragraph that is recited on both holidays, and a separate paragraph for each holiday.

ALEPH. First letter of the Hebrew alphabet.

ALIYYAH. Ascent, particularly of a spiritual nature. Also denotes the immigration of Jews to the Land of Israel.

AMEN ḤATUFAH. Lit., "snatched '*amen*.'" Response of "*amen*" to a blessing when the *aleph* of *amen* is pronounced with a *ḥataf* instead of a *kamatz*, or the *amen* is said before recitation of the blessing is completed.

AMEN YESOMAH. Lit., "orphaned '*amen*.'" *Amen* that is said in response to a blessing when the person answering *amen* is not aware of which blessing was said.

AMORAH, (PL.) AMORAIM. Aramaic for "spokesman" or "interpreter." Generic term for the rabbis of the post-Mishnaic period but prior to the redaction of the Talmud (ca. 200–500 C.E.).

ANAV. A humble person.

ANAVAH. Humility.

ANNINUT. Status of a bereaved person during the period between the death and the burial of a close relative. The bereaved person is exempt from fulfilling certain religious obligations such as reciting the daily prayers, except during the Sabbath and Festivals.

ARAVAH, (PL.) ARAVOT. Willow. One of the Four Species that the Torah requires a Jew to hold in his hand on the Festival of Sukkot.

ARAVOT. Highest heavens. See also "*Aravah.*"

ASARAH MA'AMAROT. Ten statements that Hashem made in creating the world, recorded at Genesis 1:3, 1:6, 1:9, 1:11, 1:14, 1:20, 1:24, 1:26, 1:29, and 2:18.

ASERET HA-DIBBEROT. The Ten Commandments.

AT BASH. A system in which the first letter of the Hebrew alphabet, *aleph,* is replaced with the last letter of the alphabet, *taph;* the second letter, *bet,* is replaced with the second-to-last letter, *shin,* and so forth.

ATAH YATZARTA. Lit., "You created." Refers to the special prayer that is inserted in *Musaf* when Rosh Ḥodesh coincides with the Sabbath. The prayer begins with the statement "You created Your world from the very beginning."

AVDUT. Servitude.

AVERAH, (PL.) AVEROT. Sin.

AVODAH. Service.

AVODAH ZARAH. Idolatry.

AVODAT PERAKH. Crushing labor. Typically refers to the most difficult period of the Servitude in Egypt.

AYAL. Ram.

AYIN. Sixteenth letter of the Hebrew alphabet, with a numerical equivalence of seventy.

AZARAH. Temple courtyard.

AZUT. Brazenness.

BA'AL HA-BAYIT. Householder.

BA'AL ḤESED. One who performs acts of kindness.

BA'AL KO'RE. The one who reads the Torah for the public.

BARAITA. A teaching or tradition of the Tannaim that was excluded from the Mishnah and incorporated in a later collection complied by R. Ḥiyya and R. Oshaia.

BARKHI NAFSHI. Lit., "bless my soul." Refers to Psalms 104, a tribute to Hashem for the wondrous world that He created and continuously sustains. The Psalm is recited on Rosh Ḥodesh after the recitation of the Song of the Day because the Psalm alludes to the New Moon in the verse "He made the moon for festivals" (Psalms 104:19).

BARUKH HA-BA. Welcome.

BEIN ADAM LA-MAKOM. Lit., "between man and God." Refers to the obligations between man and God.

BEIN ADAM LE-ḤAVERO. Lit., "between man and his fellow." Refers to the obligations governing interpersonal conduct.

BEIN HA-METZARIM. Lit., "between the straits." Three-week period of mourning beginning on the seventeenth day of Tammuz and ending on the Ninth Day of Av, established to commemorate the destruction of the First and Second Temples.

BEINONI. A person who is neither absolutely righteous nor absolutely wicked. His or her judgment is not sealed on Rosh Ha-Shanah but is instead suspended until Yom Kippur.

BEIT DIN. Jewish court of law.

BEIT OLAMIM. Permanent Temple.

BEKHOR. Firstborn.

BI'AT GO'EL TZEDEK. Lit., "the coming of the righteous redeemer." The coming of the Messiah.

BIRKAT HA-MAZON. Grace after Meals.

BITTAḤON. Faith.

BRIT MILAH. Circumcision.

DA'AT TORAH. Lit., "knowledge of Torah." Refers to the opinion of rabbinic scholars.

DAYYENU. Lit., "it would have been sufficient for us." Song recited as part of the Haggadah enumerating fifteen gifts that Hashem conferred upon the Jewish people, including taking them out of Egypt and giving them the Torah.

DERASHAH. Exposition. May also refer to a rabbinic sermon.

DEVEKUT. Attachment to God. Having God constantly in mind.

DIRAT ARAI. Temporary dwelling. Refers to the sukkah.

DOR YATOM. Lit., "orphaned generation." A generation that has lost its leaders.

D'TZAKH ADASH B'AḤAV. Acronym for the Ten Plagues. "*D'tzakh*" stands for *dam, tzefardde'a,* and *kinnim* (i.e., blood, frogs, and lice); "*adash*" stands for *arov, dever,* and *sheḥin* (i.e., wild beasts, pestilence, and boils); and "*b'aḥav*" stands for *barad, arbeh, ḥoshekh,* and *bekhorot* (i.e., hail, locusts, darkness, and the slaying of the firstborn).

EDUT. Testimony.

EIN OD MI-LEVADDO. "There is none beside Him" (Deuteronomy 4:35).

EMET. Truth.

EMET VE-EMUNAH. Lit., "true and faithful." Opening of the *Ge'ullah* blessing recited after the three paragraphs of *Shema* in the evening service.

EMET VE-YATZIV. Lit., "true and fair." Opening of the *Ge'ullah* blessing recited after the three paragraphs of *Shema* in the morning service.

EMUNAH. Faith.

EMUNAH PESHUTAH. Simple faith.

ERETZ YISRAEL. Land of Israel. The term is biblical, although its meaning varies, designating both the territory actually inhabited by the Israelites (I Samuel 13:19) and the Northern Kingdom (II Kings 5:2). Only from the Second Temple period onward, however, was the term used to denote the Promised Land. It was the official Hebrew designation of the area governed by the British mandate in Palestine after World War I until 1948.

ETROG. Citron. One of the Four Species that the Torah requires the Jew to hold in his hand on the Festival of Sukkot.

EVED IVRI. Israelite bondsman.

FOUR SPECIES. The four articles of plant life that a Jew is commanded to hold in his hand on the Festival of Sukkot, consisting of a branch of the date palm, a citron, willow branches, and myrtle branches.

GABBAI. Sexton.

GADOL HA-DOR. Rabbinic leader of the generation.

GAG. Roof.

GALUT. Exile. Dispersion of Jews from the Land of Israel.

GEBRUKTS. Yiddish for "broken." Refers to matzah that has come in contact with water.

GEMARA. Aramaic for "completion" or "tradition." This term is popularly applied to the Talmud as a whole, or more particularly to the discussions and elaborations by the *Amoraim* on the Mishnah.

GEMATRIA. Exegetical method by which a word or phrase is associated with another word or phrase with the same numerical value.

GEMILUT ḤASADIM. Lit., "the bestowal of loving kindness." The duty that encompasses the whole range of the responsibilities of sympathetic consideration toward one's fellow man.

GERUT. Conversion. Also refers to living in a foreign land.

GE'ULLAH. Redemption.

GLATT. Yiddish for "smooth." In reference to kosher meat, denotes that the lungs of the animal have been examined after ritual slaughter and found to be smooth, free of any defects that would render the animal non-kosher. The term is used more generally to describe a strict standard of *kashrut* for food products.

HA-ADAMAH. Lit., "the ground." Blessing recited on produce that grows directly from the ground. The blessing is "Blessed are You, Hashem, our God, King of the Universe, Who creates the fruit of the ground."

HA'ANAKAH. The gratuity that the master is enjoined to pay his Israelite bondsman when he sets him free.

ḤABURAH. Group. The paschal offering was required to be eaten in a group.

HADAS, (PL.) HADASIM. Myrtle. One of the Four Species that the Torah requires the Jew to hold in his hand on the Festival of Sukkot.

ḤADASH. Lit., "new." Grain that has taken root after the sixteenth day of Nisan, which is biblically prohibited from being eaten until the subsequent sixteenth day of Nisan. The issue of whether the prohibition applies to grain grown outside the Land of Israel is the subject of debate among halakhic authorities.

HAFTARAH, (PL.) HAFTAROT. Selection from the Prophets that is read in the synagogue after the Torah reading on the Sabbath and Festivals. The theme of the selection is usually related to the Torah reading that precedes it.

ḤAG HA-ASIF. Festival of the Ingathering. One of the names of the Festival of Sukkot.

HAGGADAH. Lit., "the telling." Book recited at the Passover Seder containing passages regarding the Exodus from Egypt. The reading of the Haggadah is based on the verse "You shall tell your son on that day, 'It is because of what the Lord did for me when I came forth from Egypt'" (Exodus 13:8).

ḤAKHAM, (PL.) ḤAKHAMIM. Sage.

HAKKARAT HA-TOV. Gratitude.

HALAKHAH. Jewish law.

HALLEL. Praise. Recitation of Psalms 113 through 118 during the morning service on the first two days of Passover, Sukkot, Shavuot, and Ḥanukkah. On Rosh Ḥodesh and the last six days of Passover, Psalms 115:1-11 and 116:1-11 are omitted from the prayer.

HAMANTASH. Three-cornered cookie traditionally filled with jam or poppy seeds, associated with the holiday of Purim. The term is commonly considered a reference to Haman, the defeated enemy of the Jews, and the shape of the cookie as reminiscent of his three-cornered hat.

ḤAMETZ. Any product made of or containing one of the five grains that are forbidden on Passover.

HARAMAT KEREN. Uplifting of pride.

ḤARATAH. Remorse for past transgressions. One of the requirements for repentance in Jewish law.

ḤAROSET. A paste composed of ground nuts and red wine eaten at the Passover Seder to recall the mortar that the Children of Israel used to make bricks during the Servitude in Egypt.

ḤAS VE-SHALOM. Heaven forbid.

HASHKAFAH. Outlook.

ḤASID, (PL.) ḤASIDIM. A member of a hasidic branch of Orthodox Judaism.

HATTARAT HA-SEFEKOT. Resolution of doubts.

ḤAVIVUT HA-MITZVAH. Endearment of the commandment.

ḤAVRUTA. Aramaic for "companionship." Study of Torah with a partner.

ḤAZAN. Cantor.

HEFKERUT. Lawlessness.

HEH. Fifth letter of the Hebrew alphabet.

HEKDESH. Consecrated property.

ḤERUT. Freedom.

ḤERUT OLAM. Everlasting freedom.

HESEBAH. Reclining while eating.

ḤESED. Kindness.

ḤESED ELYON. Act of divine kindness.

HESEḤ HA-DA'AT. Lit., "removal of thought." Inattentiveness.

ḤESHBON HA-NEFESH. Lit., "accounting of the soul." Examination of conscience regarding one's obligations to God and his fellow man. This concept is the subject of the eighth section of *Ḥovot ha-Levavot* by R. Bahya b. Joseph ibn Paquda.

ḤIBBAH. Love.

ḤIBBAH YETERAH. Abundant love.

ḤILLUL HASHEM. Lit., "disgrace of the Name." Refers to an action that brings dishonor and disgrace to God.

ḤINNUKH. Religious training.

ḤIYYUT. Life.

ḤIZZUK. Encouragement.

HOD. Splendor. One of the ten *Sefirot*.

ḤOK, (PL.) ḤUKKIM. Divine decree for which the explanation is beyond human comprehension.

ḤOL HA-MO'ED. Intermediate days of Passover and Sukkot.

HOSHANA RABBAH. Seventh day of Sukkot.

ḤOVAH. Obligation.

ḤUKKIM. See "*Hok*."

ḤUMRAH, (PL.) ḤUMROT. Stringency.

ḤURBAN. Lit., "destruction." Typically refers to the destruction of the First and Second Temples.

IKKAR. Of primary importance.

INNUI. Deprivation of sensual pleasures.

ISARUSA DE-LA-ELA. Lit., "arousal from Above." Divine inspiration or intervention.

KABBALAH. Esoteric and mystical teachings of Judaism.

KABBALAH AL HA-ATID. Resolutions for the future. One of the requirements for repentance in Jewish law.

KABBALAT OL MALKHUT SHAMAYIM. Acceptance of the yoke of Heaven.

KAL. Simple active form of a verb in Hebrew.

KAL VE-ḤOMER. A fortiori.

KARPAS. One of the rituals of the Passover Seder during which a vegetable, such as parsley or celery, is dipped in salt water and eaten.

KASHRUT. Jewish religious dietary laws.

KAVVANAH. Intention; concentration, particularly on the meaning of the words uttered during prayer.

KEDUSHAH. Holiness. Also the name of the third section of the *Shemoneh Esreh.*

KERI'AT HA-TORAH. The public reading of the Torah.

KETORET. A mixture of aromatic herbs burnt twice daily on the Golden Altar in the Temple and as part of the ritual performed by the High Priest in the Holy of Holies on Yom Kippur.

KEVES. Lamb.

KEVOD HA-BERI'OT. Concern for human dignity.

KEVOD HA-TORAH. Honor of the Torah.

KIBBUD AV VE-EM. Honoring one's father and mother.

KIDDUSH. Lit., "sanctification." A blessing recited over wine or grape juice to sanctify the Sabbath and Jewish holidays. The term is also used to refer to a reception held in the synagogue or a congregant's home after the morning Sabbath or holiday prayers where the blessing over wine is recited and refreshments are served.

KIDDUSH HASHEM. Lit., "sanctification of the Name." Refers to an observable and noble action that brings glorification to God.

KIDDUSH SHEM SHAMAYIM. Sanctification of the Name of Heaven, i.e., Hashem.

KIL'AYIM. Prohibition in Jewish law of mixing wool and linen, cross-breeding seeds, and cross-breeding animals.

KINAH. Lamentation.

KITTEL. White linen robe that serves a burial shroud for Jewish men. The robe is also worn by married men on Yom Kippur, by a groom under the wedding canopy, and by the cantor during special services during the year, such as the first night of *Seliḥot*, *Hoshana Rabbah*, and the *Musaf* Prayer of *Shemini Atzeret* and the first day of Passover.

KLAL. Community.

KLAL YISRAEL. The Jewish nation.

KNEIDLACH. Yiddish for "matzah balls."

KNESSET YISRAEL. The Jewish nation.

KODASHIM. Portions of sacrificial offerings.

KODESH. Holy matters.

KOHELET. Ecclesiastes. Also refers to King Solomon, who authored Ecclesiastes.

KOHEN. Priest. Principal functionary in the divine services. The special task of the Priests was to engage in rituals conducted mainly in the Temple. The post of the Priests is authorized by hereditary right, and they constitute a distinct class separate from the rest of the Jewish people.

KOHEN GADOL. High Priest.

KORBAN, (PL.) KORBANOT. Sacrificial offerings prescribed by the Torah. The sacrifices were offered in the Tabernacle and the Temple at the hands of the Priests.

KORBAN GERUT. An offering brought by a convert as one of the requirements to effect his conversion to Judaism. In general, in the time of the Temple, a convert to Judaism was prohibited from eating portions of sacrificial offerings until he brought this offering, even if he had undergone circumcision and performed ritual immersion.

KORBAN PESAḤ. Paschal offering.

KOR'IM. Lit., "bowing." Refers to the portion of the *Musaf* Prayer on Yom Kippur during which the members of the synagogue kneel.

LAḤLUḤIT. Lit., "moisture." Freshness.

LASHON HA-RA. Lit., "evil speech." Tale-bearing in which *A* delivers a damaging but truthful report regarding *B* to *C*, when *C* is neither the object of *B*'s mischief nor the intended target of *B*'s evil designs.

LE-ATID LAVO. Lit., "in the future." In Messianic times.

LEḤEM HA-PANIM. Showbread. Twelve loaves of unleavened bread, baked of fine flour and sprinkled with frankincense, placed on the Table in the Tabernacle and in the Temple.

LEḤEM ONI. Lit., "bread of the poor." Matzah eaten at the Seder.

LEVIRATE MARRIAGE. Biblical requirement at Deuteronomy 25:5–10 that if a man died without children, his brother is obligated to marry his widow.

LIFNIM MI-SHURAT HA-DIN. Beyond the letter of the law.

LIMMUD HA-TORAH. Study of Torah.

LISHKAT HA-GAZIT. Chamber of Hewn Stone. Chamber where the Sanhedrin would sit in the Second Temple. The chamber was built into the wall of the Temple's main courtyard to the right of the gate.

LO TAḤMOD. Thou shall not covet. The Tenth Commandment (Exodus 20:14). The prohibition is violated by pressuring another individual to sell a possession of his against his will.

LUḤOT. The Tablets on which the Ten Commandments were inscribed.

LULAV. One of the Four Species that the Torah requires the Jew to hold in his hand on the Festival of Sukkot. The obligation is based on Leviticus 23:40; the "branches of the palm tree" mentioned in the verse are identified as the *lulav*.

LUZ BONE. Lit., "nut bone." Indestructible bone at the base of the spinal column from which the future resurrection of the body will begin.

MA'AMAD HAR SINAI. Lit., "the standing at Mount Sinai." Divine revelation to the Children of Israel at Mount Sinai and the receiving of the Torah.

MAARIV. Evening Prayer.

MA'ASEH AVOT SIMAN LE-BANIM. The life experience of the Patriarchs is indicative of the further course of Jewish destiny.

MA'ASER, (PL.) MA'ASEROT. Tithe. During the time of the Temple, a portion of one's agricultural produce was required to be given to the Priests and Levites. First, *terumah* was set aside for the Priests. Next, *ma'aser rishon,* the first tithe, consisting of one-tenth of the remainder, was given to the Levites. A second tithe was then given. In the first, second, fourth, and fifth years of the Sabbatical cycle, the second tithe was called "*ma'aser sheni,*" which was generally required to be eaten in Jerusalem. In the third and sixth years, the second tithe was called "*ma'aser ani,*" which was given to the poor.

MA'ASER ANI. Lit., "poor tithe." Tithe given to the Levites and the poor in the third and sixth year of the Sabbatical cycle. See also "*ma'aser*."

MA'ASER RISHON. Lit., "first tithe." Tithe given to the Levites from agricultural produce after *terumah* was taken. See also "*ma'aser*."

MA'ASER SHENI. Lit., "second tithe." Tithe of agricultural produce set aside during the first, second, fourth, and fifth years of the Sabbatical cycle after *terumah* and *ma'aser rishon* were taken. *Ma'aser sheni* was required to be eaten in Jerusalem. If it was too difficult to carry the produce to Jerusalem, the tithe could be redeemed for money, consisting of the value of the produce plus one-fifth. The money would then be taken to Jerusalem where the owner would spend it on food or peace offerings. See also "*ma'aser*."

MA'ASIM TOVIM. Good deeds.

MAFTIR. The last verses of the weekly Sabbath and Festival reading from the Torah. On a regular Sabbath, the last few verses of the weekly portion are repeated as the *maftir*. On special Sabbaths and Festivals, the *maftir* is taken from a passage relevant to that particular day and is read from a second *sefer Torah*.

MAGGID. Itinerant preacher and skilled narrator of Torah and religious stories. Also refers to the portion of the Haggadah in which the story of the Exodus from Egypt is recounted.

MAḤAR. Tomorrow.

MAḤAR ḤODESH. Lit., "tomorrow is Rosh Ḥodesh." *Haftarah* for a Sabbath when Rosh Ḥodesh falls on the next day, Sunday, at I Samuel 20:18–42. The common name of the *haftarah* derives from its opening words "Jonathan said to him, 'Tomorrow is the New Moon.'"

MAḤATZIT HA-SHEKEL. Lit., "half of a shekel." Biblical requirement at Exodus 30:13 for each Jew to make an annual donation of a half of a shekel to fund the communal sacrifices.

MALKHUT. Royalty.

MALKHUT SHAMAYIM. Kingdom of Heaven.

MALKHUYYOT. Lit., "sovereignties." The first of the three sections of the *Musaf* Prayer on Rosh Ha-Shanah, consisting of ten verses devoted to the theme of Hashem's sovereignty.

MAROR. Bitter herbs.

MASHEHU. In a minute amount. Refers to the prohibition of *ḥametz* on Passover.

MASHIAḤ. Messiah.

MATTAN TORAH. The giving of the Torah to the Children of Israel on Mount Sinai.

MATTENAT ḤINNAM. An unearned gift.

MEDINAH. State of Israel.

MEGILLAH. Lit., "scroll." Most commonly refers to the Book of Esther, one of the Five Scrolls, but may refer to one of the other four scrolls. The Five Scrolls are a portion of the Hagiographa, each of which is read publicly on a different festival during the year. The other four scrolls are: Song of Songs, Ruth, Lamentations, and Ecclesiastes.

MEHADRIN. Beautified; enhanced. With reference to the Ḥanukkah lights, the term means the lighting of the menorah by each member of the household rather than by only the head of the household.

MEHADRIN MIN HA-MEHADRIN. Most enhanced. Refers to the practice of each member of the household lighting the Menorah on Ḥanukkah and adding an additional candle each night of the festival.

MEḤILAH. Forgiveness.

ME'ILAH. Misappropriation. Secular use of an object consecrated to the Temple, which incurs a penalty of the value of the item plus an additional fifth.

MESHIAḤ TZIDKENU. Lit., "the anointed one of our Righteousness." Messiah.

MESIAḤ DA'AT. Inattentive.

MESIRUT NEFESH. Self-sacrifice.

MEZUZAH. Lit., "doorpost." Piece of parchment containing the verses at Deuteronomy 6:4-9 and 11:13-21, affixed to the doorposts of the house. The parchment is placed in a case and is affixed on the right-hand side of the doorpost.

MIDDAH KE-NEGED MIDDAH. Measure for measure. Retributive justice.

MIDRASH. Hebrew designation of a particular genre of rabbinic literature consisting mainly of exegesis of specific books of the Bible.

MILAH. Circumcision.

MINḤAH. Afternoon Prayer.

MINYAN. A quorum of ten men necessary for public synagogue services and certain other religious ceremonies.

MISHMAR. Lit., "watch." One of the twenty-four watches of Priests and Levites who served in the Temple one week at a time on a rotating basis. The watches were subdivided into family groups, each of which served one day of the week.

MISHNAH. Designates the collection of rabbinic traditions redacted by R. Judah ha-Nasi at the beginning of the 3rd century. The purpose of the Mishnah is to elaborate, systematize, and concretize the commandments of the Torah.

MISHPAT. Justice.

MISHPATIM. Laws governing interpersonal conduct.

MITKABBED BE-KALON SHEL ḤAVERO. Elevating oneself at the expense of another person's degradation. A person who acts in such a manner is said to lose his share in the World to Come.

MITZVAH, (PL.) MITZVOT. A religious act or duty. The Bible contains 613 commandments, consisting of 248 positive commandments and 365 negative commandments.

MITZVAT ASEH. Positive biblical commandment. There are a total of 248 positive biblical commandments.

MITZVAT LO TA'ASEH. Biblical prohibition. There are a total of 365 biblical prohibitions.

MO'ED. Festival.

MOSIF VE-HOLEKH. The practice of each member of the household lighting an additional candle each night of Ḥanukkah, in accordance with the opinion of *Beit Hillel.*

MOTZI SHEM RA. The utterance or spreading of a false statement harmful to another's character or reputation.

MUSAF. Lit., "supplement." Additional sacrifice prescribed for the Sabbath and the Festivals. In the liturgy, it is the name for the additional prayer recited on the Sabbath, Rosh Ḥodesh, the Three Festivals, and Yom Kippur after *Shaḥarit.*

MUSAR. Jewish ethics or moral philosophy.

NA'ASEH VE-NISHMA. "We will do and we will listen" (Exodus 24:7). Declaration of the Children of Israel at Mount Sinai in accepting the Torah.

NAḤEM. Lit., "comfort." Prayer recited during the *Shemoneh Esreh* of *Minḥah* on Tish'ah be-Av asking for comfort for those who mourn Zion and Jerusalem.

NAZIR. A person who voluntarily took the vow described in Numbers 6:1–21. The vow required one to abstain from drinking wine, refrain from cutting the hair on one's head, and avoid coming into contact with a corpse.

NER ḤANUKKAH. Ḥanukkah lights.

NER SHABBAT. Sabbath lights.

NESHAMAH. Soul.

NESHAMAH YETERAH. Lit., "additional soul." An extra measure of spiritual energy. On the eve of the Sabbath, Hashem gives man an additional soul, which departs at the conclusion of the Sabbath. When the additional soul departs, it is referred to as "lost."

NETZAḤ. Eternity. One of the ten *Sefirot.*

NEVUAH. Prophecy.

OL MALKHUT SHAMAYIM. Yoke of Heaven.

ONEG. Enjoyment. Refers to the mitzvah to enjoy the Sabbath.

ONEN. A mourner during the period between the death and burial of a close relative. See also "*anninut.*"

OR LA-AMMIM. Lit., "light unto the nations."

PAR. Bullock.

PARAH ADUMMAH. A red cow, the ashes of which were used for the ritual purification of a person who came in contact with a human corpse.

PARASHAH. Lit., "portion." Selection of a biblical book.

PARASHAT HA-ḤODESH. Torah reading for the Sabbath immediately preceding the first day of the month of Nisan, or on the first of Nisan if that day coincides with the Sabbath. For the *maftir,* an additional Torah scroll is removed from the ark, and the laws of the paschal lamb at Exodus 12:1–20 are read.

PARASHAT SHEKALIM. Torah reading for the Sabbath immediately preceding the first day of Adar, or on the first day of Adar if that day coincides with the Sabbath. A second *sefer Torah* is removed from the ark for the reading of a special *maftir* at Exodus 30:11–16, which describes the obligation to give a half-shekel to finance the public offerings in the Temple. The tax was announced on the first day of Adar and was payable that month.

PESAḤ. Passover.

PESHAT. Literal interpretation of a verse.

PI'EL. Intensive active form of a verb in Hebrew.

POSEK, (PL.) POSEKIM. A rabbinic scholar who renders practical halakhic decisions.

RABBENU. Our teacher.

RAḤMANA LE-TZLAN. Lit., "God save us." God help us.

RASHA. Wicked person.

REBBE. Religious teacher.

RE'IYAT PANIM BA-AZARAH. Lit., "showing one's face in the Courtyard of the Temple." Requirement at Deuteronomy 16:16 for every Jewish male to appear in the Temple on the first day of each of the Three Festivals with a burnt offering.

REMEZ. Lit., "hint." Veiled reference.

RESHUT. Permissible. Optional.

RIBBONO SHEL OLAM. Master of the Universe.

RISHONIM. Early rabbinic authorities. The period of the *Rishonim* extended from the middle of the 11th century to the middle of the 15th century.

ROSH ḤODESH. The first day of a Jewish month. Considered a minor Jewish festival on which fasting is prohibited but work may be done.

ROSHEI TEVOT. An acronym.

RUAḤ. Spirit.

SA'IR HA-MISHTALE'AḤ. The he-goat that was sent off a cliff as part of the Yom Kippur service in the Temple. Also referred to as the "*Sa'ir la-Azazel.*"

SA'IR LA-AZAZEL. The he-goat that was sent off a cliff as part of the Yom Kippur service in the Temple. Also referred to as the "*Sa'ir ha-Mishtale'aḥ.*"

SANHEDRIN. Assembly of ordained scholars that functioned both as Supreme Court and Legislature before 70 C.E.

SAR HA-MASHKIM. Chamberlain of the Cupbearers to Pharaoh, whose dream Joseph interpreted.

SEDER. Lit., "order." Ritual ceremony held on the night of Passover involving the recitation of the Haggadah.

SEFER TORAH, (PL.) SIFREI TORAH. Torah scroll.

SEFIROT. Ten creative forces that intervene between the infinite, unknowable God and our created world, as taught by the Kabbalah. The Sefirot are: *keter* (crown); *ḥokhmah* (wisdom); *binah* (understanding); *ḥesed* (loving-kindness); *gevurah* (power); *tiferet* (beauty); *netzaḥ* (eternity); *hod* (splendor); *yesod* (foundation); *and malkhut* (sovereignty).

SEKHAKH. Roof covering of a sukkah.

SELIḤOT. Prayers for pardon recited a few days before Rosh Ha-Shanah and during the days between Rosh Ha-Shanah and Yom Kippur.

SEMIKHAH. Lit., "learning." Rabbinic ordination. Traditionally, ordination was passed down through generations by an individual with *semikhah* placing his hands on the head of the appointee and conferring upon him the authority to judge.

SEPHARDIM. Jews of Spain and Portugal, or their descendants, distinguished from Jews of Central and Eastern Europe (Ashkenazim) primarily by their liturgy, religious customs, and pronunciation of Hebrew.

SEUDAH. Meal.

SEVARAH. Lit., "reasoning." Process of deriving Jewish law through logical argument.

SHABBAT HA-GADOL. Lit., "the great Sabbath." The Sabbath preceding Passover.

SHABBAT MALKHETA. Sabbath Queen.

SHABBAT SHIRAH. The Sabbath when *Parashat Be-Shallaḥ* (Exodus 13:17–17:6) is read, which contains the Song of the Sea of Reeds.

SHAḤARIT. Morning Prayer.

SHALOM. Peace.

SHEGAGOT. Unintentional sins.

SHE-HA-KOL. Blessing recited before eating something other than bread, products of wheat, barley, rye, oats, or spelt, fruits, or vegetables. The blessing is "Blessed are You, Hashem, our God, King of the Universe, that everything [*she-ha-kol*] came to be through His word."

SHEḤITAH. Ritual slaughter.

SHEKHINAH. Divine Presence.

SHELAMIM. Peace offerings brought in the Temple.

SHELIAḤ TZIBBUR. Lit., "messenger of the community." Person who leads the community in public prayer.

SHELOM MALKHUT. Maintenance of a peaceful relationship with the secular government.

SHEMA. Lit., "hear." Refers to the passage at Deuteronomy 6:4, "Hear, O Israel: The Lord is our God, the Lord is One." The term is used more generally to refer to the entire portion of the daily prayers that consists of Deuteronomy 6:4–9, Deuteronomy 11:13–21, and Numbers 15:37–41.

SHEMINI ATZERET. Festival that falls on the twenty-second day of Tishrei, the eighth day of the festival of Tabernacles. The Prayer for Rain is recited on this festival during *Musaf*.

SHEMIRAH. Guarding; watching.

SHEMITTAH. Sabbatical year. Seventh year of a seven-year cycle, during which it is biblically prohibited to work the land and all loans are canceled.

SHEMONEH ESREH. Jewish prayer recited in the morning, afternoon, and evening services. Also referred to as the "*Amidah*," the standing prayer. The weekday formulation of the prayer consists of nineteen blessings, although it originally had eighteen. For the Sabbath and Festivals, the middle thirteen blessings are replaced with blessings specific to the occasion.

SHERATZIM. Animals that slither along the ground or appear to do so because they have short legs and their movement is not readily noticeable.

SHEVARIM. Lit., "broken." A series of three short blasts of the shofar sounded on Rosh Ha-Shanah. The three blasts are preceded and followed by a *tekiah*.

SHIR HA-SHIRIM. Song of Songs.

SHIRAH. Song. A triumphant hymn in praise of Hashem, such as the Song at the Sea of Reeds.

SHIUR. Torah lecture.

SHOFAR. Ram's horn sounded for memorial blowing on RoshHa-Shanah and other occasions.

SHUL. Synagogue.

SIDRAH, (PL.) SIDROT. Weekly Torah portion.

SIMḤAH. Happiness.

SIMḤAT YOM TOV. Joy of the Festival.

SINAT ḤINNAM. Baseless hatred.

SIYYUM HA-TORAH. Completion of the Torah.

SOTAH. A woman whose behavior has established her as a suspected adulteress.

SUKKAH, (PL.) SUKKOT. Temporary dwelling that the Torah instructs Jews to dwell in for the seven days of the Festival of Sukkot.

TAFEL. Subsidiary; of secondary importance.

TAḤANUN. Supplication. Petition for grace and forgiveness recited daily after the morning and afternoon *Shemoneh Esreh,* except on the Sabbath, Festivals, days of joy, on Tish'ah be-Av, and in a house of mourning during the week of mourning. Also called *nefilat appayim,* "falling on the face."

TALLIT. Four-cornered cloth with fringes that is worn as a prayer shawl during the *Shaḥarit* and *Musaf* services.

TALMID. Student.

TALMID ḤAKHAM. Rabbinic scholar.

TALMUD. The record of discussions of scholars on the laws and teachings of the Mishnah. The Talmud consists of the Babylonian Talmud, codified in ca. 500 C.E., and the Jerusalem Talmud, codified in ca. 400 C.E.

TALMUD TORAH. Learning of Torah.

TAMKHA. One of the types of bitter herbs that may be used as *maror* during the Seder. Commonly defined as horseradish.

TANAKH. Collective term for the Pentateuch, the Prophets, and the Hagiographa. The term is composed of the initial letters of the words Torah; *Nevi'im,* "Prophets"; and *Ketuvim,* "Hagiographa."

TASHLIKH. Ceremony performed typically on the first day of Rosh Ha-Shanah in which sins are symbolically cast into the water. The scriptural verses at Micah 7:18–20, Psalms 118:5–8, Psalms 130, and Isaiah 11:9 are recited near a natural body of water, preferably one that contains fish. The name of the ritual is derived from the verse "You will cast [*ve-sashlikh*] all their sins into the depths of the sea" (Micah 7:19).

TEFILLAH. Prayer.

TEFILLAT GESHEM. Prayer for rain recited during *Musaf* on Shemini Atzeret.

TEFILLAT TAL. Prayer for dew recited during *Musaf* on the first day of Passover.

TEFILLIN. Phylacteries. Two cube-shaped black leather boxes containing four biblical passages written by hand on parchment. The boxes are worn during the morning services. One box is worn on the head and the other on the arm, with leather straps affixed to the boxes for attaching the boxes to the head and arm.

TEḤIYYAT HA-METIM. Resurrection of the dead.

TEKIAH, (PL.) TEKIOT. Lit., "blowing." A long blast of the shofar.

TEKIAH AḤARONAH. Lit., "final blast." A long, drawn-out blast of the shofar that concludes the blowing of a group of blasts on Rosh Ha-Shanah. Also called "*tekiah gedolah*."

TEKIAH GEDOLAH. Lit., "great blast." A long, drawn-out blast of the shofar that concludes the blowing of a group of blasts on Rosh Ha-Shanah.

TERUAH. A series of nine staccato blasts of the shofar sounded on Rosh Ha-Shanah.

TERUMAH. Heave offering given to the Priests from agricultural produce before the first tithe was separated for the Levites.

TESHUVAH. Repentance.

THIRTEEN ATTRIBUTES OF MERCY. Divine attributes, enumerated at Exodus 34:6–7, with which Hashem governs the world.

THREE FESTIVALS. Passover, Shavuot, and Sukkot.

TIKKUN OLAM. Lit., "repair of the world." Improving the welfare of society.

TINNOKOT SHEL BEIT RABBAN. School children.

TIRḤA DE-TZIBBURA. Burden on the community.

TODAH. Thanksgiving. A type of peace offering brought by an individual in the time of the Temple to express gratitude to Hashem.

TOHU VA-VOHU. Nothingness. Refers to the condition of the earth before Hashem created the world, as described at Genesis 1:2. In the rabbinic literature, refers to the first two millennia of history, before Abraham began to spread the message of Torah.

TORAH. Lit., "instruction." Refers to the Bible as a whole.

TOSAFOT. French commentators on the Talmud who lived during the 12th to 14th centuries.

TOV ME'OD. Very good.

TUMAH HUTTRAH BE-TZIBBUR. Principle in Jewish law that if a majority of the congregation is in a state of ritual impurity, a public offering may be offered. This principle applies also to the kindling of the Menorah in the Temple.

TZADDIK. Righteous person.

TZAROT. Afflictions.

TZEDAKAH. Charity.

TZELEM ELOKIM. Lit., "image of God." Refers to the idea that all people are created in the image of God and thus have tremendous potential for righteousness.

TZENIUT. Modesty.

TZIBBUR. The collective; community.

TZILA DE-MEHEIMENUTA. Shelter of faith. Refers to the sukkah in which one is required to dwell during the Festival of Sukkot.

TZITZIT. Knotted ritual fringes attached to the four corners of a *tallit*, in accordance with the biblical mandate at Numbers 15:38 and Deuteronomy 22:12.

TZVI. Gazelle.

USHPIZIN. Aramaic for "guests." Seven celestial guests who visit the sukkah on the Festival of Sukkot. The guests are: Abraham, Isaac, Jacob, Moses, Aaron, Joseph, and David.

YAḤATZ. Portion of the Haggadah during which the middle matzah of the three matzot is broken in half. The larger piece is hidden, to be eaten as the *afikoman* later in the Seder, and the smaller piece is placed between the two other matzot.

YASHRUT. Lit., "straightness." Rectitude.

YESHIVAH, (PL.) YESHIVOT. Institute of talmudic learning.

YETZER HA-RA. Evil Inclination.

YETZER TOV. Good Inclination.

YIR'AT SHAMAYIM. Fear of Heaven.

YIZKOR. Lit., "he will remember." Jewish prayer recited in memory of close relatives on Yom Kippur, Shemini Atzeret, the last day of Passover, and the second day of Shavuot.

YOM SELIḤAH U-MEḤILAH. A day of forgiveness, i.e., Yom Kippur.

YOM TOV. Generic term for a Jewish holiday; a day of festival on which certain activities are prohibited.

YOMA ARIKHTA. Aramaic for "one long day." The two days of Rosh Ha-Shanah are regarded in the rabbinic literature as one long day.

YOTZEI. Fulfilled one's religious obligation.

ZEDONOT. Intentional sins.

ZEKHUYYOT. Merits.

ZEMAN SIMḤATENU. Season of Our Rejoicing. One of the names of the Festival of Sukkot.

ZIKHRONOT. Lit., "remembrances." The second of the three sections of the *Musaf* Prayer on Rosh Ha-Shanah, consisting of ten verses.

Bibliography

Aaron b. Jacob ha-Kohen of Lunel, R. *Orḥot Ḥayyim.*

Aaron b. Joseph ha-Levi, R. *Sefer ha-Ḥinnukh.* Edited by R. Yitzhak Yeshayah Weiss, R. David Zicherman, and R. Yitzhak Weinstein. Jerusalem: Mekhon Yerushalayim, 1992.

Abrabanel, R. Isaac b. Judah. *Yeshu'ot Meshiḥo.*

——— *Zevaḥ Pesaḥ.*

Abudirham, R. David b. Joseph. *Sefer Abudraham.*

Adret, R. Solomon b. Abraham. *Ḥiddushei ha-Rashba.*

——— *She'elot u-Teshuvot ha-Rashba.*

Albelda, R. Moses b. Jacob. *Derash Mosheh.*

Alexander, Edward. "The Academic Boycott of Israel: Back to 1933?" *Jerusalem Post,* January 3, 2003, B9.

Alfasi, R. Isaac b. Jacob. *Rif* to *Kiddushin*; *Rosh Ha-Shanah.*

Al-Hakam, R. Joseph Hayyim b. Elijah. *Torah le-Shemah.*

Alshekh, R. Moses. *Devarim Tovim.* Commentary on Ecclesiastes.

——— *Torat Mosheh.* Commentary on the Pentateuch.

——— *Marot ha-Tzove'ot.* Commentary on the Early and Later Prophets.

Alter, R. Avraham Mordekhai. *Imrei Emet.* Vol. 3. Israel, 1986.

Alter, R. Yehudah Aryeh Leib. *Sefat Emet: Mo'adim.*

Alter, R. Yitzhak Meir. *Ḥiddushei ha-Rim al ha-Torah, Mo'adim ve-Likkutim.* Jerusalem: Mossad ha-Rim Levine, 1992.

Altschuler, R. Jehiel Hillel b. David. *Metzudat David.*

Amital, R. Yehuda. "A Torah Perspective on the Status of Secular Jews Today." *Tradition: A Journal of Orthodox Jewish Thought* 23, no. 4 (Summer 1988): 1–13.

Anav, R. Zedekiah b. Abraham. *Shibbolei ha-Leket.*

Apple, Jr., R. W. "North Portrays Band of Patriots Striving to Surmount Obstacles." *Minneapolis Star and Tribune*, July 9, 1987, 09A.

Arama, R. Isaac b. Moses. *Akedat Yitzḥak.*

Arthur, Max. "New Mormon Center in Jerusalem Incites Debate." *Sun-Sentinel*, July 12, 1985, 6D.

Aschenberg, R. Simeon b. Isaac ha-Levi. *Devek Tov.*

Asher b. Jehiel, R. *Rosh* to *Berakhot*; *Kiddushin.*

Azulai, R. Hayyim Joseph David. *Ḥomat Anakh.*

______ *Ḥadrei Vaten: Derushei Musar al Seder ha-Parshiyyot.*

Ba'al ha-Turim. Commentary on the Torah.

Bacharach, R. Jair Hayyim b. Moses Samson. *She'elot u-Teshuvot Ḥut ha-Shani.* Frankfurt am Main, 1679.

Bahya b. Asher, R. *Rabbenu Beḥaye al ha-Torah.*

Bavli, R. Menahem b. Moses. *Ta'amei Mitzvot.*

Becker, Jillian. *The PLO: The Rise and Fall of the Palestine Liberation Organization.* New York: St. Martin's Press, 1984.

Bendersky, Joseph W. *A History of Nazi Germany: 1919–1945.* 2nd ed. Chicago: Burnham, 2000.

Benveniste, R. Hayyim b. Israel. *Pesaḥ Me'uvin.*

Berlin, R. Naphtali Tzvi Yehudah. *Ha'amek Davar.*

Bernfeld, R. Isaac Zvi. *Siddur Tefillah Ḥatam Sofer.* Vol. 2. New York: Gross Bros., 1966.

Besdin, R. Abraham R. *Man of Faith in the Modern World.* Hoboken, NJ: Ktav, 1989.

______ *Reflections of the Rav: Lessons in Jewish Thought.* Jerusalem: World Zionist Organization, 1979.

Besser, James D. "Rabin: Jerusalem Is Ours: Prime Minister at AIPAC Conference Emotionally Describes His Lifelong Commitment to the Israeli Capital." *New York Jewish Week* (Manhattan ed.), March 24, 1994, 35.

Blitzer, Wolf. "West Bank Decision Angers U.S.; State Dept. Calls Decision 'An Obstacle to Peace.'" *Jerusalem Post*, July 27, 1977, 1.

Bornsztain, R. Avraham. *Ne'ot ha-Deshe.* 3 vols. Tel Aviv, 1974–1997.

Bornsztain, R. Shmuel. *Shem mi-Shemuel: Al Seder Parshiyyot ha-Torah u-Mo'adei Kodesh.* 9th ed. 6 vols. Jerusalem, 1992.

Boston Globe. "Reagan Assails New W. Bank Settlements." August 28, 1983, 1.

Bunim, Irving M. *Ever Since Sinai: Essays on the Valued, the Vanishing, and the Everlasting in American Jewish Life.* Jerusalem: Feldheim, 1977.

Caro, R. Isaac b. Joseph. *Toledot Yitzḥak.*

Caro, R. Joseph. *Beit Yosef* to *Tur.*

______ *Kesef Mishneh* to *Mishneh Torah.*

______ *Shulḥan Arukh.*

Chaikin, Andrew. "Live from the Moon: The Societal Impact of Apollo." In *Societal Impact of Spaceflight*, edited by Steven J. Dick and Roger D. Launius, 53–66. Washington, DC: Government Printing Office, 2007.

Chasman, R. Yehudah Leib. *Or Yahel: Iyyunim be-Musar ve-Yir'at Hashem*. 3rd ed. Vol. 1. Jerusalem, 1969.

Cohler, Larry. "Jewish Delegation in Historic Meeting with Pope: Impetus Was Waldheim; No Change in Recognition of Israel." *Jewish Advocate*, September 3, 1987, 1.

Couch, Gregory and Greg Myre. "Major Portion of Israeli Fence Is Ruled Illegal." *New York Times*, July 10, 2004, A1.

Cowell, Alan. "Prominent U.S. Jews, Visiting Israel, Voice Unease." *New York Times*, March 2, 1988, 3.

Culi, R. Jacob. *Me-Am Lo'ez*. Translated by R. Shemuel Yerushalmi. *Yalkut Me-Am Lo'ez: Sefer Shemot*. Jerusalem: Wagshal, 1968.

______ *Me-Am Lo'ez*. Translated by R. Shemuel Yerushalmi. *Yalkut Me-Am Lo'ez*. I Kings. Jerusalem: Wagshal, 1968.

______ *Me-Am Lo'ez*. Translated by R. Shemuel Yerushalmi. *Yalkut Me-Am Lo'ez*. Esther. Jerusalem: Wagshal, 1974.

Da'at Zekenim. Commentary on the Torah.

Danzig, R. Abraham. *Ḥayyei Adam*.

Davidson, Jacob. "Carmelite Hypocrisy at Auschwitz." *Jerusalem Post*, July 25, 1989, 4.

Davis, Wade. *Into the Silence: The Great War, Mallory, and the Conquest of Everest*. New York: Vintage Books, 2012.

de Vidas, R. Elijah b. Moses. *Reshit Ḥokhmah*.

Department of Economic Affairs, Statistical Office of the United Nations. *Demographic Yearbook, 1949–1950*. New York, 1950.

Dershowitz, Alan M. *Chutzpah*. Boston: Little Brown, 1991.

Dessler, R. Eliyahu Eliezer. *Mikhtav me-Eliyahu*. Edited by R. Aryeh Carmell and R. Alter Halperin. 3 vols. Benei Berak: Hever Talmidav, 1964.

Detroit Free Press. "Malaysian Leader: Palestinian Fight Has Been Futile; Jews Rule the World, He Tells Muslim Body." October 17, 2003, A4.

Dynow, R. Zevi Elimelech. *Benei Yissaskhar*.

______ *Derekh Pikudekha*.

Edels, R. Samuel Eliezer b. Judah ha-Levi. *Ḥiddushei Halakhot ve-Aggadot*.

Eder, Elizabeth. "OPEC: Demise of a Cartel?" *Harvard International Review* 6, no. 1 (September/October 1983): 33–34.

Einhorn, R. Zev Wolf. *Perush Maharzu* on *Midrash Rabbah*.

Elijah b. Solomon Zalman, R. *Be'ur ha-Gra: Mishlei*. Edited by R. Meir Yehoshua Katzenellenbogen. Jerusalem: Mossad HaRav Kook, 2006.

______ *Ḥiddushei ha-Gra*.

______ *Kol Eliyahu*.

———. *Siddur Me'orei ha-Gra*. Jerusalem, 1999.

Emerson, Ralph Waldo. *Society and Solitude*. Boston: Osgood, 1875. "Civilization," 25.

Enoch Zundel b. Joseph, R. *Etz Yosef* to *Midrash Rabbah*.

Epstein, R. Baruch ha-Levi Epstein. *Torah Temimah*.

Epstein, R. Jehiel Michal. *Arukh ha-Shulḥan*.

Escudé, Carlos. "Argentine Territorial Nationalism." *Journal of Latin American Studies* 20, no. 1 (May 1988): 139–165.

Eybeschuetz, R. Jonathan. *Ahavat Yehonatan*.

———. *Ya'arot Devash*. Vol. 2. Jerusalem: Mekhon Or ha-Sefer, 1988.

Falk, R. Jacob Joshua b. Tzvi Hirsch. *Penei Yehoshua*.

Feinstein, R. Moshe. *Derash Mosheh: Ḥiddushei Aggadah al ha-Torah*. Benei Berak, 1988.

———. *Iggerot Mosheh*.

Feuer, R. Avrohom Chaim. *Tehillim: Psalms; A New Translation with a Commentary Anthologized from Talmudic, Midrashic and Rabbinic Sources*. Brooklyn, NY: Mesorah, 1996.

Frankel, Glenn. "Israel Launches Its First Satellite into Orbit; Major Step Seen toward Ability to Spy on Arabs from Space." *Washington Post*, September 20, 1988, A1.

Freedman, Lawrence and Efraim Karsh. *The Gulf Conflict 1990–1991: Diplomacy and War in the New World Order*. Princeton, NJ: Princeton University Press, 1993.

Friedland, R. Natan. *Kos Yeshuah ve-Neḥamah*.

Friedman, R. Israel Hayyim. *Likkutei Mahariḥ*. 3 vols. Hungary: Sziget, 1900–1911.

Friedman, R. Shelomoh. *Divrei Shelomoh: Mo'adim*. Edited by R. David Mosheh Spiegel. Jerusalem, 1961.

Ganzfried, R. Solomon. *Kitzur Shulḥan Arukh*.

Gelb, Leslie H. "A Secret Plan for Israel." *New York Times*, September 22, 1991, E17.

Gerondi, R. Nissim b. Reuben. *Ḥiddushei ha-Ran*.

Gold, Dore. "Launching of Israeli Satellite Sends a Message to Other Mideast States." *Jewish Exponent*, September 30, 1988, 3.

Goldman, Ari L. "2 Boys Held in Synagogue Fire and 10,000 Mourn 5 Torahs." *New York Times*, September 19, 1988, B1.

Gombiner, R. Abraham Abele b. Hayyim ha-Levi. *Magen Avraham* to *Shulḥan Arukh*.

Greenberg, R. Aharon Yaakov. *Iturei Torah: Likkut, Nisaḥ u-Biur*. 6 vols. Tel Aviv: Yavneh, 1967–1970.

Gruntman, Mike. *Blazing the Trail: The Early History of Spacecraft and Rocketry*. Reston, VA: American Institute of Aeronautics and Astronautics, 2004.

Gwertzman, Bernard. "Egypt and Israel Sign Formal Treaty, Ending a State of War after 30 Years: Sadat and Begin Praise Carter's Role; Ceremony Is Festive." *New York Times*, March 27, 1979, A1.

Haberman, Clyde. "Israel Dismayed by Bush Delay on Loans." *New York Times,* September 8, 1991, 3.

Haggadah shel Pesaḥ: Ashei Yisrael. 2nd ed. Brooklyn, NY: Moriah, 1988.

Hagiz, R. Moses. *She'elot u-Teshuvot Shetei ha-Leḥem.*

Harkavi, R. Shelomoh. *Me-Imrei Shelomoh.* Vol. 2. Jerusalem, 1994.

Harris, William W. *Taking Root: Israeli Settlement in the West Bank, the Golan and Gaza-Sinai, 1967–1980.* Chichester, NY: Research Studies Press, 1980.

Hart, Sergiu. "An Interview with Robert Aumann." *Macroeconomic Dynamics* 9, no. 5 (2005): 683–740.

Hezekiah b. Manoah, R. *Ḥizkuni.* Commentary on the Torah.

Hirsch, R. Samson Raphael. Commentary on the Pentateuch and the *Haftarot.*

Horowitz, R. Isaiah ha-Levi. *Shenei Luḥot ha-Berit. Shenei Luḥot ha-Berit ha-Shalem.* Vol. 3. Haifa: Yad Ramah Institute, 2006.

Horowitz, R. Naphtali Tzvi. *Zera Kodesh.* Vol. 2. Jerusalem, 1954.

Horowitz, R. Pinhas ha-Levi. *Panim Yafot.*

Houbert, Jean. "The Falklands: A Hiccup of Decolonisation." *Current Research on Peace and Violence* 5, no. 1 (1982): 1-25.

Hutner, R. Yitzhak. *Paḥad Yitzḥak: Kuntrus ve-Zot Ḥanukkah.* Brooklyn, NY: Mossad Gur Aryeh, 1984.

______ *Paḥad Yitzḥak, Rosh Ha-Shanah.* Brooklyn, NY: Mossad Gur Aryeh, 2008.

Ibn Alamani, Zadok b. Aaron. *Ezri Yavo.* Reprinted in *Siftei Renanot.* Venice, 1648.

Ibn Attar, R. Hayyim b. Moses. *Or ha-Ḥayyim.* Commentary on the Pentateuch.

Ibn Ezra, Abraham b. Meir. Ibn Ezra. Commentary on the Torah.

Ibn Janah, R. Jonah. *Sefer ha-Sharashim.*

Isaac b. Moses of Vienna, R. *Or Zaru'a.*

Ishbilli, R. Yom Tov. *Ḥiddushei ha-Ritva.*

Issachar Berman b. Naphtali ha-Kohen, R. *Mattenot Kehunnah.*

Isserles, R. Moses. *Darkhei Mosheh* to *Tur.*

______ *Rema* to *Shulḥan Arukh.*

______ *She'elot u-Teshuvot ha-Rema.*

______ *Torat ha-Olah.*

Jackson, Rev. Jesse. Speech to the Democratic National Convention ("Common Ground and Common Sense"), July 19, 1988. Reprinted in "Stresses 'Common Ground': Jackson Talks of Hope, Dreams as He Weaves 'Quilt of Unity.'" *Congressional Quarterly Weekly Report* 46 (July 23, 1988): 2057–2060.

Jad, Islah. "From the Salons to the Popular Committees: Palestinian Women, 1919–1989." In Jamal R. Nassar and Roger Heacock, eds., *Intifada: Palestine at the Crossroads,* 125–142. New York: Praeger, 1990.

Jerusalem Post. "Jordan: Offeq-I Has 'Military Role.'" September 20, 1988, 2.

______ "An Obstacle to a Negotiated Peace: West Bank Settlements 'Illegal,' Scranton Tells Security Council." March 25, 1976, 4.

______ "Poles Jeer at Jews Protesting at Auschwitz Convent." July 24, 1989, 2.

______ "Tears, Anger as Reagan Visits Belsen and Bitburg." May 6, 1985, 1.

Jewish Telegraphic Agency. "Israeli Satellite Functioning Well after First Day of Orbit." September 21, 1988.

Kaddish, R. Yo'etz Kayam. *Si'aḥ Sarphei Kodesh*. Vol. 2. Warsaw: Lewin-Epstein, 1923.

Kagan, R. Israel Meir ha-Kohen. *Mishnah Berurah*.

______ *Sefer Ḥafetz Ḥayyim*.

Kampeas, Ron. "Students: 'No' to Convent." *Jerusalem Post*, July 28, 1989, C5.

Karsh, Efraim. *The Iran–Iraq War, 1980–1988*. Oxford: Osprey, 2002.

Kasher, R. Menahem Mendel. *Haggadah Shelemah*. 3rd ed. Jerusalem: Mekhon Torah Shelemah, 1967.

______ *Torah Shelemah*. Jerusalem: Beit Torah Shelemah, 1992.

Katz, R. Reuben Hoeshke b. Hoeshke. *Yalkut Re'uveni*.

Keinon, Herb. "Israel Readies for Dirty Bombs, Missiles." *Jerusalem Post*, February 7, 2003, A5.

Kifner, John. "Israel Launches Space Program and a Satellite: Spy Craft Are Expected to Be Main Emphasis." *New York Times*, September 20, 1988, A1.

Kimhi, R. David. *Radak*. Commentary on the Prophets and Psalms.

______ *Sefer ha-Sharashim*.

Kol Bo.

Kosman, R. Joseph. *Noheg ka-Tzon Yosef*.

Kranz, R. Jacob b. Wolf. *Emet le-Yaakov, Haggadah shel Pesaḥ*. Reprinted in R. Avraham Berush Flahm. *Berit Avot al Haggadah le-Leil Shimurim*.

Kviat, R. Dovid. *Sukkat David*. Jerusalem, 2008.

Landrey, Wilbur G. "In the World of Oliver North, It's Patriotic to Lie under Orders." *St. Petersburg Times*, July 12, 1987, 5D.

Lasson, Kenneth. "Scholarly and Scientific Boycotts of Israel: Abusing the Academic Enterprise." *Touro Law Review* 21, no. 4 (2006): 989–1076.

Leibowitz, Nechama. *Gilyonot*.

Levi b. Gershom, R. *Ralbag*. Commentary on the Torah.

Levi Yitzchok of Berdichev, R. *Kedushat Levi*.

Levinsky, Dr. Yom Tov. *Sefer ha-Mo'adim: Parashat Mo'adei Yisrael*. Vol. 8. Tel Aviv: Devir, 1956.

______ *Sefer ha-Mo'adim: Sukkot*. Vol. 4. Tel Aviv: Devir, 1951.

Loew b. Bezalel, R. Judah. Commentary on Talmud.

______ *Gevurot Hashem*.

______ *Netivot Olam*.

______ *Tiferet Yisrael*.

Luntshits, R. Ephraim Solomon b. Aaron. *Keli Yakar*. Commentary on the Pentateuch.

______ *Olelot Ephraim.*

Luria, R. Isaac b. Solomon. *Sefer ha-Likkutim.* Jerusalem: Lifshitz Brothers, 1913.

______ *Siddur ha-Ari.*

Luzzatto, R. Moses Hayyim. *Da'at Tevunot.* Jerusalem: Goldblatt, 2001.

MacDougal, Douglas W. *Newton's Gravity: An Introductory Guide to the Mechanics of the Universe.* New York: Springer, 2012.

Maimon, R. Yehudah Leib ha-Kohen. *Ḥiddush ha-Sanhedrin be-Medinatenu ha-Meḥudeshet.* Jerusalem: Mossad HaRav Kook, 1951.

Maimonides. *Ma'amar Teḥiyyat ha-Metim.*

______ *Mishneh Torah.*

______ *Perush ha-Mishnayot.*

______ *Sefer ha-Mitzvot.*

Makhir, R. Moses b. Judah. *Seder ha-Yom.*

Makovsky, David. "Provided Israel's Terms for Palestinian Team Are Accepted, Shamir 'Yes' to Talks." *Jerusalem Post,* August 2, 1991, 1.

Margolioth, R. Ephraim Zalman. *Matteh Ephraim.*

Masekhet Soferim.

Mat, R. Moses b. Abraham. *Matteh Mosheh.*

McFadden, Robert D. "Americans Voice Anger on Bitburg." *New York Times,* May 6, 1985, A8.

______ "Nation Rekindles Statue of Liberty as Beacon of Hope: Light from Lasers." *New York Times,* July 4, 1986, A1.

Mecklenburg, R. Yaakov Tzvi. *Ha-Ketav ve-ha-Kabbalah.*

Megillat Antioḥus.

Megillat Ta'anit.

Meir b. Barukh of Rothenburg, R. *Haggahot Maimuniyyot* to *Mishneh Torah.*

Meir b. Jehiel, R. "*Arzei ha-Levanon.*" Reprinted in Alter Welner, *Aseret Harugei Malkhut ba-Midrash u-ve-Piyyut,* 347. Jerusalem: Mossad HaRav Kook, 2005.

Meir Simhah ha-Kohen of Dvinsk, R. *Meshekh Ḥokhmah.*

______ *Or Same'aḥ.*

Mekhilta.

Mekhilta de-Rav Shimon bar Yoḥai.

Menahem Mendel of Rimanov, R. *Menaḥem Tziyyon, Derushim le-Pesaḥ.*

Menahem b. Solomon, R. *Midrash Sekhel Tov.*

Midrash ha-Gadol.

Midrash ha-Ne'elam.

Midrash Hallel.

Midrash Ḥanukkah. Reprinted in Adolph Jellinek. *Beit ha-Midrash.*

Midrash Rabbah.

Midrash Shoḥer Tov.

Midrash Tanḥuma.

Mishnah. *Avot; Bekhorot; Ediyot; Kiddushin; Ma'aser Sheni; Megillah; Menaḥot; Nazir; Pesaḥim; Rosh Ha-Shanah; Shabbat; Sukkah; Ta'anit; Uktzin; Yadayim; Yoma.*

Mishnat Rebbe Eliezer.

Mizrahi, David Toufic. "If Oil Isn't Important, Who in the Middle East Is?" *Washington Post,* November 3, 1985, C1.

Mizrahi, R. Elijah. *Sefer ha-Mizraḥi.*

Moellin, R. Jacob b. Moses. *Sefer Maharil: Minhagim.* Edited by Shlomo Y. Spitzer. Jerusalem: Mekhon Yerushalayim, 1989.

______ *She'elot u-Teshuvot Maharil.*

Moulton, Forest Ray. *An Introduction to Celestial Mechanics.* London: MacMillan, 1902.

Nahmanides. *Ramban.* Commentary on the Torah.

______ *Torat ha-Adam.*

Nathanson, R. Joseph Saul. *Divrei Sha'ul al ha-Torah.*

New York Times. "The Democrats in Atlanta: Excerpts from Jackson's Speech; Pushing Party to Find Common Ground." July 20, 1988, A18.

______ "Israeli Settlements Criticized by Common Market Leaders." March 23, 1983, A2.

______ "Malaysian Attacks Jews." October 17, 2003, A8.

Nissenbaum, R. Issac. *Hagut Lev.* Vilna: L. Apel, 1910.

Oberlander, R. Gedaliah. "*Ḥumrat Iy Akhilat Matzah Sheruyah be-Pesaḥ.*" *Or Yisrael: Kovetz le-Inyanei Halakhah u-Minhag* 15 (Nisan 5759/1999): 134–148.

Palaggi, R. Hayyim. *Mo'ed le-Khol Ḥai.*

Passell, Peter. "Game Theory Captures a Nobel." *New York Times,* October 12, 1994, D1.

Peirpaoli, Jr., Paul G. "Madrid Conference." In Spencer C. Tucker, ed., *Encyclopedia of the Arab-Israeli Conflict: A Political, Social and Military History,* 657. Santa Barbara, CA: ABC-CLIO, 2008.

Peli, Pinchas H. *On Repentance: In the Thought and Oral Discourses of Rabbi Joseph B. Soloveitchik.* Jerusalem: Oroth, 1980.

Pendergast, Mark. *For God, Country, and Coca-Cola: The Definitive History of the Great American Soft Drink and the Company That Makes It.* 3rd ed. New York: Basic Books, 2013.

Peretz, Don. *Intifada: The Palestinian Uprising.* Boulder, CO: Westview, 1990.

______ *The West Bank: History, Politics, Society, and Economy.* Boulder, CO: Westview Press, 1986.

Perlman, Lisa. "Satellite Launch Marks Israel's Calling Card to the Space Age." *Nature* 335, no. 6189 (September 29, 1988): 387.

Perlow, R. Shalom. *Mishmeret Shalom.*

Pertman, Adam. "Panel Members Say North's Image Will Make Task Harder." *Boston Globe*, July 10, 1987, 10.

Pesikta de-Rav Kahana.

Pesikta Rabbati.

Pirkei de-Rabbi Eliezer.

Plaut, R. Hezekiah Feivel. *Likkutei Ḥever ben Ḥayyim*. Vol. 3.

Rabinovich, Abraham. "Planning for One Million New Israelis: Between a Vision and a Nightmare." *Jerusalem Post*, August 16, 1991, 5.

Rabinowich, R. Solomon ha-Kohen. *Tiferet Shelomoh.*

Rabinowitz, R. Zadok ha-Kohen. *Tzidkat ha-Tzaddik.*

Rakover, R. Nahum. *Hilkhot Yom ha-Atzma'ut ve-Yom Yerushalayim: Berurei Halakhah*. Jerusalem: Misrad ha-Datot, 1973.

Reich, R. Joseph Benjamin. *Benei Binyamin.*

Reischer, R. Jacob b. Joseph. *Ḥok Yaakov.*

______ *Iyyun Yaakov.*

Richelson, Jeffrey. "Military Intelligence: SPOT Is Not Enough." *Bulletin of the Atomic Scientists* 45, no. 7 (September 1989): 26–27.

Rokeah, R. Elazar b. Samuel. *Ma'aseh Roke'aḥ al ha-Mishnayot.*

Rosenberg, Howard. "U.S. Urges Israel Not to Deport Palestinians." *American Israelite*, March 28, 1991, A6.

Rosmarin, Rachel. *Mamma Used to Say: Pearls of Wisdom from the World of Yiddish*. Jerusalem: Feldheim, 2000.

Royal Swedish Academy of Sciences. "Robert Aumann's and Thomas Schelling's Contributions to Game Theory: Analyses of Conflict and Cooperation," October 10, 2005, 12–22.

Rubin, R. Yissachar Dov. *Talelei Orot: Mivkhar Be'urim Ḥiddushim u-Pheninim al Mo'adei ha-Shanah*. Vol. 2. Benei Berak, 1993.

Samuel b. Meir, R. *Rashbam*. Commentary on the Torah.

______ Commentary on Talmud.

Schachter, R. Jacob J. "A Little at a Time." In R. David Stavsky, ed., *Sermons for Passover: Presented by Members of the Rabbinical Council of America*, 1 (5753/1993).

Schachter, Jonathan. "UN Adjourns Discussion on Expulsions by Israel." *Jerusalem Post*, January 13, 1991, 2.

Schorr, R. Gedalia. *Or Gedalyahu: Mo'adim v-Likkutim*. Jerusalem, 2001.

Seigel, Reginald. "Arab Nations Attack Israel." *UPI NewsTrack*, May 15, 1948.

Sforno, R. Obadiah b. Jacob. *Sforno*. Commentary on the Torah. *Kavvanot ha-Torah.*

Shalev, Baruch Aba. *100 Years of Nobel Prizes*. New Delhi: Atlantic Publishers, 2003.

Shapira, R. Elijah. *Eliyahu Rabbah.*

Shapira, R. Nosson Nota. *Megaleh Amukot.*
Sharon, Moshe. "Concepts of Peace." *Jerusalem Post,* February 18, 1983, 6.
Shmulevitz, R. Hayyim Leib. *Siḥot Musar: Sha'arei Ḥayyim,* 5731–5732. Jerusalem, 2013.
Shneur Zalman of Liadi, R. *Shulḥan Arukh ha-Rav.*
Shternbukh, R. Mosheh. *Ta'am va-Da'at: Peshatim, Be'urim ve-Divrei Ḥizzuk she-Ne'emru be-Siḥot al Parashat ha-Shavua be-Yohanesburg.*
Sifrei to Deuteronomy.
Singer, Phyllis. "Views Exchanged by Pope and Jews during Meeting in Miami." *American Israelite,* September 17, 1987, 1.
Sirkes, R. Joel. *Baḥ* to *Tur.*
______ *Meshiv Nefesh.* Commentary on the Book of Ruth.
Sofer, R. Moses. *Ḥiddushei Ḥatam Sofer al Masekhet Pesaḥim.*
______ *Torat Mosheh.*
Solomon b. Isaac, R. *Rashi.* Commentary on the Torah and Talmud.
Solomon, John. "FBI, Police Prepare for Attacks in the US." *Jerusalem Post,* February 17, 2003, 5.
Soloveichik, R. Ahron. *Logic of the Heart, Logic of the Mind: Wisdom and Reflections on Topics of Our Times.* Jerusalem: Genesis Jerusalem Press, 1991.
Soloveitchik, R. Isaac Zev ha-Levi. *Ḥiddushei Rabbenu ha-Griz Soloveitchik mi-Pi ha-Shemu'ah al ha-Torah.*
Soloveitchik, R. Joseph B. *Ḥamesh Derashot.* Jerusalem: Mekhon Tal Orot, 1974.
Soloveitchik, R. Yosef Dov. *Beit ha-Levi al Derush u-Milei de-Aggadata.* Jerusalem, 1985.
Sperber, R. Daniel. *Minhagei Yisrael: Mekorot ve-Toledot.* Vol. 2. Jerusalem: Mossad HaRav Kook, 1991.
______ *Why Jews Do What They Do: The History of Jewish Customs throughout the Cycle of the Jewish Year.* Translated by Dr. Yaakov Elman. Hoboken, NJ: Ktav, 1999.
Staub, Ervin. *The Roots of Evil: The Origins of Genocide and Other Group Violence.* Cambridge: Cambridge University Press, 1989.
Tagliabue, John. "Strife Returns to a Convent at Auschwitz." *New York Times,* July 27, 1989.
Talmud (Babylonian). *Arakhin; Avodah Zarah; Bava Batra; Bava Kamma; Bava Metzia; Beitzah; Bekhorot; Berakhot; Eruvin; Gittin; Ḥagigah; Ḥullin; Keritot; Ketubbot; Kiddushin; Megillah; Menaḥot; Mo'ed Katan; Nazir; Pesaḥim; Rosh Ha-Shanah; Sanhedrin; Shabbat; Shevuot; Sotah; Sukkah; Ta'anit; Tamid; Temurah; Yevamot; Yoma; Zevaḥim.*
Talmud (Jerusalem). *Beitzah; Ḥagigah; Horiyot; Ma'aser Sheni; Makkot; Pesaḥim; Rosh Ha-Shanah; Shabbat; Yoma.*
Tanenbaum, Mare. "PLO Inspired Violence." *Jewish Advocate,* December 31, 1987, 10.
Tanna de-vei Eliyahu. Seder Eliyahu Rabba. Seder Eliyahu Zuta.

Targum Onkelos.
Targum Yonatan.
Teomim, R. Joseph b. Meir. *Peri Megadim*.
Tobiah b. Eliezer. *Midrash Lekaḥ Tov* (*Pesikta Zutarta*).
Torat Kohanim.
Tosafot. Commentary on Talmud. *Menaḥot*; *Pesaḥim*; *Rosh Ha-Shanah*; *Sukkah*.
Turkel, Eli. "The Nature and Limitations of Rabbinic Authority." *Tradition: A Journal of Orthodox Jewish Thought* 27, no. 4 (Summer 1993): 80–99.
Tyrnau, R. Isaac. *Sefer ha-Minhagim*.
Uchitelle, Louis. "American and Israeli Share Nobel Prize in Economics." *New York Times*, October 11, 2005, C2.
Vidal Yom Tov of Tolosa, R. *Maggid Mishneh* to *Mishneh Torah*.
Vital, R. Hayyim b. Joseph. *Peri Etz Ḥayyim*.
Wallfish, Asher. "Reforming the System." *Jerusalem Post*, April 4, 1990, 5.
Warburg, R. A. Yehudah (Ronnie). *Rabbinic Authority: The Vision and the Reality; Beit Din Decisions in English*. Jerusalem: Urim, 2013.
Ward, Peter and Donald Brownlee. *Rare Earth: Why Complex Life Is Uncommon in the Universe*. New York: Copernicus Books, 2003.
Weinberg, Meyer. *Because They Were Jews: A History of Antisemitism*. New York: Greenwood, 1986.
Weingarten, R. Mosheh Yaakov. *Ha-Seder ha-Arukh*. Jerusalem: Otzer ha-Mo'adim, 2011.
Weisser, R. Meir Loeb b. Jehiel Michel. *Malbim*. Commentary on the Torah.
Wertheim, R. Aaron. *Halakhot ve-Halikhot be-Ḥasidut*. Jerusalem: Mossad HaRav Kook, 2003.
———. *Law and Custom in Hasidism*. Translated by R. Shmuel Himelstein. Hoboken, NJ: Ktav, 1992.
Williams, Daniel. "Israel Fires 1st Satellite into Space; Denies It's for Spying: Impact on Mideast Arms Race Possible." *Los Angeles Times*, September 20, 1988, 1.
Yalkut Shimoni.
Yashar, R. Mosheh Meir. *He-Ḥafetz Ḥayyim be-Netivot ha-Tefillah*. Jerusalem: Mekhon Hatam Sofer, 1974.
Yehudah Leib of Zaklików, R. *Likkutei Maharil*.
Young, David. *Great Funny Quotes*. Round Rock, TX: Wind Runner Press, 2012.
Zelcer, R. Yerahmiel. *Ner le-Me'ah: Al Inyanei Ḥanukkah*. Brooklyn, NY, 1975.
Zilber, R. Yehiel Avraham. *Berur Halakhah, Oraḥ Ḥayyim*. Vol. 3. Benei Berak, 1976.
Zlotowitz, R. Meir and R. Nosson Scherman. *Shir haShirim*. Brooklyn, NY: Artscroll, 2010.
Zlotowski, Michel. "Shamir Says, 'We Will Still Go to Peace Talks.'" *Jerusalem Post*, September 13, 1991, 1.
Zohar.

Name Index

Name Index

Subject Index

The fonts used in this book are from the Arno family

Other Works by Rabbi Dr. Aaron Levine

Free Enterprise and Jewish Law: Aspects of Jewish Business Ethics (1980)

Economics and Jewish Law (1987)

Economic Public Policy and Jewish Law (1993)

Case Studies in Jewish Business Ethics (2000)

Moral Issues of the Marketplace in Jewish Law (2005)

The Oxford Handbook of Judaism and Economics (Editor) (2010)

Economic Morality and Jewish Law (2012)

Maggid Books
The best of contemporary Jewish thought from
Koren Publishers Jerusalem Ltd.